The
Romantic Ethic
and the Spirit of
Modern Consumerism

The
Romantic Ethic
and the Spirit of
Modern Consumerism

Colin Campbell

© Colin Campbell

First published 1987
First published in paperback 1989
by Blackwell Publishers ISBN 0-631-16941-5

Third edition published in Great Britain 2005 by Alcuin Academics

ISBN   1904623336

Foreword
to the Alcuin Academic Edition

The Romantic Ethic and the Spirit of Modern Consumerism was first published by Basil Blackwell of Oxford in 1987. A paperback edition appeared two years later, while in the following five years it was reprinted four times. However although the intervening years have seen the appearance of Italian, Portuguese, Slovenian and Chinese editions, no copies have been available in English since 1998.

This Alcuin Academic edition has therefore been published in order to fill this gap, and more specifically to meet the needs of those academics and students who have contacted me over the past six or seven years in search of an English-language version of the book.

Naturally I have considered writing a revised edition (which indeed some critics, as well as a few friends, have suggested is long overdue). However I have decided against doing so at this time, preferring to direct my energies elsewhere. This is a task that I do intend to undertake in the near future; and hopefully in time for the twentieth anniversary of the book's first publication in 2007. I have, however, appended to this edition a list of my publications on consumption that have appeared since 1987.

Colin Campbell
York
March 2005

Contents

to Elizabeth and Duncan

1

Introduction

Most attempts to describe the general development of modern thought tend to pay exclusive attention to the growth of rationalism. The result is a picture quite incompatible with historical facts and the world as we know it.

Karl Mannheim

The *Oxford English Dictionary* defines the word 'romantic' as meaning 'marked by or suggestive of or given to romance; imaginative, remote from experience, visionary, and (in relation to literary or artistic method) preferring grandeur or passion or irregular beauty to finish and proportion'.[1] None of these connotations would appear to have much to do with those activities which are generally covered by the heading 'consumption'. The selection, purchase and use of goods and services are all forms of everyday action which, on the contrary, we commonly tend to view as rather dull and prosaic matters, except perhaps on those rare occasions when we purchase a major item like a house or a car. It would appear, therefore, that consumption, being a form of economic conduct, should be placed at the opposite pole of life from all that we generally regard as 'romantic'. The reasonableness of this contrast is deceptive, however; something which becomes apparent once we recognize that there is one significant modern phenomenon which does indeed directly link the two.

This, of course, is advertising, for even the most cursory examination of the pages of glossy magazines and the contents of television commercials will serve to reveal how many advertisements are concerned with the topic of 'romance', or with images and copy which deal with scenes which are 'remote from everyday experience', 'imaginative' or suggestive of 'grandeur' or 'passion'. And it is not just romance in the narrow sense which features so prominently in conjunction with perfume, cigarettes or lingerie advertisements – it is also that the pictures and stories used are typically 'romantic' in the broader sense of being exotic, imaginative and idealized; whilst the very purpose of advertisements, of course, is to induce us to buy the products which are featured: in other words, to consume.[2]

The fact that basically 'romantic' cultural material is commonly used in advertisements in this fashion has often been noted and hence one could say that a general awareness of the link between 'romanticism' and 'consumption' already exists. The assumption which has largely prevailed among social scientists, however, indeed among academics and intellectuals in general, has been that it is the advertisers who have chosen to make use of this material in an attempt to promote the interests of the producers they represent, and consequently that the relationship should be seen as one in which 'romantic' beliefs, aspirations and attitudes are put to work in the interests of a 'consumer society'.[3] That view is challenged in the pages that follow (although not dismissed) where it is argued that the reverse relationship should also be taken seriously, with the 'romantic' ingredient in culture regarded as having had a crucial part to play in the development of modern consumerism itself; indeed, since consumption may determine demand and demand supply, it could be argued that Romanticism itself played a critical role in facilitating the Industrial Revolution and therefore the character of the modern economy. This is a very ambitious argument and hence I shall commence by explaining how I came to be in the position of considering it.

The events which led to the writing of this book occurred in the late 1960s and early 1970s. Like most academics in Western Europe and North America, and especially those who were in the social sciences, I found that period to be disturbing and challenging, if occasionally exhilarating. Universities appeared to be in the front line of a war which had broken out between the generations, one in which the more privileged and educated of the young seemed determined to deflect the course of history into unanticipated channels. No academic, and, least of all, no sociologist, could experience such an intellectual and cultural turmoil without being prompted to reconsider and re-examine the assumptions which guided both his professional and personal conduct. Some of my colleagues, after suitable reflexive deliberation, decided to join the young 'counter-culturalists', whilst others became more entrenched in their opposition to what they saw as youthful antinomian madness.[4] As for myself, I became increasingly intrigued by the phenomenon which presented individuals with such dilemmas; reluctant to condone or condemn that which I found I could not fully comprehend, my energies were increasingly directed toward the study of this bewildering cultural upheaval. Although at first this was a personal investigation, undertaken in the hope of permitting me the luxury of adopting a rational response to events, it quickly developed into a matter of professional concern, as indeed, I noted later, it had also become for others of my profession.

My research in the subsequent years took the form of reading the literature either produced or favoured by these heralds of 'the Age of Aquarius', or that written by their more elderly apologists, from both of which I hoped to obtain a better understanding of their world-view.[5] Whilst, at the same time, I naturally consulted those few, but increasing, sociological monographs which purported to explain this new and bewildering phenomenon.[6] What made this latter exercise such a peculiarly difficult one was that the accepted sociological wisdom of the post-war years, and indeed of the generation before that, had been founded on the assumption that modern societies would continue to progress down the road of rationality, materialism and secularity. That significant sections of the educated middle-class young should, therefore, turn to magic, mystery and exotic religion, manifesting a marked alienation from the culture of rationality and a determined anti-puritanism, was as inexplicable as it was unexpected. It was thus only with considerable difficulty that accounts of the phenomenon were developed which did not directly challenge this larger premise of long-term 'rationalization'. And yet to offer explanations which challenged that assumption was necessarily to question a tenet, held by the 'founding fathers' of the discipline and most of its present practitioners alike, concerning the fundamental rationality of modern capitalist society.

It was not long before I became convinced – the oft-repeated disclaimers not withstanding – that similar cultural revolutions had occurred before, and that the world-view espoused by the counter-culturalists could only adequately be described by the adjective 'romantic'. I was not alone in this opinion, and a comparison with the Romantic Movement was occasionally made by both advocates and critics of this latest outburst of 'romantic fever'.[7] But I did seem to be alone in regarding such an identification as less an answer than a further extension of the question. It was clear that for many commentators being able to label the counter-culture in this way served not merely to demystify it, but to solve the problem of how it should be judged, Romanticism being a phenomenon which, as always, aroused strong passions. What was most noticeable about these comparisons, however, was that whilst they served to provide the analyst with a context in which to discuss contemporary cultural change (that is, one could refer back to romantic 'equivalents' or use the beliefs and attitudes of the first Romantics to shed light on the views of their successors), little was explained as a consequence of the claimed identity. Recognition that the counter-culture was 'romantic' did not add to our understanding of why it had occurred because those 'explanations' for the Romantic Movement which I could find were predominantly historical in form emphasizing such unique events as the French and Industrial Revolutions.

It was not that there had been any lack of scholarly interest in either the Romantic Movement or the Romantics and their works; on the contrary, the body of material was dauntingly large. On the other hand, the vast bulk of it was literary, aesthetic or philosophical in form, supplemented by history of a socio-political or intellectual variety, and although I found much that these scholars produced invaluable, it did not amount to a sociological discussion. That is to say, consideration of Romanticism as a socio-cultural movement, functionally interconnected with an emerging industrial society, appeared minimal, whilst I could not find any examination of what one might call 'the romantic ingredient' in modern life, the 'romantical' as opposed to the 'rational'. For, if events in the 1960s and early 1970s were to be considered as merely the latest manifestation of Romanticism, then it clearly needed to be understood as a continuing element in modern culture.

It seemed to me that whilst the influence of romantic thought upon sociology had often been discussed, there was little sociology of romanticism with which to balance it.[8] Romantic thought, together with the ideas and attitudes of the Enlightenment to which it was, at least in part, a reaction, was the primary intellectual material out of which sociology as a discipline had been forged. But it seemed that too many of the founders of the discipline had been concerned to overcome their own romantic tendencies, and too committed to a 'progressive' view of history, to regard romanticism itself as anything other than a 'reactionary' element in modern life,[9] a phenomenon with its roots in the past and doomed to extinction at the hands of the rational elements in culture and society. This could be said to have become the established wisdom, as articulated, for example, by Mannheim.[10]

During the years when these thoughts were crystallizing in my mind and my energies were increasingly being diverted into studying romanticism, both old and new, I was still continuing work in what had, from the beginning of my career in sociology, been my principal field of interest. This was the sociology of religion and whilst teaching courses in this area I was necessarily concerned with issues relating to Weber's work, the 'Protestant ethic thesis' being a natural focus of study. Over the period in which I had taught this topic I had developed an especial interest in the fate of this ethic, an issue which began to appear more and more problematic as time went by. Although not chosen by sociologists as the object of any detailed or intensive study, inquiry in other fields, together with a persuasive popular wisdom, had together served to generate the view that the ethic which Weber identified had been displaced as the predominant societal ethic for modern, Western, industrial societies, having been superceded by some contrasting 'other-directed', 'social' or 'expressive' ethic.[11] Not at first inclined to challenge this thesis, I was nevertheless disturbed by the many difficulties and inconsistencies which it presented.

In the first place, those studies which had been regarded as lending support to this 'decline of the Protestant ethic thesis', were largely impressionistic or journalistic in character. What was even more disturbing was the fact that, as White has demonstrated, most authors were involved in developing an 'intellectual ideology', being more concerned to deplore the direction of cultural change than to chart it.[12] Then there was the methodological difficulty inherent in any study which, although itself merely a 'snapshot' in time, was used as the basis for making claims about historical processes, claims which, in the absence of proper longitudinal research, were bound to result in the hypostasizing of past and present.[13] Then, as if these difficulties were not enough, the various arguments advanced demonstrated little agreement over how, or even when, the Protestant ethic was supposedly overthrown. There had been, it transpired, a series of pronouncements concerning the actual or imminent 'death' of the Protestant ethic, which, surprisingly, always seemed to live to 'die' another day. In addition, there was a considerable difference of opinion over how this ethic was being killed off, and especially whether socio-economic or cultural forces were largely responsible for the 'murder'.[14] Then there was the intriguing issue of the historical hiatus between that initial period in the sixteenth century when the Protestant ethic was first formulated and the early twentieth century when it was usually claimed to have been overthrown. Had it really persisted unchanged and unchallenged for four hundred years? For all these reasons I had been growing more and more sceptical about the received view, and increasingly inclined to feel that whatever forces were working to challenge the Protestant ethic they were hardly recent, but could be found to have a pedigree which extended back to a time well before the twentieth century. The existence of this gap in the historical record made me feel that there was a need to bring Weber's analysis up to date; that is to say, I felt that his careful and detailed discussion of the development of the Western religious tradition and its relationship to social and economic life needed to be continued past the historical dateline represented by *The Protestant Ethic and the Spirit of Capitalism*, which was not, as some sociologists seemed to think, somewhere around 1920, but nearer to 1620, or, at best, 1720.

It was at roughly this point that my two interests came together for the first time and the idea outlined in this book formed in my mind. For it then occurred to me that if the cultural anti-puritan forces were essentially 'romantic' in character perhaps they were also associated with consumption; and if consumption and romanticism were associated in the 1960s, then perhaps they always had been? Perhaps there was a 'Romantic ethic' working to promote the 'spirit of consumerism', just as Weber had postulated that a 'Puritan' ethic had promoted the spirit of capitalism? Certainly, it was a 'romantic' cultural movement which was frequently identified as the 'natural enemy' of Puritanism.

The idea was sufficiently intriguing to prompt me to look at Romanticism in a new light as well as embark upon a search for material on consumption and consumer behaviour, and it was not long before I encountered the book by McKendrick, Brewer and Plumb discussed in Chapter 2. What I read there encouraged me to pursue the thesis further:

It will be one of the major burdens of this book to show that consumer behaviour was so rampant and the acceptance of commercial attitudes so pervasive that no one in the future should doubt that the first of the world's consumer societies had unmistakably emerged by 1800.[15]

The authors go on to employ the phrase 'consumer revolution' to refer to the changes which they document, changes which clearly corresponded in time with the Romantic Movement. Not only, therefore, did I now feel that it was worth examining the connection between these two in some detail, but a title for this work came naturally to mind. What else could I possibly call it, but *The Romantic Ethic and the Spirit of Modern Consumerism?*

Unfortunately, it was at this point, just as the evidence was accumulating to make my thesis look promising, that I encountered what was to prove a most troublesome obstacle. There was, it appeared, no satisfactory theory of modern consumerism.

Now Weber's thesis was predicated on the assumption that the Industrial Revolution constituted the most significant upheaval in the system of producing manufactured goods that the world had ever witnessed, an upheaval linked with the emergence of modern capitalism. This assumption was not his alone, but was shared by most of the social theorists of his day, being the subject of considerable investigation and debate. Controversy raged principally over its causes, not its form, however, for there was a general agreement over what constituted modern productive capitalism. The same could not be said for consumption. If, as now seemed to be the case, economic historians were coming to hold the view that the Industrial Revolution also witnessed a major revolution in consumption, there was no adequate theory as to what might be the nature of 'modern' consumption.

Largely this was because the subject of consumer behaviour had been left almost exclusively to economists, who typically operate with an ahistorical framework of assumptions, treating consumer behaviour as basically the same for all peoples at all times. Naturally I consulted those sociologists, mainly Veblen and Sombart, who had turned their attention to consumption, but here too I found little which actually dealt with the key issue in question.[16] I was left, therefore, with the daunting task of striving to formulate a theory of modern consumerism, and it is for this reason that the analogue to that topic which Weber deals with in a mere dozen or so pages (the spirit of modern capitalism) is here discussed in four chapters. First it was necessary to establish that a theory of modern consumer behaviour was needed; secondly, that neither classical economics nor Veblen had provided one which was adequate; thirdly, that a hedonistic theory of social action is fundamentally different from those utilitarian-based perspectives currently embodied in economics; and fourthly that a theory of modern hedonistic conduct can indeed account for the distinctive features of modern consumer behaviour.

I did not embark upon such an ambitious course of action without some hesitation, for I was not eager to venture far into disciplines other than my own. An examination of the account of the eighteenth-century consumer revolution provided by McKendrick, Brewer and Plumb convinced me, however, that their inability to explain that event stemmed directly from the lack of an adequate theory, and that this did not merely represent a failure on the part of economics but an indictment of all social scientists, including sociologists. Moreover, it was also clear from the material they supplied, as well as from my own studies of the 1960s and the first Romantic Movement, that other phenomena, largely neglected by social scientists, were somehow deeply implicated in both this revolution and modern consumer behaviour; phenomena such as fashion, romantic love, taste and the reading of fiction.

The fact that these topics have been much neglected now seems to me to be a matter of great regret, for although it can be argued that some, like fashion and romantic love, have largely failed to attract the attention of sociologists because of the absence of any influential theoretical perspectives which might have suggested their importance, their pervasive presence throughout the modern world is self-evident enough. Their neglect must thus be primarily understood to arise from prejudice, arising from a general tendency to assume, prior to any investigation, that such phenomena are in some way essentially trivial and not worthy of serious study. A view that derives in part from the productionist economic bias which pervades most of social science, in conjunction with an underlying strain of ascetic puritanism. The fact that these topics have not been properly investigated must be seen, however, as both cause and effect of such biases. For there is little doubt that if social scientists had indeed turned their attention to a serious consideration of these topics long ago such prejudices would not now be prevalent within these disciplines. The tendency to indulge in moralizing about consumption practices is very evident in the work of Veblen, as it is in his successor, Riesman, whilst it is trumpeted as a virtue by Galbraith. Even such widely differing contemporary gurus as Herbert Marcuse and Daniel Bell exemplify the same tendency to prefer criticism and condemnation to investigation and explanation.[17]

But another problem, equally baffling in its way, arose at this point. If, as I imagined, Romanticism served to facilitate the emergence of modern consumer behaviour in late eighteenth- and early nineteenth-century England, to legitimate, in effect, a 'consumer ethic', then how could a diametrically opposed 'production ethic', that derived from Protestantism, have been operating in the same place at the same time? Were there really two social ethics, opposed in form, existing side by side, the one legitimating production, the other consumption? If that was the case, were there also two social groups acting as the respective culture carriers? Weber's thesis had clearly linked the production ethic with the emergent bourgeoisie, so perhaps the consumption ethic was linked to the aristocracy? But then the evidence indicated that the new surge in demand came from the *nouveaux riches*. A conclusion which suggested that the bourgeoisie embraced both the Protestant ethic *and* a consumption ethic, a view consistent with what I knew to be the predominantly middle-class character of the Romantic Movement but leading, in its turn, to a fresh sociological puzzle.

I was increasingly coming to feel that the historical problem of explaining the origins of the consumer revolution could not be successfully resolved without the prior resolution of the underlying theoretical issues, especially that concerning the dynamic mechanism lying at the heart of modern consumerism, and that whatever this might turn out to be, cultural processes were fundamentally implicated. Hence, I began to view the historical, economic and sociological questions as intimately associated, as indeed Weber had perceived them to be in his original study of the origins of the production revolution.

It was at this point that I began to realize how a radical revision of the conventionally accepted view of the emergence of modern industrial society and its culture might be implied in the thesis I was developing, more so than I had originally envisaged. In the first place, that upheaval which went under the title of the Industrial Revolution had to be regarded as centring upon a revolution in consumption as well as production. This much was clearly implied by the evidence supplied by the economic historians, who it seemed, were themselves gradually coming round to that point of view. If, however, they were right in this (and logic as well as the results of their inquiries seemed to suggest that they were) then a series of other conclusions appeared to follow in its wake. It suggested, for example, that a 'consumption ethic' must have existed in industrial societies from the very beginning, rather than have emerged subsequently, whilst this in turn implied that the Protestant ethic and whatever ethic legitimated consumption were largely contemporaneous phenomena. This then led on to the thought that perhaps puritan and romantic might not be the stark cultural alternatives which sociologists generally took them to be, something which not only challenged the popular 'cultural contradiction' thesis, but even cast doubt upon the largely taken-for-granted assumption that 'rationality' was the dominant characteristic of both capitalism and modern culture. All these implications seemed to follow from a rejection of the widespread error of treating the Industrial Revolution as if it merely constituted a radical transformation in the means of production. It was, of course, because Weber took this narrow view that he singled out the rational and ascetic features of Protestantism as especially crucial influences; if, however, he was wrong in so obviously neglecting the concomitant revolution in consumption, perhaps other elements of the Christian religious tradition might have been of significance in affecting the development of the modern economy? These were some of the many thoughts which passed through my mind as I embarked on the research for this book, and I turned more and more to Weber's original essay for enlightenment and guidance in my task.

In the footsteps of Weber

Whilst most sociologists clearly hold Max Weber in very high esteem both as a scholar and as one of the 'founding fathers' of their discipline, they have usually been more eager to write about him and his work than to emulate him; that is to say, there is a much bigger Weber industry than there is an industrious effort to engage in the form of cultural sociology which he did so much to pioneer.[18] It is none too clear why this should be the case – apart perhaps from the obviously daunting nature of the task of following in his footsteps. Few scholars could successfully emulate Weber in breadth of scholarship even in his own day, with the consequence that the increased disciplinary specialization which has occurred in academia since the turn of the century now makes his style of wide-ranging and multi-disciplinary inquiry virtually impossible for any one person to emulate.[19] But this does not mean that it should not be attempted, for, as Weber himself illustrated, vital insights into the socio-cultural dynamics of modern societies are probably only to be gained through an exploration of relationships between spheres, such as religion and economics, which are normally considered unrelated, and hence by the deliberate transgressing of conventional academic boundaries. Nor have sociologists usually been over-timid in crossing these borders, even if scholars in other disciplines tend to look askance at such improper conduct. Part of the answer clearly lies in the fact that many of those sociologists who praise Weber so highly actually choose to follow the example of Marx when it comes to the study of culture, focusing, not so much on any of the distinctive categories which Weber employed so successfully, but on the concept of 'ideology'.[20]

The other main reason probably stems, ironically, from the very esteem accorded to Weber's work and hence to the world-view which it embodies, for the rationalistic *Weltanschauung* which he espoused envisaged the actual disappearance of that very phenomenon to which he devoted a lifetime of study. Although Weber's broad interests encompassed institutions, such as bureaucracy, the division of labour, the law and the state – which have remained a significant part of the modern world – his predominant focus was upon religion, and here his emphasis upon disenchantment and the overall processes of rationalization suggested the clear loss of influence, if not the actual disappearance, of this phenomenon. Whilst of crucial significance to the birth of the modern world, his view seems to have been that, religion's mid-wifely duties accomplished, it would then cease to have any significant role to play upon the world stage. To the extent, therefore, that sociologists have accepted the Weberian view (which was not, of course, limited to him alone) then they might be forgiven for assuming that there is little point in engaging in that particular form of cultural analysis which he made his forte, for many of the concepts which Weber employed, such as theodicy, asceticism and prophecy, seem to apply specifically to 'religious' systems of beliefs and values.

A little reflection soon reveals the error of this assumption, however, for these terms, as developed and used by Weber, have no more necessary connection with religion than does the term 'charisma', that most notable of all Weberian terms to break out of such conceptual 'ghettoization'; in which case, of course, Weber's style of analysis is then seen to be no less applicable to contemporary cultural phenomenon than to the historic forms of religion which he studied. This is certainly the assumption underlying this work.

But then those sociologists who have taken religion as their particular field of study have typically adopted strangely ambiguous attitudes toward their subject-matter, being characteristically Durkheimian in their approach to the present, but Weberian when viewing the past. That is to say, they have proved themselves to be highly ingenious in seeking out contemporary activities and institutions to which Durkheimian insights concerning the nature and function of 'religion' can be applied in an insightful fashion, whilst following Weber in adopting a more conventional view of what might be considered 'religious phenomena' when examining the past. This in itself might not have mattered had Weber's extraordinarily ambitious scheme to survey the world's religions and their historical development actually been continued up to his own time.[21] But as Weber did not carry his analysis of the evolution of theological systems into the eighteenth century, an awkward time-shadow has developed within the sociology of culture. This separates that essentially feudal and pre-modern time, when it is assumed all significant socio-political and cultural movements were likely to be manifest in a 'religious' form and be accompanied by a recognizable theology, from the contemporary world in which, if anything, the opposite assumption prevails. As for the intervening age – that crucial period between *c.* 1650 and 1850 – here the assumption seems to be that Weber's 'Protestant ethic thesis' says it all. Unfortunately, it is too easy to forget that this thesis was developed as an answer to a very specific problem, why modern capitalism emerged first in Western Europe, and hence cannot be considered to constitute a complete or comprehensive account of the development of Western religious thought down to modern times.

This book expresses the belief that the best way to honour a great man is to imitate and not simply praise him, and so is intended as both a compliment to Weber the scholar and a complement to his most famous work. Although not intended as either a companion volume or a commentary on *The Protestant Ethic and the Spirit of Capitalism*, it has perhaps acquired something of the flavour of both. It is a companion text in the sense that the main argument developed here aims to complement Weber's, to be, in effect, its mirror image. Weber's claim concerning the nature of the link between Protestantism and capitalism is not denied, but extended such that both the rational ascetic and the sentimental Pietistic sides of that religious movement are seen as contributing to the development of the modern economy. It is true that, in order to achieve this more ambitious integral account, some refinements of Weber's views are suggested, especially with respect to his treatment of Protestantism and what might reasonably be regarded as constituting its 'ethic', as well as what has subsequently been its fate. But such modifications are not seen as in any way fatal to Weber's argument; on the contrary, such modifications are essential in order to resolve some of the long-standing problems which acceptance of his thesis has created.

Weber's example has been followed to the extent of first outlining the 'Spirit of Consumption' in Part One and then subsequently discussing a 'Protestant' ('Romantic') ethic in Part Two, but this procedure has been complicated by the necessity of discussing the nature of modern consumerism at some length. That accomplished, its 'Spirit' is then specified as being autonomous, self-illusory hedonism, making it possible to move on to outline the cultural ethic which has facilitated its emergence.

The difference in treatment here is a direct consequence of Weber's own work. For, whilst he concentrated on outlining those Protestant teachings which he considered had influenced the development of an ethic favourable to a capitalist spirit, it is necessary here to disentangle the origins of another ethic from those self-same teachings. Thus the basis of an ethical code which served to justify consumption is described largely by a process of distinguishing it from that 'Protestant ethic' described by Weber. Despite these differences, the underlying structure of the argument advanced mirrors that of Weber's, stressing the central role of a cultural 'ethic' in enabling the introduction of a 'modern' form of economic action, demonstrating both their 'congruence' and their psychological and cultural connections.

This is not an exercise in the history of ideas in any conventional sense, but like Weber's own work, possesses something of the flavour of that approach. Thus whilst not subscribing to the one-sided view that mind or spirit is the ultimate force behind the development of history, the claim that the movement of ideas can be a major cause of social change when constituted as the 'living faith' or 'formulated aspirations' of people is taken seriously.[22] Following Weber's example, however, the precise nature of the conduct which issues from acceptance of a given belief is treated as problematic, and becomes itself the central focus of investigation. Hence the principal concern is to trace the manner in which changes in society's conceptions of the true, the good and the beautiful influence patterns of conduct, not in any direct prescriptive fashion but through the way that ideals give direction to character-confirming conduct. It does not follow, nevertheless, that the influence of material forces upon the construction and adoption of ideas is neglected, whilst some suggestions are made in the concluding chapter concerning the way in which 'idealistic' and 'materialistic' modes of explanation might be more successfully related.

A further similarity with the history of ideas, as exemplified by such an eminent exponent as Arthur Lovejoy, is a concern with ideas and 'thought' in the form of tacit assumptions and presuppositions in addition to explicit systems of beliefs.[23] What Lovejoy called the 'unconscious mental habits' of people may clearly be as significant for understanding their ethical conduct as their professed creeds,[24] and it is in this context that material from literary criticism has been found to be especially valuable. At the same time, like intellectual history but unlike cultural history in the full sense of that term, there is a tendency to ignore popular and folk belief in order to concentrate upon 'higher' if not merely 'high' culture. The justification for this lies in the greater influence which the latter has upon the general climate of thought, and especially upon the formulation of ethical ideals. It is for this reason that there is little reference to the working classes in the pages that follow.[25]

At the same time, this inquiry shares that interdisciplinary quality so characteristic of the history of ideas, and makes extensive use of those 'gates' which Lovejoy has suggested it constructs in 'the fences which separate academic disciplines'[26] As a result it has a certain cross-grained character, derived, not merely from examining topics outside their usual disciplinary context, but according them a significance normally denied within it. Thus Sentimentalism is considered here as a socio-ethical movement of great importance rather than as a somewhat unfortunate literary trend significant merely for its subsequent influence upon Romanticism; similarly fashion is considered a major socio-aesthetic phenomenon indicative of the central values of a modern society, rather than as just an ingenious and exploitative retailing device.[27] This book therefore involves a certain amount of reading between the lines of the conventional story of the birth of modern society, presenting an account which challenges not only the productionist bias in both history and social science, but the accompanying assumption that modern cultural development is best characterized by ever-increasing rationality.

One cannot, of course, claim to 'complement' Weber's argument in this way without giving rise to a range of further questions concerning the whole which is created through the attempted integration of the two theses. If it is accepted that parallel cultural processes occurred in relation to both the development of modern production and modern consumption, what is the precise connection between these two sides of the equation? Given that the productionist bias which characterized Weber's view of the industrial revolution requires some correction, should it be replaced by a consumptionist one, or is there some integrated 'balanced' account of the emergence of the modern economy which escapes from the necessity of having to take sides on such an issue? The questions are intriguing and remain to be considered in some other, subsequent, work.

Lastly, it should be remembered that this book, like that upon which it is modelled, is essentially an essay.[28] Thus despite its length, it remains an attempt, an experiment, arising out of a deep dissatisfaction with the doubtful cultural contrasts and marked productionist biases of most contemporary discussions, to see if a more plausible and acceptable account of the development of modern consumerism and the culture of modernity can be constructed. It is not a detailed scholarly study, but a broad-ranging and fundamentally speculative attempt to draw together a highly diverse and apparently unrelated body of material to form a meaningful and coherent story.[29]

This story starts, in Part One, with the puzzle presented by modern consumerism and the eighteenth-century consumer revolution, and the subsequent development of an hedonistic theory of modern consumer behaviour. Then, in Part Two, Protestantism's relationship with hedonism is explored by examining the cults of benevolence and melancholy, prior to a discussion of Sentimentalism and Romanticism. Lastly, the conclusion attempts to explicate the complex relationship between idealistic and self-seeking aspects of social action, as well as that between rational puritanism and romanticism within the culture of the West.

Part One

The Spirit of Modern Consumerism

2

Accounting for the Consumer Revolution in Eighteenth-Century England

If consumer demand, then, was the key to the Industrial Revolution, social emulation was the key to consumer demand.

Harold Perkin

Over the past two decades economic historians have increasingly come to recognize that their discipline has been marked by a tendency to over-emphasize the factor of supply and that, too closely following the lead of the classical economists, analyses of the industrial revolution have tended to concentrate upon changes in the techniques of production rather than changes in the nature of demand.[1] As a consequence of this realization more attention has been paid to the problems which relate to the demand side of market expansion and the necessity of providing an explanation for this phenomenon which does not treat it as little more than 'a reflex to the rising tide of mechanized production'.[2] At the same time, there has been a belated recognition of the fact that any understanding of the industrial revolution as constituting a dramatic transformation in supply logically 'presupposes a concomitant development and extension of consumption'[3] and hence that a consumer revolution forms the 'necessary analogue to the industrial revolution, the necessary convulsion on the demand side of the equation to match the convulsion on the supply side'.[4] Put together, these insights result in the view that a crucial part of any understanding of the emergence of the economic basis of modern societies lies in an appreciation of those forces which brought about a dramatic increase in demand or, in Perkin's words, that 'consumer demand was the ultimate key to the Industrial Revolution'.[5] This, quite naturally, makes the explanation of that demand a matter of more than ordinary interest and significance.

At first, historians directed their attention to what appeared to be the most obvious influence upon demand for goods, the size of the market, with the consequence that population growth became the focus of attention. This 'extension of the market' thesis raised certain difficulties, however, not least the circularity of causation which it seemed to suggest. What is more, the evidence from the Third World did not support such an argument, pointing instead to the probability that increases in population, if taken by themselves, simply lead to greater poverty without any effective increase in demand.[5] Attention therefore shifted to the idea that the crucial event must have been an increase in spending power consequent upon a rise in the standard of living.[6] This thesis was also soon recognized as presenting difficulties as there is ample evidence to show that consumers do not automatically use surplus income to satisfy new wants. Indeed, only the modern consumer typically does this; the traditional consumer being more inclined either to save or to translate his extra wealth into leisure. As Perkin observes, peasants characteristically hoard a surplus against the day when they may need to replace an ox or dower a daughter,[7] whilst both Hoyt and Nair[8] describe how, when peasants suddenly acquire wealth through the introduction of a cash crop, they are inclined to pay others to do their work, translating their new-found prosperity into leisure.[9] Even if one accepts that the attitudes of consumers in the eighteenth century were not identical to those of Third World peasants, it is still highly important to distinguish, as Eric Jones does, between the presence in a population of 'a new *ability* to buy inessentials and a new *willingness* to do so',[10] and hence to explain how traditional attitudes are overcome. In fact, William Cobbett provides evidence to support the view that in England at the time the yeomanry did not immediately employ their extra wealth to satisfy new wants, observing in 1825 of one family that, 'they had long been in command of income sufficient to acquire new possessions, but only now felt compelled to do so'.[11]

Recognizing that the solution to the problem of accounting for increased demand cannot be found in a consideration of either numbers or spending power alone, economic historians have been forced to accept that the answer must be sought in some change in those values and attitudes which govern consumption. Increasingly, therefore, one finds references to the crucial part played by 'a new moral attitude towards consumer spending', or to an important change in the 'attitude of mind' toward buying, whilst Jones emphasizes the factors of taste and fashion.[12] Such arguments tend to take the debate out of the realm of traditional economic theory and place it in the broader context of social science.[13]

Scrutiny of the literature reveals that a 'standard' or conventional explanation of the increased demand which accompanied the Industrial

Revolution has now emerged which does accept as its premise the centrality of a change in attitude on the part of consumers. Instead of dealing with such straightforwardly material factors as population or income this perspective recognizes the importance of the motivation lying behind consumer behaviour, considering that it is here that the critical change occurred. What McKendrick calls the 'increased propensity to consume'[14], and which was considered an essential accompaniment to the Industrial Revolution is thus now commonly accounted for by reference to the motive of social emulation. Harold Perkin has popularized this view:

If consumer demand, then, was the key to the Industrial Revolution, social emulation was the key to consumer demand. By the eighteenth century nearly everyone in England and the Scottish Lowlands received a money income, and nearly everyone was prepared to spend a large part of it in 'keeping up with the Joneses'.[15]

This, he feels, was a particularly effective motive in Britain where a comparatively open and finely graded system of social stratification allowed for easy interchange between adjacent ranks, with the consequence that social emulation was an important factor spurring individuals both to work hard and to increase consumption. Perkin's argument has been readily adopted by others and constitutes a major plank in McKendrick et al.'s more detailed discussion of the nature and origins of the consumer revolution.[16]

Economic and social historians characteristically employ theory, whether drawn from economics or sociology, in a very informal and 'informative' manner and hence, even though one can identify a 'standard' interpretation of the consumer revolution in which Veblenesque theories of social emulation predominate, it is not an easy matter to identify the precise nature of the claims made nor the exact interpretation given to certain terms and phrases. To make matters worse, other theoretical perspectives are frequently mixed in with the emphasis upon emulation in an apparent attempt to compensate for some of this theory's shortcomings, with the consequence that the resulting melange of assertions are hard to interrelate or evaluate. Nevertheless, the critical importance of the issue in question requires that an attempt should be made to disentangle and evaluate these claims, and so McKendrick's discussion will be taken as the focus for such an endeavour.

It is clear that Veblen's theory of conspicuous consumption together with the stress which he placed upon the role of the leisure class occupies a central position in McKendrick's account of the emergence of a modern consumer society. In the first place, he attributes a key role to the part played by the rich, whom he considers to have 'led the way' in ushering in the new era of consumption through a veritable 'orgy of spending' in the

1760s and 1770s.[17] Additionally and crucially, however, he stresses how it was the fact that the middle ranks of society imitated the rich in this extravagance, and were in turn imitated by those beneath them, which constituted the critical development giving rise to a new propensity to consume. The story which he tells therefore is one of 'social imitation and emulative spending penetrating deeper than ever before through the closely packed ranks of eighteenth century society',[18] a process which he explicitly refers to as the 'Veblen Effect', and considers to have become a force throughout society 'only in the last two centuries'.[19]

The theme of emulation as a central mechanism accounting for the dramatic upsurge in demand is repeated several times as reference is made to the growing practice of individuals emulating 'their betters', or being 'propelled' by the power of envy and ambition.[20] Like Perkin, McKendrick stresses the fact that the comparatively open structure of British society greatly facilitated this 'restless striving to clamber from one rank to the next', whilst the domestic servant class is identified as an especially vital link in the 'chain' of emulative imitation, as too is London in the equally crucial geographical spread of consumption habits.[21]

Although Veblen's theoretical insights are here employed, as so often by economists and economic historians, without any discussion of their limitations, the most obvious criticism of the emulative theory of consumption as an answer to the problem of the origin of the increased eighteenth-century demand for goods does occur to McKendrick, who states it thus:

One of the weaknesses, however, in arguments drawing attention to the domestic servant class, or the role of London, or the character, structure and mobility of English society as explanations of increasing home demand and rising levels of spending is that critics can promptly point out that none of them were new to the eighteenth century. Servants mimicking their masters are an age-old phenomenon, one rank in society being eager to join a higher group is just as old, and London as a centre of conspicuous consumption was by no means new.[22]

His response to this serious objection is to point to the development at this time of a new 'commercial capacity' and 'techniques' in the spheres of marketing and distribution and, in particular, to the rise of advertising. These events, he suggests, constituted the crucial innovations for:

The long-felt desire of so many members of English society to ape their superiors had to be given a fresh impetus to do so, a new spending ability to enable them to do so, and easier access to a greater variety of amply available new commodities. A mass consumer market awaited those products of the industrial revolution which skilful sales promotion could make fashionably desirable, heavy advertisement could make widely known, and whole batteries of salesmen could make easily accessible.[23]

As can be seen, several factors are invoked to explain why it was only in the mid-eighteenth century that emulative motives should have become so especially effective in stimulating consumer demand. Some of these, such as 'a new spending ability', have already been encountered and dismissed, whilst 'amply available new products' is merely a re-statement of the 'demand as reflex of supply' thesis. This means that the crucial claims are those contained in the last sentence with its reference to skilfully directed and controlled advertising and sales campaigns, and this does indeed turn out to be a central part of McKendrick's subsequent discussion, as the subtitle of the book – 'The Commercialization of Eighteenth Century England' – suggests.

There are several aspects to this process of commercialization and they are discussed in some detail by McKendrick and his colleagues Brewer and Plumb, but what is of particular interest is the role which it is attributed in the creation of a new level of consumer demand and this, as the above quote implies, turns out to be the factor of conscious manipulation. It is this ingredient which McKendrick clearly feels explains why emulative motives should have become especially significant at this time, and in his conclusion to the chapter on fashion he writes: 'I have tried to show ... how the manipulation of social emulation made men pursue "luxuries" where they had previously bought "decencies", and "decencies" where they had previously bought only "necessities"'[24] The emergence in this period of modern advertising and sales techniques and their successful exploitation by such entrepreneurs as Josiah Wedgwood and George Packwood is then cited in support of this general claim.

Unfortunately, McKendrick does not perceive the obvious objection against this stress upon manipulation as clearly as he did earlier with respect to social emulation. For here too there is a problem in accounting for the sudden appearance and spread of aggressive advertising and sales campaigns. Had not manufacturers long sought to control the market for their goods? Had they not always tried, by whatever means at their disposal, to persuade consumers to buy their products? How is it then that they were immeasurably more successful in achieving these goals in the later decades of the eighteenth century than they had been previously? In fact, McKendrick does recognize the importance of the phenomenon which represents the answer to this conundrum, but fails to give it an unambiguously definite location in his causal account of the generation of demand. The phenomenon in question would appear to be fashion, or more precisely, its modern variant.

McKendrick provides evidence to show how what he calls the 'Western European fashion pattern' came into being for the first time in the eighteenth century.[25] Fashion, in the sense of the prevailing custom, is, of course, a universal social phenomenon and is subject to change even in traditional societies. What characterizes modern fashion, by contrast, is the very rapid pace of change which occurs in shape, material and style, and evidence suggests that this quickened tempo began in the middle of the eighteenth century, the turning point being the reign of George II, to be followed by a certain 'fashion frenzy' early in the reign of George III.[26] Consequently, whereas previously modifications in styles of dress had taken generations to reveal themselves now they occurred within the space of a few years, even in some cases annually. In 1753, for example, purple was the 'in' colour, whilst in 1757 the fashion was for white linen with a pink pattern; in 1776 the fashionable colour was 'couleur de Noisette'; in 1777 it was dove grey.[27] The enthusiasm for fashion was by no means limited to the rich, but rapidly spread throughout society, extending from the domestic servant class to industrial employers and eventually even to agricultural workers: all began to feel some compulsion to be 'in fashion'.[28] London was the geographical and social centre of fashion and innovation spread outward to the provinces in such a way that it was claimed one could trace fashionable gradations in dress according to the distance travelled from the city.[29] The central and distinctive feature of this new phenomenon was the sheer rapidity with which novelty was consumed; as McKendrick's evidence clearly shows, 'Fashions changed with kaleidoscopic speed' with – as far as the design of shoes was concerned, for example – 'Toes [going] from sharp pointed to. round pointed to square toed, as remorselessly as they do in the twentieth century, and at roughly the same speed'.[30]

A chapter is devoted to a discussion of the emergence of modern fashion and its significance in the commercialization of consumption and here, as elsewhere in the book, its key role is illustrated and affirmed. It is made clear, for example, that the manipulation of demand was only really possible through the control of fashion, or if this is too grand a claim, through its careful exploitation, as Josiah Wedgwood did so successfully. Indeed, the manipulation of social emulation was itself only possible via the medium of fashion, there being no other available mechanism through which manufacturers could so directly affect the ambitious or envious desires of consumers. The emergence of the modern fashion pattern is thus the crucial ingredient in any explanation of why either emulation on the part of consumers or manipulation on the part of producers should have begun to take such novel and dynamic forms in the eighteenth century.

Such a conclusion naturally leads to yet one further question, one which McKendrick does recognize and attempt to answer, that concerning the universality of fashion and the uniqueness of its modern form. For, once again, if fashion is to be advanced as the crucial factor making for change then some account of why it only became operative in this manner in the mid-eighteenth century is required. The answer given is rather perplexing.

At first, McKendrick seems tempted to resort to notions of inherited need in order to explain the existence of fashion, referring to the desire to be fashionable as a 'constant of the human condition'.[31] Such an argument naturally directs attention to those economic and commercial developments which 'allowed' this 'need' to be fully expressed for the first time.[32] Happily he does not pursue this sterile course of argument but turns instead to place an emphasis upon the role of manipulation in the 'creation' of the Western European fashion pattern, suggesting that

potent as the force of fashion was, it needed to be released and mobilized and exploited before it could significantly add to aggregate demand. The conditions making this possible grew steadily more favourable. . . . But it still required active and aggressive selling to reach that market and exploit its full potential.[33]

Finally concluding that the significant element of the new commercial approach was that it 'deliberately and consciously aimed at controlling the market, sustaining consumer interest and creating new demand'.[34] The question of the origin of the modern fashion pattern does appear, however, to have become lost as McKendrick returns to the issue of its role in the generation of new levels of consumer demand. What is to be especially noted though, is that in so far as any explanation of its origin is offered, it is in terms of a factor, the conscious manipulation of the market, which it has already been suggested is itself dependent upon the prior existence of the Western European fashion pattern. Obviously there are some unresolved problems in this account.

In fact, one can conclude more broadly that the 'standard' account of the consumer revolution in the eighteenth century, of which McKendrick et al.'s is the most detailed version to date, does not constitute an adequate explanation of either the origin of the new propensity to consume or indeed of modern consumerism more generally. All that such an account contains is an itemization of those factors considered relevant to such an explanation, factors such as emulative spending, fashion and deliberate attempts to manipulate the market, but there is no worked-out understanding of the relationship between these, or any statement of the precise manner in which they might be considered to have interacted so as to have brought about such a transformation. The key problem, as far as each factor is concerned, is to provide a convincing account of its increased effectiveness at this time, something which it is apparently easier to do for fashion – where the contrast with what came before is very marked – than for the others. If, however, the novel force of the modern Western fashion pattern is to be explained in its turn by reference to factors already considered, then all explanatory power is lost. The extent of this failure is glossed over by constant cross-referencing to each of the factors in turn and by the fact that the theoretical perspectives employed contain fundamental but unacknowledged inadequacies.

Something of the full extent of the inadequacy of this 'standard' account of the consumer revolution can be gauged as soon as one probes the common understanding of the phenomenon of modern fashion which lies at its centre, only to discover that this is in turn explained in terms of social emulation; social scientists typically adopting Simmel's view that fashion is basically an emulation of prestige groups.[35] In which case, it really would appear as if one has finally closed the circle of explanation. The new demand for goods, it is claimed, arises from the sudden operation of new emulative motives for spending, these being exploited and manipulated by manufacturers because of the presence of a novel and dynamic form of 'fashion'. It now transpires, however, that this phenomenon does itself entirely presuppose the presence of such motives. The account is clearly tautological and does not provide us with any insight into the dynamics of the consumer revolution. A conclusion which strongly suggests fundamental weaknesses at the level of theory.

Consumption and cultural change

Before leaving the discipline of economic history and the enigma of the origin of the new consumer demand which accompanied the Industrial Revolution, there are certain characteristics of eighteenth-century consumerism which it is important to record.

The first of these concerns that section of society which was to the fore in this revolution, and hence played the significant role in its accomplishment. As McKendrick pertinently inquires:

Who bought the cottons, woollens, linens and silks of the burgeoning British textile industries? Who consumed the massive increases in beer production? Who bought the crockery which poured from the Staffordshire potteries? Who bought the buckles, the buttons, the pins and all the minor metal products on which Birmingham fortunes were built? Who bought the Sheffield cutlery, the books from the booming publishers, the women's journals, the children's toys, the products of the nurserymen? Which families purchased the products of the early consumer industries?[36]

He answers these questions by quoting Professor Eversley to the effect that 'the foundation of the industrial revolution was laid by the home sale of articles of everyday life to a section of the labour force which was neither very poor nor very rich'.[37] In other words, to a 'middle-income market', a 'nascent bourgeoisie consisting of artisans, tradesmen, the more substantial farmers, engineers and clerks'.[38] Pawson agrees that 'it was essentially a middle-class demand, supported by the farmers and gentry in the countryside, and the professional and tradespeople of the towns'.[39] Of course, the rich consumed lavishly, making a contribution to overall demand which was out of proportion to their numbers, but then they had always done so. Also, it is correct to point out that, as the Industrial Revolution gained momentum, so the contribution made by the lower classes to overall demand increased. None the less, it seems to be the case that the very considerable expansion of demand in the early part of the Industrial Revolution was essentially middle class in origin.

The second significant feature of the consumer revolution of the eighteenth century which research has revealed concerns the products listed in the quotation from McKendrick given above, in other words, the actual nature of the items which were so much the object of this new demand. For, contrary to popular impression, the manufacturing industries most closely associated with the early Industrial Revolution were those producing consumer rather than capital goods and among these, those which produced objects for 'luxury' consumption predominated. Thirsk has shown how the vast majority of the economic 'projects' and associated 'industrial by-employments' of the seventeenth century were concerned with the production of 'non-essential' goods; those occupations which emerged in rural areas at this time being predominantly concerned with the manufacture of such products as 'toys, buttons, pins or lace, items which politicians labelled as frivolities, as indeed they were'.[40] She lists among other luxury products looking-glasses, brooches, cards, puppets and even toothpicks.[41] McKendrick, Brewer and Plumb's study of the later period does little to dispel the general impression that the new demand was indeed for anything but 'essentials', although, as they observe, what could be considered to fall into that category was constantly being redefined. It is clear from the examples they give, none the less, that such products as toys and games, novels, beauty products, flowering plants and above all, fashionable clothes, were hardly the sort of purchases which those other than the very rich could easily designate as 'necessities'.

Closer examination of the consumer revolution in eighteenth-century England also reveals that a wider cultural revolution was involved. This is hardly a surprising conclusion, for not only is 'consumption' largely an economists' abstraction from the complex pattern of humanly meaningful conduct, but it has already been noted how the new propensity to consume stemmed from a change in values and attitudes; a change which presumably was not confined to the economic significance of gratificatory behaviour. This fact is also appreciated, if only in part, by economic historians, for their discussion of this topic extends to include such general issues as the growth of leisure and changing attitudes towards children.[42] What remains unclear, however, is how the revolution in demand was related to these wider developments, or even which of the many innovations which occurred at this time should be considered as either part of the consumer revolution or closely related to it.

What is clear, as Professor Plumb has demonstrated,[43] is that a leisure revolution was an integral part of this overall pattern of change. A very wide range of activities which we now accept as a normal part of recreation, such as the theatre and horse-racing, took their modern form during this period. In this respect, it is even more obvious that the expenditure involved can hardly be classed as anything other than luxurious, leisure being, almost by definition, a non-essential activity, the modern view of 'healthy recreation' as an important human need having not as yet become widely accepted. Here too the middle classes constituted the dominant new market, as Professor Plumb makes clear, commenting at the end of his survey that 'All the activities that I have so far described point to the growth of a middle-class audience.' These he specifies as the theatre, music, dancing, sport and 'cultural pastimes' generally, for which 'the prosperous gentry and the new middle class hungered'.[44]

Another facet of the eighteenth-century consumer revolution only referred to in passing by McKendrick et al. was the development of the modern novel and the emergence of a fiction-reading public. There occurred a tremendous expansion in the market for books, especially fiction, during the century with the annual publication of new works quadrupling; at the same time, new marketing and distributing techniques were introduced, most noticeably the circulating library, whilst the profession of 'author' also became more or less established.[45] Here too commercialization was very apparent with the development of a 'fiction-manufacturing industry'[46] being linked to aggressive advertising, with special subscription plans and part-publication designed to overcome the high cost of books. Also there is widespread agreement that the major part of the demand came from the middle classes and more particularly still, from women. As Taylor observes, the fact 'That women constituted by far the greater part of the readership for these novels was never disputed.'[47] This latter observation serves to direct attention to another significant socio-cultural development which occurred at this period; the rise of romantic love. Whether this could be said to be a 'part' of the consumer revolution is unclear but it was very closely associated with the growth of a market for fiction.

Although the novels published during the later eighteenth century did deal with other topics, they had this one overriding subject. Less prominent perhaps in the Gothic novel than in the 'sentimental' or explicitly 'romantic' genre it pervaded most of the fiction of the time, as indeed it has tended to do down to the present day. The fact that love was a near-universal theme was one of the principal reasons for the moral objections commonly raised against novels, for they were considered to serve as 'silent instructors in the art of intrigue', and by 'corrupting female hearts' thought to incite young women to disobey their parents by eloping.[48] This strongly suggests that love in the novel and love in the real world were closely related, and this is indeed what Professor Stone has argued:

Despite . . . objections, romantic love and the romantic novel grew together after 1780, and the problem of cause and effect is one that it is impossible to solve. All that can be said is that for the first time in history, romantic love became a respectable motive for marriage among the propertied classes, and that at the same time there was a rising flood of novels . . . devoted to the same theme.[49]

Although love was no eighteenth-century discovery, attitudes toward it did change significantly at this time, making it not only fashionable, but as the above quote indicates, a sufficient motive for marriage. This was clearly something new, for although young people had often fallen in love before, marriage for this reason alone was not acceptable, and relatives and friends would act to prevent any such unsuitable match.[50] Now, for the first time, romantic ideas so elevated the status of the emotion that no such obstacles were to be endured; love, and love alone, was the sovereign consideration in the choice of partners. Indeed, all the features which we recognize today as characteristic of romantic love become clearly outlined for the first time during this period, such as:

the notion that there is only one person in the world with whom one can fully unite at all levels; the personality of that person is so idealized that the normal faults and follies of human nature disappear from view; love is often like a thunderbolt and strikes at first sight; love is the most important thing in the world, to which all other considerations, particularly material ones, should be sacrificed; and, lastly, the giving of full rein to personal emotions is admirable, no matter how exaggerated and absurd the resulting conduct may appear to others.[51]

Exactly why this complex of beliefs should emerge to prominence in Britain in the late eighteenth century has not been fully explained, although it has been suggested that, as a development out of courtly love, it represents the further extension of religious teachings about passion transplanted into a purely secular context.[52]

The general expansion of leisure-time activities, including the reading of novels, can, together with the rise of fashion and romantic love, all be seen as part and parcel of a cluster of cultural phenomena which first appeared in England in the eighteenth century, and which, in some way as yet unclear, relate to what has been called the consumer revolution. The explanation for the appearance of each of these is no more adequate than that for the consumer revolution itself, and yet it does seem that all involve fundamental changes in beliefs, values and attitudes.[53]

The problem of justification

Naturally changes of this order do not occur within a society without both comment and opposition as they constitute a departure from traditional and approved forms of conduct. Neither, of course, can they gain acceptance or become widespread unless some currents of thought serve to legitimate them by countermanding such condemnation. This problem – which can be dubbed the issue of justification – has been noted in connection with the consumer revolution if not for the larger cluster of cultural innovations mentioned above. Typically, the problem is simply recorded, or treated as a self-evident consequence of economic change.

Thus Thirsk, for example, does little more than observe that consumer goods 'taken for granted in the English home' in Adam Smith's day, 'had been condemned in the 1540s as childish frivolities or unnecessary, even harmful, indulgences'.[54] Whilst Minchinton, discussing convention and fashion in relation to consumption, sees economic change itself as inevitably leading to the abandonment of asceticism:

But important too for changes in consumption was the attitude of mind. The Puritan was typically associated with a wish to limit expenditure on material desires. . . . (These) religious attitudes seemed appropriate when output was growing slowly but when with industrialization the speed of growth not only quickened but appeared to be sustained and cumulative, then the old precepts of poverty ceased to appeal. The quickening pace of technological change began to provide glimpses of abundance which made dreams of affluence possible. To reinforce the material desires, philosophers and economists came to expound a hedonistic calculus rather than asceticism and helped to undermine the restraints of custom and convention.[55]

The argument that economic change and increases in the standard of living lead to the weakening of ascetic attitudes rather begs the question under discussion if we assume that a surge in consumer-led demand was the factor which initiated economic growth in the first place. Thus we are left with the suggestion that a 'consumption ethic' was justified by the writings of philosophers and economists.

This theme is taken up by McKendrick, using material from Joyce Appleby, and he shows how, by the end of the seventeenth century, there existed 'an impressive array of contemporary writers who saw the constructive and beneficial aspects of progressive levels of spending'.[56] These were men like Dudley North, John Houghton and Nicholas Barbon, and McKendrick quotes Professor Appleby to the effect that 'the idea of man as a consuming animal with boundless appetites, capable of driving the economy to new levels of prosperity, arrived with the economic literature of the 1690s'.[57] Yet, as he also notes, such ideas did not gain widespread acceptance for almost a century. In fact, the intensity of moral opposition to these views became apparent with the universally hostile reception given to Mandeville's *Fable of the Bees*, published in 1724. This allegory argued that the pursuit of such private vices as avarice, prodigality, pride, envy and vanity stimulated the demand for luxury goods and in so doing created employment, increased wealth and generally contributed to the public good. It was widely condemned as an immoral and wicked book.

There are reasons for being sceptical, however, about the extent to which politico-economic theorizing can be seriously regarded as contributing to the justification of consumer behaviour. McKendrick credits such writers as Dudley North, Adam Smith and (in an ironic fashion) Mandeville, with supplying what he calls the 'intellectual origins' of the consumer revolution because they attacked the conventional wisdom.[58] The essence of this had been that whilst the rich could be expected to spend in an extravagant fashion (creating patronage, employment and wealth in the process) all other sections of society should uphold an ethic of frugality and restraint. The counter-arguments presented by these apologists for consumption were overwhelmingly utilitarian in character, stressing (as in Mandeville's case) the general benefits which could be expected to follow from encouraging higher levels of consumption; the principal of these being the increased stimulus to production. But apart from the fact that justifying consumption in terms of its contribution to production does nothing whatever to alter the predisposition to value the latter over the former,[59] such arguments cannot be considered to carry much weight compared with the moral objections ranged against them. After all, the primary grounds for advocating such values as humility, abstinence, frugality, thrift and industry, and condemning luxury, greed, avarice, indulgence, idleness and envy, were not that the former were useful and the latter useless, but that moral virtues were being contrasted with vices, and although (as Mandeville was detested for noting) it may be true that, under some circumstances, desirable consequences may follow from the practice of vice, that is not a good enough reason to turn it into a virtue.[60] In other words, moral arguments are unlikely to be overthrown by utilitarian considerations; on the contrary, they are only likely to be successfully countered by other moral arguments.

It is thus pertinent to consider more closely what a 'defence' of luxury might be. Vichert refers to Boswell's observation that Dr Johnson characteristically 'defended luxury' on the grounds that he advocated spending money 'in luxury' because by so doing one was doing good to the poor, that is inducing them to 'exert industry', rather than by keeping them in idleness (which would be the consequence if one was to give out alms).[61] But apart from the fact that this appears to be merely an argument in favour of luxury spending as opposed to charity, it does not constitute a sanctification of luxurious consumption as such. Vichert actually excludes the following line from the quotation, 'I own, indeed, there may be more virtue in giving it immediately in charity, than in spending it in luxury'; which clearly demonstrates that pointing to the benefits of luxury is not the same as morally justifying it. Dr Johnson goes on to criticize Mandeville for not defining vice or public benefit, and for assuming that whatever contributes to wealth is thus a public benefit.[62] In fact, Johnson's advocacy of luxury is purely utilitarian in character and not at odds with a personal asceticism.

It is clear that such intellectual defences of the freedom to produce and distribute luxury goods should not be confused with the moral legitimation of their consumption. One may well support the former (especially if you are yourself a merchant who profits from the trade in luxury goods) without in the least approving of this form of conduct. The practice of a personal asceticism is thus not incompatible with a recognition of the general utility of luxury consumption.

The fact that intellectual justifications of luxury tended to be purely utilitarian in form, and did not confront the fundamental moral objections which constituted the essence of the ascetics' case, is admitted by Eli Heckscher, who observes that

Mercantilism rejected in principle any ethical attitude towards luxury. The only consideration that carried weight was how far a particular measure furthered or obstructed economic life in the direction which mercantilism tried to lead it. Thus, finally, in strictest contrast to the medieval standpoint, there arose a conscious and frankly admitted tendency to justify luxury, indeed to stimulate it, quite irrespective of the status of the purchaser, in all cases in which it guaranteed a market for the country's products and 'put money into circulation'.[63]

This kind of 'justification' takes the issue of motivation for granted; that is, it assumes that people desire to consume luxury goods and merely require such arguments as these to be able to do so with a good conscience. The alternative would involve assuming that the desire to stimulate trade, 'keep money in circulation' or (in Dr Johnson's case) provide potential beggars with work, constituted the real motives of the consumers of luxury goods. That this was the case seems unlikely, for these are surely the arguments favoured by the manufacturers and traders who fear that the upholders of an ascetic morality will interfere with their trade in an attempt to control the spread of 'vice'. Now it may well have been the case that such pleas for an uncontrolled market in luxury commodities became more common and forceful during this period, but it cannot seriously be proposed that these constitute the 'intellectual origins' of the consumer revolution as they patently fail to address the moral issues of concern to consumers.[64]

Consumption and the Protestant ethic

It is at this point that it becomes possible to see how the problem of explaining the consumer revolution, and hence the emergence of modern consumer society, connects with a central issue in sociology, that of the fate of the Protestant ethic, for in pursuing the argument over the justification of luxury consumption it is clear that the principal objections derived from this source. Puritanism, even today, is recognized as a tradition of thought which, out of a basis in intense moral and religious concern, condemns all idleness, luxury and indulgence, espousing in contrast an ethic of asceticism and industry – and this, it must be assumed, was the primary source of the moral objections levelled against the new propensity to consume. This in itself is hardly surprising, for less than a century earlier Puritanism had been the dominant cultural force in English society as a consequence of the victory of the Parliamentarian forces in the Civil War.

What is surprising, however, constituting one of the central conundrums of cultural history, is that the evidence strongly suggests that the consumer revolution was carried through by exactly those sections of English society with the strongest Puritan traditions, that is, the middle or trading classes, together with artisans and sections of the yeomanry. This was the conclusion, noted earlier, of investigations into the primary source of the new demand. At the same time, it was observed that this demand was for such luxury goods as toys and fashionable clothes, whilst also involving the pleasurable indulgencies of dancing, sport and novel-reading. In other words, it was exactly that kind of conduct which, it could be assumed, would be most likely to incur disapproval from those with a 'Puritan' outlook which formed the very substance of this middle-class consumer revolution. How could this have come about?

The answer to this especially puzzling problem which most immediately suggests itself is, in effect, an extension of the emulation theory so widely used in the 'standard' accounts of the consumer revolution. There, as has been noted, it is employed in order to try and explain how the new propensity to consume occurred, the assumption being that much luxury consumption is significant as a sign of the social status of the consumer, and hence emulation of the patterns manifested by those above one in rank is tantamount to upward social mobility. Such a theory naturally makes those at the pinnacle of the system of social stratification the dominant influence and arbiters of taste, with the consequent result that, sooner or later, all inferior ranks will seek to adopt their values and attitudes. Regarded in this way, it is natural that those who see emulation as the key to the origin of consumer demand should also see it as the mechanism through which the once Puritanically inclined middle ranks of English society came to abandon this commitment and adopt a more indulgent and 'aristocratic' way of life. Such a view is then strengthened by the historical sequence of events which marked the late seventeenth and early eighteenth centuries for, as Professor Stone believes, it was during this period that

two different world views, the Puritanically ascetic and the secularly sensual, were competing for the allegiance of the ruling classes. Between 1640 and 1660 the former won, abused its victory by attempting to impose its values by force and then collapsed. The result was a strong reaction to hedonism, while Puritanism persisted as a viewpoint adhered to by a minority. There was thus a major oscillation between two predominant personality types in England in the seventeenth century. . . . But it was the post-1660 cultural supremacy of the anti-Puritan character type which built on this foundation decisively to change attitudes toward authority, affection and sex within the middle and upper ranks of society.[65]

This argument has certain obvious attractions. It would appear, for example, that the aristocratic way of life both prior to the Civil War and during the period of the Restoration, was one which was favourable to luxury and pleasure-seeking, and might indeed serve as a basis for stimulating consumer demand were it to be imitated at all levels of society. At the same time, the majority of the nobility were, understandably, hostile toward the Puritans and their intolerant and dogmatic ascetic outlook, and thus could indeed serve as the rallying point for any general 'anti-Puritan' cultural movement.

By the same token, however, such a thesis only appears to resolve the problem, for if the Puritanically inclined middle classes are to be considered to have abandoned their inhibitions against luxurious consumption as a consequence of imitating the upper classes, whatever happened to the tendency for them, in their turn, to despise the aristocracy? After all, Puritanism was itself a response against those very laxities in morality and religion which had traditionally characterized the upper classes; and had not the most bitter and damaging of wars been fought by a religiously inspired bourgeoisie against that very class and its cultural ethos? Could it be possible that in less than a century the descendants of Oliver Cromwell's Roundheads would scramble to imitate the way of life most closely associated with those of the Cavaliers?[66]

The Puritan antipathy toward the aristocracy was deeply grounded in their religious world-view which, placing the highest value upon work and frugality, considered the nobility to be corrupted through idleness and indulgence. Since the poor were considered to be corrupted in their turn by deprivation, they held to the belief that only the middle ranks could maintain virtue. In addition they asserted their own aristocracy of the spirit against the earthly aristocracy of blood, something which led to a marked hostility toward the very notion of social status, as they set spiritual condition, character and inner worth above any such worldly considerations. This tendency was a marked feature of many of the religious movements, such as the Levellers and the Diggers which appeared in the period of the Commonwealth and was also evident long after that in the Quaker refusal to address anyone, no matter what their status, in any other manner than 'thee' or 'thou'. Given this religious inheritance, it does seem difficult to accept the idea that it was among this section of society that the new enthusiasm for social emulation which was responsible for creating a consumer revolution first appeared.[67]

In any case, the evidence does not really support the 'abandonment of asceticism through emulation of the aristocracy' thesis, for if one looks closely at some of the cultural innovations referred to above it would appear that they originated with the middle classes in the first instance. The habit of novel-reading, for example, seems to have developed among the middle ranks of society rather than as a fashionable practice which was taken over from the aristocracy. The vogue for the Gothic novel, in particular, embodying an essentially middle-class taste. Similarly the cult of romantic love flourished here rather than among the nobility. No doubt there were ways in which the emerging bourgeoisie of the period 'imitated' the aristocracy, but it is also quite clear that in certain fields they, and not the nobility, functioned as the tastemakers for society, and in so doing gave expression to values and attitudes very different from those which had long characterized the way of life of the English elite. The critical question therefore concerns the origin and nature of those values and attitudes which facilitated the new propensity to consume; were these indeed no more than traditional aristocratic ones, newly adopted by those beneath them in social status, or were they perhaps novel values, expressive of the ethos of a social group which had gained power and influence for the first time?

Looked at in a broader perspective, the idea that modern mass luxury consumption has come about as a consequence of the dissemination downwards through society of that way of life which had previously prevailed among a small aristocratic elite does involve something of a paradox. For although this theory has received some support following its initial formulation (in very different ways) by Sombart and Veblen, with the consequence that it is built in to such theories of economic modernization as Rostow's, it is at odds with that view of the Industrial Revolution and the emergence of modern industrial societies which was advanced by Marx and Weber. For, in the opinion of these theorists, the emergence of a modern 'capitalist' society was achieved by a bourgeoisie who confronted and overcame the existing ruling class, displacing their feudal world-view with a modern, 'rational' ideology. In this view, the ethic of the triumphant bourgeoisie, whether Protestant or merely capitalist in form, is asserted against the older, aristocratic one, eventually sweeping it aside.[68] How could it be, therefore, if this argument is accepted, that the middle classes are cast in such contradictory roles in relation to the production and consumption sides of the drama of the Industrial Revolution? On the one hand, regarded as defying the aristocratic ethic, and on the other, as adopting it.

In setting out to find an explanation for the consumer revolution of the eighteenth century, the 'standard' account accepted by economic historians has been considered and found to be wanting. In essence it is a model which places the emphasis upon emulation, and yet no good reason is given to explain why people should have become more actively emulative at this time. The factors mentioned are either self-conscious manipulation of the market – which is rightly seen to be largely dependent on the prior existence of the modern fashion pattern – or fashion itself, which, on closer examination, appears to be emulative behaviour under another name. It may well be that if demand was the key to the Industrial Revolution, then fashion was the key to that demand, but as yet no adequate explanation for either the origin or functioning of that phenomenon has been offered.

Certain crucial features were noted, however, about the consumer revolution. It was, for example, a predominantly middle-class affair (at least in this early stage), and consisted chiefly of a new demand for luxury or non-essential products. At the same time, it was clearly related to larger changes that were taking place in English society, ones which involved a shift in values and attitudes. Obvious examples here are the enthusiasm for leisure and leisure-time pursuits, the rise of the novel with the associated demand for fiction, and the cult of romantic love. These changes were, in their turn, observed to provoke opposition from those who adhered to traditional values, and thus required some justification.

The standard account sees this process as being successfully accomplished by various economists and thinkers who published arguments in favour of consumption itself during the late seventeenth and early eighteenth centuries. Essentially, these were observations on the utility of allowing the production, distribution and sale of luxury goods to proceed unhindered, rather than claims for the intrinsic merit of either consumption or luxury. As such, it is hard to see how they can have served to overcome the deep-seated moral antipathy to indulgence, or enabled luxurious consumption to be regarded as a form of virtuous behaviour. This issue is crucial because of the difficulty of understanding how the essentially Puritanical, English middle classes could have come to compromise their asceticism to the extent of indulging in a frenzied bout of spending on luxury goods and services. The answer conventionally provided – that they overcame their inhibitions in this respect through imitation of the extravagant life-style of the aristocracy – is very difficult to accept, and only serves to raise yet further problems. Hence the only reasonable alternative which suggests itself is that the consumer revolution was in fact carried through by means of a specifically bourgeois consumer ethic; a set of values and beliefs which were distinct to this section of English society, and which served to justify not only the reading of fiction and romantically motivated behaviour, but also indulgence in luxury consumption. It is intriguing to speculate on what this might have been and how it could have developed, but first it is necessary to consider more carefully why the standard account fails to provide a satisfactory explanation of modern consumer behaviour.

3

The Puzzle of Modern Consumerism

In the modern world the production of consumption becomes more important than the consumption of production.

John Lukács

In exploring the issues raised by attempts to explain the consumer revolution in England in the eighteenth century it has become apparent that the principal difficulty is a theoretical one; that is to say, the conceptual framework employed to account for the origins of the new propensity to consume is simply not adequate for the task. Ideas about increased demand stemming from a new outburst of social emulation, coupled with strenuous attempts at manipulation of consumer wants by producers, do not amount to a logically related set of propositions from which cause might effectively be separated from effect, or even a convincingly meaningful pattern of subjective action constructed. In particular, the central role played by changed values and attitudes is not properly explored, nor integrated with observations concerning intellectual movements which might have served to justify the resulting changes in conduct. The blame for this deficiency should not be placed on the historians, however, for it is a characteristic of those social sciences – principally economics and sociology – upon which they are forced to rely. No satisfactory account of the consumer revolution is possible because no satisfactory account of modern consumer behaviour exists, although, ironically, this is due at least in part to the past failure of historians to appreciate the importance of that revolution.[1] It follows from this that the problem of explaining the conduct of modern consumers – and that of accounting for events in the eighteenth century – is, at root, one and the same, with the heightened propensity of contemporary consumers to want goods no easier to account for than that which first appeared over 200 years ago. This is a fundamental truth which is obscured both by a widespread ethnocentricity and a tendency for social scientists to overlook what are the most characteristic features of modern consumerism.

For the truth is that a mystery surrounds consumer behaviour, or, at least, there is a mystery surrounding the behaviour of consumers in modern industrial societies. It does not concern their choice of products, nor why some groups manifest patterns of consumption different from others. Neither does it involve the question of how much of a product a person is willing to purchase at a given price, nor what kind of subconscious forces might influence that decision. The mystery is more fundamental than any of these, and concerns the very essence of modern consumption itself – its character as an activity which involves an apparently endless pursuit of wants;[2] the most characteristic feature of modern consumption being this insatiability. As Fromm observes, 'Contemporary man has an unlimited hunger for more and more goods',[3] or, as O'Neill expresses it, the modern consumer must learn 'economic tension', that is, the realization that all his wants and desires will never be satisfied.[4] This can never happen because of the apparently endless process of replacement which ensures that 'When one want is fulfilled, several more usually pop up to take its place.'[5]

This is not to say that insatiability itself is especially hard to understand, or that it is confined to modern society. For there is plenty of evidence to suggest that human beings in all cultures are capable of developing addictions. One could say that the Spanish Conquistadors had an insatiable greed for gold, or that Don Juan was similarly hard to satisfy when it came to women. Such non-satiable appetites, however, typically have a single product focus, as is the case with alcoholism or drug addiction; by contrast, the modern consumer (although not proof against such temptations) is characterized by an insatiability which arises out of a basic inexhaustibility of wants themselves, which forever arise, phoenix-like, from the ashes of their predecessors. Hence no sooner is one satisfied than another is waiting in line clamouring to be satisfied; when this one is attended to, a third appears, then subsequently a fourth, and so on, apparently without end. The process is ceaseless and unbroken; rarely can an inhabitant of modern society, no matter how privileged or wealthy, declare that there is nothing that they want. That this should be so is a matter of wonder.[6] How is it possible for wants to appear with such constancy, and in such an inexhaustible fashion, especially when they typically concern novel products and services?[7]

This endless wanting has been described as arising out of the 'revolution in rising expectations' which occurs when traditional societies undergo the series of changes associated with the process of development or modernization.[8] This revolution appears to have the consequence of causing consumers to develop expectations which consistently outstrip realization, something which has led observers to redescribe the change as a 'revolution in rising frustrations'.[9] Whether frustration exceeds satisfaction or not depends upon what Lerner dubs, the 'want-get ratio'. No matter how limited the feelings of frustration, however, and hence how close this ratio comes to one, it is a central fact of modern consumer behaviour that the gap between wanting and getting never actually closes.

It may be objected that the dynamism characteristic of modern consumerism has its origin in the inventiveness which so typifies modern man; an inventiveness which leads to an endless production of novel products and services. Whilst there is truth in this observation, a crucial gap exists between a new 'invention' and a new 'want'. Without claiming that all inventions arise to meet existing needs, the vast majority could be said to arise as a result of attempts to satisfy present needs more efficiently, and if they fail to do this then no new want will result. This rational, instrumental dynamic may have little effect upon the basic pattern of gratifications typical of a consumer, whilst profoundly affecting the economic use of resources. In this respect it is crucial to distinguish between a purely economic and a wider social action conception of what 'consumption' means.

In a purely economic sense, consumption refers to those processes through which economic resources are used up; it is, in this respect, the logical opposite of production. This may not, however, involve any human gratification (as is the case, for example, when referring to objects which are accidently 'consumed' by fire). Humanly conceived, therefore, consumption refers to 'the use of goods in the satisfaction of human wants',[10] and is typically the outcome of consciously motivated behaviour. Human beings may, however, also obtain gratification from activities which do not, in any conventional economic sense, involve the use of resources at all (except those of time and human energy), such as the appreciation of natural beauty or the enjoyment of friendship. Consumption habits may alter as a consequence of either an innovation in the use of resources or a modification to the pattern of gratifications. The position adopted here, as will be seen, is that the latter has a more intimate connection with the insatiability of wants than the former.

The continual extinction of wants is as much of a puzzle as their creation, for a natural corollary of endless wanting is the high rate of product (and hence want) obsolescence. How is it that wants depart as suddenly and as effortlessly as they arrive? How is it that individuals manage to cease to want that which they ardently desired only a little while before? For modern consumer society is symbolized at least as much by the mountains of rubbish, the garage and jumble sales, the columns of advertisements of second-hand goods for sale and the second-hand car lots, as it is by the ubiquitous propaganda on behalf of new goods.

There is a widespread tendency to take such behaviour for granted and to assume that, even though it might not be morally desirable, it is at least a perfectly 'normal' or 'rational' mode of acting. It takes only a little reflection to realize, however, that such a view is neither supported by psychology nor anthropology, but is merely the product of a deep-seated ethnocentricity.[11]

For this is certainly not the traditional pattern. In non-literate and pre-industrial societies, consumption, like other aspects of life, is largely governed by custom and tradition, and these forces specify a fixed rather than an open-ended notion of wants. It is not merely that in such societies habit has gained an encrustation of normative approval, but that an endlessly changeable pattern of consumption is impossible for the individual to contemplate, or for the society as it is constituted to tolerate. Riesman and Lerner have stressed how, for the 'tradition-directed' person, 'what exists ... is all that can exist'.[12] At the same time, the efforts of any one individual to 'better' his condition by striving after new wants are not only seen as threatening to the whole community but as fundamentally immoral. Since peasants typically operate with a notion of the 'limited good', that is with the view 'that [since] all the desired things [in] life such as land, wealth, health, friendship and love ... [exist] in finite quantity and [are] always in short supply', an apparent improvement in the position of one person threatens the entire community.[13] In addition, since the traditional way of life has divine legitimation, such 'self-seeking' is also regarded as blasphemous.[14] Most crucially, however, what separates the traditional consumer from his modern counter-part is his view that the novel is to be feared, if not actually regarded as the embodiment of evil.[15]

Thus it is not consumption in general which poses special problems of explanation, so much as that particular pattern which is characteristic of modern industrial societies.[16] It is, after all, easy enough to appreciate the necessary biological basis of many of the acts of consumption involved in the pattern of life exemplified by non-literate, pre-industrial peoples. What is more, consumption in these societies is not an activity clearly set apart from that of production. Consequently, there are few problems of explanation presented by consumption itself, there is merely a need to understand the way of life as a whole. Thus whatever consumption practices are observed require no separate theory, just a thorough understanding of the culture and traditions of the group. Hence the idea that human beings somehow have a 'natural' tendency to display insatiable wanting does not derive any support from history or anthropology. On the contrary, if there is such a thing as a 'normal' pattern in these matters, it is the traditional one of a fixed, limited and familiar set of wants.

Unfortunately this point tends to have been overlooked by social scientists, who consequently have been tempted to develop universal, ahistorical theories of consumer behaviour. The failure to perceive the truly puzzling nature of modern consumer behaviour derives in large measure from this absence of a proper historical sense and the ethnocentricity which it naturally produces. Thus instead of contemporary practices being regarded as exceptional, pre-modern peoples are typically considered to be merely prevented from behaving like us because of the lack of an industrial economy. In this way, the modern pattern is presented as immanent in history and its peculiarity given a teleological justification.

The approach to the phenomenon of consumption which predominates within the discipline of economics is that associated with the microeconomic theory of marginal utility; utility being the name given to that quality intrinsic to the item of consumption from which the consumer derives satisfaction whilst he, in turn, is always assumed to behave in such a way as to maximize his utility and hence his satisfaction. This he will endeavour to do by acting rationally in the market within those limits set by his disposable income and prevailing prices, his motive in entering the market being the need to satisfy his wants and tastes. These are generally regarded as originating within the personality of the consumer (or are at least assumed to do so for the sake of the theory) and are revealed in choice, it being assumed that actual behaviour is a faithful reflection of underlying preferences. In the classical formulation of this perspective no explanation is offered for the origin of wants or tastes, nor of how they might develop or change. In addition, although the theory offers predictions concerning the degree of interest which a consumer might have in a product depending upon the amount of it that he already possesses, it does not offer any insight into the possible differential preferences which a consumer might have for the satisfaction of various wants. Each want is, in that sense, assumed to possess an equal urgency.

Although the theory of marginal utility has proved to be a powerful tool for the analysis of certain aspects of consumer choice it has long been obvious that it does not constitute a theory of consumer behaviour. The familiar criticisms of utility theory, such as the dubiousness of the assumptions concerning rationality and the intention to maximize satisfaction, are less pertinent in this respect than the simple observation that far too much is omitted. A theory which does not even attempt to account for the nature or origin of wants and tastes, and offers only the most attenuated suggestion concerning why people buy goods, hardly deserves to be called a theory of consumer behaviour.

These deficiencies have long been apparent, to economists as well as others, and yet little effort has been directed at remedying them.[17] Instead, theoretical perspectives drawn from elsewhere have been attached to marginal utility theory in an attempt to compensate for the more obvious of these inadequacies, a strategy which is clearly a poor substitute for the development of a satisfactory overall theory of consumer behaviour. Before looking at these 'incorporated' perspectives, however, and the extent to which they can be said to serve to fill these gaps, it will be useful to specify how it is that utility theory is unable to explain exactly that feature which (with the exception of rationality) is most characteristic of modern consumption. This, as we have seen, is the preference for new wants and, in particular, their rapid and seemingly endless creation.

Given that marginal utility theory assumes that the consumer is seeking to maximize his satisfactions it is not at all clear how a want for a novel product develops, for this offers unknown and hence unestimable satisfactions to set aside the known ones gained from the products presently consumed. How, rationally, could any consumer justify transferring some of his scarce resources from habitual purchases, when all he could be absolutely sure of would be the loss of current satisfactions? As Henry Waldgrave Stuart outlined the problem as long ago as 1917:

How are we to understand the acquisition, by an individual, of what are called new economic needs and interests? Except by a fairly obvious fallacy of retrospection we cannot regard this phenomenon as a mere arousal of so-called latent or implicit desires. New products and new means of production afford 'satisfactions' and bring about objective results which are unimaginable and therefore unpredictable, in any descriptive fashion, in advance.[18]

It follows from this argument that the truly 'rational' consumer, determined to maximize his satisfaction at all costs, would simply not strive to obtain new products or services as this would, as Stuart observes, be more in the nature of an adventure or a gamble than 'calculation'.[19] Thus it is that the very assumptions introduced to account for that 'rationality' which is considered to characterize instrumental consumer action actually have the consequence of making its other dominant characteristic – insatiability for new products – appear as an especially 'irrational' and puzzling form of behaviour.

In order to see how economists (and some other social scientists) characteristically supplement these deficiencies of marginal utility theory in an effort to build a theory of consumer behaviour, it will be useful to look briefly at Galbraith's discussion of consumption as outlined in chapters 10 and 11 of *The Affluent Society*.[20] This book was not intended to supply a fully developed theory of consumer behaviour, the aim of its author being to expose what he regarded as the outdated and unhelpful economic myths of the age. This, nevertheless, is an advantage because it means that the discussion is especially revealing of those assumptions which economists commonly make when called upon to consider consumption as a real phenomenon rather than as an abstract aspect of behaviour.

Galbraith's main concern is to demonstrate how irrational is that view which regards all increases in production – as indicated for example by increases in the Gross National Product – as necessarily good irrespective of the nature of the products which are manufactured or the wants which they satisfy. In order to develop a critique of this assumption he examines the sources of consumer demand for goods in modern society and questions the tendency of classical economic theory not to inquire into the origin of wants, but to assume none the less that their urgency does not diminish appreciably as more of them are satisfied.[21] Galbraith challenges this position with the argument that

If the individual's wants are to be urgent, they must be original with himself. They cannot be urgent if they must be contrived for him. And above all, they must not be contrived by the process of production by which they are satisfied. For this means that the whole case for the urgency of production, based upon the urgency of wants, falls to the ground. One cannot defend production as satisfying wants if that production creates the wants.[22]

Leaving aside for the moment the question of what arguments might or might not be considered to 'defend' the production of goods in a society, Galbraith's subsequent development of this position is of interest because he simultaneously employs the three main strands of thought which can be found in the social sciences as proffered explanations of the origin of consumer wants.

The first of these is the instinctivist tradition, which by locating wants in the biological inheritance of human beings, attempts to assimilate them to the category of 'needs'. This view is clearly visible in Galbraith's subsequent reference to 'independently established need', and 'independently determined desires' and 'wants';[23] obviously what these desires are taken to be 'independent' of, are both the activities of others and the constraints of culture. This is clear from his above reference to 'urgency' and his employment of this as a criterion of 'independence', citing the example of a hungry man as one who is subsequently 'immune' to attempts at persuasion.[24] From this perspective wants are pre-programmed into consumers and will manifest themselves when goods are supplied without the benefit of any additional action to 'create' them. The second tradition, by contrast, emphasizes the idea of active want creation. Here the assumption is that a 'want' does not arise from any inherent force within the consumer, but is deliberately manufactured within him through such agencies as advertising and salesmanship. These wants he assumes to be 'non-urgent', and hence in some way not 'really' wanted, observing, 'Is a new breakfast cereal or detergent so much wanted if so much must be spent to compel in the consumer a sense of want?'[25] This perspective (echoing the 'compel' in the above sentence) will be called the manipulationist tradition of theorizing about wants. The third, and last strand, which Galbraith refers to as 'passive' want creation, also assumes that wants are manufactured rather than inborn (and hence, in his sense, 'non-urgent') but does attribute a key role to the consumer himself, since he acquires new wants as a consequence of imitating or emulating the behaviour of other consumers. Here Galbraith cites Keynes's observation concerning 'needs of the second class', that is those which follow from efforts to keep abreast or ahead of one's fellow beings.[26] This tradition, in view of its heavy indebtedness to the writings of Thorstein Veblen, will be called the Veblenesque perspective on want creation.

Instinctivism

The instinctivist perspective is built in to economic theorizing about consumption as a result of the very language which is standardly employed, most especially through the use of the concepts of 'latent want' and 'latent demand'. In one sense, this usage is unimportant, for, as has been noted, the classical approach does not involve consideration of the origin of wants. To that extent it would make little difference to the theorizing engaged in by economists whether wants were thought to be the product of instinct, the activities of others or the result of divine intervention. This is because the concept of want has a taken-for-granted or axiomatic status within economic theory and is not, in any real sense, the product of empirical investigation. On the other hand, there is a tendency for economists to forget this when discussing the real world of human affairs, as it appears does Galbraith. Whilst for economic historians, who are more especially charged with the task of accounting for actual events, the temptation to fall into this trap is a constant one.

This last point is well illustrated in *The Birth of a Consumer Society* discussed in the previous chapter, for there is ample evidence to show that the contributors to that book presuppose that wants are indeed inherent within individuals, merely becoming operative when the circumstances are right. McKendrick, for example, when discussing the increased sales of printed calicoes in the 1670s, refers to an 'unleashing of latent home demand'.[27] He also writes of the 'propensity to spend' having previously been held in check by an inadequate supply of goods, and to the factors which 'released' the 'force of fashion'; whilst, in discussing the activities of producers, reference is made to 'the kind of latent demand they were attempting to release'.[28] The instinctivist basis of this kind of emanationist phraseology is best revealed in an early reference to 'the unleashing of acquisitive instincts'.[29] These examples will suffice to indicate the nature of the underlying assumption, which is that consumer behaviour is best understood in terms of inherent forces which pre-date their actual expression in the form of demand for goods.

No doubt some of the appeal of such language is that it manages to provide connotations of intensity and urgency by the suggestion that 'instinctive' agencies are at work, and in this way succeeds in conveying something of the dynamism which accompanied this early explosion in demand. Unfortunately, the evidence suggests that it is not used simply to add colour to what might otherwise be a rather dull description of events but is regarded as possessing some explanatory power. What this might be, however, is hard to determine.

On the one hand, the plausibility of the instinctivist or latency assumption rests upon the obvious fact that human behaviour does have a biological basis in such real needs as those for food and shelter. The behaviour motivated by these drives, however, is unspecific and contrasts sharply with the consumer's determined and sharply defined conduct in pursuit of particular products. It is indeed this very difference between needs and wants which argues against any inherited basis for the latter. If, on the other hand, all that is being implied by the use of the term 'latent' is the observation that all human beings have the potential to become willing consumers of any kind of product or service, then it is precisely because this is true that the idea of want as an inherent category is nonsensical. One is left with the suggestion that consumer behaviour might involve some processes of 'manifestation', that is to say, the 'realization' of something which had previously only been 'potential'. To the extent that this is an accurate description of consumption it derives logically from its definition as motivated action. All purposive human conduct is teleological in form and hence possesses the quality of being a 'manifestation' of something 'latent'. It is, however, the precise nature of these motivating processes which is the key issue under debate.[30]

An associated feature of the instinctivist position is the assumed existence of a 'needs-wants' hierarchy in the structure of human motivation. Needs, being biologically based, must be met before the less-basic 'wants' can be experienced;[31] clearly in this view, the satisfaction of given 'needs' immediately brings certain 'higher-order' wants into being, which when met are then replaced by others even 'higher' in the hierarchy. Markin associates this concept with the work of

Abraham Maslow, listing the needs (in ascending order), as first those for oxygen, food, water, relief from pain and others with a physiological basis, then those for safety, such as security, protection and routine, followed by the 'love motives' of affection and affiliation. Next come the 'esteem motives' of self-respect and prestige and finally the self-actualization motive of self-fulfilment.[32] Galbraith's subscription to this view is revealed by his observation that 'When man has satisfied his physical needs, then psychologically grounded desires take over.'[33]

The postulation of such a hierarchy is obviously an attempt to cope with the problem of the non-universality of 'instinctivist' desires, that is, the fact that the whole of humanity does not display one common set of consumer wants. The absence of those wants which is manifested by modern man is thus accounted for by claiming that traditional peoples are still preoccupied with attempts to 'satisfy' basic needs. Such an argument rests upon dubious foundations, for not only is the evidence in support of the existence of such a hierarchy highly debatable (with plenty of data to show that human beings will override the imperatives of biological urges for the sake of a 'higher-order' need such as love or self-respect)[34] but in addition, the evidence in favour of the 'satisfaction' of a need at one level tends to be the appearance of a 'higher' one, thus giving an aura of tautology to this model.[35]

The presentation of individual consumer wants as the emanation of pre-formed, inherited inclinations makes it extremely difficult to understand either the variation or changeability which characterize human desires. If the diversity of human wants is inherited in origin how is it that individuals change their pattern of wanting over a lifetime? Or if wants are akin to needs why is it that they do not take the same form in all societies? If, in addition, a latent want only becomes manifested once the appropriate product is presented to the consumer, how is it that consumption of the product often appears to extinguish the want altogether? Surely, if it sprang from a genuine biological basis it would continually reassert itself? How is it, indeed, that not-wanting occurs? Do individuals also possess latent non-wants? It should be clear by now that the instinctivist position is quite unsupportable. It is, in any case, based on the fallacy of retrospection, as was noted long ago,[36] for it attempts to invoke as evidence in support of the existence of the concept of latent want exactly that behaviour (the presence of demand for a product) which the latent want is supposed to explain.

Manipulationism

The second of the two perspectives employed by Galbraith in an effort to compensate for the inability of economic theory to account for the origin of wants is that of manipulationism, or the view that consumers are 'compelled' to want products as a consequence of the actions of outside agencies; an argument which, as was noted, figures prominently in the standard account of the eighteenth-century consumer revolution. Interestingly, it contrasts sharply with instinctivism since it tends to treat individuals as lacking in any pre-formed tendencies to act in pursuit of particular goals, regarding them as motivationally 'empty' until 'injected' with wants through the medium of advertising. As this metaphor suggests, this perspective derives from what has been called the 'hypodermic' model of the workings of the mass media, one which implies that the various media of modern society – such as film, television and newspapers – each function like a hypodermic needle to inject a given message into their audience. In this case, what is introduced into the 'blood stream' of consumers is the 'want' for a particular product or service. Clearly, this theory attributes a passive role to the consumer, whilst the onerous task of ensuring that the endless and continuous creation of new wants occurs is attributed to such agents of the producers as advertisers and market researchers.

There are different versions of this manipulationist position with the variations concerning the degree to which the consumer is a willing, if naïve, participant in the process, and the specificity of the intentions implanted in him. At one extreme, there is the claim that consumers have their buying habits directly controlled through sublimilal techniques, which was Vance Packard's sensational thesis in the *The Hidden Persuaders*.[37] This view has little empirical support and need not be taken too seriously. At the other extreme, there is the idea that mere exposure to information and exhortation is sufficient to generate wants in consumers.[38] Although it is necessary to recognize the obvious fact that consumers are influenced in their actions by the information which they receive from producers it is only the most hypersuggestive of individuals who are likely to rush out and buy products merely because they have been brought to their attention. Hence the fact that advertising exerts an influence over consumers' demand for goods neither helps to explain the origin of wants nor proves that manipulation has taken place. In between the extremes of suggesting that consumers are subject to subliminal control, or prone to act hypersuggestibly when presented with such simple injunctions as 'Buy Blogg's Biscuits', are those theories which imply that consumers are 'persuaded' or even 'forced' in some way or other, through processes of which they are conscious, to act in a manner which is either against their inclinations or contrary to their best interests, but which is in the interests of producers.[39]

Naturally many of the criticisms of this view are the same as those which have long been levelled against the hypodermic model in general.

Firstly, there is the obvious fact that advertisements (and other product-promoting material) only constitutes one part of the total set of cultural influences at work upon consumers.[40] Among the rest are those which represent the outlook of groups and agencies with very different interests, such as the unions, churches, professions and government agencies.[41] Secondly, the market for goods like the audience for any one medium, is not homogeneous and hence the effect of a message will vary considerably depending upon who receives it. Thirdly and lastly, there is plenty of evidence to show that consumers do not simply 'accept' or 'ingest' commercial messages in an unthinking or unselective fashion, but respond, if only to a degree, in a discriminatory and purposeful manner.[42] This last point is, after all, hardly surprising, for 'manipulation' can only be attempted if there is indeed something to manipulate, and this in turn necessitates some accommodation to whatever might constitute the existing motives of consumers. To be successful in making others act in accordance with one's wishes, therefore, it is necessary to know something about their motives, for only then can one hope to turn their dispositions to one's own advantage. The central importance of this fact for those who would seek to 'manipulate' consumers is revealed by the development of motivation research as an integral feature of modern marketing and advertising. Activity under this heading is largely directed at discovering the dreams, desires and wishes of consumers so that advertisers may build upon these when devising product 'messages'. The common desire to be attractive to the opposite sex, for example, may be used in this way to help sell anything from spot-cream and cigarettes to aperitifs, and it is in this sense that it is often claimed that peoples' 'wants' for products are the result of 'manipulation'.

It is crucial to note two things, however, about this position. Firstly, it is not the basic motivational structure of individuals which is being 'manipulated'. On the contrary, that is precisely what the 'manipulation' is being accommodated to take into account. Thus, although one might argue that the desires and dreams of the consumer are 'exploited' in this way, one cannot claim that they are simply constructed by the actions of advertisers. Secondly, what the producers of goods and services actually manipulate, through their agents, are not consumers or their wants but, in the first instance at least, the symbolic meanings which are attached to products. They, in effect, manipulate messages. The crucial question then becomes: how does receipt of a message lead to the creation of a want in the consumer? Instead of focusing upon the problematic issues raised by this question and those related ones concerning the consumer's regular and endless wanting, social scientists have become overly preoccupied with the issues of 'manipulation' and 'exploitation', something which appears to be due to the predominant influence of utilitarianism and the two central assumptions which it generates.

The first of these is the idea that the only genuine gratification which consumers can obtain from products and services is that provided by their intrinsic utility. Hence, if consumers are persuaded to buy products for 'other' reasons (that is to say, for reasons to do with messages relating to non-utilitarian aspects of the product) then they are being duped in some way. This is the basis of the frequent objection levelled against 'non-informative' advertising of the kind which merely tries to associate a product with a desirable image. It should be obvious, however, that the gratification obtained from the use of a product cannot be separated from the images and ideas with which it is linked, in the way, for example, that eating caviare or drinking champagne is popularly associated with luxurious living. To concentrate the advertising of such products upon these associations (whilst ignoring the presentation of such information about their 'utility' as calorific or alcoholic content) is, therefore, not to mislead the consumer but to stress information directly relevant to potential gratification. In other words, images and symbolic meanings are as much a 'real' part of the product as its constituent ingredients.[43]

The second, and closely related assumption, is that in so far as emotion and imagination, rather than rational calculation, enter into the processes through which the consumer chooses and purchases goods and services, then 'manipulation' or 'exploitation' is involved. This view is predicated on the axiom that consumption is, by definition, a rational process and should approximate to one in practice. If, therefore, advertising and marketing strategies can be seen to bypass these, being patently aimed at influencing the feelings and imagination of the consumer, then, in this sense too, 'manipulation' if not 'exploitation' is involved. Here too, however, the assumption is invalid, for consumer behaviour is just as much a matter of emotion and feeling as it is of cognition, as the centrality of issues of liking and disliking clearly reveal. In fact, the dimension of affective attachment can be said to be more basic to consumption than any issue of rational calculation. There is, therefore, no good reason whatsoever for assuming that the emotional nature of many advertising 'messages' is indicative of the existence of 'manipulation' (or at least, no more than is true of all messages about the product).[44]

This discussion of the issue of manipulation tends to divert attention from the crucial questions concerning how it is that wants come to be formed in consumers. It is quite possible, for example, to accept that the agents of producers, in the form of advertisers, do indeed attempt to manipulate the symbolic meanings or 'messages' which are attached to products in an effort to induce consumers to want them, and that they seek to do this by trying to identify their product with peoples' general desires. This still leaves open the issue of how this is actually accomplished (in some cases, if not in others) and what part the individual consumer plays in that process. There is also the outstanding question of the regular and continuing sequence of want-creation to be accounted for together with the problem of disposal or not-wanting.

The Veblenesque perspective

The last of Galbraith's three strands of consumer theorizing is the one in which the consumer is seen as actively engaged in the creation of his own wants. This he accomplishes, however, in a somewhat incidental fashion, as a by-product of an overriding concern with the maintenance and enhancement of social status; a perspective which derives almost entirely from the writings of Thorstein Veblen. Once again, the centrality of this argument to the standard historical account of the consumer revolution has already been noted, where it occupies an even more important position than claims concerning the manipulationist creation of wants.

Veblen's theory of consumer behaviour rests upon an insight which had long been familiar to anthropologists but had become obscured by the influence of utilitarianism as far as the behaviour of modern man was concerned. This is the simple fact that the act of consumption has profound socio-cultural significance, and should not be viewed in simple economic terms, commodities having importance as signs or symbols and not merely for the intrinsic satisfaction which they might bring. Consequently, as Diggins observes, Veblen suggests that the ultimate problem in understanding industrial societies is not how goods come to be made but how they take on meaning.[45] Such an observation is a very necessary corrective to the naïve materialism of the utilitarian tradition, and promises to provide a more realistic basis from which to tackle the problem of accounting for the characteristics of modern consumer behaviour.

Unfortunately, Veblen was a little too single-minded in his consideration of the kind of meanings which consumption might signify, concentrating almost exclusively upon issues of social status. His view, as outlined in *The Theory of the Leisure Class*[46] stressed that the consumption of goods serves, in addition to the conventionally accepted function of satisfying needs, to indicate a person's level of wealth or 'pecuniary strength', and that this is, in turn, a primary index of social status. Hence acts of consumption are also manifest signs of one's social status. This function of consumption is well understood by the consumer, and may indeed rival the direct satisfaction of needs in importance, as Veblen explains:

No class of society, not even the most abjectly poor, foregoes all customary conspicuous consumption. The last items of this category of consumption are not given up except under stress of the direct necessity. Very much of squalor and discomfort will be endured before the last trinket or the last pretence of pecuniary decency is put away.[47]

This view is based upon certain key assumptions concerning both human motivation and the nature of societies. Veblen assumes, for example, that the motive behind much human activity is emulation and that since 'the possession of wealth confers honour',[48] the 'end sought by accumulation is to rank high in comparison with the rest of the community in point of pecuniary strength',[49] a view which would appear to make pride and its companion, envy, the root causes of human action. Clearly, if consumption is regarded as essentially a manifestation of a competitive striving for the scarce commodity of high status, then it would indeed appear as if one had at last provided an answer to the problem of the source of its dynamic. Not surprisingly, therefore, economists have come to employ the term 'Veblen effects' to refer to phenomena which are not explicable within the parameters of marginal utility theory.[50]

Economists typically employ Veblen's name in making two kinds of modification to their essentially individualistic and utilitarian model of consumer behaviour. The first, which is more specifically called *the* Veblen effect, involves recognizing that the price of a commodity is a culturally significant symbol in its own right, and not merely an index of economic worth or utility. Following Veblen's argument, therefore, they accept that demand for goods may increase with price where the function of consumption is to manifest pecuniary strength. The second, which embraces what are called the 'bandwagon' and 'snob' effects, involve recognition of the fact that an individual's consumption of goods is affected by the behaviour of other consumers. Either an individual's demand for goods or services is increased by the fact that others are seen to be consuming them (bandwagon), or decreased by the fact that others are consuming them (snob).[51]

These Veblenesque modifications to utility theory are notable for their extreme simplicity, as well as the conception of human motivation which they contain. They are very limited assumptions which patently fail to grasp the full complexity of either the symbolic meanings possessed by consumer products and services, or the communal and associational dimension of the act of consumption. Clearly, the price of a commodity is a cultural symbol of some importance and in purchasing and conspicuously displaying it a consumer conveys a message to those around him; a message which may indeed amount to saying, 'see how rich I am, I can afford this very expensive item'. But products and services are redolent with other cultural meanings, notably those which pertain to the issues of 'taste' and 'style', and the purchase and display of a product or service may thus stem more from a desire to convey messages of this kind. In which case price may be a comparatively irrelevant symbol, and not at all central either to the consumer's decision or the message he wishes to convey. Similarly, the fact that an individual's consumption habits are affected by the actions of others cannot be adequately described by the simple alternatives offered above. It would be more realistic to note that consumers are typically striving to make their consumption conform to the pattern exhibited by one group and deviate from that manifested by another; bandwagon and snob are not therefore alternatives but integral features of one 'other-related' pattern of behaviour. More to the point, however, is the fact that reference group theory shows how complex is the real nature of imitative and emulative behaviour, and that any one person may make use of a variety of positive, negative, comparative and normative reference groups (or role models) when deciding what course of action to take.[52] What this means is that the explanations of consumer behaviour offered under the heading 'Veblen effects' are obviously inadequate and do not deserve to be taken too seriously. At best they constitute no more than an outline of the direction in which social science should develop if an adequate understanding of the social dimension of consumer behaviour is to be obtained.[53]

The interpretation given by economists to 'Veblen effects' is also revealing for the nature of the assumptions about human motivation which they contain, the use of the terms 'bandwagon' and 'snob' being especially indicative. Whilst all that is at issue is the fact that a consumer's behaviour is influenced by the actions of others, the gratuitous assumptions made are that this takes the form of getting 'into the swing of things', wishing to be 'one of the boys', or a desire to 'dissociate oneself from the common herd'; motives generally considered to be among the least creditable of those which impell people to act. There is no justification for this (apart from the precedent set by Veblen) and one could equally suggest other accounts of associational and disassociational action which did not carry such disreputable overtones. To emulate others or to seek to disassociate oneself from others is neither praiseworthy nor blameworthy in itself but must be judged by the conduct of the 'others' taken as the point of comparison, and upon the motives for acting. What these accounts therefore illustrate is the widespread bias in social science against luxury consumer behaviour, and its taken-for-granted basis in 'other-directed' patterns of motivation.[54]

Veblen's argument is not without its ambiguities and difficulties, and one of these lies at the very heart of his description of that which drives the consumer to engage in conspicuous consumption. Whilst in some places in *The Theory of the Leisure Class* it appears as if he regards the competitive striving for status as the primary dynamic mechanism, at others it is a desire to aspire to that ideal way of life exemplified by those of superior rank; whilst he uses the same term 'emulation' to refer to both processes. At one point, for example, Veblen observes that the standard of expenditure which guides the efforts of the consumer is not that already achieved but one which is just out of reach, commenting that the motive for straining to reach this higher level is 'emulation – the stimulus of an invidious comparison which prompts us to outdo those with whom we are in the habit of classing ourselves'.[55] This seems to imply that any attempt to compare our standard of life with that of our peers will result in feelings of envy and dissatisfaction followed by renewed efforts to improve our status. Studies in reference group theory have shown, however, that this is by no means the necessary outcome of comparisons made with those whom we consider to be our equals, and that satisfaction with one's position is just as likely an outcome as dissatisfaction.[56] Veblen is, in any case, obviously assuming the prevalance of an 'aggressive' rather than 'defensive' form of conspicuous consumption,[57] since he refers to individuals being prompted to 'outdo' each other. In this sense he can be said to be assuming that social life is like a race in which everyone wants to be first rather than a procession in which the predominant concern is to maintain one's position in the line.[58] At other places in the book he presents a somewhat different account of the reasons why people strive for higher levels of consumption, one which relates more to the predominant influence of the leisure class.

Veblen's claim that social status is intimately linked with wealth is but a variant of a more fundamental argument concerning the centrality of a leisured class. Accepting the logic of the claim that time is money, Veblen argues that wealth and leisure are alike in being symptoms of privilege and high status, and that conspicuous consumption and conspicuous leisure are both ways of gaining honour through displaying waste. What he calls the leisure class is thus at the pinnacle of the system of social stratification and sets the standards which all below must aspire to:

The leisure class stands at the head of the social structure in point of reputability; and its manner of life and its standards of worth therefore affords the norm of reputability for the community. The observance of these standards, in some degree of approximation, becomes incumbent upon all classes lower in the scale. In modern civilized communities the lines of demarcation between social classes have grown vague and transient, and wherever this happens the norm of reputability imposed by the upper classes extends its coercive influence with but slight hindrance down through the social structure to the lowest strata. The result is that the members of each stratum accept as their ideal of decency the scheme of life in vogue in the next higher stratum, and bend their energies to live up to their ideal.[59]

It is clear that this account of status striving differs markedly from the earlier one. Here the motive is the desire to live up to an ideal, rather than to outdo one's peers, an activity which can also be labelled 'emulation'. Although Veblen's use of the term 'ideal' is ambiguous, at times apparently signifying simply that pattern of life which people aspire to (as opposed to that which they exhibit) and at others that which is considered to embody the highest moral and aesthetic standards, it would seem to be the latter which he has in mind here. From this perspective, therefore, the dynamic ingredient in status striving derives not from attempts to outdo or upstage others in a context of taken-for-granted competition, so much as the necessarily ceaseless efforts involved in attempting to live up to an ideal way of life. Veblen appears to try to reconcile his two uses of the term 'ideal' by assuming, firstly that the leisure class actually lives up to its own cultural ideals, and secondly by claiming that each class sees the one immediately above it as embodying these values to a higher degree than does their own. In this way, Veblen attempts to assimilate the competitive striving for status with idealistically motivated behaviour. It is clear, none the less, that they need have no necessary relationship with each other. In fact, it seems that Veblen confuses two different types of social situation. One is the kind of close-knit community of peers in which intense rivalry for prestige often occurs, say among athletes or actors; this may well be the sort of context in which there is a concern to out-perform one's rivals. The other is the phenomenon of social mobility in a fairly 'open' society, that is to say, one without clear legal or religious barriers to movement between adjacent strata. Upward social movement in this kind of situation clearly requires the adoption of a new style of life, a process which might reasonably involve imitative 'emulation'. This does not, however, necessarily mean that one is trying to compete with anyone out of envy or pride, as an improved standard of living may simply be regarded as attractive in its own right. This error is closely related to Veblen's mistake in assuming an identity between competition and imitation, arguing as he does that where a contest between individuals or groups for higher status exists, then this will take the form of behaviour which imitates those who already hold the higher status. But this is to overlook two important points: firstly, that individuals may gain success over their competitors through innovation rather than imitation (as many entrepreneurs have shown) and, secondly, that social groups (especially social classes) may actually be in conflict over the very question of the criteria to be employed in defining status.[60] This latter case is the more important as it denies Veblen's assumption concerning a consensus of values in modern society and hence the existence of a single agreed status system. A more successful way of improving one's own social position may thus be to deny the moral validity of the claims of those above you, asserting in their place grounds for prestige which favour those like yourself. That Veblen did not consider this alternative appears to follow from his assumption that the leisure class held an unchallenged as well as a pre-eminent position in modern societies.

Once one abandons Veblen's insistent emphasis upon the invidious aspects of consumption to concentrate upon the extent to which this feature of life is expressive of basic cultural values then further difficulties are encountered.[61] As we have seen, Veblen considered the cultural significance of consumption to lie in its index of status, something which was measured in terms of wealth and leisure, with all other values being treated as either synonyms or derivatives of these. At the same time, he considered modern societies to possess a single elite leisure class constituting the highest embodiment of these values, with all subordinate classes ranked to the extent to which they lived up to this ideal.

A little reflection will be sufficient to reveal some of the many objections to this view. In the first place, high status in modern societies is clearly associated with values other than wealth and leisure, noble birth being merely the most obvious of these. Secondly, the treatment of wealth and leisure as interchangeable both signifying the honorific value of 'waste' is unconvincing in the light of the Protestant tradition of applauding the first and deploring the second, and the Bohemian inversion of this view. Thirdly, the treatment of modern societies as culturally monolithic with one class providing all the cultural leadership does not fit with the considerable evidence suggestive of a more complex picture. As Riesman notes:

Contrary to the situation described by Veblen, it does not seem to us to be the members of the upper class who dictate life styles, which then filter down; these residual legatees of the past are influenced as much as they influence, and the location of style leadership, is ramified and, to our mind, obscure.[62]

Other attempts to validate Veblen's thesis have provided further support for this conclusion. The study of Laumann and House, for example, showed that the *nouveaux riches* were the group most likely to engage in conspicuous consumption, largely because of their especially strong need to validate a newly acquired social position.[63] Groups who felt secure in their social status, or who manifested no particular desire to be upwardly mobile, displayed no such marked tendency to conspicuously consume. At the same time, the *nouveaux riches* were very conscious of the necessity to consume conspicuously with 'taste' if their claim to higher status was to become accepted. Those who they regarded as the 'tastemakers', however, were not members of the traditional elite 'leisure class' but professionals whose job it was to advise on such matters, people like architects, decorators, interior designers and fashion correspondents. In accepting their definition of what was regarded as tasteful, the *nouveaux riches* were in effect rejecting the standards of the more traditional upper class. Apart from supporting the suggestion that the status system of modern societies is more complex than Veblen claimed, this research suggests that the social dimensions of status and taste do not necessarily coincide, and that one cannot simply be subsumed under the other.[64]

Fourthly, Veblen's central assertion that the primary cultural meaning of consumption behaviour is to be found in what it indicates about the consumer's social status cannot pass unchallenged, for it is clear that among the many meanings commonly attributed to such behaviour are those which have primary significance for character. Fifthly, Veblen's gratuitous equation of the cultural significance of the act of consumption with inter-peer competition for status meant that he unnecessarily limited his analysis to socially visible or conspicuous actions, thereby giving impetus to the long-standing tendency to assume that consumption is an essentially 'other-directed' pattern of behaviour. There seems to be no reason, however, to assume that private or inconspicuous consumption should be any less culturally meaningful than its public counterpart nor any the less expressive of basic cultural values.[65] Sixthly, Veblen offers no explanation of the mechanisms through which individuals manage to achieve changes in their pattern of consumer wants. Once again, the way in which a want is itself generated, only later to be extinguished and supplanted by another, is simply not explicated. Beyond the suggestion that pride or envy might be the predominant motives, and that imitation is implicated in the process, these mechanisms remain a mystery.

Lastly, but most important of all, Veblen does not provide a basis for distinguishing traditional from modern consumer behaviour, and hence does not account for that insatiability and desire for novelty which is such a crucial hallmark of the latter. His theory of conspicuous consumption – which intriguingly seems to have been inspired by a traditional ritual in the first place[66] – applies with equal force to all human communities, members of tribal, non-literate societies being just as prone to engage in intense status-competition as any individuals in contemporary society, whilst all communities encourage people to live up to ideals. Why then is it commonly thought that Veblen's theory provides an answer to the problem of the dynamic of modern consumerism? For the truth is that his approach only appears to offer an explanation for the extraordinary insatiability which is such a marked feature of this pattern. In so far as Veblen's theory rests upon the assumption that modern consumers are all committed to a policy of aggressive conspicuous consumption, then one form of insatiability is only 'explained' in terms of the problematic assumption of another; in this case the claim that people are motivated by an overwhelming desire to get the better of their fellows, a psychological reductionism about as useful (and convincing) as the older explanation of insatiable consumption as motivated by greed.[67] If, on the other hand, 'defensive' conspicious consumption is assumed to be widespread, then some other factor must be invoked to explain how change is introduced into the system.

One can easily understand why, in a society in which patterns of consumption are rapidly changing for other reasons, individuals would constantly need to adjust their consumption habits so as to continue to give the correct signals concerning their social status. This does not have to be seen as a 'defensive' response to someone else's efforts to 'steal a march' in the status rankings so much as a 'corrective' manoeuvre. That is, people might make the wrong assessment of an individual's status if he continued to wear out-of-date clothes or to drive an old model of car. The dynamic ingredient here, however, is not status competition or emulation, or even imitation, but the phenomenon of fashion itself, and it is only because this is so closely identified with status emulation that the Veblenesque model gives the appearance of accounting for change.

This combined fashion emulation explanation typically has the following form. Those at the top of the social scale have a need to invent new fashions in order to maintain their superiority over those immediately below who, out of emulative desires, are copying their patterns of consumption. This is equally true for those in the next subordinate stratum, and so on, down to the bottom of the status system. As soon as any one social group looks like catching up with the fashion prevalent among those above, the members of the superordinate group will adopt a new fashion in order to maintain their superiority. In this way, fashions are introduced, spread and replaced all through the power of social emulation.[68] Puzzlingly, however, this view makes the introduction of a new fashion a response to emulative behaviour (this is what prompts the elite to innovate) whilst also presenting emulative behaviour as a response to the introduction of a new fashion. Indeed, as Herbert Blumer observes, 'most sociological explanations [of fashion] center on the idea that fashion is basically an emulation of prestige groups',[69] a view which ignores the fact that there is no good reason whatever why status competition or emulation should require an institution which functions to supply continuous novelty. In this way, the introduction and spread of any one fashion, which is clearly facilitated – like all innovation – by imitation, is confused with an understanding of the modern Western fashion pattern as a whole. Empirical evidence does not really support this model, for, as we have seen, fashionable innovations are not by any means always introduced by the societal elite. Hence, although it is possible to see how both modern fashion, and the desire to emulate one's social superiors, might serve to encourage what appear to be similar patterns of action (to the extent that both are envisaged as imitative behaviour this is bound to be true), it is far from obvious how they came to interact so as to produce insatiable wanting in consumers. For, whilst 'fashion' appears to be precisely the ingredient which, when added to Veblen's emulative theory, provides it with its dynamic, there is no adequate explanation of fashion-oriented behaviour which does not, in turn, rest upon theories of emulation. Obviously, one or more crucial elements are missing from the sought-after theory of modern consumerism.

4

Traditional and Modern Hedonism

I will offer one thousand gold pieces to any man who can show me a new pleasure.

Xerxes

Heard melodies are sweet, but those unheard
are sweeter.

Keats

The preceding discussion has revealed a clear need for a more adequate theory of modern consumption, one which addresses the central question of how individuals manage to develop a regular and endless programme of wanting in relation to new goods and services. Existing theories tend not to focus on this issue, treating it as the unproblematic by-product of exposure to the media, or the stimulation of emulative desires, and concentrate instead upon the rationality of product selection within a framework of taken-for-granted wants and tastes. In addition, the discussion of consumption by social scientists is singularly marked by a tendency to substitute moralizing for careful analysis, thereby causing existing theorizing to be marred by intrusive observations of an ideological nature. These two factors operate, when combined, to generate a view of modern consumer behaviour as a form of conduct which is both 'irrational and reprehensible'. 'Irrational' in the sense that such endless wanting is 'meaningless' from the point of view of the individual consumer, who is impelled to behave in this fashion by forces beyond his control; and 'reprehensible' in so far as the image of human nature appealed to in explaining this conduct presents individuals in an unfavourable light. Such a view is unjustifiable, for if behaviour is not perceived as 'rational' then the blame lies with social scientists for failing to see the structure of the meanings employed, and it is they, and not consumers, who should be reprimanded. Hence instead of indulging their prejudices so readily, social scientists would be better occupied concentrating their efforts on the development of a more adequate theory of modern consumerism. This is what will now be attempted.

There appears to be general and widespread agreement that modern consumption is characteristically 'luxury' consumption, and whilst that word has been variously defined, it does typically possess two different, if related, connotations. The first is the idea that a 'luxury' is in some sense a superfluous item, something which is desired yet is additional to need. Indeed, it is the very contrast between the concepts of 'need' and 'want' which lies at the heart of this formulation of the term, as Sombart makes clear in his assertion that 'luxury is any expenditure in excess of the necessary'.[1] Like others who make this distinction, Sombart recognizes that it cannot be absolute but varies between individuals and groups as well as over time, and he would have agreed with McKendrick's description of the consumer revolution in eighteenth-century England as a process in which yesterday's luxuries become today's necessities;[2] a transition which has been identified as the primary purpose of the contemporary advertising industry.[3]

The second of the two meanings found in the word 'luxury' is the reference to sensuous or pleasurable experience. Here the emphasis is upon the verb rather than the noun, and hence upon activities rather than objects. One may contrast a 'luxury item' with a 'basic necessity', but to 'luxuriate', for example in a hot bath, is to contrast a richly sensuous and pleasing experience with an ordinary, unstimulating or unpleasant one. A similar contrast applies when one 'luxuriates' in the sun, or, more metaphorically, in praise. In each case, the common feature is the enjoyment of the pleasurable dimension of an experience. Now this aspect of the concept of luxury has rather tended to elude the attention of economists. Of the classical writers only Sombart has clearly elucidated what Trilling has called, the 'pleasure–sensuality–luxury complex',[4] and perceived that 'at base' a 'love of luxury' might derive from 'purely sensuous pleasures',[5] with Scitovsky the only contemporary economist to attempt to pursue this line of thought.[6] From this perspective luxuries constitute the means to pleasure, whilst necessities are merely whatever is needed for the maintenance of existence, a state best described by the word 'comfort'. In this way, the original contrast between need and want can be related to the difference between activities which aim to relieve discomfort and those which yield pleasure, and although one might try to claim that these are congruent categories, such an argument is unconvincing.[7]

This interpretation of the concept of luxury does not figure at all prominently in theories of consumption and consumer behaviour, as the common assumption appears to be that pleasure-seeking is assimilable into an existing utilitarian framework.[8] Once it is recognized, however, that pleasure and utility are very different concepts, relating to contrasting aspects of human conduct, the way is open to develop a theory of consumer behaviour which is predicated upon a hedonistic rather than an utilitarian framework of thought. The error of equating the two appears to stem from Bentham's original careless formulation, in which utility is described as 'that property which produces benefit, advantage, pleasure, good, or happiness'.[9] Since these are very different concepts (or, at least, the third is not equatable with the first two), the subsequent development of utilitarianism required that some selection should be made from this list, and, in the event, the 'good' became identified with the 'necessary', that which served to meet human needs, with the consequence that the concept of pleasure was largely ignored.[10] Leaving aside the question of the significance of the concepts of pleasure and necessity for any theory of ethics, the key point to be emphasized here is that, sociologically speaking, they are implicated in contrasting modes of action. That is to say, a model of human motivation which assumes that action is oriented to 'the satisfaction of needs' has to make different assumptions from one which takes an orientation to the pursuit of pleasure as its axiom, whilst neither can sensibly be reduced to the other.

A theory of hedonistic conduct

Central to this contrast is the difference in meaning between the concepts of need and satisfaction on the one hand, and those of desire and pleasure on the other. The former relate to a state of being and its disturbance, followed by action to restore the original equilibrium. Hence a state of need is a state of deprivation, in which one lacks something necessary to maintain a given condition of existence, and realization of this leads to exploratory activity in the environment in order to find whatever is capable of remedying this lack. The paradigm for this model is food-seeking arising from an awareness of hunger. By contrast, pleasure is not a state of being so much as a quality of experience. Not properly in itself a type of sensation, pleasure is a term used to identify our favourable reaction to certain patterns of sensation.[11] Desire is the term used to refer to a motivational disposition to experience such patterns, and this is typically triggered by the presence in the environment of a recognized source of pleasure. The paradigm for this model is the initiation of sexual activity following an encounter with a potential mate. It can be seen from this that satisfaction-seeking and pleasure-seeking are basically very different kinds of activity, the first suggesting a process of being 'pushed' from within to act so as to restore a disturbed equilibrium, whilst the second implies one of being 'pulled' from without in order to experience greater stimulation.[12]

Now it might be argued that pleasure-seeking is merely a form of satisfaction-seeking in which pleasure is the commodity of which one feels deprived, and that consequently one's search is for the 'satisfaction' which pleasure can bring. Equally, one could claim that satisfaction-seeking is merely a form of pleasure-seeking, in which satisfaction is the name we give to conditions produced by the experience of pleasure. Interestingly, however, although such a juggling with words appears to bring the two conceptions close together, it is clear that a difference remains. For, in the one case, the stress is upon a state of being, whilst in the other, it is upon a quality of experience, and although interrelated these cannot be directly equated. Consequently, conduct directed towards satisfaction and that directed towards pleasure necessarily have a tendency to take different forms, and lead individuals to direct attention to contrasting aspects of their environment.

Objects possess utility or the capacity to provide satisfaction. It is, in this sense, an intrinsic attribute of real things: food can relieve hunger, clothes provide warmth, houses shelter, people affection. Pleasure, on the other hand, is not an intrinsic property of any object but is a type of reaction which humans commonly have when encountering certain stimuli. Pleasure is not even a property of stimuli, but refers to the capacity to react to stimuli in a certain fashion. To search for satisfaction is thus to engage with real objects in order to discover the degree and kind of their utility, whilst to search for pleasure is to expose oneself to certain stimuli in the hope that they will trigger a desired response within oneself. Hence, whilst one typically needs to make use of objects in order to discover their potential for satisfaction, it is only necessary to employ one's senses in order to experience pleasure, and, what is more, whereas an object's utility is dependent upon what it is, an object's pleasurable significance is a function of what it can be taken to be. Thus whilst only reality can provide satisfaction, both illusions and delusions can supply pleasure.

This can be illustrated from the simple example of eating, for while, on the one hand, one can mainly be concerned with the utility of the food and its function in remedying a state of deprivation, one can, on the other, direct one's attention to the pleasures to be gained from this activity, mainly (though not exclusively) those yielded through taste and smell. Neither concern need involve the other, for very nourishing substances can be experienced as highly unpleasant, whilst pleasing substances (like saccharin) may have no calorific or nutritional value whatever. In addition, food and drink can provide pleasure via the senses without any being ingested, as is the case with the aroma of a steak or the bouquet of a wine, whilst the body's need for nourishment may be met by a process of direct injection which bypasses the taste buds entirely.

This example serves to draw attention to a crucial difference between a state of satisfaction and the experiencing of something as pleasant, which is that the second is inseparable from our paying attention to it. Thus, whilst it is not absurd to ask whether an unconscious person is in a 'satisfactory' condition, it does seem rather silly to ask if he is experiencing pleasure. It is necessary to be conscious of sensations in order to be able to derive pleasure from them, for 'pleasure' is, in effect, a judgement made by the experiencer. As Gilbert Ryle observes,

It is impossible, not psychologically but logically impossible, for a person to be enjoying the music while paying no heed at all to it, or to be detesting the wind and sleet while completely absorbed in quarrelling with his companion. There is a sort of contradiction in describing someone as absent mindedly enjoying or disliking something.[13]

Satisfaction, on the other hand, is the name for an effect of action, one which, in principle, is open to anyone to assess. It is for this reason that it is more common for others to assure us that we will indeed find something 'satisfactory', than it is for them to assure us that we shall find something 'pleasant'.

This does not of course preclude the possibility that a group of people might judge a common stimulus to be pleasant or that individuals are unable to predict each other's likes and dislikes. Such communality of judgement, however, is crucially dependent upon the existence of shared tastes, backed up by extensive knowledge of other people's values, beliefs, attitudes, and even possibly moods. In other words, a high degree of knowledge and sympathetic identification is required before it is possible to make anything like an accurate judgement concerning someone else's experience of pleasure. This is much less true of satisfaction, which one might say possesses a higher degree of inter-subjective validity, deprivation being observable to an extent to which 'unpleasure' is not.

Typically, comfort-seeking behaviour is initiated by the recognition of a specific need, and consequently the sought-after satisfactory state is very particular in form, such that other objects, which may none the less also possess 'utility', lack the capacity to provide it. Thus clothing will not bring relief from the pangs of hunger, nor food shelter from the cold. Pleasure-seeking, on the other hand, does not characteristically take this form, for although some 'pleasures' may be preferred to others, this quality can be found in a wide range of experiences, ones which are hence interchangeable to a considerable degree. Frustrated by the bad weather in our desire for the pleasures to be gained from sunbathing on the beach, for example, we may find alternative enjoyment in a funfair or amusement arcade, the constraint limiting our search for pleasure lying more in our 'tastes' than in our environment.

Pleasure would appear to derive from the capacity of sensations to act as stimuli and hence to produce an 'excited' state within us. It is thus not the substantive nature of sensations but their stimulative potential which is most directly pertinent to pleasure-giving. Since, however, a stimulus can only be identified (and indeed defined) contextually as something apprehended by a sense organ against an existing background of sensations, continual stimulation necessitates continual change. A given stimulus, if unchanging, rapidly ceases to be a stimulus, and thus cannot give pleasure (like a single note of music if held indefinitely without variation in volume or pitch). It is, therefore, the changes in monitored sensations which yield pleasure rather than anything intrinsic to their nature, and while a totally unchanging environment could be satisfying it is unlikely that it could be experienced as pleasant. It follows from this that the capacity to experience pleasure repeatedly from the sensations derived from activities is threatened by a too frequent or too extended exposure to them; it is, in this respect, a function of prior experience. The capacity to gain the satisfaction of needs from objects, however, is a function of the general use which has been made of them, and hence of the degree of utility which they still possess. Thus, whilst the pleasure-potential of any situation is crucially a function of its stimulative power in conjunction with past experience, its satisfaction-potential is a function of the degree to which the objects present have in general been 'exploited'.

Pain and pleasure are implicated in contrasting ways in these alternative models of purposive, human behaviour. Since they are not really opposites, they cannot be regarded, in Benthamite fashion, as if they were the motivational north and south poles of conduct. Pain is a sensation, and as such can be identified and described: we may note that it is an 'aching', 'throbbing' or 'burning' pain, and is located in our foot or our head. Pleasure, on the other hand, is less an individual sensation than a quality of an experience and if asked to locate and describe pleasure we are normally forced to respond by elaborating on the nature of that experience. We are certainly not in the habit of saying that we have a pleasure in our foot, or of classifying pleasures according to their different 'sensational' qualities, as Gilbert Ryle observes.[14]

Pain is in fact most commonly one of the sensations which serves to warn us of existing or impending need, as with the 'pangs' of hunger. Consequently it is an important ingredient in the satisfaction-seeking model of human behaviour which can, with a fair degree of accuracy, be said to be 'driven' by the primary necessity of avoiding pain and discomfort. The fact that the alleviation of need is also commonly a pleasant experience is a reason why a flight from pain and a search for pleasure are often confused. Where, however, pleasure-seeking is a primary motive (rather than the incidental accompaniment) of action, there are unlikely to be any urgent needs demanding attention, and thus no 'pains' to be avoided. On the contrary, the hedonist's overriding desire is for stimulating experiences and pain itself can be an extremely effective means of providing just such pleasurable excitation.

As has been noted, an isolated or unchanging stimulus is unlikely to be experienced as pleasant; it can, however, be painful. Pleasure thus appears to arise from a pattern and more usually a sequence of stimuli; it is in that sense a function of the process of continuing stimulation. Pain, on the other hand, seems to be primarily related to the intensity of a stimulus, occurring once this reaches a given threshold. This seems to be the main reason why 'a' pain characteristically refers to an individual sensation whilst 'a' pleasure usually implies a complete activity. In addition this would account for the fact that pleasure is much less localized than pain, for the flow of stimuli typically engages a larger area of receptors. There also appears to be something intrinsically rhythmic or wave-like about the patterns which yield pleasure, as is implied by the essential nature of sexual activity, and the enjoyments of both movement and massage.[15] Pleasure thus appears to be a tune made from the notes of individual stimuli, whilst pain is one or more notes of excessive volume. Comfort is a state in which one is not exposed to any over-loud noise, whilst boredom is the product of experiencing nothing but tuneless stimuli. If this is indeed a relevant metaphor, then it should not be surprising that some people develop a taste for 'explosive bangs' in their favourite tunes.[16]

Finally, to reiterate the main conclusion of this discussion, even though much human activity is of a kind which yields both satisfaction and pleasure, the fact that these derive from different aspects of the individual's relationship with the environment means that a fundamental choice of orientation exists. To pursue the example of eating, an interest in enjoyment will direct attention to the first mouthfuls and toward sampling different courses in order to experience fresh stimuli, whilst an interest in satisfaction will direct attention to the amount eaten and the point when all bodily 'needs' are completely gratified. Each orientation works to exclude the other with the focus of attention placed either upon the quality of an experience or a resultant state of being.

This choice between action directed toward maximizing satisfaction and that directed at maximizing pleasure is not likely to be especially apparent to people who rarely escape from the experience or threat of deprivation. This is because activity which relieves the discomfort of need also brings pleasure. There is therefore no necessity for such people to make a choice between these goals, for merely by concentrating upon satisfying their needs they will naturally encounter enjoyment. Thus, although the pleasure which the eating of food can provide to the hungry man is, in effect, a by-product of his endeavour to end his state of hunger, it is a real and integral part of his experience. When, however, the satisfaction of such needs becomes a regular and guaranteed event, and the discomforts associated with deprivation cease to be routinely experienced, then so too will the pleasures which accompany their relief. Supplied with regular and ample meals, for example, modern man rarely experiences real hunger, or the intensity of pleasure which eating can provide under such circumstances.[17]

In this respect it is crucial to recognize that were an individual to experience a state of permanent and perfect satisfaction then he would also be deprived of pleasure. This follows naturally from the fact that it would be necessary to allow the discomforts associated with a need to develop before pleasure could be gained from the process of its alleviation. In fact, extinction of the experience of need involves the elimination of all such naturally arising powerful stimuli and hence the very possibility of intense pleasure. Thus, as long as the discomforts of deprivation and need are part and parcel of an individual's everyday life there is no dilemma as to whether satisfaction or pleasure should be accorded the higher priority. It is the arrival of 'affluence' which brings this problem in its wake.[18]

Traditional hedonism

Historically, therefore, it is with the development of an economy efficient enough to provide a permanent food surplus that the beginnings of civilization and the first experiences of this dilemma both occur. For members of the small elite who enjoy the privileges of power and wealth, regular satisfaction of needs can be guaranteed, with the result that they experience a loss of pleasure in their lives. This then becomes, in effect, the crucial, sought-after, scarce commodity, with the consequence that for the first time the pursuit of pleasure for its own sake, rather than its mere appreciation as an adjunct of action pursued for other purposes, takes on the character of a clearly defined and distinct goal of action.[19]

The initial response of the traditional hedonist, when faced with the loss of naturally occurring pleasure as a consequence of guaranteed satisfaction, is to attempt to re-create artificially the cycle of need–satisfaction experience. The Romans, for example, deliberately made themselves sick so that they might be able to continue to enjoy the pleasures of eating beyond the point at which they were replete. Along with such attempts to replicate situations of secondary pleasure, an epicurean response to the problem of increasing one's enjoyment also develops. This involves the skilful manipulation of sensations associated with appetites so as to maximize their stimulative impact and it is in this context that such 'arts' as those practiced by the cook and the concubine develop. This manipulation, however, is restricted to activities customarily identified as 'pleasures' and features the deliberate modification of real stimuli.

A crucial feature of this process is an inherent tendency toward despotism. Since pleasure can only be successfully assessed subjectively yet is a function of the sensations arising from objects and events in the environment, the pleasure-seeker will naturally be pushed toward acquiring greater and greater control over all that surrounds him. Such control is not merely a question of ensuring that others submit to his will, but is more a matter of possessing complete power over all sources of sensations so that the continuous adjustments can be made which ensure prolonged pleasure. There will, however, be an irreducible element of frustration for even the most powerful of individuals as not only will some actions fail to have the kind of stimulative power anticipated of them whilst some stimuli remain 'out of reach', but it will also prove impossible for those who seek to please their master to anticipate successfully all his changes of taste and mood.

The potentate will nevertheless employ his considerable power over others so as to select and manipulate the stimuli he experiences. The most obvious way of doing this is by varying the means employed to yield satisfaction in catering for needs. Thus his table is spread with an assortment of exotic foods, prepared in different ways, and complemented by various wines. In addition, his harem caters for variety with regard to sexual needs, whilst entertainers of all kinds seek, in a different manner, to stimulate his jaded senses. This latter point shows that it is not only through the 'contact' senses of taste, smell and touch, as they relate to 'appetites', that pleasurable stimulation can be experienced, but also through the 'distant' ones of sight and hearing. It is in this latter context, of course, that the pleasures of the arts are developed. Finally, the potentate might attempt to expand his pleasurable experiences by personally undertaking energetic activity which in itself provides direct stimulation, such as hunting or even warfare. Each of these paths to pleasure, however, contain serious limitations which act to block the further rationalization of hedonistic action.

The acquisition of pleasure through the manipulation of the means of satisfying appetitive needs is severely limited by the small number of human contact senses and the restricted range of sensations which they can distinguish. The sense of taste (which is also the sense of smell), for example, is only capable of distinguishing the four categories of salt, sweet, bitter and sour. Clearly, any moderately powerful figure may soon exhaust the potential for fresh stimulative pleasures which these can afford. The non-appetitive, distant senses of sight and hearing are, by comparison, capable of much finer discrimination, and hence present greater possibilities for pleasurable stimulation; something which is well illustrated by the enormous range of artistic styles present in cultures past and present. Unfortunately, this increased power of discrimination is associated with a greatly diminished power of arousal, such that aural and visual stimuli do not, in themselves, have anything like the same capacity of physical excitation as those mediated through taste or touch.

Thus, although the despot will be entertained by jugglers, acrobats and dancers, and possibly even by such spectacles as athletic or gladiatorial games, the pleasures which these supply (initially judged to be weak in comparison with those of the appetites) will rapidly pall. The arts, on the other hand, as represented by music, poetry and drama, do seem to have more potential for gratifying the hedonist, if only because they offer a greater variety and complexity of stimuli than is possible with traditional 'entertainments'. It is therefore the aesthetic dimension of experience which seems to offer the greatest promise for the further rationalization of pleasure-seeking. Unfortunately, unlike simple entertainment, the arts do not exist for the sole purpose of yielding pleasure. Indeed, it is not even their primary function. They serve to uphold and transmit central religious, political and moral values and beliefs, with the consequence that considerable constraints are placed upon the possibility of deliberately manipulating aesthetic stimuli in order to maximize pleasure. In any case, the potentate has a clear interest in not pursuing his own pleasure to the extent of undermining the legitimate basis of his authority, and so he will not be inclined to disinvest the arts of their central ideological functions.

There is, however, another path which seems to offer a rather different solution to the problem. This is to pursue pleasure as it manifests itself as an accompaniment of intensive or fateful activity. Action constitutes its own stimulus through its general arousal effect on the body, and, if it is associated with events which pose an element of risk, uncertainty or danger, there will be the added element of emotional arousal as well. Hunting is the classic elite activity which can provide pleasure from these sources, but fighting (whether in earnest or play) is another possibility. The overwhelming problem here for the hedonist is the inherent difficulty of concentrating upon the element of pleasure. The exigencies of action demand that the focus of attention is upon the immediate task in hand, especially if real dangers exist (and yet without them, arousal is diminished). Any awareness of pleasure is thus likely to be retrospective, or, of course, anticipatory, rather than a concommitant of the experience itself. There is, in addition, the very real disadvantage that pursuing primary pleasure through 'action' of this kind is to seriously endanger one's level of 'satisfaction', exposing oneself to the potential 'pains' of injury, hardship, discomfort or death. Finally, here too, the activity concerned is usually highly significant for the attribution of status and thus the need for prestige works to impose stoicism upon any hedonistic tendencies.[20]

The fact that activities which yield pleasure also fulfil other important functions is a major obstacle to the further rationalization of hedonism in traditional societies. Even the pursuit of appetitive pleasure is compromised in this respect by a continuing predominant concern with the maximization of satisfaction. The possibility that it might be necessary to sacrifice some of this in order to increase one's pleasure is not recognized, or, if it is, rejected because of the symbolic importance of the signs of comfort-luxury. For luxury in the form of opulent excess is more than an insurance against possible deprivation, it is also the very manifest evidence of power and wealth; hence to sacrifice some of this in the interests of greater pleasure would be to endanger once again the basis of the potentate's authority. In fact, because the fundamental conflict between comfort and pleasure is not recognized, there merely being an awareness that pleasure appears to be harder and harder to obtain, the symbols of luxury in both its aspects tend to be closely identified. Banquets, for example, constitute an excess and a wide variety of food whilst numerous servants attend to one's needs and one's desires. Wealth and power have common symbols.

A more basic problem stands in the way of the further rationalization of pleasure-seeking, however; one which arises from the intrinsically subjective nature of this form of activity. As noted above, pleasure is really only open to assessment by the stimulatee, and can at best only be guessed at by the stimulator on the basis of experience, knowledge of the subject and an insightful reading of behavioural cues. It obviously follows from this that no other person is in such a good position to provide pleasurable stimulation as the hedonist himself, for then the problems attendant upon assessing the precise nature of the stimulation desired and successfully communicating this to another are dispensed with. Thus the potentate, no matter how extensive his powers, can never experience that intensity of pleasure which, in principle, would be available were he in a position to create and control stimuli directly. It is the realization of this possibility of autonomous hedonism which, after a gap of many centuries, constitutes the major advance in the rationalization of pleasure-seeking. Such a development is also required before hedonism can be a truly universal orientation rather than simply a concern of the powerful few.

Traditional hedonism involves a concern with 'pleasures' rather than with 'pleasure', there being a world of difference between valuing an experience because (among other things) it yields pleasure, and valuing the pleasure which experiences can bring. The former is the ancient pattern, and human beings in all cultures seem to agree on a basic list of activities which are 'pleasures' in this sense, such as eating, drinking, sexual intercourse, socializing, singing, dancing and playing games. But since 'pleasure' is a quality of experience, it can, at least in principle, be judged to be present in all sensations. Hence the pursuit of pleasure in the abstract is potentially an ever-present possibility, provided that the individual's attention is directed to the skilful manipulation of sensation rather than to the conventionally identified sources of enjoyment.

These two orientations involve contrasting strategies. In the former, the basic concern is with increasing the number of times one is able to enjoy life's 'pleasures'; thus the traditional hedonist tries to spend more and more time eating, drinking, having sex and dancing. The hedonistic index here is the incidence of pleasures per unit of life. In the latter, the primary object is to squeeze as much of the quality of pleasure as one can from all those sensations which one actually experiences during the course of the process of living. All acts are potential 'pleasures' from this perspective, if only they can be approached or undertaken in the right manner; the hedonistic index here is the extent to which one is actually able to extract the fundamental pleasure which 'exists' in life itself. To pursue this aim, however, it is necessary not only for the individual to possess special psychological skills, but for society itself to have evolved a distinctive culture.

The growth of modern hedonism

The key to the development of modern hedonism lies in the shift of primary concern from sensations to emotions, for it is only through the medium of the latter that powerful and prolonged stimulation can be combined with any significant degree of autonomous control, something which arises directly from the fact that an emotion links mental images with physical stimuli. Before the full potential of emotionally mediated hedonism can be realized, however, various critical psycho-cultural developments have to have taken place.

That emotions have the potential to serve as immensely powerful sources of pleasure follows directly from their being states of high arousal; intense joy or fear, for example, produces a range of physiological changes in human beings which for sheer stimulative power generally exceed anything generated by sensory experience alone. This is true no matter what the content of the emotion. It is certainly not the case that some emotions, such as gratitude or love, are pleasant, whilst others, such as grief or fear, are not, for there are no emotions from which pleasure cannot be obtained.[21] Indeed, since the so-called 'negative' emotions often evoke stronger feelings than the others, they actually provide a greater potential for pleasure. The question, therefore, is not which emotions can supply most pleasure but what are the circumstances which must prevail before any emotion can be employed for hedonistic purposes.

An emotion may be represented as an event which is characteristically 'outside' an individual's control (or, at least, this is true biographically and historically, if subsequent developments are ignored). It is, in that sense, a behavioural storm which is endured, rather than an activity which is directed. Under the influence of very intense emotions, the behaviour of people is frequently so extreme and chaotic that they are said to be 'out of their minds', or 'to have taken leave of their senses', even, to be 'possessed'. Individuals may laugh or cry uncontrollably, dance, or run wildly about, even beat themselves or pull out their hair. Clearly experiences of this kind inundate the individual with such an excess of stimulation that there can be little possibility of enjoying it. What is more, as the examples suggest, such emotional arousal is merely part of a larger directive behavioural complex, involving overt motor activity, in the way in which fear is linked to flight or anger to aggression.[22] Thus not only is the individual's capacity to 'appreciate' his aroused state negated by his being subjected to a form of sensory overload, but he also has his attention directed away from any introspective appreciation of the subjective dimension of his experience by the preparation and implementation of action. Before any emotion can possibly be 'enjoyed', therefore, it must become subject to willed control, adjustable in its intensity, and separated from its association with involuntary overt behaviour.

This form of emotional control is not to be confused with that ordering and regulation of affective responses which must necessarily be a feature of all social life. That process is primarily concerned with the co-ordination of patterns of emotional restraint and display, and is primarily achieved through common socialization experiences. It is obvious that all cultures require individuals to learn both when and how to suppress, as well as express, emotions – a process which consists, in essence, of learning which situations are associated with what emotions. Control rarely extends, however, beyond the exercise of restraint in circumstances where no expressive response is permitted. In other words, it does not embrace a process of self-determination with regard to emotional experience, yet it is precisely in the degree to which an individual comes to possess the ability to decide the nature and strength of his own feelings that the secret of modern hedonism lies.

Such self-regulative control is clearly more than a mere capacity to suppress, although this is the connotation most usually associated with the expression, 'controlling one's emotions'. Obviously this is a necessary part of such a skill, and a soldier who endeavours to subdue his fear when in battle can indeed be said to be trying to 'control' both his state of arousal and its manifestation in observable actions. If he succeeds his fear will not be translated into the action of fleeing from the battlefield, and perhaps, in time, a certain diminution in the tendency to experience the emotion may occur. This ability, however, is one of limited behavioural, rather than full emotional, control; power being exerted over overt action rather than the psycho-physiological dimension of emotional experience itself.[23] The term 'self-control' or 'self-discipline' is appropriate to describe success in this respect.[24] A more crucial part of the capacity for emotional control concerns the deliberate cultivation of an emotion, especially in the absence of any 'naturally occurring' stimulus, and although this is, in part, a corollary of the power to suppress feeling, it also transcends it.[25] The attainment of emotional 'self-control' in the negative sense is hence both a precursor and a prerequisite of the development of full voluntaristic emotional control, for, whilst it is perhaps natural that problems presented by the presence of unwanted emotions should be more pressing than those created by the absence of desired ones, efforts directed at suppressing emotion succeed in breaking the intimate association between feeling and overt behaviour. By thus separating anger from aggression, or fear from flight, a start is made on the process by which emotion becomes defined as a largely interiorized facet of human experience.[26]

Of course, if an individual is to determine his own emotional state, then it is necessary to be 'insulated' in some way from those inevitable exigencies of life which typically prompt such responses. To the extent, therefore, that advances in knowledge, wealth and power reduce a person's exposure to the threats of famine, disease, war or disasters in general, one might anticipate an increased possibility of emotional control. Although this is true, the development of cultural resources to provide such 'insulation' would seem to be an occurrence of far greater significance, for this process allows considerable latitude in the way in which any situation is defined. Thus, to take an example, a clergyman may organize the frightened passengers of a sinking ship into a religious congregation joined in prayer, and in this way counter the environmentally stimulated fear and panic with ritually stimulated hope and calm. Alternatively, a commander-in-chief, like Henry V, might employ a rhetoric rich in powerful and suggestive images to instil courage and determination into his exhausted and demoralized troops. In this fashion the symbolic resources of a culture can be employed to re-define the situations in which groups find themselves and thus bring about changes of mood, a process which extends beyond mere self-control to embrace the substitution of one emotion for another. The trouble, of course, with using symbolically triggered emotions in this way to combat environmentally prompted ones, is that the individual may simply be exchanging one form of external determination for another. Only if the individual is himself in control of the employment of symbolic resources can true emotional self-determinism emerge. For this reason, a decline in the importance of the collective symbolic manipulation of emotion is important. Literacy, in conjunction with individualism, would seem to be the key development in this respect, for this grants the individual a form and degree of symbolic manipulation which was previously restricted to groups.

The central point to be emphasized in this context is that only in modern times have emotions come to be located 'within' individuals as opposed to 'in' the world. Thus, whilst in the contemporary world it is taken for granted that emotions 'arise' within people and act as agencies propelling them into action, it is typically the case that in pre-modern cultures emotions are seen as inherent in aspects of reality, from whence they exert their influence over humans. Thus Barfield has pointed out how, in the Middle Ages, words like 'fear' and 'merry' did not denote a feeling located within a person, but attributes of external events; 'fear' referring to a sudden and unexpected happening, and 'merry' being a characteristic of such things as the day or the occasion.[27] The attitude and emotion of 'awe' is another good example of an aspect of experience which was regarded as primarily a characteristic of God rather than of a man's typical reaction to his presence. These examples show how the main sources of agency in the world were viewed as existing outside of man, from whence they not only 'forced' him into actions but also 'filled' him with those distinctively aroused states called emotions.[28]

This view of man and his relationship to the world was to change dramatically as a consequence of the process which Weber called 'disenchantment'; that is, the collapse of the general assumption that independent agents or 'spirits' were operative in nature.[29] The origins of this development can be traced back as far as ancient Judaism but it was accelerated by the Reformation, attaining its most complete expression in the Enlightenment. A significant corollary of disenchantment was the accompanying process of de-emotionalization such that the environment was no longer seen as the primary source of feelings but as a 'neutral' sphere governed by impersonal laws, which, whilst they controlled natural events, did not, in themselves, determine feelings. A natural consequence of this fundamental shift in world-view was that emotions were re-located 'within' individuals, as states which emanated from some internal source, and although these were not always 'spiritualized', there is a sense in which the disenchantment of the external world required as a parallel process some 'enchantment' of the psychic inner world.[30] A new set of terms was required in order to describe this transition, and to this end old words were pressed into fresh uses. Examples would be 'character', 'disposition' and 'temperament', all words which had originally referred to some feature of the external world and which now came to stand for a subjective influence upon behaviour.[31]

This increasing separation of man from the constraining influence of external agencies, this disenchantment of the world, and the consequent introjection of the power of agency and emotion into the being of man, was closely linked to the growth of self-consciousness. Such a uniquely modern ability is itself a product of these processes, as, in becoming aware of the 'object-ness' of the world and the 'subject-ness' of himself, man becomes aware of his own awareness poised between the two. The new internal psychic world in which agency and emotion are relocated is that of the 'self', and this world is, in its turn, also increasingly subject to the cool, dispassionate and inquiring gaze which disenchanted the outer, with the result that consciousness of 'the world' as an object separate from man the observer, was matched by a growing consciousness of 'the self' as an object in its own right. This is revealed by the spread of words prefixed with 'self' in a hyphenated fashion, words such as 'self-conceit', 'self-confidence' and 'self-pity', which began to appear in the English language in the sixteenth and seventeenth centuries, and became widely adopted in the eighteenth; 'self-consciousness' itself apparently being first employed by Coleridge.[32]

Associated with this development were attempts to understand the laws which link the inner and the outer worlds: to grasp how exactly certain features of each are connected. In part, this meant examining the way in which aspects of externality tend to prompt particular emotional responses from within. Hence the proliferation of words which relate to the effects which objects can have upon people, words like 'amusing', 'charming', diverting', 'pathetic' and 'sentimental', whilst the effects which the 'self' has on the environment are summarized by the terms, 'character', disposition', 'taste' and the like mentioned above.

Of crucial significance for this discussion is the fact that the growth of self-consciousness had, as one of its many consequences, the effect of severing any remaining necessary connection between man's place in the world and his reaction to it. Objective reality and subjective response were now mediated through consciousness in such a way that the individual had a wide degree of choice concerning exactly how to connect them. Beliefs, actions, aesthetic preferences and emotional responses were no longer automatically dictated by circumstances but 'willed' by

individuals. Such a contrast is, of course, exaggerated, but, in so far as
individuals gained control over their own tendency toward impulsiveness,
and could, on the other hand, manipulate the symbolic meanings of
events, then it is indeed reasonable to speak of the growth of an
autonomous control of emotional expression.

The first major historical expression of success in this direction was
apparent in Protestantism, and it is natural that one should automatically
think of the Puritan ethic when discussing the issue of emotional control,
as the success obtained by the Puritan 'saints' in suppressing all
manifestation of unwanted emotion was formidable indeed. But it would
be wrong to envisage such control in the purely negative form of
suppression, for once this power has been attained then some controlled
expression also increasingly became possible. In fact, not even the
Puritan ethic prohibited the expression of emotion upon all occasions.[33]

To stress the crucial part played by Puritanism in the evolution of
modern hedonism may seem, at first sight, to be somewhat strange, and
yet as far as the emergence of sentimental hedonism is concerned,
Protestant religion, and especially that harsh and rigorous form of it
which is known as Puritanism, must be recognized as the primary source.
This is precisely because as a movement it adopted a position of such
outright hostility to the 'natural' expression of emotion, and consequently
helped to bring about just that split between feeling and action which
hedonism requires. In addition to this, however, it also contributed
greatly to the development of an individualistic ability to manipulate the
meaning of objects and events, and hence toward the self-determination
of emotional experience.

Religion is the most important of all areas of culture as far as the
evolution of an ability to cultivate emotion is concerned. This is because
such intensely fateful issues as one's state of sin (or grace) and one's
hopes for salvation, together with the extremely powerful emotions which
they can arouse, are coupled with the necessity of presenting invisible
divine agencies by means of symbols. Naturally enough, the potential to
arouse these feelings then becomes attached to the symbols themselves.
This is in marked contrast to the powerful emotions aroused by such real
events as a battle or a shipwreck, where the emotion arises from the
experienced reality rather than a 'symbol'. In fact, as has been noted,
religious symbols can serve to counteract such experientially induced
emotion, just as, more significantly, they can serve to induce emotion in
the absence of any discernible environmental stimulus.

That individualism was carried to unprecedented lengths in Protestantism is particularly significant in relation to this last point, for whilst in
Roman Catholicism symbols also served to arouse (and allay) powerful
emotions, their control was kept firmly in the hands of the priesthood, and

hence situationally located in communal ritual. In Protestantism, by contrast, not only was there no one to act as mediator between the individual and the divine, but both 'magical' ritual and the use of idols was proscribed. The consequence of this was that those symbols which did serve to arouse religious emotion were of an abstract and general character. Death and mortality, for example, which were commonly regarded as evidence of man's inherently sinful state, could be represented by a very wide range of objects and events in the world, from coffins, graves, churchyards and yew trees, to sickness, worms and church bells, with any one of these acting as the 'trigger' for emotional experience. Such a situation clearly gives the individual considerable scope to decide when and where he will choose to undergo a particular emotion. It is, however, the religious beliefs which ultimately underpin these emotions, and hence, as long as the beliefs are accepted as true, then this ability to manipulate symbolically the occasion of their expression is of comparatively little relevance; but when such beliefs begin to atrophy, a significant change can occur.

Clearly belief dependent emotionality is a rather different phenomenon from that which is event dependent in so far as the potentiality exists for the individual to gain control over his own emotions without first having to obtain mastery over the real world. As long as the validity of the beliefs is taken for granted, however, there is little obvious difference between an individual's terror on encountering the devil and that on meeting a lion. But the waning of conviction inevitably affects the intensity of the emotion even if it still occurs: of more significance, however, is its probable effect on the emotion's genuineness. For as doubts about the truth of beliefs crystallize, the likely initial consequence is to remove the basis for the emotion rather than the emotion itself, which has, over time, become habitually associated with the given symbols. There thus remains a tendency for it to occur even though the individual knows that it is not entirely necessary. It is under these circumstances that the real possibility of gaining pleasure from emotion can arise.

This is best illustrated by reference to the fate of beliefs concerning hell, eternal damnation, the Devil and sin in the late seventeenth and early eighteenth centuries when they gradually faded in the face of the scepticism and optimistic rationalism of the Enlightenment. As they did not disappear altogether, the powerful emotional resonances which such beliefs created remained in the minds of many, and their conventional symbols became employed as a means of gaining emotional pleasure. Thus out of a background of real religious terror there developed such artistic genres as graveyard poetry and the Gothic novel both of which catered for the 'thrill' of being frightened.

In order, therefore, to possess that degree of emotional self-determination which permits emotions to be employed to secure pleasure, it is necessary for individuals to attain that level of self-consciousness which permits the 'willing suspension of disbelief';[34] disbelief robs symbols of their automatic power, whilst the suspension of such an attitude restores it, but only to the extent to which one wishes that to be the case. Hence through the process of manipulating belief, and thus granting or denying symbols their power, an individual can successfully adjust the nature and intensity of his emotional experience; something which requires a skilful use of the faculty of imagination.

Whilst it is possible to employ the power of imagination to summon up physical sensations such as the feel of the sun on one's back or the taste of grapes, this is an exceptionally difficult exercise. To that extent it is almost impossible to gain real pleasure from directly imagined sensations. By contrast, it is comparatively easy (at least for modern man) to use imagination to conjure up realistic images of situations or events which produce an emotion in the imaginer; an emotion, which, if controlled, can itself supply all the stimulation necessary for a pleasurable experience. This is an ability which it is all too easy to take for granted, forgetting that it is a comparatively recent addition to mankind's repertoire of experiences.[35]

Modern hedonism presents all individuals with the possibility of being their own despot, exercising total control over the stimuli they experience, and hence the pleasure they receive. Unlike traditional hedonism, however, this is not gained solely, or even primarily, through the manipulation of objects and events in the world, but through a degree of control over their meaning. In addition, the modern hedonist possesses the very special power to conjure up stimuli in the absence of any externally generated sensations. This control is achieved through the power of imagination, and provides infinitely greater possibilities for the maximization of pleasurable experiences than was available under traditional, realistic hedonism to even the most powerful of potentates. This derives not merely from the fact that there are virtually no restrictions upon the faculty of imagination, but also from the fact that it is completely within the hedonist's own control. It is this highly rationalized form of self-illusory hedonism which characterizes modern pleasure-seeking.

5

Modern Autonomous Imaginative Hedonism

There are two tragedies in life. One is not to get your heart's desire. The other is to gain it.

George Bernard Shaw

Like its traditional predecessor, modern hedonism is still basically a matter of conduct being pulled along by desire for the anticipated quality of pleasure which an experience promises to yield. The contrast is considerable, however. In the first place, pleasure is sought via emotional and not merely sensory stimulation, whilst, secondly, the images which fulfil this function are either imaginatively created or modified by the individual for self-consumption, there being little reliance upon the presence of 'real' stimuli. These two facts mean that modern hedonism tends to be covert and self-illusory; that is to say, individuals employ their imaginative and creative powers to construct mental images which they consume for the intrinsic pleasure they provide, a practice best described as day-dreaming or fantasizing.

Imagination is a common human faculty and has a part to play in traditional hedonism. In that context, images deriving principally from memory are brought (or, more likely, force themselves) into consciousness with the consequence of creating an effective anticipation of events; a process essential to the birth of desire itself. Such images, however, are seldom crafted self-consciously by the individual, but are largely just taken from the past and employed as they are. To this extent, imagination is not under self-direction to the extent that it is in modern cultures, and an individual's 'imaginings' when awake are not very different in status from those which occur when asleep. They can, of course, give pleasure, just as night-dreams may, but they can equally well be distressing. This lack of personal autonomy is reflected in the fact that artistic creativity, like dreaming, is commonly considered to derive from the activity of external agencies.

By contrast, in modern, self-illusory hedonism, the individual is much more an artist of the imagination, someone who takes images from memory or the existing environment, and rearranges or otherwise improves them in his mind in such a way that they become distinctly pleasing. No longer are they 'taken as given' from past experience, but crafted into unique products, pleasure being the guiding principle. In this sense, the contemporary hedonist is a dream artist, the special psychic skills possessed by modern man making this possible. Crucial to this process is the ability to gain pleasure from the emotions so aroused, for, when the images are adjusted, so too are the emotions. As a direct consequence, convincing day-dreams are created, such that individuals react subjectively to them as if they were real. This is the distinctively modern faculty, the ability to create an illusion which is known to be false but felt to be true. The individual is both actor and audience in his own drama, 'his own' in the sense that he constructed it, stars in it, and constitutes the sum total of the audience. All this drastically alters the nature of hedonism, for not only does modern man take pleasure in his day-dreams, but obtaining enjoyment from them radically changes his view of the place of pleasure in real life.

The nature of modern autonomous illusory or imaginative hedonism is best illustrated by reference to two fictional creations, Thurber's Walter Mitty and Hall and Waterhouse's Billy Liar, for although these are both 'unreal' characters, they do present, albeit in an exaggerated form, a characteristic and unique feature of the psychic experience of modern man.

Walter Mitty's 'secret life', as revealed in the original, very short, story by James Thurber,[1] is the existence which he creates for himself in his imagination. Thus whilst on a brief shopping trip with his wife into the town of Waterbury, during which he is charged with the job of buying overshoes for himself and puppy biscuits for the dog, Walter constructs alternative adventures for himself; including piloting a navy plane through a hurricane, taking over at a critical stage in an important operation, making a dramatic court-room confession, and carelessly volunteering to fly a bomber single-handed on a hazardous, 'dare-devil' mission. Each of these day-dreams is triggered by some real activity or incident, although the connection is sometimes fairly vague; the scene in the operating theatre is conjured up as a consequence of his wife prompting him to put on his gloves, whilst the court-room scene is, in part, initiated by his attempt to remember what it was he had been asked to buy, and starts with the District Attorney saying 'perhaps this will refresh your memory'.[2] Once set in motion, however, the fantasy experience takes on a life of its own, with the introduction of other characters and a dialogue in keeping with the overall theme. None of these day-dreams appears to last more than a few minutes, and is usually terminated by the abrupt and unwelcome intrusion of reality, Walter's attention having been deflected from the world about him by his reverie.

Billy Fisher has earned the sobriquet 'liar' because of his tendency to invent preposterous stories about himself and other people, his father observing that he 'can't say two words to anybody without it's a bloody lie'.[3] In fact, he tells one of his girlfriends, Barbara, that his father was in the merchant navy and had been a prisoner of war, whilst he misleads his parents into believing that his friend Arthur's mother is pregnant. In part, the lying is necessitated by his general incompetence and irresponsibility, as is the case when his employer rings up to discover why he hasn't turned up for work, or is prompted by a desire to enhance his reputation, as in the instance when he impulsively declares that he has made the cocktail cabinet which Barbara had admired. But, generally, his lying does not seem to have a purpose and, far from advancing his interests, works in the end to his disadvantage. As his mother observes,

I don't know why he says these things. I mean what good does it do him? It's not as if he gets anything out of it. . . . He says things we can find out about, that's what I don't understand. He told me that young lad who works in the fruit shop had gassed himself – and he knows I go in there every Tuesday.[4]

As this passage suggests, Billy is continually being found out in his lies, and when this happens he either tries to bluff or claims that it was 'only a joke'. In fact, he confesses to Barbara that he possesses a 'fairly vivid imagination', and that at times it is 'inclined to run away with' him,[5] implying that the jokes stem from this tendency to day-dream. Billy's apparent congenital inability to tell the truth, therefore, derives from his inveterate fantasizing, constituting its intrusion into everyday reality.

At one level, Billy's fantasies resemble Walter Mitty's by being private, covert acts. That he often engages in such fantasizing is revealed when he confesses to another girlfriend, Liz, that he 'goes' to an imaginary country of his making whenever he feels the need to be 'invisible', and that he has sketched out the government and people of this country in some detail.[6] Such fantasies also resemble those of Walter's by having the dreamer cast in the central, 'starring' role (Billy is the Prime Minister of this country). It is also clear that in both instances the fantasizers dislike the mundanity and boredom of the everyday, real world, and are markedly incompetent in coping with it. Thus, Walter Mitty, when jolted out of his day-dream by his wife, finds her 'grossly unfamiliar',[7] whilst he hates the regular, enforced shopping trips into town. He also resents those people, like the parking-lot attendant, who display an easy competence in those everyday tasks which he finds so difficult to accomplish. Billy too resents his life in a Northern, industrial town where he finds himself trapped between nagging, insensitive parents at home, and a dull, boring routine at work. He also manifests a marked lack of worldliness and competence, failing to get up in time to go to work, forgetting to shave or clean his shoes, and is unable to perform his job in an even moderately adequate fashion. For both, therefore, fantasizing would seem to offer an escape not merely from a world of boredom, but also from one of failure.

In other respects, however, Billy's fantasizing has dimensions which are not present in Walter Mitty's. In the first place, it includes real people other than himself, indeed, this habit leads to many of his lies. Thus, even in his most extended 'private' fantasy – the 'major-general' sequence in the garden – he invents an imagined history for his just-deceased grandmother. But, secondly, and more significantly, Billy's fantasies are often anything but covert, manifesting themselves to others through the content of his speech, and, occasionally by non-verbal behaviour. In one instance he has an imaginery conversation over the phone with his employer, whilst in another, he day-dreams about his future life in London, ostensibly in the course of a conversation with his grandmother (only she isn't listening). These overt manifestations of his vivid imagination sometimes produce accommodating responses from others, and thus merge into communal make-believe or pretend play. Using an exaggerated, North-country brogue, he acts out a 'trouble up at mill' routine with his friend Arthur, whilst shortly afterward the two of them engage in a mock presentation ceremony in honour of Billy's services to television.[8] By sharing his fantasies in this manner, Billy gains at least the partial social approval of having his behaviour identified as 'playing about', or a 'game'. When, however, he is found acting them out by himself, his behaviour produces bewilderment and ridicule. Finally, unlike Walter Mitty, Billy also day-dreams rather than fantasizes; that is to say, he envisages possible (if not especially probably) outcomes of present and future actions. In this sense, he imaginatively extends present experience. He does this, for example, when speculating upon what he would be doing in a week's time were he to go to London. All Walter Mitty's fantasies, on the other hand, seem to be totally divorced from the possible outcomes of existing actions.

There can be little doubt that the motive for fantasizing is in both cases a desire for the pleasure which it brings. Walter Mitty lapses into fantasy easily and quickly, and has to be jolted back to reality, whilst Billy 'creates any situation he wants to in his head . . . and thoroughly enjoys them', or, as the drama critic of *The Times* expresses it: 'the most commonplace remark suggests . . . a personal fantasy which he at once indulges for the sheer pleasure of the indulgence'.[9] Of course, the journey into fantasy is also prompted by a desire to escape from reality, but then this can be seen as closely associated with the fact that everyday experience does not offer much in the way of enjoyment. Thus fantasizing is fundamentally a form of hedonism, its distinguishing feature being that pleasurable sensations derive from images which the hedonist himself creates, images which are known to be illusory but are yet treated as real in order to gain a stimulative effect.[10] Walter Mitty's wife, for example, comments that he appears to be 'tensed up', and is driving too fast,[11] features of his behaviour which are direct psycho-physiological consequences of his fantasizing.

To associate modern hedonism with the construction of imaginatively mediated illusions is apparently to suggest that the search for pleasure should cause individuals to withdraw from engagement with real life, as they pursue that reclusive enjoyment only to be found in their dreams. To a considerable extent this is indeed the case, a certain 'other-worldly' hedonism characterizing contemporary culture.[12] In fact, Billy Liar demonstrates this tendency, refusing, when the opportunity presents itself, to embark upon that course of action which could 'make his dreams come true'; that is, to go to London with Liz and try to make a living as a script-writer, preferring to continue his fantasy-imbued current existence. His commitment is, in this sense, to fantasy itself, rather than to any programme of action which would make his dream a possibility, something which becomes apparent when he impulsively confesses his secret desires to Liz:

I want a room, in the house, with a green baize door. It will be a big room, and when we go into it, through the door, that's it, that's our country. No one else would be allowed in. No one else will have keys. They won't know where the room is. Only we'll know. And we'll make models of the principal cities. You know, out of cardboard. And we could use toy soldiers. Painted. For the people. We could draw maps. It would be a place to go on a rainy afternoon. We could go there. No one would find us. I thought we could have a big sloping shelf running all the way down one wall, you know like a big desk. And we'd have a lot of blank paper on it and design our own newspapers. We could even make uniforms, if we wanted to. It would be our country . . .[13]

It is clear that this conception of a 'play-room' is really a place in which he can fantasize, and that what Billy wants most out of life is to be free to do this to his heart's content. Admittedly, he expressed his desire to share this activity with Liz, but basically, he is, like Walter Mitty, simply hooked on the pleasures of fantasy and requires little from life except the freedom to indulge his addiction undisturbed. A concern with the pleasure which can be gained from the covert consumption of self-constructed illusions need not lead in the direction of such a complete withdrawal from everyday life, however, at least, not for most adults. This is because it is more commonly sought for in day-dreams than fantasies.

It is not too easy to distinguish clearly between the various mental processes and activities which are relevant to this discussion, and terms like illusion, fantasy, day-dream, make-believe, imaginative speculation and stream of consciousness all appear to be pertinent in one way or another. In addition, the usage of these words is not standardized, and various influential writers, most especially Freud, have given very distinctive interpretations to some of them. It should be clear, however, that the meaning which he attributed to the term 'illusion' is not the one employed here. Freud identified a belief as an illusion 'when a wish-fulfilment is a prominent factor in its motivation',[14] whereas here it is being used in a more conventional manner to refer to a false or deceptive impression. Thus, the essence of an illusion is not a matter of what people believe, or why, but the contrast between what they know to be true and what their senses report. The illusion of depth provided by a mirror or, indeed, by perspective in a painting, is not the product of wish-fulfilment, but a phenomenon in which one accepts as natural the discrepancy between our knowledge and our experience of objects. The crucial point is that we typically respond by 'seeing into' them, even though we are not deluded into believing that the objects in question are anything other than flat. It is this 'as if' response which is at the heart of modern hedonism; the ability to treat sensory data 'as if' it were 'real' whilst knowing that it is indeed 'false'. Now although the illusion of depth provided by a mirror is a simple function of the laws of optics, and owes nothing to the intentional mental activity of the observer, the fantasies of a Walter Mitty or a Billy Liar can be said to illustrate the same basic principle. Whilst they react to their imagined environments as if they were real, they both know that they are actually 'false'.[15]

In so far as the other categories of image construction mentioned above can be successfully distinguished, the relevant dimensions would appear to be pleasant–unpleasant, probably–improbable, possible–impossible, consciously directed–sub consciously directed, and vividly conceived–dimly conceived. Vivid images which are not consciously called to mind, for example, need not be pleasant but may arise from a deep-seated anxiety: equally one may consciously direct one's mind to conjure up highly impossible scenes (perhaps for artistic purposes). The category of most interest in this discussion is that which has here been designated as 'day-dreaming', and this is taken to be that form of mental activity in which fairly vivid future images are brought to mind (either deliberately or not in the first instance) and are either found to be pleasant or elaborated in a way which renders them so. These pleasing images are then explored for the potential enjoyment which they can yield, perhaps being returned to on subsequent occasions. This exploration may take place in a more or less 'directed' fashion, with the individual perhaps content at times to allow the imagery to evolve 'as it wishes', whilst at others 'intervening' to make 'adjustments'. These may either be those thought necessary in order to make the imagined scene more pleasant to contemplate, or more commensurate with the constraints of reality; imagery which is allowed to develop because of the pleasure which it yields without being adjusted to take the latter into consideration will be dubbed 'fantasy'. On the other hand, the development of imagery which does conform closely to that which experience and understanding leads the individual to believe will occur, and which is not modified in any way so as to provide pleasure in its contemplation will be dubbed 'imaginative construction' or anticipation.

Fantasy usually implies the exercise of imagination in ways unrestricted by reality, and may thus involve such impossibilities as being invisible, or picturing oneself as a historical figure like Christopher Columbus or Winston Churchill; hence although the imagined scenario will unfold according to its own internal 'logic', it will not be constrained by those factors which limit the possibilities of ordinary life. In contrast to this, a day-dream can be defined as the imaginative elaboration, in a pleasurable direction, of a forthcoming or anticipated, real event, and, as a consequence, requires that incidents should be kept within the bounds of the possible (even if highly improbable). In this respect, day-dreaming involves the introduction of the principle of pleasure-seeking into the normal process of imaginative anticipation of, or speculation about, the future. Hence children and adolescents may day-dream about what they will be when they grow up, or who they are going to marry, whilst adults may day-dream about what they will do if they win a large sum of money. The key point about such exercises is that images are elaborated in order to increase pleasure and not for any other reason, yet they still contain that element of possibility which separates them from pure fantasy.[16]

The imaginative anticipation of the way in which an existing course of events might develop is, of course, an integral ingredient of all social action. Much of the time little real imagination is required in order to be able to accomplish this, because most conduct follows regular and repeated routines in which 'things turn out' as expected. We know, as it were, what is round the next bend, because we have been along the road before, and we know too, from long experience, what others will do and say. To this extent, therefore, memory serves as a reliable source of images such that recollection and anticipation become commensurate activities. But we also know from experience that we should expect the unexpected, there being an irreducible element of surprise in life. The forms which this takes – such as the car accident or the uninvited guest –

may not be welcome, whilst those which are, may not be novel, but the chance remains, none the less, that something new and exciting could happen at any time, and it is this very possibility which is the starting-point for much day-dreaming.

This does not mean that all day-dreams have to begin in the present for the extrapolation may be from a future point in time.[17] One may, for example, imagine incidents set in a forthcoming holiday, or at that unknown time when a hoped-for event finally occurs. Equally, the day-dream does not have to stem fron one's present course of action in the sense of being consequential upon it, for although one may have to visit a casino in order to day-dream about breaking the bank, one does not have to do anything in order to dream that one day a handsome stranger will sweep you off your feet.

The way in which mental images are most likely to be modified in imagination so as to deviate from a 'realistic' path is by the simple omission of those elements which, although inherent in life, interfere with the pursuit of its pleasures. Just as in romantic novels and films, heroes and heroines rarely have hiccups, headaches or indigestion unless this proves essential to the plot, so too are our dreams purged of life's little inconveniences. In a similar fashion, what would be happy coincidences in life become routine events in our dreams; we look our best on the important occasions, the waiter arrives just as we are ready to order, and other people utter exactly those words we had hoped to hear. In this way our imagined experience characteristically comes to represent a perfected vision of life, and from these apparently small beginnings, our dreams may gradually develop into elaborate works of art, deviating more and more from that which anyone has good reason to expect.

It would seem that, at least in principle, fantasies present greater possibilities for pleasurable experiences than do day-dreams, as no restrictions are set upon the circumstances and events which can be conjured up. This advantage is offset, however, by the loss of 'possibility' associated with the more extravagantly fanciful scenarios, and thus some of the vividness and power which comes with a sense of 'reality'. There is thus a basic tension in imaginative hedonism between the pleasures of perfection and those of reality potential, between the joys of unbridled imagining and those of anticipation. It is for this reason that dreaming of a fairly modest alteration in an existing pattern of life may actually provide more pleasure than the most magnificently impossible fantasy, an awareness that the former might come true more than compensating for the greater theoretical pleasure afforded by the latter.[18]

As this observation suggests, day-dreaming possesses a dimension which is not present in fantasizing proper, one which stems less from the nature of the images brought into view than the contemplation of these becoming real. This is the excitement of anticipation which arises when a foreseen pleasure draws near, in other words, the ingredient of desire. One can, of course, desire the pleasures which fantasy provides, as both Walter Mitty and Billy Liar do, but in the case of day-dreaming it is possible to have double-desire; that is, to desire the pleasure yielded by the day-dream as well as that associated with the contemplation of its actualization (indeed the two become inseperable).[19] Unlike fantasy, therefore, day-dreaming is intimately linked with a key component of modern hedonism, that of longing.[20]

The generation of longing

The capacity to gain pleasure from self-constructed, imaginative experience crucially alters the essential nature of all hedonistic activity. The important point is less that modern hedonism includes within it a form of pleasure-seeking unknown in former times, than that the capacity to day-dream, when made an integral feature of hedonistic conduct, dramatically modifies its character. As indicated earlier, pleasure-seeking is essentially activity motivated by desire for contact with a given pleasure-source. What happens in its modern form is that the process of day-dreaming intervenes between the formulation of a desire and its consummation; hence the desiring and dreaming modes become interfused, with a dream element entering into desire itself.

Day-dreaming can perhaps best be envisaged as an activity which mixes the pleasures of fantasy with those of reality. It is possible, as we have seen, to gain pleasure from purely imaginary situations, whilst, on the other hand, there are real-life activities which yield enjoyment. Bringing these two together requires envisaging different forms of real experience from those so far encountered, ones which include existing pleasures whilst corresponding more closely to the contents of one's 'fantasies'. Although fantasies cannot, by definition, 'come true', there is always plenty of room for the 'perfection' of real experience along the lines which they exemplify. Hence activity directed at enhancing the pleasures to be gained from reality merges into attempts to actualize the 'dream'.

In the simple, more traditional pattern of hedonistic conduct imagination does not have a significant role to play because the nature of anticipated pleasure is known from past experience. The expectation of pleasure triggers desire but what one 'expects' to enjoy is mainly what one 'remembers' enjoying. Novel objects or activities thus tend to be regarded with suspicion as their potential for pleasure is as yet unknown. In modern hedonism, on the other hand, if a product is capable of being represented as possessing unknown characteristics then it is open to the pleasure-seeker to imagine the nature of its gratifications and it thus becomes an occasion for day-dreaming. Although employing material from memory, the hedonist can now imaginatively speculate upon what gratifications and enjoyments are in store, and thus attach his favoured day-dream to this real object of desire. In this way, imagined pleasures are added to those already encountered and greater desire is experienced for the unknown than the known.

The introduction of day-dreaming into hedonism thus not only strengthens desire, but helps to make desiring itself a pleasurable activity. Whilst for traditional man deferred gratification had simply meant the experience of frustration, for modern man it becomes a happy hiatus between desire and consummation which can be filled with the joys of day-dreaming. This reveals a unique feature of modern self-illusory hedonism – the fact that the desiring mode constitutes a state of enjoyable discomfort, and that wanting rather than having is the main focus of pleasure-seeking.[21]

It follows from this that attaining an object of desire is likely to eliminate the pleasures associated with anticipatory day-dreaming, replacing them with those arising out of the stimulatory nature of the 'real' experience. Such actual pleasures are unlikely to compare favourably, however, with those encountered in the dream, not necessarily in impact – few people have such a powerful imagination as to be able to conjure up images which match reality in stimulative intensity – but rather in perfection. For it is in the nature of the images which we construct purely for pleasure that they are free of all blemishes and imperfections (they are the soft-focus photographs of life). Unfortunately, real life is different, and hence it is bound to be the case that whilst 'heard melodies are sweet, those unheard are sweeter'.[22]

The consummation of desire is thus a necessarily disillusioning experience for the modern hedonist as it constitutes the 'testing' of his day-dream against reality, with the resultant recognition that something is missing. The real experience in question may yield considerable pleasure, some of which may not have been anticipated, but despite this, much of the quality of the dream-pleasure is bound to be absent. In fact, the more skilled the individual is as a 'dream artist', then the greater this element of disillusionment is likely to be. A certain dissatisfaction with reality is thus bound to mark the outlook of the dedicated hedonist, something which may, under appropriate circumstances, prompt a turning to fantasy. It is more likely, however, that the dream will be carried forward and attached to some new object of desire such that the illusory pleasures may, once more, be re-experienced. In this way, the modern hedonist is continually withdrawing from reality as fast as he encounters it, ever-casting his day-dreams forward in time, attaching them to objects of desire, and then subsequently 'unhooking' them from these objects as and when they are attained and experienced.

It can easily be appreciated how this alters the very nature of desiring from that which characterizes traditional hedonism. There it is usual to desire that which one knows, and has had experience of in the past, or alternatively, perhaps, to be curious (if apprehensive) about something new which one is introduced to in the present. But in modern hedonism the tendency to employ imagination to perfect pleasures and project these on to future experience means that one will probably desire that which one has had no experience of at all. This may, however, be more than a matter of casting an illusory spell over a real object and then identifying it with something in our dreams, as we may believe in the reality of our dreams before actually 'discovering' anything in reality which corresponds to them. To that extent, our behaviour may correspond to an imaginatively initiated, diffuse search for an 'unknown' object to desire. This characteristic feature of modern hedonism is best labelled 'longing', something which differs from desiring in so far as it occurs without the presence of any real object. In other words, although one must always desire something, one can long for . . . one knows not what.

Longing and a permanent unfocused dissatisfaction are complementary features of that distinctive outlook generated by self-illusory hedonism, and both can be said to be inevitable consequences of the practice of day-dreaming. For no matter how far individuals attempt to exercise restraint over their individualistic pursuit of imaginary pleasure, either in order to pay greater attention to the exigencies of reality or in order to prevent the development of extravagant fantasies, there is a sense in which this will always be left too late. It will be too late because they will have already eaten of the forbidden fruit of the tree of dreams; that is, they will have 'lived' that particular slice of unreal life and sampled its delights, with the consequence – whether they wish it or not – that actuality will now be judged by its standards. To this extent, day-dreaming makes an irreversible difference to the way people feel about the life they lead.

Of course, this does not mean that they cannot 'wake up to reality', or recognize the difference between their dreams and the real world about them; in truth, this is appreciated more than ever. They may even remonstrate with themselves, saying that they were 'just day-dreaming' and that, naturally, 'life is not like that'. They may even attempt to 'correct' their day-dream, using knowledge and reason to construct a more 'realistic' anticipation of those events yet to come. But none of this alters the fundamental fact that considerable pleasure was gained, not merely from the dream, but from imagining that dream as actuality.

Consequently, the desire to have the dream come true remains in existence despite these corrective endeavours. They may not expect this to happen, but the hope is ineradicable. Thus all that they generally succeed in doing by 'shaking off' the day-dream is to ignore or suppress the desire which has been generated, a desire which, in all probability, will sooner or later strike out, and like lightning seeking the earth, connect with some object, person or event.[23]

It follows from the above analysis, that, contrary to popular wisdom, pleasure-seeking in its distinctly modern form is not in opposition to the practice of deferred gratification but its basic ally. Since the focus of concern is with desiring and the pleasures of day-dreaming, the postponement of real gratification is readily accepted. Indeed, this permits more opportunities for extracting pleasure than does the rush to experience consummation, for, in addition to the pleasures derived from the anticipatory drama of fulfilment, there are those associated with the present, deprivation-induced, 'suffering' which create the enjoyable discomforts of desire. The intimate association between pleasure and pain, which is so characteristic of modern hedonism, derives in large measure from this source. Thus the contemporary hedonist not only tends to welcome deferred and interrupted gratification, but may also prematurely abandon a source of pleasure, as, by so doing, he maximizes the opportunities for indulging the emotions of grief, sorrow, nostalgia and, of course, self-pity.

The spirit of modern consumerism

It is now time to return to the problem of finding an adequate theory to account for the nature of modern consumerism. The difficulty here, it will be remembered, stemmed from the prevalence of deterministic theories of consumer behaviour which emphasized instinct or external manipulation, whilst the only tradition of thought which presented the individual as actively involved in formulating his own wants placed the emphasis on emulative desires; a solution which fails to distinguish modern from traditional consumerism, and, in addition, merely relocated the enigma in the equally unexplained phenomenon of modern fashion. The puzzle to be resolved involves not only the question of where new wants originate, or why there appears to be an inexhaustible supply, but also how it is that individuals become detached from those products and services which supply their existing satisfactions. It should now be possible to see that answers to these questions can be formulated by viewing such activity as an outgrowth of modern, autonomous, imaginative hedonism. Indeed, it should be possible to see how that distinctive cultural complex which was associated with the consumer revolution in eighteenth-century England, and which embraced the rise of the novel, romantic love and modern fashion, is related to the widespread adoption of the habit of covert day-dreaming. The central insight required is the realization that individuals do not so much seek satisfaction from products, as pleasure from the self-illusory experiences which they construct from their associated meanings. The essential activity of consumption is thus not the actual selection, purchase or use of products, but the imaginative pleasure-seeking to which the product image lends itself, 'real' consumption being largely a resultant of this 'mentalistic' hedonism.[24] Viewed in this way, the emphasis upon novelty as well as that upon insatiability both become comprehensible.

The modern consumer will desire a novel rather than a familiar product because this enables him to believe that its acquisition and use can supply experiences which he has not so far encountered in reality. It is therefore possible to project onto this product some of that idealized pleasure which he has already experienced in day-dreams, and which he cannot associate with those familiar products currently being consumed. The fact that a so-called 'new' product may not, in reality, offer anything resembling either additional utility or a novel experience is largely irrelevant, as all real consumption is a disillusioning experience in any case. What matters is that the presentation of a product as 'new' allows the potential consumer to attach some of his dream pleasure to it, and hence to associate acquisition and use of the object with realization of the dream. As soon as this identification has taken place, the product will be 'desired', as some of that intense longing which is generated by the practice of day-dreaming becomes linked to the product in question. The visible practice of consumption is thus no more than a small part of a complex pattern of hedonistic behaviour, the majority of which occurs in the imagination of the consumer.

Since the very practice of day-dreaming generates that diffuse desire which has been designated as longing, all that is required for the creation of new wants is the presence of objects in the environment which can be 'taken as new' to some degree. That is, objects which can be differentiated from those currently consumed to a sufficient extent to be identified with illusory images.[25] Obviously, the 'real' nature of products is of little consequence compared with what it is possible for consumers to believe about them, and hence their potential for 'dream material'.

It should be clear from this interpretation that the spirit of modern consumerism is anything but materialistic. The idea that contemporary consumers have an insatiable desire to acquire objects represents a serious misunderstanding of the mechanism which impels people to want goods. Their basic motivation is the desire to experience in reality the pleasurable dramas which they have already enjoyed in imagination, and each 'new' product is seen as offering a possibility of realizing this ambition. However, since reality can never provide the perfected pleasures encountered in day-dreams (or, if at all, only in part, and very occasionally),[26] each purchase leads to literal disillusionment, something which explains how wanting is extinguished so quickly, and why people disacquire goods as rapidly as they acquire them. What is not extinguished, however, is the fundamental longing which day-dreaming itself generates, and hence there is as much determination as ever to find new products to serve as replacement objects of desire.

This dynamic interaction between illusion and reality is the key to the understanding of modern consumerism and, indeed, modern hedonism generally. The tension between the two creates longing as a permanent mode, with the concomittant sense of dissatisfaction with 'what is' and a yearning for 'something better'. This is because wish-directed day-dreaming turns the future into a perfectly illusioned present. One does not repeat cycles of sensory pleasure-seeking as in traditional hedonism so much as continually strive to close the gap between imagined and experienced pleasures. Whatever one experiences in reality it is possible to 'adjust' in imagination so as to make appear more pleasurable; thus the illusion is always better than the reality: the promise more interesting than actuality.

What this means is that in modern hedonism pleasure is not simply a quality of experience, but a self-illusioned quality of experience. Increasingly pleasure is a commodity associated with experiences which we have had a hand in constructing; something which we have 'tailored' to suit our own needs. Yet we are aware that we have done so; we recognize our 'day-dreaming' and fantasizing for what they are (or rather what they are not – that is, 'real'). Such 'realism', however, merely has the effect of making us dissatisfied with a life which provides actual pleasures so far short of those which illusion can supply; somewhere, we are convinced, it must be possible to experience the latter in reality. Hence that dissatisfaction with existence and the consequent readiness to seize whatever new pleasures are promised, which characterize the modern attitude of longing.

It should also be obvious that this dynamic owes little or nothing to the activity of other consumers, and that neither imitation nor emulation are required to ensure that the momentum is maintained. The cycle of desire-acquisition-use-disillusionment–renewed-desire is a general feature of modern hedonism, and applies to romantic interpersonal relationships as much as the consumption of cultural products such as clothes and records. It is therefore a feature of both 'invisible' and conspicuous consumption, and does not necessitate any presuppositions concerning attitudes towards status or prestige, although it may well be the case that the activities and attitudes of others exert an influence over which new products become the focus of desire.

That there is a close relationship between people's day-dreams and their selection, purchase, use and disposal of goods and services is patently revealed in the character of many advertisements. These typically address themselves to dreams rather than to needs in an attempt to associate given products with cherished illusions and hence awaken desire. But the processes through which dreams become attached to products do not depend entirely upon the efforts of advertisers, for individuals may spin fond fantasies around something seen in a catalogue or in a shop window without the benefit of their images and copy. Thus although advertisers make use of the fact that people day-dream, and indeed feed those dreams, the practice of day-dreaming is itself endemic to modern societies and does not require the commercial institution of advertising to ensure its continued existence.

Something of the relationship between day-dreams and the use of products is suggested by Virginia Woolf in her short story *The New Dress*.[27] A young woman has a dress made to her own, somewhat idiosyncratic, design, and, when trying it on for the first time and looking in the mirror, she is delighted with what she sees:

Suffused with light, she sprang into existence. Rid of cares and wrinkles, *what she had dreamed of herself was there – a beautiful woman.* Just for a second . . . there looked at her, framed in the scrolloping mahogany, a grey-white, mysteriously smiling, charming girl, the core of herself, the soul of herself; and it was not vanity only, not only self-love that made her think it good, tender, and true.[28] (Italics added.)

Unfortunately, later, when she first wears the dress at a party, the dream vanishes, as, tortured by the conviction that everyone considers her to look ridiculous, she is 'woken wide awake to reality'.[29] Here one can discern the basic pattern of first associating a dream with a product, followed by the disillusionment consequent upon its use. Of course, the initial conviction that one's dream had come true need not be so total, or so intense, as portrayed here, nor the eventual disillusionment so swift and complete; but the cycle itself would nevertheless seem to be a universal one. Note how the quote reveals that she had been accustomed to day-dream about herself as 'a beautiful woman' and that in this instance the dress is the magical means through which the dream becomes reality. One also suspects that the subsequent disillusionment was limited to that particular dress, and not the dream, leaving open the possibility that it might become attached to another dress on a later occasion.

That the imaginative enjoyment of products and services is a crucial part of contemporary consumerism is revealed by the important place occupied in our culture by representations of products rather than the products themselves. This not only embraces overtly commercial advertisements and catalogues, but magazines, periodicals, posters, cards, calendars and even works of art. In many of these the line between representation in the interests of a particular manufacturer and distributor (i.e. advertising), and images produced primarily for entertainment is barely distinguishable, suggesting that they both fulfil the same function of facilitating imaginative hedonism. In other words, people 'enjoy' these images in much the same manner that they enjoy a novel or a film.[30] Certainly the dream nature of the images suggests that this is the case, as is the fact that people regularly enjoy looking at pictures of products which they cannot – nor are ever likely to be able to – afford.

This in turn relates to another feature of modern consumerism – the practice of window-shopping. Now although people can 'shop around' for goods in the sense of comparing prices, thereby attempting to ascertain what might be the 'best buy', they also indulge in 'shopping' without actually buying anything at all, although clearly deriving pleasure from the experience. In part, of course, the enjoyment is strictly aesthetic, involving an appreciation of the art of the designers and window-dressers involved. On top of this, however, there is the pleasure which comes from the imaginative use of the objects seen; that is, from mentally 'trying on' the clothes examined, or 'seeing' the furniture arranged within one's room.[31]

It follows from this observation that many of the cultural products offered for sale in modern societies are in fact consumed because they serve as aids to the construction of day-dreams. This is most clearly the case with novels, but it also applies to paintings, plays, records and films as well as radio and television programmes. Whilst in most cases there is a direct sensory gratification to be gained from the patterned stimuli which the product represents, the greater pleasure is likely to be derived from its open invitation to be used as material for illusory enjoyment. Such usage is necessarily covert and individualistic in character and cannot, by its very nature, be communal.[32]

This does not mean that individuals may not sit side-by-side whilst lost in private worlds of their own, as may be the case with audiences at concerts, plays or films. Also, since in some of these examples the nature of the illusion is strongly structured by what is represented, different individuals may have approximately parallel experiences. None the less, even here individuals can identify with different fictional characters, or react with varying degrees of emotion at contrasting points in the story. In this respect no two individuals' experience of the product will be the same, just as no two people ever read the same novel. It is for this reason that it is more apt to conceive of these cultural products as providing the material for day-dreams rather than as being day-dreams. This is important not only because the individual has to actively use the words, pictures, and sounds to construct an 'as-if' world for himself to inhabit, but also because the process of day-dreaming (which has in any case preceded contact with the cultural item in question) may well continue long after direct contact has ceased; images relating to a particular film or novel being brought to mind subsequently and embroidered in a pleasurable fashion. In this respect individuals may have predominant or recurrent day-dreams or fantasies, as Billy Liar did with his imaginary country, returning to them over and over again. Fragments of stories or images taken from books or films are often used as the foundation stones for these continually extended dream edifices, constructions which can take on quite mammoth proportions with time.[33]

It also follows from this argument that 'taste', regarded as the typical pattern of a person's preferences, is largely a function of day-dreaming. At one level this is obvious enough, for if one person has a 'taste' for detective stories, and another a 'taste' for Westerns, it can be seen that this is simply another way of saying that the character of their fantasy-pleasure differs. It may be much less obvious, however, in what way a person's preference for, say jazz as opposed to classical music, or red rather than white wine, connects with his day-dreams, and it is necessary to recognize that factors such as personality and biographical experience may also be influential. Nevertheless, it can still be assumed that there is a general connection between those activities which give an individual most pleasure, and the self whom he enjoys imagining himself to be in his 'mind's eye'.

A more fundamental point is that recognition of the importance and universality of day-dreaming helps to account for that basic taste for novelty which is shared by all modern consumers, and hence also for the existence of that most central of all institutions of modern consumerism – the phenomenon of fashion. It provides an answer to the question of why individual consumers should be eager to embrace new fashions, without resorting to the suggestion that they are manipulated into doing so, or that it is an outcome of an obsession with social status. Instead it is possible to understand how the regulated introduction of controlled elements of novelty into those products with a high aesthetic significance is necessary in order for the continued attempt to realize day-dreams to occur.[34] In theory, covert imaginative hedonism could exist without the modern Western fashion pattern, as is the case with the phenomenon of romantic love. Here, the required novelty is guaranteed by the very number and diversity of persons which an individual will normally encounter in a life-time of social interaction, consequently ensuring that there are plenty of 'strangers' upon whom one can project one's dreams. With man-made products, however, 'strangeness' cannot be guaranteed, but must be programmed for in some particular way. This is generally achieved by the regular importing of 'foreign' styles or, alternatively, the creation of new ones.[35]

Taste is the crucial phenomenon which links imaginative hedonism with the institution of modern fashion, for, as its linguistic usage suggests, taste embraces both the patterning of pleasures and the processes of aesthetic discernment. Since the permanent consumption of 'novelty' lies at the heart of self-illusory hedonism, patterns of 'taste' – in the sense of our choices of those things which yield pleasure – must themselves be undergoing endless, if gradual, change. This means that aesthetic standards are continually evolving, whilst the necessity for order in social interaction means that control must be exercised over such a process. The outcome is the Western European fashion pattern. The modern consumer is able to adjust his tastes rapidly and continually in a way which traditional consumers find impossible because of his possession of the psychological skill of autonomous day-dreaming. This enables him to experiment, in imagination, with different 'pleasures', and imaginatively explore new tastes before risking doing so in reality.

This does not mean that the modern consumer typically gives expression to idiosyncratic tastes. Rather it means that the only fixed, or 'basic' standard of taste adhered to is a preference for proximate or 'fresh' pleasures, those on the borderline between the experienced and the yet-to-be-experienced, those where imagination embroiders existing reality in tantalizing ways. The fundamental 'taste' for novelty can only really be understood in these terms; as a consequence of trying to maximize the pleasures of reality and illusion by projecting the second into the near-future, with the result that the maximum-pleasure horizon always remains just out of reach.

It has been argued that modern consumerism is characterized by the abandonment of the practice of deferred gratification and its substitution by instant or immediate gratification, a change accomplished by the development of mechanisms for granting credit to consumers.[36] The fact that such facilities permit people to enjoy the use of objects before they have been able to save the full amount necessary to cover their cost does not, however, mean that individuals are freely able to indulge all their desires as soon as they have taken shape. No doubt some wants are almost immediately created and satisfied: the sweets and chocolates offered for sale at the point of sale in supermarkets are placed there on exactly this premise. But even with credit, a modern consumer's resources are still limited, whilst wants are not. It therefore follows that at any one time a consumer will have desires which cannot be gratified but must, if only temporarily be postponed. Thus the fact that wants are continually being indulged should not cause us to overlook the fact that they are also continually being created, with the consequence that 'frustration' is a permanent state. Admittedly, the purchase and or use of a particularly long-desired product may yield such delight as to temporarily obscure this fact, but it is assuredly the case that an awareness of unsatisfied wants will quickly surface. It is therefore the case that although specific gratifications may not be deferred for long, the individual consumer is none the less permanently exposed to the experience of wanting, something which is only periodically and briefly interspersed with soon-to-be disillusioned consummations of desire.

The fact that wanting is a permanent condition helps in its turn to explain why the consumer is impelled to day-dream, as a preoccupation with what one has not displaces an interest in what one has. Thus, whilst day-dreaming works to generate the pleasurable imaginative experiences from which desire is created, wanting also generates that dissatisfaction with reality which facilitates imaginative speculation about the gratification novel products might bring.

The inexhaustibility of wants which characterizes the behaviour of modern consumers has to be understood as deriving from their permanent desiring mode, something which, in turn, stems from the inevitable gap between the perfected pleasures of the dream and the imperfect joys of reality. No matter what the nature of the dream or, indeed, of reality, the discrepancy between them gives rise to a continuing longing, from which specific desires repeatedly spring.[37] It follows that not being a modern consumer would mean either failing to day-dream or restricting one's imaginative activity to non-real fantasizing. The former is, in effect, the option of traditionalism, whilst the latter approximates to the rare, 'other-worldly' response of a few Bohemians or those labelled as eccentrics.

Part Two

The Romantic Ethic

6

The Other Protestant Ethic

It is hard to distinguish between a Sentimentalist and a Calvinist who believes himself saved.

John W. Draper

Identification of autonomous, imaginative pleasure-seeking as the force which was largely responsible for the dynamic form taken by modern consumerism naturally directs attention to those cultural developments which can be identified as creating and justifying this type of hedonism, for, whatever these might have been, there is now good reason to view them as crucial to the emergence of the modern economy. Since it has already been established that the consumer revolution occurred among the middle ranks of English society in the second half of the eighteenth century, it would seem that one must first turn to examine the distinctive experience of this stratum. When, in addition, one bears in mind that this new propensity to consume was associated, as noted, with other significant socio-cultural innovations – such as the emergence of the Western European fashion pattern, the popularity of the novel and romantic love – then an obvious premise which suggests itself is that the intellectual and aesthetic movement which has been labelled Romanticism, together with its affiliated precursor, Sentimentalism, might have served to fulfil this function. This will indeed be the hypothesis explored in the pages which follow. Before taking up this theme, however, there is a prior puzzle to be examined, one which, although pertinent to the issue of the cultural origins of Sentimentalism and Romanticism, arises more directly out of Weber's thesis concerning the link between Protestantism and capitalism.

This puzzle was alluded to earlier,[1] in connection with the debate over those currents of ideas which it had been contended served to justify the new patterns of consumer behaviour. There it was noted that a particular difficulty existed in claiming that new economic arguments would be compelling enough to counteract the powerful Puritanical suspicion of luxury consumption, which, it was assumed, would have been widespread among the lesser yeomanry and trading and artisan classes of the time. Certainly Weber's thesis that it was within these groups in particular that a 'Protestant ethic' prevailed, stimulating both dedicated industriousness in a calling and a frugal asceticism, makes it exceptionally difficult to understand how they could have been prominent in any movement to display a new propensity to consume. Whilst, in that context, this argument was employed to advance scepticism concerning the suggestion that the writings of such advocates of consumption as Dudley North or Adam Smith could be credited with making middle-class consumers consider it morally right to purchase luxury goods, it has now, in the light of the preceding discussion, taken on the character of a seemingly even-stronger objection against the contention that modern consumerism is dependent upon a form of hedonism. For now it becomes necessary to regard these self-same groups as not merely purchasing 'luxury' goods, but as being motivated to do so by a desire for pleasure; something which it seems especially difficult to believe of the inheritors of a Puritan outlook. This then is the puzzle which will now be considered, focusing as it does upon the central issue of the relationship between Protestantism and pleasure, whilst Weber's analysis, from which, as we have seen, the problem derives, will be taken as the point of departure.

Protestantism and pleasure

Max Weber, in his attempt to explain the origins of the modern capitalist spirit, and having demonstrated how the attitude of the Roman Catholic Church toward profit-taking was rarely less than hostile, asks the crucial question, 'how could activity, which was at best ethically tolerated, turn into a calling in the sense of Benjamin Franklin?'[2] He goes on to answer by arguing that particular Protestant doctrines, especially the Lutheran interpretation of the calling and the Calvinist teaching concerning predestination, had the effect of sanctifying not only work but the conscientious and legal accumulation of wealth. In this way he showed how certain religious ideals served to overcome traditional moral and religious objections and hence assisted in the legitimation of new economic practices. A fundamentally similar question naturally arises in relation to the problem of explaining modern consumerism; how could an activity – in this case the pursuit of pleasure – which was at best ethically tolerated, turn into the acceptable life-goal of the citizens of contemporary society?[3] Such a question is, in fact, the logical counterpart to Weber's, since the industrial revolution involved the clear separation of human life into the two distinct spheres of production and consumption, each governed by its own imperatives, and although, like most economic theorists of his age, Weber treated the issue of consumption as being, in essence, unproblematic, this is clearly not the case. Thus one can say of the spirit of modern consumerism, what Weber said of the spirit of capitalism: which is that its prime aim appears 'absolutely irrational'.[4] For the endless striving after stimulative pleasure, the gratification of each new want, is no more a rational life-goal than the earning of more and more money.

That eighteenth-century Britain had inherited a religious tradition which did not look with favour upon the pursuit of pleasure would seem indisputable, for Puritanism, if not Protestantism in general, must surely rank as one of the most powerful anti-hedonistic forces which the world has known. Some of the evidence for this view is referred to by Weber himself in the course of his demonstration of the thorough-going asceticism which characterized Calvinism, that is to say 'the attempt to subject man to the supremacy of a purposeful will, to bring his actions under constant self-control with a careful consideration of the ethical consequences'.[5] In order to achieve this end it was necessary to destroy all that was impulsive in man, and hence Puritan asceticism 'turned with all its force against one thing: the spontaneous enjoyment of life and all it had to offer'.[6]

Weber illustrates this point by reference to the struggle that occurred over the *Book of Sports*, which both James I and Charles I had made into law expressly to counter the spread of such ascetic attitudes. The opposition which they encountered was intense, for not only did the Puritans resent the breach of the Sabbath which these ordinances permitted and what Weber calls 'the intentional diversion from the ordered life of the saint' that followed, but also those opportunities for the 'spontaneous expression of undisciplined impulses' which were created.[7] Their deep suspicion of sport was aroused in so far as 'it became purely a means of enjoyment, or awakened pride, raw instincts or the irrational gambling instinct',[8] an attitude which was held in respect of all human activities which permitted any impulsive response to life.

This view arose from the emphasis which was placed upon man's depravity, with the consequent distrust of any natural feelings or desires. It was for this reason that children were so detested, whilst not merely unchastity but any concupiscence attached to sexual intercourse within marriage was considered a sin.[9] The arts and nearly all forms of entertainment were similarly suspect, with the consequence, as Weber puts it, that 'asceticism descended like a frost on the life of "Merrie old England"'.[10] Such traditional rural pleasures as maypole dancing were proscribed, theatres were closed, novels contemptuously dismissed as 'wastetimes', and poets declared to be wantons; whilst all activities not judged to be in accord with God's will or the ideal of sober utility were condemned. To illustrate this point, Weber cites Barclay on what recreations (and what expenditure) it is legitimate for Quakers to pursue. These are listed as: visiting of friends, reading of historical works, mathematical and physical experiments, gardening, discussion of business and other occurrences in the world.[11]

We can see from this that Puritanism did not attempt to banish all pleasure from life; 'rational recreation' was permitted, that is recreation which could be seen to serve a useful purpose. In this context, they didn't prohibit alcohol, as their nineteenth-century successors, the evangelicals, were to strive so hard to do. Nor, for example, did they uphold the Catholic ideal of celibacy; continence was a virtue but abstinence was in conflict with God's commands. Hence their clergy married young and often, and women had a right to expect more from their husbands than duty.[12] In fact, as Carroll observes, the Puritans did a good deal to promote a 'new fusion of sensual and spiritual love in marriage'.[13] The pleasurable ingredient, however, in all these activities, was most definitely not to be taken as an end in itself, but was acceptable merely because it accompanied acts demanded by God or supported by reason. In this respect it is clear that it was only secondary pleasure which the Puritans tolerated, that which accompanied conduct engaged in for other reasons, and that the pursuit of pleasure for its own sake was totally unacceptable.

It is important to note, however, that if anything the Puritans were even more hostile to opulence than they were to voluptuousness; their objection being that 'vain ostentation' – that is anything which, neither glorying God nor being useful to man, served merely to promote human pride – was sinful. An obvious target here was the decoration of the person, especially clothing, as any unnecessary elaboration in this context was seen as a sure sign of the idolatry of the flesh.[14] The plain and simple clothes favoured by the Quakers exemplified this attitude, whilst Weber mentions in a footnote how a pious congregation of exiles in Amsterdam at the beginning of the seventeenth century were thrown into a turmoil for a decade over 'the fashionable hats and dresses of a preacher's wife'.[15] He goes on to explain how the Puritan's attitude toward the use of wealth tried to steer a middle course between vain ostentation on the one side and mortification of the flesh on the other. That is, needs had to be met in as sober and sensible manner as possible, whilst wants were not to be pandered to. Comfort but not comfort-luxury was the ideal.

The Protestant ethic did not prohibit acquisition; obviously not, for it seemed to justify the accumulation of wealth. What it did render unjustifiable was the enjoyment of possessions. As Weber observes, it had the psychological effect of freeing the acquisition of goods from the inhibition of traditionalistic ethics, making such activity something willed by God.[16] It was the irrational use of wealth which was condemned; covetousness, the pursuit of riches for their own sake; 'This irrational use was exemplified in the outward forms of luxury which their [Puritan] code condemned as idolatry of the flesh. . . . On the other hand, they approved the rational and utilitarian uses of wealth which were willed by God for the needs of the individual and the community'.[17] This, as Weber comments, is the limitation of what is ethically permissible by way of expenditure to that which constitutes the idea of comfort. At the same time, the Puritan was required to lead an ordered and disciplined life in which time and talents were not to be wasted. As a result, 'Forms of indulgence which dissipated both wealth and energy were sternly denounced and repressed', with the consequence that 'Puritanism cut men off from wasteful expenditure and worldly pleasure'.[18] Weber's overall conclusion being that, 'this worldly Protestant asceticism . . . acted powerfully against the spontaneous enjoyment of possessions whilst also [restricting] consumption, especially of luxuries'.[19]

This apparently unequivocal conclusion would appear to leave little room for any further debate on the question of the relationship between Protestantism and luxury, whether the latter is conceived of as a matter of pleasure-seeking or of the provision of goods surplus to need. Yet there is more to the relationship than this, although, perhaps understandably, Weber might be considered to have had good reasons for not thinking this was the case. After all, his primary concern was not the link between Protestantism and economic action in general so much as that between certain forms of Protestantism and a philosophy or 'spirit' of wealth creation, and it was in this connection that he focused his attention not merely upon Calvinism and Lutheranism but upon that idealized construct which he called 'inner-worldly asceticism'. This has prompted his critics to accuse him of having taken an unrepresentative selection of religious texts upon which to base his arguments, and what is more, to have given these a far from uncontentious interpretation.[20] The position adopted here is that the completeness rather than the correctness of Weber's thesis is the point at issue. That is to say, given the nature of the task which he set himself, there would seem to be little reason to cavil overmuch at his account of what constituted the critical features of Protestantism, but the problem as defined here requires that this phenomenon should be considered more broadly and not be contained within the boundaries which he imposed.

The fact that our interest is in the modern economy as a system of consumption rather than one of production means that we have good grounds for making a different evaluation from Weber concerning which

Protestant teachings are of most relevance. In fact, it seems very likely that such a contrasting concern would lead to an inverse valuation of the various strands of Protestant thought, with those accounted by Weber to be of least significance for the development of a rationalized ethic of worldly conduct being the most important in leading to the appearance of imaginative hedonism. To some extent this is true, and yet surprisingly perhaps, it is also the case that Calvinism once again proves to be of disproportionate significance, and in this context there is reason to challenge Weber's rather selective interpretation of the doctrine of signs. More importantly, a concern with the cultural environment surrounding the consumer revolution of the eighteenth century means that it is necessary to pursue the development of Protestant thought into the late seventeenth and early eighteenth centuries, something which Weber omitted to do.

Weber's sources for his discussion of Protestantism (in addition, that is, to the writings of Luther and Calvin) are the works of English and European Puritan divines of the sixteenth and seventeenth centuries, especially Baxter (1615–91), Bailey (1643–97) and Spener (1635–1705), together with others found in the ten-volume *Works of the Puritan Divines*.[21] In addition, he makes use of such official statements of church doctrine as the Savoy Declaration of 1658, the Confession of the Particular Baptists of 1644 and the Westminster Confession (1643–47), supplemented, here and there, by illustrative material drawn from his voluminous knowledge of the writings of individual religious thinkers and reformers. The vast majority of this material covers the period up to the end of the seventeenth century, Weber's principal concern being, firstly, to contrast Protestant and Roman Catholic teachings, and, secondly, to draw out some of the major differences between the various Protestant churches. He does not, however, discuss the development of Protestant religion, either in the form of theology or practical ethics, after this date. In fact, only two of the long list of thinkers and reformers whom he discusses can be said truly to belong to the eighteenth century, and these are Zinzendorf (1700–60) and John Wesley (1703–91), Methodism being the only religious movement occurring in that century to which he devotes any consideration. Thus, although he does cite studies of Calvinism, Lutheranism and Baptism which encompass the period up to the end of the nineteenth century, and makes comments in passing concerning the fate of particular teachings in 'later' times, his analysis effectively stops at 1700.

Methodism is, of course, the exception to this, and, in a footnote, Weber does acknowledge that it differs from the other ascetic movements he considers by occurring much later in time.[22] He continues, however, by describing it, in association with the Zinzendorf form of Pietism (which was also an eighteenth-century phenomenon), as constituting a 'reaction' against the Enlightenment; a position which enables him, in effect, to treat Methodism as if it were contemporaneous with Calvinism, Lutheranism, Pietism and Baptism. Certainly, in his brief discussion of Methodism, there is little indication that he regarded it as representing a further development, rather than as simply a variant, of Protestant thought.

This means that Weber's position must be taken to be one in which Protestantism as he outlined it constituted its fully developed form, and that all that subsequently happened was a process of slow decline and decay in the face of the forces of secularization and rationalization; a process which he eloquently summarized in the famous last few paragraphs of the book. Thus, although evidence is cited to show how certain Protestant traits persisted well into the nineteenth century,[23] the assumption made is that the eighteenth century witnessed Puritanism's evolution into utilitarianism. It is not intended to challenge this latter thesis here. On the contrary, it is indeed accepted that modern rationalism and utilitarianism had their principal origins as philosophical systems in certain strands of Protestant thought.[24] What is at issue is whether religious systems continued to evolve after the end of the seventeenth century, and if they did, whether they can be considered to have exerted any significant influence upon the nature of economic conduct; a question which turns, in particular, upon whether it is correct to characterize the Enlightenment as an unequivocally 'secularizing' influence.

Weber on theodicy

Weber's discussion of the issue of theodicy,[25] that is the problem of explaining the ways of God to man with special reference to the issues of suffering, evil, death and injustice,[26] must especially be judged to be incomplete. In the religions of the West the conception of the divine as transcendental, unchangeable, omnipotent and omniscient focused attention upon the problem of how the power and goodness of such a God can be reconciled with the imperfections of that world which he created.[27] Even in the East a conception of the divine as impersonal and supertheistic still raises the issue of accounting for the world's imperfections. Hence, in one form or another, this problem exists in all religions, and Weber outlined what he considered to be the 'various theoretically pure types' of solution which can be found.[28]

The first possibility he considers is that involving messianic eschatologies and the belief in a coming revolution which will bring the world into accord with God's nature; that is, the establishment of a Kingdom of God on earth. But he goes on to show how this view is likely to develop into a belief in predestination, as more and more emphasis is placed upon the chasm between a totally transcendent and inscrutable God and human beings enmeshed in the coils of sin: 'God's sovereign, completely inexplicable, voluntary, and antecedently established (a consequence of omniscience) determination has decreed not only human fate on earth but also human destiny after death.'[29] This, as Weber notes, is less a solution to the problem of theodicy than a way of defining it out of existence.

Besides predestination Weber specifies two other religious outlooks which he suggests provide 'systematically conceptualized' treatments of the problem of the world's imperfections.[30] These are dualism, as represented mainly by Zoroastrianism and Manicheism, and the Indian doctrine of *karma*. The latter Weber describes as 'the most complete formal solution of the problem of theodicy', since the world is regarded as a completely connected and self-contained cosmos of ethical retribution in which each individual forges his own destiny, with guilt and merit in this world unfailingly compensated for in the succeeding incarnation.

Now Weber makes it clear that these are ideal type 'solutions' to the problem of theodicy and that in reality religions of salvation combined ingredients from these three types together in various mixes, with the consequence that 'the differences among various religious theories of god's relation to the world and to man must be measured by their degree of approximation to one or another of these pure types'.[31] Whilst bearing this proviso in mind, the question must still be posed as to whether Weber was right in imagining that there were only these three idealized solutions to the problem of theodicy. For there would appear to be other traditions of thought dealing with the problem which, whilst not discussed by Weber, do not seem to be merely ingredients in, or combinations of, these ideal types. It is not clear, for example, that the full complexity of Greek thought on these issues, whether Platonic, Epicurean or Stoic can be successfully incorporated into this triadic scheme, whilst it is also difficult to see precisely where one would place what John Hick has called the 'Irenaean type of theodicy'.[32] For this reason there must be some doubt about Weber's claim that all theodicies can be understood in terms of the types which he outlines, as there must be also over the suggestion that they represent a form of treatment of the problem of the world's imperfections which is more especially 'systematically conceptualized' than those he omits to discuss.[33] There is, in any case, one significant theodicy missing from Weber's list, and it is an omission which is closely connected with his failure to carry the analysis of religion in the West much beyond the end of the sixteenth century.[34] This is the eighteenth-century philosophical theology of optimism most closely associated with the name of Leibniz. But, since this arose in part as a reaction against Calvinism, it is necessary, first of all, to inquire more closely into the fate of that particular 'systematically conceptualized' theodicy.

Calvin's doctrine of predestinarian determinism cannot justifiably be regarded as either the logical or historical end-point of Western theological endeavours to resolve the problem of theodicy, nor can the thinkers who came after him be considered to have done no more than elaborate or refine his views, or, alternatively, to have rejected religion entirely. On the contrary, a succession of seventeenth- and early eighteenth-century philosophers including such eminent figures as Pascal, Spinoza, Leibniz and Kant, devoted considerable effort to the construction of a philosophical theology which would serve in place of an increasingly discredited Calvinism.[35] The need for such a theodicy had become urgent as a consequence of the attacks on traditional theology made by the sceptical and atheistic thinkers of the Enlightenment. It was these two factors, the need to transcend the inadequacies of Calvinism and the necessity of combating anti-religious propaganda which together provided a fresh impetus to the constructing of theodicies during the seventeenth century, with Calvin's thought generally providing the common starting point for such endeavours.

The doctrine of predestination and the Cambridge Platonists

There were, of course, specific historical factors associated with the decline of Calvinism in England, for, after twenty years in which nearly all prominent men were Calvinists, it was 'cast out' when Charles II was restored to the throne, an event described by Cragg as representing both the 'overthrow of the Puritan party and the defeat of Puritan theology'.[36] In reality, Calvinism was still a powerful force, but in the political and ecclesiastical struggles which ensued between the Puritans and the Laudians it was clear that the tide had turned and the supporters of Calvinism were increasingly on the defensive. This decline was to some degree an inevitable consequence of the intolerance, fanaticism and sectarian bickering which the Puritans had displayed during the period of the Commonwealth, with the result that their eventual overthrow was greeted with relief together with a general rejection of a dogmatic attitude to questions of faith by the population at large.[37] To this extent, therefore, the collapse of Calvinism should be seen as a process which stemmed from its very nature as a closed and uncompromising system of doctrine, something which was bound to generate a powerful reaction. Criticisms of Calvinist doctrines, however, rested on more than a mere dislike of fanaticism and bigotry, gaining their intellectual force from a sustained theological attack on what were seen to be its central deficiencies.

Although the Reformation represented the first significant expression of the principal of individual autonomy in matters of religious inquiry, the major Protestant creeds were all largely systematized well before the end of the sixteenth century, with the consequence that there was little further scope for intellectual initiative and development. At the same time, Calvin had obtained apparent logical closure in his theodicy by stressing the justice rather than the love of God, and by making faith rather than reason the basis of belief. In retrospect it seems inevitable that certain individuals would be drawn by the free spirit of rational inquiry to challenge these fundamental tenets, especially in the light of the harsh form of the teachings which they generated. Tulloch summarizes the general nature of this reaction against the completeness of Calvinist dogmatism:

Satisfactory in the highest degree to those who accepted its main principles and identified them without hesitation with the teachings of St. Paul, to other minds of a less unquestioning character it left no scope for the free play of Christian thought, while its stern logical consecutiveness directly tended to grate against the edge of this thought. The system, in short, broke down just where its triumphant logic topped its highest summit. The doctrine of absolute Predestination was the keystone of the whole. Augustine himself had not shrunk from the most extreme consequences of this doctrine, and neither did Calvin. But these consequences were such as to revolt many minds more Christian, so to speak, than logical. The very enthusiasm of spiritual feeling which made their own religious interest so vital to them, drew them back from the results of a logic which seemed harsh and unchristian. They felt there must be a flaw somewhere in a system which, however consecutive, terminated in such results. For, after all, the idea of the divine benevolence is as essential as that of the divine omnipotence; and if we cannot separate from God the thought of absolute will, neither can we separate from Him the thought of absolute good. The same Grace which on one side issues in predestinarian Determinism – saving whom it will according to its own elective arbitration or 'mere good pleasure' – on the other side takes the form of divine Love which instinctively desires the good of all, and 'wills all men to be saved'.[38]

This then represented the basis of the revolt against Calvinism, and it is important to recognize that its origins were within rather than without Puritanism, as doubts and difficulties increasingly beset the faithful. Thus Arminianism, which represented the first significant break with orthodoxy, occurred among Calvinist communities in Holland in the 1580s being precipitated by the Supralapsarianism versus Infralapsarianism debate. This was the question of whether God's eternal decrees should be considered to have predestined Adam and Eve's fall into sin; if they had, as Calvin asserted, then it could be protested that God was made the author of sin, but if not, then why shouldn't the children of Adam and Eve also be considered able to 'freely' determine their fate? This issue, focusing as it did upon the key Calvinist teaching of predestination, necessarily raised in its wake a range of related problems. The Calvinist God, for example, appeared both vindictive and cruel by giving commands to men which he then forced them to disobey, and in apparently offering salvation to those he had already condemned.[39] Although, in theory, orthodox Calvinism did allow for the human will to make some contribution to the work of salvation, the emphasis upon the independent activity of divine grace was so strong as to make divine will appear to be mere fate and God himself to be an arbitrary rather than a moral and loving figure. Arminius himself, who had been an orthodox Calvinist prior to his apostasy, advocated the view that the free activity of the human will was a necessary co-determinant in salvation; a position which opened the way to the belief (as expressed by John Wesley, who was an Arminian) that 'God willeth all men to be saved'.[40] Calvinists counteracted this 'heresy' by claiming that it denied the work of divine grace by exalting the purely human element in redemption, thus committing the ancient heresy of Pelagianism. Despite this charge and a savage programme of repression directed against the 'heretics', Arminianism continued to gain converts and was widespread in England by the mid-seventeenth century, the majority of the King's supporters in the civil war adhering to an Arminian position in theology.

The Arminian revolt against Calvinism represented more, however, than a doctrinal dispute leading to the addition of one more sect to the rapidly multiplying number of religious groups comprising Protestantism. For it constituted a 'method' as much as a 'dogmatic theory', and can be viewed as reviving 'the suppressed rational side of the Protestant movement'.[41] Not that one should underestimate the long-term implications of the challenge to predestinarian principles for these had guided Christian thinking since St Augustine's time, and their abandonment signalled a radical shift in the nature of that tradition. But it was the new intellectual climate created by the Arminian revolt which made these developments possible, and, in particular, the establishment of the principle of private judgement in the interpretation of scripture; that is, the idea that every man had an indefeasible right to examine and decide the truth of scripture for himself.[42] This was something which Calvinism simply did not permit as the nature of religious truth was considered to have been successfully encoded in dogma. By disputing the very idea of dogma and asserting that no one Christian could decide what was in fact true for another, whilst at the same time asserting that no profession of doctrine or creed was really necessary to Christian communion,

Arminianism represented a truly new spirit in Protestant theology, one which was to find its fullest expression in the writings of the Cambridge Platonists.

It has already been noted how the Calvinism which prevailed in England prior to 1660 was effectively eclipsed by the Restoration, and that Arminianism constituted a feature of the Anglo-Catholic 'Laudian' party who came to power at that time. The theology of this group, however, was as dogmatic in its way as that of the Puritans they opposed, incorporating little of the spirit of free inquiry which was such a feature of Arminianism in the broader sense. This was represented in England by a third group who appeared at this time but who were independent of both the Puritans and the Anglo-Catholic Laudians. Identified as a liberal, or 'Latitudinarian', group of thinkers, and mostly scholars connected with Emmanuel College, Cambridge, they have come to be known to posterity as 'the Cambridge Platonists', and had an important part to play in bringing about those developments through which Protestantism came to justify emotional pleasure-seeking.

Not really a 'school' in the proper sense so much as a small group of scholars who shared a common point of view,[43] all of them had a Puritan, if not a distinctly Calvinist, background, but had come to develop convictions which 'cut across all the prevailing orthodoxies of a dogmatic age'.[44] In this respect they form the beginnings of liberal rational theology in England.[45] As Cragg expresses their position:

With scarcely an exception, the Cambridge Platonists came out of a Puritan background. For the most part they were educated in the very citadel of Puritan zeal. But they cannot be classified as Puritans. They retained some of the finest qualities of Puritanism – its moral earnestness for example – but they abandoned its theology. Nevertheless, it did not follow that, having shed their Calvinism, they accepted the principal alternative then available. They disliked the rigidity of Archbishop Laud as much as they did the dogmatism of the Puritans.[46]

Consequently, whilst accepting the Anglican church (they were not dissenters) they disliked the nature of Anglicanism and can be said to have occupied the middle ground in the religious conflicts which characterized seventeenth-century England, preaching a message of reasonableness, tolerance and deep ethical and religious concern to both parties.[47]

Like the Dutch Arminians, the Cambridge Platonists reacted vigorously against the Calvinist doctrine of predestination, expressing a profound revulsion at both the concept and its implications. Again and again they attacked what they called 'this divine fatalism arbitrary',[48] or the 'divine Fate immoral'[49], arguing that such eternal decrees cannot have been issued by God 'because this grates upon the notion that mankind have of goodness and justice. This is that which no good man would do, and therefore it cannot be believed of infinite goodness.'[50] "There is that in God', claimed Whichcote, 'that is more beautiful than power, than will and Sovereignty, viz. His righteousness, His goodwill, His Justice, wisdom and the like.'[51] Consequently they accused the Calvinists of publishing *unworthy and dishonourable opinions ... concerning God* by identifying him with a doctrine which condemned men to everlasting torment, asserting that it was impossible that 'Infinite Goodness should design or delight in the misery of his Creatures'.[52] Such a rejection of the Calvinist image of God frequently arose out of a deep personal conviction concerning his goodness, not infrequently experienced, as in Henry More's case, early in life. He reports that he was

bred up, to the almost fourteenth Year of my Age, under *Parents* and a *Master* that were great *Calvinists*. . . . But neither there [at Eton], nor yet anywhere else, could I ever swallow down that hard Doctrine concerning *Fate*. . . . Moreover, that I had such a deep Aversion in my Temper to this Opinion, and so firm and unshaken a Perswasion of *Divine Justice* and *Goodness;* that on a certain Day . . . *musing concerning these Things with my self, and recalling to my Mind this Doctrine of Calvin,* I did thus seriously and deliberately conclude with my self, viz. *If I am one of those that are predestined unto Hell, where all Things are full of nothing but Cursing and Blasphemy, yet will I behave my self there patiently and submissively towards God.* . . . Being certainly perswaded, that if I thus de-meaned my self, he would hardly keep me long in that place. Which *Meditation* of mine is as firmly fixed in my Memory, and the very place where I stood, as if the Thing had been transacted but a Day or two ago.[53] (Italics in original.)

What is especially interesting about More's account is the implication that God should be bound in some way by a higher constraint than his own decrees. That the demands of justice might, in effect, require them to be countermanded. This suggestion is in keeping with an important strain of thinking present in the writings of the Cambridge Platonists, the idea that moral values have a basis independent of God's will and that consequently not even God could condemn the innocent without violating justice. Thus whilst the Calvinists insisted that right is right because God wills it so, the Platonists argued that the distinction between right and wrong is eternal and immutable.[54] This point reveals the important and significant difference between this and earlier, more distinctly Arminian, attacks on predestination. For the Cambridge Platonists were, as their name implies, drawing upon material from philosophy in order to construct their theological alternative to Calvin's system.

The Greek philosophers, though nominally heathens, had long been recognized as having a part to play in the correct interpretation of faith, and Plato's teachings in particular had been commonly employed by the

early church fathers in the task of constructing theology. By the time of
the Reformation, however, greater emphasis had come to be placed upon
scripture and the importance of revealed religion such that the
contribution of philosophy, in the form of natural theology, had become
neglected. So much so that the Puritans typically relied on no other
source than the Bible, condemning any resort to 'heathen' books for
enlightenment on religious matters.[55] An interest in classical philosophy
had been revived by the Renaissance however and subsequently kept
alive by scholars. Thus it was in their capacity as members of a university
college (albeit a Puritan one) that the Cambridge divines were heirs to
this tradition, and employed it to reconstruct theology upon a Platonic
rather than an Augustinian basis. A sympathetic contemporary observer
remarked that it was the purpose of the Cambridge men to 'bring the
Church back to her old loving nurse, the Platonic philosophy',[56]
although as Willey notes, 'whilst the Greek Fathers of the second century
grafted Christianity onto a recognized philosophy, with the Platonists it
was a question of grafting philosophy on to a recognized Christianity'.[57]
In either event, what was created was a 'new force in Protestantism', one
which did not resemble either Calvinism or Lutheranism.[58] It was this
use of philosophy which marked a critical turning point in the evolution
of religious thought and which laid the basis for the sentimental deism of
the eighteenth century, for, as Cassirer notes,

it is philosophy which first succeeds in awakening those forces of Protestantism
which were finally invoked in order to extricate Protestantism from the
narrowness of Pauline and Augustinian dogma. In the Netherlands it is Bayle
and Hugo Grotius, in Germany Leibniz, in England the Cambridge thinkers,
who deliberately adopt and persistently maintain this goal, all obstacles
notwithstanding.[59]

The philosophical tradition employed for this purpose was derived from
the Platonic Academy at Florence being introduced into England by John
Colet, Erasmus and Thomas More. It was one which relied on Plotinus
as much as Plato, and focused upon the role of ideas, the nature of the
soul, the place of reason and the eternity of moral concepts.

Plato's doctrine of Eros and his teachings concerning the self-
sufficiency of the moral life, especially as developed by Plotinus, were
eagerly taken up by the Cambridge Platonists in order to deny the
Calvinist doctrine of the incurable corruption of the human will. As a
consequence, the previous emphasis upon God's grace was replaced by
that on God's love with faith no longer set against reason. On the
contrary, they advocated a reasonable faith, reason and benevolence being
the divine qualities present in all men. This reason was not, however, the
narrow faculty of *raison* as idolized by the rationalists of the eighteenth

century, but a 'spiritual faculty whereby spiritual things are discerned'.[60] In line with the ancient doctrine of Right Reason, the Platonists held that reason was not merely a matter of a clear head, but also of a pure heart, with true knowledge of God only attained by both head and heart working in alliance. God felt as a living principle within was the goal to be aimed at, and this meant that religion was a matter of deep moral conviction with humility and charity counting for more than ritual or dogma. In this way, the Cambridge Platonists carried forward the moral intensity and disdain for the outward world so characteristic of the Puritans whilst rejecting a Calvinist theology. This served to shift the focus of attention from gaining salvation in an after-world to living a truly spiritual life in this one, and hence laid the basis for the development of a Christian humanitarianism. The stress upon God as a God of love and upon the creation of man 'in his image' naturally led to a stress upon benevolence as the primary characteristic of a good Christian, whilst scriptural authority, together with the example of Christ, was employed as the basis for emphasizing charity and the associated feelings of pity and sorrow. But such an evolution of Protestant thought required that a new theodicy should replace that of Calvin's, and the man who did most to do this was not actually a member of the Cambridge school – although there are many affinities – but the German philosopher, Leibniz.

Leibniz tackled the age-old problem of reconciling the nature of God with the presence of evil in the world in the only full-scale philosophical work published in his lifetime, namely the *Theodicy*. He was, in fact, attacking the arguments presented by the French sceptic Pierre Bayle, who had argued that religious belief could only depend on faith as the problem of evil meant that Christianity itself was contrary to reason.[61] Leibniz does not so much prove that the presence of evil is compatible with an omnipotent, benevolent creator, as concentrate upon turning back objections against the idea, thereby maintaining that it is not irrational to hold to a theistic belief.[62]

Leibniz advances three discernible strands of argument in dealing with the conundrum presented by God's characteristics of omnipotence and benevolence as identified by Epicurus: is he willing to prevent evil, but not able? Then he is impotent. Is he able but not willing? Then he is malevolent. Is he both able and willing? In which case where does evil come from? Firstly, he argues that the imperfection of the universe was logically necessary in order to preserve its distinctiveness from God, the only perfect being. Such a distinction is required by the laws of logic and God cannot be blamed for failing to contravene these. Secondly, he advances a variety of arguments to show that what appear to us to be evils can, from a wider perspective, be seen to do good, and that a deficiency in the part, therefore, may actually enhance the whole; as in the case of a painting in which parts may be ugly when viewed in isolation, but taken in conjunction with the rest of the painting serve to enhance its beauty. But thirdly, and most importantly, he advances the general argument that 'this is the best of all possible worlds', and it was this claim, in particular, which became famous.

Its essence involves the elevation of God's goodness and wisdom over his omnipotence such that he is, to an extent, 'constrained' by his own benevolence. The argument is that the world we know can only be but one of an infinity of worlds which it would have been possible for God to create. God's 'supreme wisdom', however,

united to a goodness that is no less infinite, cannot but have chosen the best. For as a lesser evil is a kind of good, even so a lesser good is a kind of evil if it stands in the way of a greater good; and there would be something to correct in the actions of God if it were possible to do better.[63]

God was therefore morally obliged to choose to create the best universe possible – including the world with the maximum amount of good – without actually making it collapse back into himself. God is assumed to have no control over which possibilities are mutually compatible and which are mutually exclusive, and hence to blame God for creating this universe as he did would be tantamount to saying that he should not have created anything at all. This argument, together with the assertion that all 'evils' should be seen in the context of a larger good, led to Leibniz's theodicy being characterized by the view that all is for the best, in this, the best of all possible, worlds.

Leibniz's views were widely disseminated, Gottfried Martin claiming that

It is scarcely possible to imagine the impact which this work [*Theodicy*] made upon the eighteenth century; it was probably the most widely read book of the century, at least in Germany, and it is in a sense the embodiment of the Enlightenment.[64]

Certainly followers like Wolff did a great deal to popularize (and, it could be said, distort) Leibniz's theodicic arguments, whilst Voltaires's attack on them in *Candide* is testimony to their influence. Whether or not Arthur Lovejoy is right in seeing the *Theodicy* as containing an appeal to the principle of plenitude, and hence as one of the sources for the idea of 'the great chain of being',[65] it is clear that Leibniz did help to provide the philosophical theology which underpinned Deism and the natural religion of the Enlightenment. Leibniz's solution to the problem of theodicy does not appear to correspond to any of Weber's ideal types. Instead of projecting a resolution of the world's imperfections into some future time it claims that they are, in reality, 'resolved' now. Dualism is obviously rejected whilst it is only with difficulty that it can be linked to

Hindu teachings.[66] Admittedly, there is a sense in which the contribution which certain evils make to the good of the whole is inscrutable to man, much as is God's plan in Calvinism, but the elimination of any element of predestination and the emphasis upon benevolence clearly distinguish the two.[67]

This philosophy has been dubbed an 'optimistic' one, and as such a major contributor to the general 'progressive' outlook which prevailed throughout Europe in the eighteenth century. Whether it logically justifies optimism is debatable; after all, it does involve a resigned acceptance of the inevitability of evil, as Voltaire bitterly observed. It could thus be said to lead more properly to a stoic attitude toward life. What it did do, however, was to rescue the idea of the fundamental benevolence of God from the dark shadow cast on it by Calvinist doctrines, and in addition, present both man and nature as exemplifying that benevolence by being 'the best' the God could devise. Hence it was crucial in displacing that negative judgement on human nature and natural feelings which Puritanism had established.

There was, however, another crucial factor which operated to push the development of the Cambridge Platonists' theology in the direction of a Christian sentimentalism and this was their fierce opposition to the emerging empiricist tradition in philosophy, as represented by Bacon and Hobbes. This constituted a more formidable and dangerous enemy than Calvinism, which it was rapidly replacing. Indeed, as noted above, it was in many respects the inheritor of that tradition, carrying forward its values and attitudes within a secular framework of assumptions. As Cassirer observes, both were active faiths stressing doing above knowing in an attempt to obtain mastery over nature whilst manifesting a legalistic style of thought.[68] In addition, a fundamentally pessimistic evaluation of human nature led to a common stress upon the crucial disciplinary role of social institutions, a view forcefully expressed by Hobbes in *The Leviathan*.

Hobbes represented almost everything that the Platonists rejected, that is an atheistic, materialistic, deterministic and pessimistic philosophy. Indeed he epitomized the very use of philosophy against religion, when they believed passionately in the unity of the two. Willey has shown, with quotations from John Smith and Ralph Cudworth, how the Platonists endeavoured to counter Hobbes's arguments, asserting an idealistic theory of perception and knowledge against his materialism, a theory of freedom of the will against his determinism, and arguments for the immortality of the soul and the existence of God against his atheism.[69] But the most significant effect of their quarrel with Hobbes was the impetus it gave to their ideas about morality and the consequent emphasis which they placed upon the inherent goodness of man.

Just as they detested the Calvinists' reduction of morality to little more than the will of an awesome, if just, God, so the Cambridge Platonists could not accept Hobbes's treatment of morality as either simply 'relative' to our affections or determined by the edict of any earthly Leviathan. Against both, they insisted that the distinctions between right and wrong were eternally fixed in the very nature of things. What is more, since the mind of man is a finite repetition or reflex of the divine mind, its ideas, when true, represent readings of the divine thoughts.[70] In this way, it is possible for individuals who are spiritually aware to possess direct intuitive knowledge of what is good and right. At the same time, the Platonists protested in the strongest terms against Hobbes's picture of human beings as fundamentally motivated by the egoistic passions of pride and self-esteem and hence, if not governed by a 'common power to keep them all in awe', likely to be in that 'condition which is called Warre; and such a warre, as is of every man against every man'.[71] Since, once again, man is a partial image of God, he shares with him that central quality of benevolence, and hence is naturally inclined to join harmoniously with other men, not merely because his reason tells him that kindness to others is the best means to the end of his own private happiness, but because of an inherent tendency to acts of love and goodwill. This theme was reiterated again and again in the years after the Restoration by what Crane calls 'the anti-Hobbesian preachers of "natural goodness"',[72] with the result that from the middle 1680s, 'it had become part of the recognized duty of the preacher of a charity sermon to picture human beings in an amiable light as creatures naturally disposed to impulses of pity and benevolence'.[73]

It will be useful at this point to pause and briefly reconsider the way in which religious and moral beliefs may be considered to exert an influence upon social action. Here, as before, Weber's work will be taken as the starting-point for discussion.

A reading of *The Protestant Ethic and the Spirit of Capitalism* reveals that Weber did not consider religious teachings to have much of an effect upon individual behaviour in any direct didactic fashion. That is to say, whether or not the theologians or ecclesiastical authorities actually proscribe or prescribe an activity is not in itself a matter of prime importance when evaluating religion's impact on conduct. Neither is the nature of that impact to be deduced from what may appear to be the logical consequences of a given theodicy; predestination, for example, as Weber notes, has fatalism as 'its only logical consequence'. What is of significance, by contrast, are 'the psychological consequences for the practical religious attitude to be derived from certain religious ideas',[74] which, as he notes, constitute anything but fatalism in the case of Calvinism. The relevant questions, therefore, relate to the implications which theology has for the direction taken by practical religious conduct, and thus must start from a correct identification of the essential nature of the believer's principal concerns; for only by taking these as a focal point can the effect of changes in doctrine be truly assessed. Thus Weber traces the way in which the doctrine of predestination gives rise to the believer's search for proof that he has attained a state of grace. If, bearing this in mind, we now turn to the post-Calvinist theodicy and philosophy of religion advocated by Leibniz and the Cambridge Platonists, we can similarly ask, what consequences did these teachings have upon the conduct of those latitudinarian Protestants open to their influence?

Whilst the abandonment of the doctrine of predestination can be seen to have eliminated that especial urgency which Weber rightly notes must have characterized the Calvinist's search for proof of his election, it does not follow that Arminians were likely to be indifferent to the goal of salvation. The crucial shift in this respect occurs with the change to 'natural religion' and the apparent unconcern among deists toward the issue of other-worldly salvation, for then the questions which Weber considered central to Christianity – What must I do to be saved? And how can I be certain of my salvation? – gradually fade away. This does not mean, however, that individuals could no longer be credited with possessing any effective religious concerns as there were other forms which these could take. For the Cambridge Platonists, for example, the relevant questions would have been, what must I do in order to realize the divinity which is within me? And how can I be certain of my status as one of the spiritually elect? Questions which merge into (and are eventually replaced by): what must I do to realize my true goodness? And how can I be certain of my status as one of the virtuous?

This last point serves to reveal that Weber's concern with the impact of religious teachings upon practical conduct is but a special case of the analysis of the way in which the formulation of a society's ideals (whether of the good, the true, the just or the beautiful) come to affect behaviour. All these question can thus be more generally rendered as: what must I do to realize these ideals in my own character and conduct? And how can I be certain that I do indeed constitute the ideal? Hence, in all societies, whether they embody religious or non-religious systems of belief in their cultures, it will be possible to adopt an essentially Weberian approach to the way in which the content of ideals affects practical conduct; the crucial link being that form of behaviour which one is called upon to adopt in order to realize the ideal and, more especially, to gain reassurance that one has attained it.

Turning back then to the ideal Christian as advocated in the writings of the Cambridge Platonists, we have noted this to be the benevolent, empathizing man who, moved by pity and compassion to perform acts of charity towards his fellows, exemplifies the idea of holiness as goodness. To achieve this goal it is necessary to attain a true understanding of religion and of God's design as indicated in scripture and in the world, but it is more important to give full expression to the divine which is within by allowing oneself to be affected by the plight of others, and, being so moved, to act with genuine love and compassion toward them. Only if one is indeed so moved, and consequently experiences these emotions, can any assurance that one possesses true holiness and virtue be obtained. This is a doctrine of signs which specifies that individuals of genuine goodness are distinguished by the fact that their charitable acts spring from the tender emotions of pity and compassion.[75] In this way, an optimistic theodicy of benevolence, linking a pietistic strand of Puritan thought to a neo-Platonic philosophy, served to create an 'emotionalist' ethic of Christian sensibility.

Whilst it may well be accepted that Leibniz's theodicy was, in effect, that which, in one form or another, constituted an essential basis for the world-view of the Enlightenment, it could be contended that this was, in general, a secularizing or disenchanting movement; one which served to diminish the role which religion played in life. Thus, to present this as associated with a new religious movement is to overlook or downplay the more significant, long-term, anti-religious features of this momentous turning point in Western civilization. This objection cannot be ignored, for the Enlightenment certainly witnessed the emergence of currents of thought which were to provide the basis for widespread scepticism and unbelief,[76] but to regard this as its principal effect would be to confuse short-term with long-term consequences, as its most immediate effect was to create a new form of religion, that which became known as Deism or 'natural religion'.

Deism and the theology of benevolence

Lovejoy identifies 'uniformitarianism' as the central principle underlying Deism, whilst that which was most crucially considered to be uniform or identical in all men was the faculty of reason.[77] It followed from this that differences in opinion or taste were considered evidence of error, whilst what was universally accepted had the mark of truth. 'Nature' was the key word here, used to mean the standard and universal, and constituting the ultimate court of appeal in all disputes. Thus, as far as religion was concerned, the very obvious differences in belief and practice, not only within Christianity, but among the world's religions in general, suggested that the only beliefs which could be true were those found among man as a whole; what came to be called 'natural religion'. The truths of this religion could be discovered by one of two methods: by each individual employing his own power of reason uninfluenced by tradition or external authority; or by examining the beliefs and values actually held in common by all mankind, the *'consensus gentium'*, as it was known. It was assumed that both methods would lead to the same conclusions and that these would represent the true voice of God. Neither appeal to the 'inner light' of reason nor to the *'consensus gentium'* was new in theological and philosophical debate, but what was different was the exclusive use of these criteria to determine truth to the neglect of both revelation and ecclesiastical authority.[78] Naturally a central problem was encountered when individuals did not arrive at similar conclusions when exercising their reason, or indeed at the same judgements concerning what was, or was not, commonly accepted by all humanity. But, at first, this was not regarded as damaging to the assumptions of natural religion since the light of reason was considered to be obscured by prejudices arising either from the peculiar history of a people or the idiosyncratic experiences of an individual.

The rejection of revelation and ecclesiastical authority meant that the traditional Christian explanation for the existence of evil could no longer be accepted; original sin, the Fall, the Devil, rewards and punishments in another world, all were discarded on the grounds of being no more than local 'superstitions' unsupported by reason and not accepted by mankind in general.[79] The deistical religion of the Enlightenment did not, however, succeed in totally displacing distinctively Christian traditions of thought, nor indeed, did it always take the highly rationalistic form so distinctive of the French *philosophes*. In England, in particular, it tended to constitute an ingredient rather than a complete perspective in the philosophy of religion; the Cambridge Platonists employing Enlightenment ideas to fit in with the anti-stoic and emotional predispositions of a middle-class, Puritan-based religiosity. They accepted much of the content of natural religion, downgrading the supernatural teachings in Christianity and relying upon what was uniform in all men as the basis of their beliefs. What the Platonists emphasized, was not merely man's common possession of reason, but his common possession of sympathy, benevolence and fellow-feeling; in this way they effectively interpreted Deism on a 'sentimental' rather than a rationalistic basis.

In the years following the Restoration this theology of benevolence spread outside the small circle of scholars who constituted the Cambridge Platonists to meet with increasing acceptance among the more influential clergy. Crane mentions Isaac Barrow, Robert South, John Tillotson, Richard Cumberland, Samuel Parker, Hezekiah Burton, Richard Kidder, John Scott, Edward Pelling, William Sherlock, Gilbert Burnet, Richard Bentley, Samuel Clarke, as well as 'many lesser men who yet occupied important livings in the days of the later Stuarts and the early Hanoverians'.[80] All were united in their exaltation of 'goodness', and in preaching the virtues of charitable feelings and actions.

In part, they presented charity – in the form of a general kindness to all men – as the essence of religion in an attempt to escape from the interminable wrangles and disputes over doctrine which had characterized the period of Calvinist supremacy. They were, as Willey expresses it, prepared to 'let sleeping dogmas lie',[81] arguing that it is much better to do good than to quarrel about doubtful and uncertain opinions.[82] But they could, in addition, point to excellent scriptural authority for this emphasis, especially I Corinthians 13 and the extolling, not simply of benevolent actions, but of charitable feelings. Christ himself was also presented as the very exemplification of goodness because he was so moved by pity and compassion for the plight of man that he sacrificed his life in a supreme act of charity. But then these arguments were supplemented by ones which were more distinctly recognizable as deriving from natural religion.

There were three key strands. Firstly, the primary emphasis which was placed upon God's goodness and love meant that these qualities constituted what was most divine in man, who was made in his image in this respect.[83] This argument did not rest merely upon scriptural authority, however, for the essential 'good nature' of all men (when not overlaid by prejudice or ignorance) was taken to be an observable fact of life. Secondly, this goodness sprang from feelings, as with God's love, and did not by any means merely consist of philanthropic actions. In this sense, what was being advocated was less that men should *do* good as *be* good, or rather, allow their natural benign feelings to express themselves in charitable acts. It was in this connection that certain, distinctive, novel teachings emerged concerning man's susceptibility to feelings. Essentially, it was claimed that man's capacity for sympathy and empathy with others was an especially divine quality implanted in man by God so that goodness would ensue. As William Clagett expressed it:

to *Man* only of all Creatures under Heaven, God has given this quality, to be affected with the Grief and with the Joy of those of his own kind; and to feel the Evils which others feel, that we may be universally disposed to help and relieve one another.[84] (Italics in original.)

Samuel Parker had earlier made the same claim that God had endowed men with the passions of 'Natural Pity and Compassion', so that each individual would act for the good of mankind as a whole,[85] a process, which as Crane observes, is not only taken to be true in fact, but to occur in an almost mechanical fashion:

As for the generality of Men their hearts are so tender and their natural affections so humane, that they cannot but pity and commiserate the afflicted with a kind of fatal and mechanical Sympathy; their groans force tears and sighs from the afflicted, and "tis a pain to them not to be able to relieve their miseries'.[86]

This argument was also advanced by Isaac Barrow, who similarly contended that no one could see, hear, or even imagine, another's grief without being affected.

Thirdly, and lastly, as one moves into the early eighteenth century it becomes more and more common for these arguments to be supplemented by references to the inherent pleasure which accompanies benevolent emotions and their ensuing acts of kindness. The idea that pleasure was a natural accompaniment of virtue was commonly expressed by the classical philosophers, and seems to have become emphasized in this context both in reaction to the Calvinist stress on other-worldly rewards, and in order to entice the errant Christian away from more fleshy enjoyments. For whatever reason, it is a theme which receives much attention, Tillotson observing that 'There is no sensual Pleasure in the World comparable to the Delight and Satisfaction that a good Man takes in doing good', whilst Richard Kidder declared that 'There is a Delight and Joy that Accompanies doing good, there is a kind of sensuality in it.'[87] Once again, Isaac Barrow was to the fore in presenting this argument, writing in 1671 that

As nature, to the acts requisite toward preservation of our life, hath annexed a sensible pleasure, forcibly enticing us to the performance of them: so hath she made the communication of benefits to others to be accompanied with a very delicious relish upon the mind of him that practices it; nothing indeed carrying with it a more pure and savoury delight than beneficience. A man may be virtuously voluptuous, and a laudable epicure by doing much good.[88]

This passage is of considerable interest, for although Barrow was no Puritan he was still, as a devout Anglican, the inheritor of an intense and sober-minded Protestant moral tradition. Hence his advocacy of voluptuousness, even if only in the cause of goodness, is worthy of note. But then so too is his reasoning, reminiscent as it is of the Puritan justification for accepting pleasure. That, it will be remembered, was similarly based on the argument that certain activities were so designed as to be accompanied by enjoyment (eating or the procreation of children were the obvious examples) and that this supported the view that it was God's intention that one should engage in them. Only, of course, in so far as it was necessary in order to fulfil God's purposes, and not for the sake of the pleasure itself. The same argument is used here by Barrow, and although it is unlikely that he intended to advocate indulgence in benevolence for the sake of the pleasure to be gained from so doing, his choice of words is suggestive of such an attitude of mind.

Others writers did allow their enthusiasm for the cult of benevolence to take them this far, revealing what Crane refers to as a strain of 'egoistic hedonism'. He gives the following example from Samuel Parker:

Acts of Love and Kindness are in themselves grateful and agreeable to the temper of humane Nature; and all Men feel a natural Deliciousness consequent upon every Exercise of their good-natur'd Passions; and nothing affects the Mind with greater Complacency, than to reflect upon its own inward Joy and Contentment. So that the Delight of every vertuous Resolution doubles upon it self; in that first it strikes our Minds with a direct Pleasure by its suitableness to our Natures, and then our Minds entertain themselves with pleasant Reflections upon their own Worth and Tranquility.[89]

Clearly such an obviously self-regarding complacency concerning one's own goodness as is presented here is effectively akin to an indulgence in benevolence for the pleasures which it can bring, whilst is must be remembered that it is upon feelings and not actions that the focus is fixed. It is therefore possible to conclude that the cult of benevolence, as preached by the Cambridge Platonists and Latitudinarian Anglican divines of the late seventeenth and early eighteenth centuries, did indeed help to stimulate an 'altruistic' form of emotional hedonism.

Now it could be objected against those like Barrow and Samuel Parker that our natural sympathy and pity for others could equally well cause us to experience pain as we vicariously experience the privation, grief and suffering of those worse off than ourselves, and although this feeling might well move us to acts of charity, the 'voluptuousness' of such virtue may not outweigh the antecedent anguish. This view is indeed expressed, but, instead of proving an objection against the hedonistic advantages of the cult of benevolence, it becomes yet a further source of them. The following quotation concerning the emotional pleasures open to the benevolent man is from the Scottish moralist David Fordyce:[90]

His Enjoyments are more numerous, or, if less numerous, yet more intense than those of bad Men; for he shares in the Joys of others by Rebound; and every Increase of *general* or *particular* Happiness is a real Addition to his own. It is true, his friendly *Sympathy* with others subjects him to some Pains which the hard-hearted Wretch does not feel; yet to give a loose to it is a kind of agreeable Discharge. It is such a Sorrow as he loves to indulge; a sort of pleasing Anguish, that sweetly melts the Mind, and terminates in a Self-approving Joy.[91] (Italics in original.)

Here, in the reference to 'pleasing Anguish', and the indulgence in sorrow, a new note is sounded. It is still very much a question of the pleasures of feeling, but the emotions now implicated in hedonism are not simply the positive ones of joy and delight but embrace the darker variety of sadness, pain and despair. In order to understand how these emotions also became crucial to the eighteenth century ethic of sensibility it is necessary to look once again at the fate of Calvinism and, in particular, at those teachings which concerned the emotions.

Calvinism and emotion

Given that Weber's central concern was to provide an explanation for the origin of the spirit of modern, bourgeois capitalism it is understandable that he should have stressed the rational nature of Protestant asceticism, and of Calvinism in particular, both in relation to the generally 'unrationalized' nature of the ethics of Roman Catholicism, and the greater emotionality of Pietism. In this context his emphasis upon the manner in which the 'unique consistency' of Calvinist teachings led to a rigorous attempt to subject man to the supremacy of a purposeful will, and hence 'to enable a man to maintain and act upon his constant motives, especially those which [asceticism] taught him itself, against the emotions' is also understandable.[92] Thus the picture one forms from Weber's discussion of the typical Calvinist is of an intensely serious, sober and rational individual who manifests no emotion, and this, of course, connects, if in muted form, with our present-day usage of the term 'puritan'. Some important qualifications need to be made, however, to this stereotype.

In the first place, this emphasis upon the formal rationality of Calvinist asceticism should not cause us to overlook the key role which Weber accords to emotional forces in his account of the psychological effects which Calvinist teachings, and especially predestination, have upon believers. The ethical demands may cause an individual to act, as Weber says, 'against the emotions', even to the extent of not manifesting any signs of grief at the funeral of one's next of kin, but this does not mean that no emotions are present. On the contrary, Weber's argument involves asserting that such individuals experienced greater emotions than followers of other faiths. They must, for example, have experienced 'a feeling of unprecedented inner loneliness',[93] as well as immense agonies of self-doubt related to the terrible fear of damnation. Indeed it is just these enormously powerful emotions, arising from unresolved internal tensions, that create the desperate need for some reassuring sign that one is of the elect. The Puritan is thus not characterized by the absence of emotion but by the presence of very powerful emotions of particular kinds; what is distinctive is the generally negative attitude toward their expression.[94]

This emotional dimension of Calvinism was especially significant in England where, as Haller notes, the Calvinists were unable to establish a

Geneva-style theocracy, or even a uniformity of belief and doctrine, as was the case in Scotland. As a consequence, not only were they obliged to tolerate wide differences of opinion in matters of belief, but they were forced to establish some degree of doctrinal orthodoxy by making the key teaching of predestination seem attractive.[95] This they did by stressing its profoundly equalitarian implications (as far as this-world was concerned) and by appealing through the imagination to men's emotions. Hence those whom Haller calls the 'affectionate practical English writers', whilst nominally adhering to Calvin's deep suspicion of emotion, actually aimed in their sermons and writings to arouse the most powerful feelings in their listeners and readers.[96] They quite deliberately played upon the doubts and fears of ordinary people concerning their ultimate fate, with the consequence that many men and women were racked by anxiety; the early period of Puritanism especially being, as a result, a period 'of storm and stress seldom equalled and probably never surpassed'.[97]

In view of this, it is hardly surprising to discover that outbursts of 'enthusiasm' or intense emotional release did characterize religious movements during the period of the Commonwealth, or that Calvinists were not exempt from these occasional eruptions of undisciplined feeling; a fact which helps to explain how it was that the banner of cool reasonableness was eventually raised against them. Now although communal forms of emotional expression had little theological justification, and can be duly regarded as deviations from a strict Calvinist ethic, it is not true to portray the individual orthodox believer as someone who could not legitimately manifest feeling under any circumstances.[98] For, in addition to their self-confidence, the Puritans were famous for another personal trait redolent with emotional overtones; one they did little to suppress and which, almost to this day, has remained a hallmark of the dedicated Calvinist. This, of course, is the tendency to melancholia. Weber does note that 'a deep melancholy and moroseness' is characteristic of the Puritans having its psychological basis in the 'breaking down of [the spontaneity] of the *status naturalis*',[99] but he does not examine what significance such an emotional predisposition might have, either in the context of the pastoral need for proof of election, or for the long-term processes of cultural change.

That melancholia was endemic among Puritans was evident to contemporaries. Burton, in his *Anatomy of Melancholy* observes that 'They are certainly far gone with melancholy, if not quite mad, and have more need of hellebore than those that are in Bedlam.'[100] The Puritans themselves, of course, did not consider that their condition warranted any kind of medical treatment, for they accorded it a genuine spiritual significance. Periodic descents into the Slough of Despond, with accompanying bouts of sadness, gloom, dejection, grief, self-pity and despair, were not therefore merely the natural accompaniments of a creed as uncompromisingly pessimistic and frightening as Calvinism; they were also something which the devout Calvinist was advised to experience. Thus it was for the sake of their souls that Puritans were encouraged to wear a ring garnished with a death's head to act as a permanent reminder of their mortality, and spend a part of each day imagining their own funeral or the vivid realities of an eternity spent in the torments of hell.[101] The same rationale was invoked for advocating the contemplation of corpses, tombs, graveyards, charnel-houses and everything associated with dying and death, whilst suffering, pain and even disease were also to be welcomed.[102] It was hardly surprising, under these circumstances, that the various manifestations of melancholia should not only have been prevalent but widely greeted with approval. There was, however, a more fundamental incentive for displaying grief, despair and its cognate traits than the view that such gloomy spiritual exercises were of value in preparing one's soul to receive the gift of grace, one which, in accord with Weber's own argument, derived from the most powerful psychological sanction possible.

An alternative doctrine of signs

In his discussion of the consequences of Calvin's teaching for practical conduct Weber stresses the importance to the individual believer of the questions, 'Am I one of the elect?', and 'how can I be sure of this state of grace?'[103] As he notes, this was not a problem for Calvin who felt himself to be a chosen agent of the Lord and was certain of his own salvation. None the less, Calvin taught that the individual Christian could not know for sure whether he was one of the elect but could only put his trust in Christ. He specifically rejected the idea that one could deduce whether or not individuals were chosen on the basis of their conduct, as this was an unjustifiable attempt to force God's secrets; the elect are truly God's invisible church.

Such a rigorous position was, however, impossible for the majority of Calvin's followers to accept, and so it became overwhelmingly important to be able to have some recognizable sign by which they could identify a state of grace (either in themselves or others) and hence from which a certainty of salvation might be inferred. This was crucial, not only so that the individual could attain some peace of mind, but also because, as Weber observes, on it depended admission to communion and thus membership to the Church.[104] Pastoral work was especially preoccupied therefore with the difficulties presented by attempts to ascertain a man's state of grace, and various solutions were developed. Two are specifically identified by Weber. One is the belief that an individual had an absolute duty to consider himself to be one of the chosen as doubts in this respect are most likely to be implanted by the Devil, whilst a lack of self-confidence may also indicate a lack of faith. The other was to recommend intense worldly activity as the most suitable means of overcoming doubt, and thus generating certainty concerning one's election.[105]

It is at this point in the argument that Weber invokes one of his central conceptual dichotomies, that between the exemplary and instrumental models of religious prophecy, for he describes how the religious believer can 'make himself sure of his state of grace either in that he feels himself to be the vessel of the Holy Spirit or the tool of the divine will'.[106] The former model he associates with Luther and Pietism, the latter with Calvinism, on the grounds that Calvin viewed all pure feelings and emotions with suspicion, and considered that faith had to be proved by its objective results alone. Consequently, the Calvinist was one who came to see the fruits of true faith in a particular type of conduct, and thus 'however useless good works might be as a means of attaining salvation . . . nevertheless, they are indispensable as signs of election. They are technical means, not of purchasing salvation, but of getting rid of the fear of damnation.'[107] It is in this way that the Calvinist came to create, as it were, the conviction of his own salvation.

Weber's use of ideal-typical constructs in this instance and his close association of Lutheranism with the one and Calvinism with the other does, however, seem to have caused him to overlook another response which arose to deal with the problem of attaining reassurance of one's membership of the elect. For, although he was undoubtedly correct to stress the greater emphasis within Lutheranism and indeed Pietism generally upon the subjective experience of the gift of grace, this wasn't absent from Calvinism.[108] Indeed, he seems to have ignored his own warning against confusing the teachings of Calvin with the content of the pastoral advice typically given, in later periods, to ordinary Calvinists. Thus although Calvin's deep hostility to all feelings and emotions may have caused him to place an overwhelming emphasis upon the significance of rational ethical conduct, this was not true for all subsequent generations of Calvinists. Indeed, it could be said that it was inevitable, in Calvinism as in Lutheranism, given the importance attached to the state of grace, that the precise nature of that experience was bound to be a focus of concern. To this extent, therefore, Calvinists were naturally interested in all attitudinal changes (including emotional ones) associated with this experience. It might be true that this was less of an end in itself for the Calvinist than the Lutheran, merely heralding a dedicated and rigorous life of good works, but it was still an event which had to be recognized as well as one which changed the behaviour of the individual concerned. It is for this reason that every Calvinist had an interest in subjective experience, even if he did not take the path to mysticism and emotionalism typically followed by the Lutheran. For, no matter how suspicious of natural feelings a Calvinist might have been, he still had to be able to recognize the workings of the saving grace of Christ in his own heart, and hence succeed in manifesting the 'correct' attitudes and feelings throughout the various stages of that process. Grief and sorrow were prominent among these. As John Bunyan comments in *Pilgrim's Progress*, 'A sight of sin, a sense of sin, and a sorrow for sin, with a desire to be saved by Jesus from all sin, as well as from wrath, do really bespeak the workings of the grace of Christ in the heart.'[109] A tendency thus developed to look for signs of a state of grace in character traits and not just conduct. Intense self-confidence was one such, but there were others which derived from what were considered to be the characteristic features of experiencing saving grace.

There therefore emerged an alternative Calvinist ethic, or ideal of character, which was to undergo important changes as Calvinism in general, and the doctrine of predestination in particular, went into decline; whilst the idea that emotional states had a special spiritual significance and that consequently certain displays of feeling were to be considered as signs of godliness was to outlast the collapse of Calvinism as a coherent theological system to become incorporated into the Enlightenment-based theodicy of benevolence which replaced it.[110] As it happened, the question of determining whether or not an individual had experienced saving grace became most crucial in relation to the issue of membership of the Church, and it was in the Puritan colony of New England that pastoral teachings concerned with identifying these signs first developed.

The principal issue which had given rise to the Puritan party within the Church of England in the first instance had been, as the name suggests, a desire to 'purify' that organization of all those clearly unworthy to be members. The basis for this purge was the doctrine of the visible and invisible Church which St Augustine had developed in response to the Donatist heresy. He had argued that the invisible Church was composed of every person living, dead and yet to be born, whom God had predestined for salvation, whilst the visible Church included only living persons who professed to believe in Christ. Not all of these were destined to be saved as the visible Church was bound to contain sinful men. That the Church of England in the seventeenth century did contain many sinful men was manifestly obvious to the Puritans, and hence they urged that steps be taken to make it a closer approximation to the invisible one. However, efforts to reform the Church were, from their point of view, frustrated, and thus many separated to form a more genuinely Christian movement.

At first, the separatists demanded little of their members except rejection of the Church of England and consent to the basic Christian doctrines. Being committed to making the visible Church as close an approximation as possible to the invisible, however, and seeing themselves as a group of true believers set apart from the wicked, they had a critical, but difficult problem to solve. If the Church was to be seen as a company of the faithful, who was to be judged faithful? Who should be allowed to join? As Morgan explains their problem:

In order to make the visible church as much like the invisible as possible one should look for signs of saving grace in potential members. Even though it was known that signs were fallible (only God *knew* who he had elected for salvation), it was necessary to try to form an estimate of the probability of faith in every candidate for membership.[111] (Italics in original.)

This concern with the signs of saving grace had come about because of the obvious deficiencies in existing criteria. A confession of faith was required, as indeed it had been in the Church of England, but this was recognized as an inadequate test of true faith, even though the Puritans demanded clear evidence of an understanding of the creed and were not satisfied with simple recitation. At the same time, an emphasis upon 'good works' could not be guaranteed to exclude hypocrites. Thus the Puritans were necessarily drawn to place an ever-greater importance upon signs of saving grace as the crucial ingredient in any test of suitability for membership of the Church of Christ.

What this meant in practice was that the test adopted was one in which the confession of faith included a declaration of the experience of the work of grace, that is, of how the individual became convinced that he had experienced such an event. As Schneider summarizes the process:

To be accepted as a saint it was necessary to know the principles of the religion, to be blameless and free from scandal and provide a public confession of one's faith in which an elaborate and explicit statement of the experience of redeeming grace in their souls was a prerequisite.[112]

In fact, applicants for membership were likely to be cross-examined about the nature of their experience in order to assess its genuineness, and although these rigorous tests of suitability for membership had originally stemmed largely from a desire to exclude the ungodly, with the elders accepting that no man could know who was or was not one of God's elect, they gradually came more and more to resemble an examination to establish the validity of an individual's claim to have signs of grace.[113] For, as Morgan observes,

Although Calvin had made it quite clear that it was impossible to form a reliable opinion about whether or not a man is one of God's elect, he had nevertheless furnished a number of clues by which anxious Christians could predict their chances.[114]

In particular, he had made it clear that sanctification – that is the gradual improvement of a man's behaviour in obedience to God – though it could not in itself assist a man toward salvation, could be a sign that he was saved. However, since even the damned could perform charitable works, the real emphasis fell upon the problem of determining whether or not one had experienced saving grace, and in relation to this problem a body of literature gradually accumulated which supplied a general outline of the experience. That is, convinced 'saints' described events in such a way that a common pattern could be discerned, and using this as a guide, an individual could judge how far his own experience gave grounds for hope or despair. As Morgan comments, 'The marks of faith in a Puritan were painful to behold and sometimes deceptive, but they ran so much according to form . . . that Calvin's injunction against seeking to discover a particular man's eternal condition seemed to be overstated.'[115] Obviously, if true faith could be recognized with a high degree of probability in this way, then it could be used as a test of membership of the Church, for a man simply had to show that his experience followed this pattern. At first individuals were merely encouraged to test themselves, and this self-searching did itself become a mark of faith, but subsequently candidates for admission to the Church were required to give a public recital of the way in which God's grace had come to them.[116] This practice was established in New England by 1640, from whence it was subsequently introduced into Britain. Morgan provides a summary account of a typical description of such an experience:

first comes the feeble and false awakening to God's commands and a pride in keeping them pretty well, but also much backsliding. Disappointments and disasters lead into other fitful hearkenings to the word. Sooner or later true legal fear or conviction enables the individual to see his hopeless and helpless condition and to know that his own righteousness cannot save him, that Christ is his only hope. Thereafter comes the infusion of saving grace, sometimes but not always so precisely felt that the believer can state exactly when and where it came to him. A struggle between faith and doubt ensues, with the candidate careful to indicate that his assurance has never been complete and that his sanctification has been much hampered by his own sinful heart.[117]

What is of particular interest about this account is that an intensely personal, subjective experience is here being used as the crucial test of religious worth. It is not the individual's knowledge or conduct which is under scrutiny so much as the nature and quality of his inner state of being. The queries raised were typically about such issues as the depth and genuineness of his 'humiliation' or conviction of sin, the authenticity of his grief for his sinfulness, the pervasiveness of doubt, and the continuing presence of bouts of despair. Certain rules of thumb in these matters seem to have been commonly applied, such as, for example, that an 'unfeigned grief for the want of faith' was itself a sure sign of faith, and that the surest earthly sign of a saint was his uncertainty.[118]

Haller shows how the same ideas were prevalent among Puritans in England where the general assumption made was that 'the manifestation of grace in the elect was faith'.[119] Since these 'saints' truly believed in Christ's power they waged an incessant war against sin, hating the evil they committed, with this continuous struggle against the flesh being seen as evidence of their election. At the same time there developed a 'descriptive psychology of sin and regeneration', which became the basis for a kind of spiritual self-help, something which brought into being a body of literature aimed at teaching people how to 'cure' their own souls.[120] Haller observes that since

Every man was either a convert or susceptible of conversion, and the inner life of any man, once converted, was fraught with daily possibilities for struggle and adventure. It followed that every man's state of spiritual health was the subject of acute concern to the man himself and of sympathetic curiosity to others. Naturally this gave occasion to the reporting and comparing of individual case histories, to the endless retailing of confession, reminiscence and anecdote. Out of such spiritual gossip arose a body of legend and a type of popular literature which was soon found to be quite as edifying and certainly as fascinating as the more formal tracts and sermons.[121]

The spiritual autobiography or diary was an essential tool in this cult of spiritual self-help, and by committing one's experience to paper it was even possible to persuade others that one had indeed actually experienced saving grace; such documents serving, in effect, as a kind of 'diploma from the Holy Ghost'.[122]

Crucially, therefore, it was possible to know if one was saved, but in order to possess this knowledge it was necessary first to scrutinize one's inner experience with great care, and then secondly, to observe in it that pattern which had already been identified as signifying saving grace, for

In sermons and popular treatises almost beyond number, the Puritan preachers described the psychological pattern which exemplified the working of the formula, which all the saints were supposed to have exemplified and which every man who desired to be saved must hope would be exemplified again in his own case ... men ... were taught to follow by intense introspection the working of the law of predestination within their own souls. Theoretically, there was nothing they could do of their own will to induce or further the process of regeneration.

They were only the witnesses of a drama which moved to its predetermined end according to a law they could do no more than marvel at. But the theatre of that drama was the human breast, and their own fate right up to the deathbed scene hung upon its outcome. With the most anxious curiosity, they looked into their own most secret thoughts for signs that the grace of God was at its work of regeneration, and what they so urgently looked for they naturally saw.[123]

Having witnessed this longed-for event, they then naturally manifested the outward signs of one of the elect, such as a true grief for sin, as well as confidence interspersed with intense despair and despondency in the continuing struggle against temptation.[124]

This doctrine of signs, like the one which Weber identified, is something of a perversion of Calvin's original teaching, and emerged out of the same desperate need for reassurance. It seems to have existed alongside the emphasis upon worldly success, and, because of the stress upon humiliation, grief and despair, was often simplified into the assumption that 'a melancholy demeanour and emotionalized self-debasement' were the 'outward signs of godliness within',[125] and even, that 'a longing for death and a delight in musing upon it' was overt proof of election.[126] However, whether the emotion stressed was self-pity, self-debasement or morbidity, the point to be emphasized is that its expression was not merely permitted but actually endorsed by the most powerful religious sanction. True faith, holiness, sanctity, the mark of the 'saint', could not only be manifest to the individual within his own heart, he could also manifest it to others, not by any particular action but through a distinctive form of profound emotional sensibility, and not just when seeking membership of the church, but throughout life. In this way, a link was forged between displays of feeling and assumptions about the fundamental spiritual state of an individual which was to long outlive the decline of Calvinism and to influence profoundly the eighteenth-century movements of sensibility and Romanticism.

From Calvinism to Sentimentalism

It is now possible to appreciate how even Calvinistic Puritanism came to place a special value upon the possession and manifestation of feelings, and although these were apparently very different from those stressed in the cult of benevolence they had the same general significance as indicators of a truly godly person. The way was open, therefore, once the distinctive Calvinist doctrine of predestination had been abandoned, for these two strands of Protestant pastoral thought to be woven together.

We have already had occasion to note the reaction against Calvinism

which occurred in the second half of the seventeenth century, and to
trace the development of the Arminian- and Platonic-inspired doctrines
that replaced it. The Enlightenment optimism which was associated with
this movement, however, also affected those Calvinists who continued to
adhere to the principles outlined in the Westminster Confession, with
the consequence that 'there was a certain falling away from the strict
spirit of the doctrine' among them, and their religion 'lost its revivalist
force'.[127] Or, as G. M. Trevelyan expressed it, 'in the reign of Queen
Anne, the dissenting sects hold with easy minds the doctrines their
grandfathers sought sorrowing, and reached with doubts and divisions,
groans and tears'.[128] Hence, even though no formal changes were made
to theology, Calvinists themselves became less and less preoccupied with
God's eternal decrees, the preaching of hell-fire and brimstone sermons
fell away, and Calvinism became more of an 'abstract Scriptural
dogmatism'.[129]

Such a change was closely related to the different political and
economic circumstances which non-conformists were now experiencing,
ones which seem guaranteed to have prompted 'secularization' in the
sense which Burke suggests, of 'the expression of hopes and fears in
increasingly worldly terms'.[130] The practical removal of the disabilities
laid upon dissent, and the consequent weakening of a 'sectarian'
mentality, clearly contributing to this process. As too, of course, did
increasing prosperity. Trade grew rapidly in these years, especially trade
with India and the East and the merchant classes naturally benefited.
That this should be to the detriment of piety was widely recognized.
Wesley was later to comment that 'I fear wherever riches have increased,
the essence of religion has decreased in the same proportion',[131] whilst
Weber observed that 'Puritanical ideals tended to give way under
excessive pressure from the temptations of wealth', and that 'with great
regularity we find the most genuine adherents of Puritanism among the
classes which were rising from a lowly status . . . are often found tending
to repudiate the old ideals'.[132] One suspects that this process is by no
means a simple matter of the 'temptations of wealth' working to
undermine asceticism, but that the experience of an improved quality of
life, including a lengthening of life expectancy, is involved in bringing
about significant changes in attitudes toward the world. In this case, the
change of attitude was, as one might expect, in the direction of optimism,
with, as Draper dryly observes, a paradoxical outcome:

The new liberation at first affected only the wealthier and more intellectual
dissenters, the *haute bourgeoisie*: but, as this upper stratum included in large
measure the dissenting clergy, these bodies, and especially the Presbyterians,
were gradually brought over to the new point of view, which in its early stages may

be described – if one may be allowed the appearance of a *contradicto in adjecto* – as an optimistic Calvinism.[133]

The optimism which he goes on to outline is a product of the confluence of Enlightenment thought with material success, for, as he suggests, 'An expansive sense of the rightness of everything, especially human nature, seemed the natural attitude of life for a class of persons who were exchanging the battlefield of religious strife for the primrose path of peace and plenty.'[134]

What then happened to religious emotions during these years of increasing 'secularization'? Did the 'tumultuous and exalted depression', the melancholia which signified godliness, simply die away as the old doctrines faded in face of the new optimism? It would seem that they did not, but rather they were transformed, both in their function and meaning.

The waning of a traditional religious conviction seems to have been accompanied by a subtle but highly important shift in the relationship between belief and emotion, one aptly summarized by Sir Leslie Stephen when he remarked that, 'We are not melancholy because we believe in Hell, but we believe in Hell because we are melancholy.'[135] In other words, whilst the old beliefs in sin, hell and eternal damnation were no longer held with the intense conviction of former decades, there was a reluctance to abandon the subjective states with which they had been associated. Perhaps, for the reasons given above, the belief and the emotion has become identified in such a way that an expression of feelings was thought to serve in place of an expression of faith. Draper does observe that there were those who considered 'religion and sadness to be the same'.[136] In any event, the important point is that these religiously generated emotions had become a source of pleasure in themselves and hence there was a widespread reluctance to abandon them.

For religious doctrines of a Calvinist character to give rise to emotions which might be 'enjoyed' it was clearly necessary that belief should have become considerably attenuated; few individuals could possibly have found much pleasure (even bearing in mind the lessons which Freud has taught us) in the total despair or abject terror which the first Puritans commonly experienced. Once convictions become conventions, however, the possibility of emotional self-indulgence is a real one. At the same time this possibility is extinguished if the beliefs really are abandoned, in form as well as in substance, as some of the Enlightenment rationalists desired. In between the two extremes of conviction and dismissal, however, there is a position in which the belief becomes merely a symbol representing an emotional condition or mood, manipulable more or less at will in order to obtain pleasure. Of course, it is not always easy to determine whether an individual's feelings stem from genuine religious conviction or arise out of spurious sentimentality. As Draper asks in relation to Young's poem *Night Thoughts*, 'Did Young write of night because it was auspicious of his soul's future or because it was "delightful" to his present experience?'[137] The difference, he notes, is that between a Calvinist and a Sentimentalist. The fact that the emotion is not truly genuine but is, to an extent at least, artificially stimulated for the pleasure it yields, is usually discernible, nevertheless; firstly, by the fact that the intensity of expression tends to be somewhat in excess of that which the occasion would 'naturally' demand, and, secondly, by the indications of self-consciousness and reflexiveness contained in its expression. These are typical hallmarks of Sentimentalism.

It would seem to be around this period that individuals began to gain pleasure from their religious meditations. In his discussion of the material contained in Puritan funeral elegies, Draper notes that, 'As time passes it becomes more and more obvious that a pleasure is being derived from the horrors and grief conjured up'.[138] and that, in the second half of the seventeenth century, a 'new mental attitude' emerged in which 'the melancholy of life and death was cultivated for its own sake, and found to be agreeable'; a change which he identifies as 'the beginnings of Sentimentalism among the Calvinistic non-conformists'.[139] The seventeenth-century horror of death begins to give way to a typical eighteenth-century liking for pensive sadness. As Sickels observes, death, having lost some of its power to sting, becomes romanticized.[140] Genuine religious motives, such as the fear of damnation, developed gradually into a form of spurious religiosity, whilst melancholy, which was at first merely the manifestation of a deeper religious sentiment, is increasingly cultivated for its own sake.

One way of looking at this change is to regard the Puritans as having developed a 'taste' for the strong meat of powerful religious emotion, and when their convictions waned, seeking alternative fare with which to satisfy their appetite. Draper refers to the middle classes 'craving' the feeling they could no longer express in their religion,[141] and needing to express their 'surplus' feeling in melancholy, whilst Sickels comments that 'the intensity of belief and emotion which we have lost for ourselves we not infrequently seek to regain through vicarious experience – nor are fear, remorse, and despair by any means exceptions to this rule'.[142] One could say that the Puritans, or those who inherited their mentality, had become addicted to the stimulation of powerful emotions and were now seeking substitutes for the original.[143] An obvious place to find them was in literature where artificially created feelings could be experienced by 'living' real-life situations vicariously; this was certainly what the graveyard poets and the Gothic novelists sought to provide. There is, as

Sickels points out, an obvious psychological as well as an historical connection between the decline of religious terrorism and the rise of terror-romanticism.[144] Except that, as Bredvold observes, the Gothic cult which by 1750 had been grafted on to the exploitation of melancholy, was strictly to do with horror, not terror. The latter, a 'real' emotion, had long been employed in tragedy and was intended to make one tremble with fear. Horror, on the other hand, is a more self-conscious and disingenuous emotion, from which we typically obtain a pleasurable shiver.[145] It is clear that we have now arrived at the point of being able to conclude, with Draper, that what happened to Puritanism between 1660 and 1760 was that 'the middle classes reinterpreted Protestantism on a Sentimental, rather than a Calvinistic basis'.[146]

It is now possible to perceive how the two strands of Puritan 'emotionalism', that sympathetic kindliness associated with the cult of benevolence, and the Gothic self-pitying morbidity of the Calvinists, eventually meet in a common concern with the pleasures of feeling. Both, as has been noted, were critical signs of godliness within, and thus had theological and philosophical justification for their expression, whilst there had also been an increasing tendency within the benevolentist tradition to emphasize the intrinsic pleasures of such good-natured feelings. All that remains, in order to indicate the clear basis of Sentimentalism in Protestantism, is to show how these two strands can be intertwined via an emphasis upon the empathetic faculty. This, which was strongly stressed in the cult of benevolence, opened up the possibility, as we noted with David Fordyce's quotation, that one's sympathetic incorporation of the experiences of others may expose one to unwanted pain and anguish. Intriguingly, Fordyce judges this an advantage, as the good man actually 'loves' to indulge 'in sorrow', gaining a 'sort of pleasing Anguish' from it.[147] We can now recognize this form of emotional masochism as stemming from the Calvinist strand and note how easily it can be assimilated into an apparently altruistic Sentimentalism. The concern with displaying sadness, melancholy and self-pity, together with the desire to experience pain, suffering and death, is easily linked to an expressed sympathy for the plight of all the wretched and miserable people in the world. At the same time, the idea that it is good for one's soul to contemplate such ennobling prospects as death and disease can be assimilated to the injunction to empathize with the unfortunate so that one will be moved to assist them. Pity and self-pity become interchangeable as the cult of Sentimentalism is born.

The other crucial ingredient in Sentimentalism is belief in the natural goodness of man. At first sight diametrically opposed to Calvinistic Puritanism, this belief could develop from several sources. Firstly, Arminianism itself, by rejecting predestination and teaching that salvation is open to all, can, as we noted, develop in this direction. As Fairchild outlines this process:

Without a firm setting in Catholic orthodoxy, Arminianism loses its equilibrium. Remove the conception of Holy Church and the sacraments as real means of grace, blur the traditional images of mediation, over-emphasize the human need of divine aid, let the transcendent Deity be felt less vividly than the Deity within us – and there arises an Arminianism which is little more than a restatement of the Pelagian heresy, and which points directly toward the cult of natural goodness and universal benevolence.[148]

Secondly, a similar teaching could emerge from the centrality accorded to the doctrine of the Inner Light emphasized by the more 'enthusiastic' Separatist sects. Their claim of an immediate and private revelation which takes precedence over scripture, revelation and ecclesiastical authority, meant that each believer could come to see himself as the 'Word made flesh'.

There existed, however, a third path within Protestantism by which one could pass from the doctrine of original sin to that of original genius or goodness. This, unlikely as it may seem, was via Calvinism itself. This argument, as presented by Fairchild, rests on Haller's analysis.[149] It starts from the perception of Calvinistic Puritanism as a faith which encourages enormous self-confidence in the individual who believes himself saved, a self-confidence built around the conviction that worldly rank and distinctions count for nothing in comparison with character and inner worth. In addition, as all things are predestined, there could be no fear concerning the outcome of life's ordeal. Fairchild describes what happens to this character type under the impact of Deism:

Under the rationalistic influences of the Enlightenment the Calvinist's formal beliefs decay more rapidly than his inward religious emotions. He loses most of his creed, but he retains, in a blurred and softened form, the emotions which his creed had both reflected and fostered. The God above him becomes more shadowy than the God within him, until at last he is left with the basic attitude of sentimentalism – a sense of inward virtue and freedom which must somehow find corroboration in the nature of the universe. Just enough brimstone remains to tinge his optimism with melancholy, just enough other-worldliness to make him shrink at times from the civilization which he has built.[150]

It is on these grounds that Draper remarks on the difficulty of distinguishing 'between a Sentimentalist and a Calvinist who believes himself saved'.[151] whilst Fairchild rounds of the above paragraph with the reflection that 'It is fitting that Jean-Jacques should have been reared in Geneva.'[152]

It is now possible to conclude that there were two, and not one, powerful cultural traditions of thought and associated 'ethics' which developed out of English Puritanism in the eighteenth century. The first, which corresponds to that identified by Weber and is consequently commonly referred to as 'the Protestant ethic', stressed rationality, instrumentality, industry and achievement, and is more suspicious of pleasure than of comfort; here the impact of Enlightenment scepticism produces an atheistic and empiricist outlook which finally develops into utilitarianism. The second, traceable from the Arminian revolt against predestination to the Cambridge Platonists and Latitudinarian Anglican divines, and incorporating an 'optimistic', 'emotionalist' version of the Calvinist doctrine of signs, develops first into the cults of benevolence and melancholy, and then into a fully fledged Sentimentalism. For both, the culture-carriers are the middle classes, and each, in its own way, has a vital contribution to make to the accomplishment of the Industrial Revolution and the legitimation of an essentially 'bourgeois' way of life.

7

The Ethic of Feeling

We must judge the soul of every man by the degree of emotion he displays in the theatre.

Sebastien Mercier

Although it is usual to describe the eighteenth century as the Age of Reason this can be a deeply misleading title if left unqualified, as Bredvold suggests:

We no longer accept as adequate Matthew Arnold's dictum that the eighteenth century was an age of prose and reason; we are well aware that it was also an age of sentiment and that more tears were probably shed both in literature and in real life in that century than in the nineteenth.[1]

Barfield makes the same point when he refers to the 'imaginative double life' of the typical eighteenth-century gentleman; his life in 'the order and reason of the moral and material universe' on the one hand, and of 'sensibility in the little universe of himself' on the other.[2] As intimated earlier, the two parts of this 'double life' should not be regarded as at odds with one another, for the process of disenchanting the world served both to permit and to prompt the accompanying voluntaristic re-enchantment of experience. The Age of Reason was also necessarily therefore the Age of Sentiment. There is a danger, however, of failing to perceive the proper significance of this latter term for everyday conduct during this period unless some care is taken to avoid anachronistic interpretations.

The word 'sentimental' together with the closely associated 'sensibility', although dating back to the fourteenth century, first became widely used in England in the eighteenth and particularly in the 1740s and 1750s when it was especially fashionable.[3] Raymond Williams cites a certain Lady Bradshaugh as commenting in 1749 that the word 'sentimental' is 'so much in vogue among the polite. . . . Everything clever and agreeable is apprehended in that word . . . a *sentimental* man . . . a *sentimental* walk' (italics in original).[4] Today 'sentimental' typically means 'tending to indulge the emotions excessively',[5] and this is more or less the interpretation given to 'sentimental', 'sentimentality' and 'sentimentalism' by literary commentators and critics. Thus, the author of the article 'Sentimentality' in *The Princeton Encyclopedia of Poetry and Poetics*, describes its meaning (in rather pejorative language) as 'an indulgence of more emotion . . . than seems warranted by the stimulus' often suggesting 'the presence of self-pity and the absence of mature emotional control';[6] whilst Sickels, more guardedly, translates 'sentimentalism' as, 'the doctrine or practice of cultivating – and expressing – the emotions for their own sake'.[7] Indulging in emotion 'for its own sake' is, of course, another way of saying that it is done for the pleasurable stimulation which it provides, and this was explicitly recognized by Virginia Woolf, who dubbed 'sentimentalism' a 'philosophy of pleasure', whilst Frances Bickley called it 'a pleasant philandering with emotion'.[8]

Now it cannot be doubted that the man, the party and the walk, itemized by Lady Bradshaugh, were judged to be sentimental because they served as sources of emotional pleasure, but it is doubtful if this was all that she meant, for, as Erametsa's study has clearly shown, the word had a somewhat different meaning at the beginning of the eighteenth century.[9] Then it meant 'of thought, or opinion' where the noun 'sentiment' means a judgement, as indeed it may still do today, especially when used in the plural (we refer to someone expressing those 'sentiments' which are appropriate to the occasion).[10] Since, however, the opinion expressed was commonly a moral one, this sense passed into the adjective 'sentimental'; when, subsequently, in the second half of the century, the word came increasingly to signify 'of thought and feeling', the implication of moral relevance continued, until eventually, in the last few decades, all reference to thought disappeared, and the term meant 'of refined, or moral feeling'.[11] Bearing this in mind therefore, it can be noted that the word so much in vogue in 1749 implied not merely something which yielded emotional pleasure but also that which was in some way expressive of a moral attitude. It is, of course, this close association between feeling and morality which clearly demonstrates the kinship between Sentimentalism and earlier Protestant thought; an association which was even more apparent in the case of the word 'sensibility'.

The cult of sensibility

In the eighteenth century sensibility was a 'significant, an almost sacred word, for it enshrined the idea of the progress of the human race. Sensibility was a modern quality; it was not found among the ancients, but was a product of modern conditions.'[12] As this quote from Tompkins suggests, sensibility was regarded as a personal quality; but it was also the name for an ideal of character, and the two tended in practice to shade into each other. In the first sense, it was conceived of as an inherited attribute, an aspect of one's temperament or disposition, such that one could not help but respond in this way if possessed of a 'natural sensibility'.[13] But as these qualities became increasingly admired and praised, so too did they come to be built into an ideal character type, that of the Man of Feeling.[14]

But what did sensibility involve? Basically it was a susceptibility to tender feelings, typically exhibited by a show of tears; but the physical symptoms could be far more extensive than mere lacrimosity, as indicated by the following passage from Diderot, in which he is describing the state of ecstasy he experiences when contemplating a good man or a good deed:

Such a sight fills me with sweetness or kindness, kindles in me a heat and an enthusiasm in which life itself, if I had to lose it, would mean nothing to me; then it seems as if my heart were distended even beyond my body, as if it were swimming; a delicious and sudden sensation of I know not what passes over my whole body; I can hardly breathe; it quickens over the whole surface of my body like a shudder; I feel it most of all at the top of my brow, at the roots of my hair; and after that the indications of admiration and pleasure appear in my face mingled with those of joy, and my eyes fill with tears. That is what I am like when I am really interested in a man of virtuous life.[15]

The range of objects, situations or events which could prompt such responses as this in the Man of Feeling was considerable, as Sickels indicates:

He is exquisitely attuned to the slightest touch of joy or pain either in himself or in another. He is capable of swooning with joy or dying of a broken heart, or rejoicing in the good fortune of a rival or weeping over the sad tale from the antipodes or the death of a pet mouse. If poetically inclined – as he usually is – he may write love elegies, not only about Negroes, whom he does not understand, but even about a turtle-dove who dies of a broken heart, or a nightingale who has lost her mate.[16]

As Sickels also observes, the Man of Feeling usually finds it easier to enter into the woes of others than their happiness, with the result that the sentimental literature is predominantly melancholy in tone; sensibility and melancholy being 'close sisters'.[17] In fact, that association between sensibility and benevolence present in the arguments of the Cambridge divines is also close and similarly rests, as we have seen, upon an ability to enter into the sufferings of others, empathetic ability being a common theme throughout the literature of Sentimentalism.

This character ideal can thus be seen to centre upon a susceptibility to emotions of particular moral significance. As Vickers expresses it, sensibility meant 'an ideal sensitivity to – and spontaneous display of – virtuous feelings, especially those of pity, sympathy, benevolence, of the open heart as opposed to the prudent mind'.[18] Viewed in this way, it is possible to see sensibility as a charismatic quality akin to the gift of grace itself. Indeed, it would seem that it was not uncommonly regarded in this manner, as evidence of the goodness, if not superiority, of a person's soul. There was certainly a tendency to judge the soul of a man by the degree of emotion he displayed, as Wellek observes.[19] Laurence Sterne, in particular, seems to have held the view that sensibility was a gift from God, regarding the faculty as 'a mixture of the physiological and the spiritual, of those feelings in the human nervous system that correspond to God's contact with mankind, elevating it to the force underlying human love and charity'.[20] In line with this view, Sterne's readers seem to have experienced a degree of self-congratulation for their emotions, 'Like him they easily persuaded themselves that the gift of tears is a proof of the excellence and loftiness of [their] nature, and exclaimed when the tears were over: "I am positive I have a soul".'[21]

It is now possible to see how displays of emotion served to fulfil two functions within the cult of sensibility. On the one hand, they were necessary to the Men (or Women)[22] of Feeling if they were to succeed in convincing others, and more critically, themselves, that they did indeed possess that most vital of personal qualities. As Lady Louisa Stuart recalled, when she first read Henry Mackenzie's *The Man of Feeling* at the age of fourteen, she was 'secretly afraid lest she should not cry enough to gain the credit of proper sensibility'.[23] On the other hand, in addition to serving in this fashion as a sign of virtue, emotional expression was indulged in for the intrinsic pleasure which it yielded; thus it was that sound ethical justification was provided for an emotionalist hedonism.

That the emotions associated with a proper sensibility were in practice experienced as pleasurable is clearly revealed in the expressions popular at the time, many of which refer to the 'pleasures' to be gained from pity, sorrow, benevolence, love, grief or horror.[24] Interestingly enough, from the point of view of the overall argument presented here, the word 'luxury' featured prominently and Tompkins provides a useful collection of examples from novels published between 1760 and 1790. 'Never before have I revelled in such luxury of tears'; 'pity ... the greatest luxury the soul of sensibility is capable of relishing'; sensibility as 'luxurious woe'; 'it might yield to some of your readers a portion of that luxurious pity which I felt'. Finally, she completes the list with 'indulge in all the voluptuousness of sorrow', and 'a pleasing kind of distress'.[25] Many more examples of the delight afforded by emotion could be given both from life and literature of the period. Among others cited by Tompkins, for example, is the character who is made to cry out, 'Go on, I insist upon it! I love to weep, I joy to grieve; it is my happiness, my delight, to have my heart broken in pieces.'[26]

Sense and sensibility

Jane Austen's novel *Sense and Sensibility* not only provides us with a valuable insight into sensibility as an ideal of character, but also serves to remind us that its opposite may be considered to be 'common sense' – the two sisters, Elinor and Marianne, embodying the alternatives given in the title. Although it is necessary to bear in mind that Jane Austen was to some extent engaged in a satire and that the word 'sensibility' may be considered to have 'burlesque overtones' in her fiction, whilst, as the novel progresses, Marianne acquires some sense and Elinor some sensibility,[27] this does not render the accounts of their attitudes and behaviour any the less useful for our purpose. On the contrary, the element of satire can be said to render the underlying 'ideal types' more discernible.

The first point which can confidently be made is that the ideal of sensibility, as presented in the character of Marianne, clearly embraces a readiness to indulge emotions for the pleasures which they can supply. She rarely lets such opportunities pass by, and the leaving of Norland is one such, prompting her to declaim:

when shall I cease to regret you! – when learn to feel a home elsewhere! O happy house, could you know what I suffer in now viewing you from this spot, from whence perhaps I may view you no more! And you, ye well-known trees! – but you will continue the same. No leaf will decay because we are removed, nor any branch become motionless although we can observe you no longer! No; you will continue the same; unconscious of the pleasure or the regret you occasion, and insensible of any change in those who walk under your shade! But who will remain to enjoy you?[28]

This passage clearly displays those features of self-conscious responsiveness and excessive emotionalism which, as we have seen, are the hallmarks of sentimentalism. That pleasure is being derived from this display of emotion cannot be doubted, and, in a later passage, Marianne obtains a similar delight from another exhibition of feelings concerning Norland, one which is sparked off on this occasion by her imaginative remembrance of the falling leaves in autumn:

'Oh!' cried Marianne, 'with what transporting sensations have I formerly seen then fall! How have I delighted, as I walked, to see them driven in showers about me by the wind! What feelings have they, the season, the air altogether inspired! Now there is no one to regard them. They are seen only as a nuisance, swept hastily off, and driven as much as possible from the sight.[29]

This is a good example of that modern ability to use the imagination to create an illusioned environment which, in turn, prompts a sought-after emotion. Marianne is here choosing to experience nostalgia by deliberately employing the falling leaves which she sees as a means of conjuring up 'unseen' but desired images. Nostalgia is an especially appropriate emotion for the self-illusory hedonist, for, although there are common ideas and symbols concerning what is meant by 'home', the specific triggers for such a feeling are necessarily largely self-referential. Thus, whilst some stimuli may remind all those in one society of their 'home', others will depend upon the individuals' distinctive personal experiences. This serves to give considerable latitude to a person to decide whether or not a particular object, scene or event will be chosen as a trigger for nostalgia.[30]

The moral ingredient that enables sensitivity to function as an ideal of character is also well illustrated in Marianne's behaviour, for it can be said to embody an 'ethic' of feeling, central to which is the obligation to express powerful emotions without constraint. As Elinor observes, Marianne considered it a 'disgraceful subjection of reason to common-place and mistaken notions' to restrain sentiments which were not in themselves illaudable.[31] Moderation in feeling was for her a vice not a virtue, for she considered that the woman of feeling had a duty to give full expression to her passions. This is clear from Elinor's reflection on that 'violent sorrow which Marianne was in all probability not merely giving way to as a relief, but feeding and encouraging as a duty'.[32] Later, we read,

Marianne would have thought herself very inexcusable had she been able to sleep at all the first night after parting from Willoughby. She would have been ashamed to look her family in the face the next morning, had she not risen from her bed in more need of repose than when she lay down in it.[33]

Then, after Willoughby's rebuff and Elinor's attempts to persuade her to exercise a little self-control, at least in public, Marianne declares that she 'must feel' and that she 'must be wretched' no matter what other people may think. In part, of course, this determination to manifest emotion is prompted by the view that self-command is itself a sign of weak affections and thus an indication of a lack of sensibility,[34] this being an accusation which Marianne levels at her sister. But, it is also clear that indulgence in emotion is seen as a duty important enough to override convention, even indeed to justify behaviour considered improper or impolite by others.

When Elinor upbraids her sister for being too forthcoming with Willoughby, Marianne replies that she had indeed been 'open and sincere' where presumably Elinor thinks that she should have been 'reserved, spiritless, dull and deceiptful'.[35] On subsequent occasions, Marianne's commitment to being 'open and sincere' leads to behaviour which causes embarrassment to others. Not that this concerns Marianne very much; her attachment to 'sincerity' means that she dislikes convention and is inclined to ignore it, whilst she is not averse to being rude to those people whom she considers to lack taste or sensibility.

This point is worth noting because it reveals the extent to which the ethic of sensibility had an 'inner-directed' quality. All too often, eighteenth-century sensibility has been referred to as a 'fashion', and not only is this patently not an explanation of the phenomenon, it is also misleading in its implication that the behaviour simply arose out of the social forces of imitation and emulation. Obviously there are elements of imitation in all forms of social conduct, but in so far as middle-class character ideals are concerned, orientation to the approval of others is likely to be less important than self-esteem. At the same time, an overwhelming desire to hold a good opinion of oneself is independent of the values contained in the ideal, which may be either ascetic or hedonistic; the assumption that inner-directedness is more closely associated with Puritan asceticism than Puritan emotionality being unwarranted.

There is another sense in which the ideal of sensibility could be said to be 'inner-directed' and this is with respect to the faculty of imagination. It was this that helped to determine Marianne's actions once Willoughby had entered her life, as 'he was all that her fancy had delineated' for her in day-dreams,[36] his person and air 'being equal to what her fancy had ever drawn for the hero of a favourite story'. Marianne had an 'active' imagination of the kind which, in her day, was considered to derive from reading too many novels, and this led her to have extravagant expectations of reality; expectations which were quite capable of distorting her perception, as happens when she mistakes Edward for Willoughby.[38] However, her strong imagination and penchant for dreaming also meant that she had the power to turn inwards, settling, for example, into 'a gloomy dejection' whilst 'brooding over her sorrows in silence',[39] in addition to being able to 'collect her thoughts within herself' in a crowded shop as easily as if she was in her own bedroom.[40] In other words, whilst she could employ her imagination to construct an illusioned view of the world about her, she could also retreat into the private and secluded inner world of imagination itself. This feature of sensibility is proto-romantic and anticipates the direction of later development.

The moral duty to give full expression to all emotions, together with the pleasures which feelings can supply, naturally tend to support one another in pushing the person of sensibility into orgies of emotional indulgence, there being neither any inclination nor any obligation to exercise restraint. This point is stressed repeatedly with respect to Marianne's conduct. When distraught at Willoughby's sudden departure, she was 'without any power, because she was without any desire of command over herself',[41] whilst the next day she was busy indulging her feelings of misery to the full, visiting those places where they had been alone together and playing their favourite pieces at the piano.[42] Later, when she discovers Willoughby's change of heart toward her, she exhibits 'torrents of unresisted [and] impetuous' grief.[43] All of which is in sharp contrast to her sister's behaviour, representing as it does the apparent embodiment of stoicism. She consistently displays a remarkable 'composure of mind' which is attained by 'constant and painful exertion',[44] and when Marianne recovers from her fever and is no longer in any danger of dying, Elinor does not take part in the general celebration:

[She] could not be cheerful. Her joy was of a different kind, and led to anything rather than to gaiety. Marianne restored to life, health, friends, and to her doting mother, was an idea to fill her heart with sensations of exquisite comfort, and expand it in fervent gratitude; – but it led to no outward demonstrations of joy, no words, no smiles. All within Elinor's breast was satisfaction, silent and strong.[45]

This appears to be less stoic than Calvinistic in the coupling of a fierce determination not to display emotion with a confident, if not actually smug, sense of self-satisfaction. It is interesting to note, however, that strong feelings were experienced (as 'exquisite comfort' and 'fervent gratitude' imply) and were not considered undesirable in themselves, as true stoicism would require. Thus only in their attitudes towards the expression of emotion do the sisters seem to represent a true contrast.

Most of the ingredients which go to make up the cult of sensibility are united in Marianne's character. She is full of powerful feelings, impulsively expressed, and 'her opinions are all romantic';[46] she knows when it is her duty to cry or avoid company, and how to judge sensibility in others. Whilst the strand of melancholy is well represented for she knows how to make the most of those 'moments of precious, of invaluable misery', when she can 'rejoice' in 'tears of agony' and wallow in 'luxurious solitude'.[47] Yet she is also capable of 'affectionate', if not exactly benevolent, sensibility in relation to the plight of others; something she is moved to express, for example, when she feels that her sister has been slighted,[48] whilst she is quick enough to feel pity for Willoughby. But above all, perhaps the characteristic of sensibility which is most prominent in Marianne (and indeed central to the plot of the book) is her enthusiasm for romantic love.

It is important to recognize that romantic love is little more than one element in the total ethic of sensibility, and hence that its rise to prominence in the eighteenth century can only be understood in terms of this more-embracing cultural movement. Its beliefs exactly parallel those present in the wider context, simply being applied to interpersonal heterosexual relationships. In that sense, romantic sensibility is but a special instance of sensibility in general. The key ingredients of romantic love have been outlined earlier and it was noted there how central is the idea that 'the giving of full rein to personal emotions is admirable, no matter how exaggerated and absurd the resulting conduct may appear to others',[49] and, as we have seen, this is a keystone of sensibility. The other ingredients Stone mentions also have their parallel in general sensibility; love at first sight, for example, is but a special case of the importance attached to 'first impressions' in the philosophy of sensibility.[50] Then again, the idea that 'love is the most important thing in the world, to which all other considerations, particularly material ones, should be sacrificed'[51] is but an echo of the general affirmation of the superiority of the spiritual over the material encountered in sensibility. 'What has wealth or grandeur to do with happiness?' asks Marianne, proceeding to upbraid her sister for believing that money can bring happiness; 'beyond a competence it can afford no real satisfaction, as far as mere self is concerned'.[52] Lastly, the idealization of character, and the belief that there is only one other person in the world with whom complete intimacy is possible, does have its non-lover counterpart in sensibility with the idea of 'true', 'special' or 'bosom' friendships. As Mansell notes, 'in the novels of sensibility it is just short of obligatory for young ladies to meet and fall into sudden, apocalyptic friendships'[53] and cites the example of Laura and Sophia in Jane Austen's *Love and Friendship* where the two, having just met, 'flew into each others arms and after having exchanged vows of mutual Friendship for the rest of our Lives, instantly unfolded to each other the most inward Secrets of our Hearts'.[54] A similar sudden intimacy, ending in 'sisterly happiness' occurs between Catherine and Isabella in *Northanger Abbey*, and reaches such a state that, after only a very short acquaintance, Isabella is able to declare to Catherine that she knows her better than she knows herself.[55] Mansell is very specific about the relationship between the concept of 'love' and that of 'friendship' in the novels of sensibility. After observing that they frequently occur coupled together in a single phrase, he comments that '"Love" in these cases is the heterosexual manifestation of "friendship", the two together making up the sum total of sensibility'.[56]

Marianne is portrayed as a firm believer in the creed of romantic sensibility. Love to her means 'falling a sacrifice to an irresistible passion'[57] for a man whose tastes reflect her own so exactly that 'one can enter into all feelings of the other'.[58] This mutual empathy arises out of a compatability of temperament or 'disposition', and cannot be acquired if that is lacking.[59] Such a relationship can only be encountered once, with just one other person and hence only one 'true' love can be experienced in a lifetime. Thus second marriages, indeed second attachments with any pretence of romance, are an anathema to her.[60] We have already seen that she knows how to behave when 'in love'; that is to say, with joyous impetuosity when with one's loved one, and with indulgent sorrow and melancholy when apart, being especially dejected at separation.[61] All of which adds up to a clearly defined role of 'lover' that can be seen to derive its form from the wider philosophy of sensibility.

One especially crucial question now requires consideration. From whence does the obligatory ingredient in the ethic of sensibility derive? Given that indulgence in emotion is given legitimacy as a consequence of being linked to a display of virtuous feelings, what makes them so? What are the reasons which cause Marianne to feel that she 'must' indulge her feelings to the full? How is it that she can feel that it is right to behave in such an impulsive manner, with excess of emotion, when it is clear that this frequently contravenes convention, distresses her relatives and friends, and does little or nothing to serve her own interests? Obviously she feels that this is how she should behave, and although, toward the end of the novel, she can be said to have acquired some 'sense', this merely makes her earlier conduct seem unwise rather than unethical. References to religion are few indeed and there is little evidence to suggest that a benevolentist Protestant theology is still operative to provide sensibility with its ethical justification, so from whence does this derive?[62] Some indications of where one should look for an answer to this question can be found in the text of the novel. One of them is the common tendency to use the term 'taste' as a cognate term for sensibility, whilst another is the inclusion of references to the cult of the picturesque. But there is one incident which is perhaps especially revealing.

This concerns the intended excursion to Whitwell. On that occasion Marianne and Willoughby steal away from the rest of the party in order to spend the day alone viewing the house at Allenham, and she is subsequently reprimanded by her sister for the impropriety of this conduct. By way of a defence Marianne observes that she had 'never spent a pleasanter morning in [her] life', words which lead Elinor to remark, somewhat priggishly, that 'the pleasantness of an employment does not always evince its propriety'. This calls forth the following rejoinder from Marianne:

On the contrary, nothing can be stronger proof of it, Elinor; for if there had been any real impropriety in what I did, I should have been sensible of it at the time, for we always know when we are acting wrong, and with such a conviction I could have had no pleasure.[63]

Marianne's confident assertion that 'we always know' when we are doing wrong does not seem to stem from any assumed familiarity with the norms and conventions governing social intercourse. On that basis, she would have known that she was doing wrong, as her sister did. Her certainty that she wasn't therefore must have derived from some other source, and the implication is that it was acquired intuitively. At the same time, Marianne appears actually to aver the opposite of Elinor's statement about the relationship between pleasure and propriety, seeing the former as 'proof' of the latter. This is a rather startling suggestion, as there is a very profound difference between claiming that the knowledge that you are doing something wrong prevents you from enjoying it, and the assertion that because an action is pleasurable it must be right. This quotation is thus of special interest because of its implication of a direct connection between pleasure and virtue, something which seems to transcent the previous association of goodness with displays of approved emotion, and hence represents an evolution beyond the Protestant cults of benevolence and melancholy. It is also a cultural development of the most crucial importance for the emergence of modern hedonism. In order to understand how this shift occurred, it is necessary to consider the one area of cultural life where the pleasant and the good had long been intimately linked.

A middle-classicist aesthetic

The classical aesthetic tradition, which derived its ideas principally from Aristotle, was built upon the axiom that the function of art was to please whilst providing moral instruction, beauty being the distinctive quality of those works which achieved this end through techniques in conformity with long-established principles. These specified that art should 'imitate' nature, not in a straightforward, naturalistic fashion, but via an idealized representation of content and form in which the values of harmony, balance and order predominated. The principal subject-matter, also largely Graeco-Roman in inspiration, consisting of epic themes featuring the exploits of noble heroes.

Eighteenth-century neo-classicism reaffirmed much of this whilst attempting to link these assumptions to more specifically Enlightenment ideas. Uniformitarianism, for example, was applied enthusiastically to aesthetics as elsewhere, and in accord with the view that there was only one human nature, a vigorous attempt was made to discover those universal laws which governed the creation of beauty. Here too the assumption made was that such immutable rules could be discovered either by direct rational reflection or through observation of that which did, in practice, please all. As Lovejoy explains:

Uniformitarianism is, moreover, worked out in the same dual way in the neo-classical aesthetics as in deism: on the one hand, the reader or beholder is sometimes bidden to rely solely upon his own judgement or feeling – once it is purified of prejudices and is a genuine expression of 'common nature' – in judging the value or 'beauty' of a work of art; on the other hand, he is bidden to accept the *consensus gentium* as the test of merit, and allow himself to like only what everybody else has always liked.[64]

Somewhat safer than either of these methods, however, is the process of studying the classics, for that which has been esteemed over a long period must be in accord with the true standards of beauty. All three methods, it was assumed, would ultimately lead to the discovery of the same truths, which were considered to be as equally self-evident to the artist as to his patron. Both saw themselves as representatives of humanity, giving expression to, and appreciating, that which all human beings recognized as truly beautiful. Such a philosophy did not allow much room for the idiosyncratic, or the original, whilst 'enthusiasm' was as suspect in art as in religion.[65]

This neo-classical aesthetic tradition had little direct appeal to the newly affluent and increasingly influential tradesmen, merchants, yeoman farmers and skilled artisans of eighteenth-century England, as the principal subject-matter was too far removed from their interests, whilst the treatment was to unemotional to cater adequately for their tastes. At the same time, some of them felt a certain respect for the venerable nature of the tradition and recognized that considerable prestige was attached, not merely to the artist working within it, but to anyone who could reasonably claim to appreciate his work. It was in the context of such attitudes of ambivalence, therefore, that aesthetics itself became a battleground in the class struggle for cultural hegemony waged in the second half of the century. For as the middle classes sought to contest the elite's taken-for-granted claim to moral and cultural superiority, they increasingly found that their own lack of any legitimate claim to aesthetic distinction counted against them.

Just as the eighteenth-century English aristocracy were most vulnerable to the criticisms of immorality and extravagance, so were the rising middle classes most vulnerable to the charge of being vulgar, that is, of lacking 'taste' in both the behavioural and aesthetic senses of that word. In order to counter this accusation, there was a move to develop an essentially 'bourgeois' aesthetic and norm of conduct, and to argue that it, and not

upper-class neo-classicism, represented 'good taste'.[66] To a considerable extent, this could only be achieved by adopting some of those
classical ideas concerning aesthetics which had been a part of this elite
tradition, for no indigenous bourgeois school of aesthetics really existed.
But, at the same time, no matter what aesthetic was adopted, it still had to
reflect the real pattern of preferences for pleasure characteristic of these
classes or, of course, it would not be accepted. The solution was to adapt
essentially neo-classical ideas in such a way as to permit the incorporation of fundamentally Protestant attitudes; something which individual
artists had been struggling to achieve for some time, giving rise to a
tradition which Fairchild punningly dubbed 'middle-classicism'. As he
observed, many bourgeois writers and poets who aspired to neo-classical
forms and ideals imposed upon them 'something of the religiosity, the
moral urgency, sober utilitarianism, the suppressed emotionalism, of the
rising middle class'.[67] The trouble with the ensuing 'bastard' products
was that they ran the risk of pleasing no one, whilst still laying their
creators and appreciators open to the charge of not possessing true taste.
Only by replacing the aristocratic neo-classical system of aesthetics with
a bourgeois version could one successfully cater for both middle-class
taste and pride. This was eventually achieved by blending the moral and
emotional features mentioned by Fairchild with certain classical ideas in
such a way as to produce the philosophy of sentimentalism, and ironically
enough, it was an aristocrat, the Third Earl of Shaftesbury (1671–1713),
who was to contribute most to this alternative ethico-aesthetic tradition.[68]

We have already seen how the Cambridge Platonists had developed a
theory of ethics in which a sympathetically inspired capacity for
benevolence was substituted for 'reason' as the characteristic possession
of man. Shaftesbury, in *Characteristics of Man, Manners, Opinions, Times*,
published in 1711, built upon this foundation, and drawing extensively
from a wide range of classical sources, proposed that man – more than
simply having a conscience – possessed an intuitive moral sense; a 'sense'
or understanding of what is good and right, as well as a natural desire to
carry it out. One cannot be good, according to Shaftesbury, out of either
a desire for reward or a fear of punishment; virtuous behaviour can only
be conduct which is freely chosen, arising directly out of one's very
being. The good man is simply incapable of doing harm, and hence has
no need to ponder the rights and wrongs of different courses of action:

He never deliberates . . . or considers of the matter by prudential rules of
self-interest and advantage. He acts from his nature, in a manner necessarily,
and without reflection; and if he did not, it were impossible for him to answer his
character, or be found that truly well-bred man of every occasion.[69]

As Bredvold comments, such a doctrine reduces the idea of virtue to little
more than 'a matter of passions and feelings', elevating the 'moral sense'

above judgement, conventional morality, the law or even conscience. Yet this is indeed Shaftesbury's position, for he claims that such an intuitive faculty is, in the last resort, sovereign:

After all . . . it is not merely what we call principle, but a taste that governs men. They may think for certain, 'this is right, or that wrong' . . . yet if the savour of things lies cross to honesty . . . the conduct will infallibly turn this latter way.

Even conscience, I fear, such as is owing to religious discipline, will make but a slight figure where this taste is set amiss.[70]

It is obvious how such a doctrine served to support the cult of sensibility, asserting as it does that only feelings can be truly relied upon to indicate that which is good,[71] and it is perhaps now possible to perceive from whence Marianne might have derived her belief that 'we always know' when we have done wrong.

Yet what is of greater interest than Shaftesbury's observations on the existence of an intuitive moral sense *per se* is the fact that he extended the same argument to aesthetics. Following the classical association of goodness and beauty, he claimed that the virtuous soul must necessarily be characterized by harmony (as is the case with the natural world, being the creation of God) with the consequence that there is a beauty in goodness and a goodness in beauty. 'Will it not be found', he argues, 'that what is beautiful is harmonious and proportionable; what is harmonious and proportionable is true; and what is at once both beautiful and true is, of consequence agreeable and good?'[72]

Now Shaftesbury was not the first to link goodness with beauty: that was an axiom of classical thought. Nor indeed was he the first to speculate on man's possession of innate faculties through which one might gain knowledge of these, or indeed, to observe that pleasure was a natural link between them. What he did claim, which was essentially novel, was that it was through feelings rather than reason that these insights were to be obtained. This has the consequence of making formal rules appear irrelevant, both to the identification of beauty and the formulation of the good, as these could now be ascertained merely by 'trusting to one's feelings'. Since, however, pleasure had long been a defining characteristic of the beautiful, it could now also serve – in the form of emotional indulgence – as an indicator of virtue, a natural conclusion being that whatever aroused feelings of pleasure was both beautiful and good.

This was a revolutionary conclusion, opening up new possibilities for moral action. Whereas it had been theoretically possible within the classical tradition to argue that obtaining pleasure was an indication of the virtue of an act, this line of argument had been severely restricted by the supreme position accorded to reason, supported by a deep suspicion of all strong emotion. When combined with the unquestioned authority of the ancients this meant that unchanging rules governed what was deemed good and beautiful, closely constraining what anyone might experience as pleasurable. Morality, like art, involved both restraint and the following of rules. Thus by making both morality and aesthetics a matter of emotional intuition, Shaftesbury left the way open for the classical test of beauty to be applied to virtue independently of reason or tradition. The fact that a course of action not only 'felt right' but, in addition, gave pleasure, could now be advanced as a forceful argument in favour of its propriety.[73]

What Shaftesbury's theory did, therefore, was to make ethics and aesthetics virtually interchangeable, with sensibility the term which embraced them both.[74] Typically it covered feeling sorry for oneself, feeling sorry for others, and being moved by beauty, and yet all responses had equal significance as indications of goodness. Responsiveness to beauty thus became a crucial moral quality, such that any deficiency in this respect became a moral lapse, whilst correspondingly virtue became an aesthetic quality, such that, in turn, any moral lapse was 'bad taste'. This is a significant extension of the doctrine of signs for it makes 'taste' the most important of an individual's qualities, a point which can be illustrated by turning back to *Sense and Sensibility* and noting how it is that an individual's 'taste', 'sensibility' and 'virtue' (the terms are, significantly, used almost interchangeably by Marianne) is actually assessed.

A person's ethical sensibility was understandably largely judged by their treatment of others, especially such stock symbols of pathos as small children, the poor and animals, and if they did indeed possess a 'true delicacy', then they were expected to experience and display a genuine pity; an emotion which, it was assumed, would lead on to generous, philanthropic actions. It is in this regard that 'insensibility' came to be a synonym for cruelty.[75] A more direct and convenient way of assessing an individual's sensibility, however, especially at first meeting or where their treatment of others could not easily be observed, was through their aesthetic taste or sense of beauty. This could be done indirectly, as Marianne does in establishing Willoughby's feelings about Scott, Cowper and Pope or,[76] more directly, by observing an individual's reaction to specific works of art, such as Elinor's drawings; or indeed through their appreciation of the performing arts, by the necessity of reacting to Marianne's piano playing, for example. More critically, one could be asked to demonstrate sensibility through one's own performance, as poor Edward is called upon to do by reading Cowper, and is judged 'insensible' by Marianne for his failure to read him in a sufficiently animated spirit.[77] Equally, one's reaction to the beauties of nature could serve as a measure, with appreciation of the picturesque the critical test.

The picturesque was a term, much in vogue in the 1770s and 1780s, which stood for that which was visually striking in nature: literally, like a picture. Praz suggests that 'a hovel beneath a gnarled oak, with an aged gipsy, a rusty donkey, mellow tints and dark shadows' would be a typical example of a picturesque subject, along with a cross-eyed parson's daughter,[78] and that the fashion for the picturesque profoundly affected garden design as well as painting. Edward teases Marianne about her liking for it by observing that if she were rich she would 'buy every book that tells her how to admire an old twisted tree',[79] but he has to confess that he lacks such a taste, preferring that which is sensible or useful:

I like a fine prospect, but not on picturesque principles. I do not like crooked, twisted, blasted trees. I admire them much more if they are tall, straight, and flourishing. I do not like ruined, tattered cottages. I am not fond of nettles, or thistles, or heath blossoms. I have more pleasure in a snug farm-house than a watch-tower, and a troop of tidy, happy villagers please me better than the finest banditti in the world.[80]

Since it is clear that Edward does not really subscribe to that cult of sensibility at whose shrine Marianne is such a devout worshipper, he can presumably accept her necessarily negative judgement of him with some degree of equanimity. For those who do share her values, however, such is not likely to be the case, for they will see the failure to express 'correct' aesthetic judgements as direct evidence of a lack of virtue. This view has profound implications for patterns of consumption since these individuals are bound to regard all those objects which advertise their taste as also indicating their moral standing. Here, surely, is the probable answer to that conundrum of how the middle classes could change their attitudes toward luxury consumption so markedly from the seventeenth to the eighteenth centuries. Whilst in both periods the predominant concern was with moral issues, and especially with gaining reassurance concerning the essential goodness of one's soul, changes in ethical theory meant that this was sought in different forms of conduct. Asceticism was now less significant than manifesting sensibility, something which required continuing evidence of one's good taste.

As noted earlier, McKendrick described the consumer revolution as occurring because families which 'had long been in command of income sufficient to acquire new possessions . . . now . . . felt *compelled* to do so' (italics added)[81], whilst adding that 'in the late eighteenth century large numbers in society felt that they *must* be in fashion, whether they liked it or not' (italics in the original).[82] Surely the nature of such compulsion could only be moral in essence? Something which can now be appreciated given the aesthetico-ethical nature of the concept of taste. It was, therefore, precisely because the middle classes had such a strong Puritan inheritance that they were so eager to 'follow fashion' and hence to consume 'luxury' goods with avidity. This they did out of a deep-seated fear that they might be (and be thought to be) lacking in virtue. Their predominant concern was thus to protect their character by manifesting 'taste', rather than improve their status by exhibiting pecuniary strength.

A matter of taste

It should be clear at this point how central the phenomenon of taste is to the solution of the general problem which is the focus of this work. At one and the same time implicated in pleasure-seeking and the formulation of ideals of character, it serves to articulate consumer behaviour with changes in the intellectual content of aesthetic and ethical systems of thought. What is more, it is clearly fundamental to that institution which has repeatedly surfaced as the epitome of modern consumerism, to wit, the Western European fashion pattern. It is therefore important to examine briefly the historical background to eighteenth-century discussions of this concept before identifying those different strands of thought about taste found in modern society.[83]

Although in its strictly gustatory sense the word had long been employed prior to the seventeenth and eighteenth centuries, it was at that time, as Spingarn notes, that it first became an important term in European criticism;[84] whilst Wellek states that it became 'the subject of elaborate theorizing only in the early eighteenth century'.[85] The main reason for this upsurge of interest lay in the neo-classical attempt to discover the universal rules or laws which determine why it is that some objects in nature and in art are regarded as pleasing or beautiful. Classical standards themselves were not at first called into doubt, being merely subject to examination in accord with the new empirical spirit of the age. As the century progressed, however, and these standards became opposed by emotional sensibility, whilst empirical enquiries raised more problems than they solved, the search for a new and acceptable universal standard of taste increasingly became the focus of concern.

Addison, in a series of articles in his *Spectator* in 1712, in which he outlined many of the topics that were to be among the main subjects of debate for the next seventy to eighty years, defined taste as 'that faculty of the soul which discerns the beauties of an author with pleasure, and the imperfections with dislike'.[86] He goes on to make it clear that he is using the term as a metaphor, based on the likeness of 'mental taste' to that 'sensitive taste which gives us a relish of every different flavour that affects the palate',[87] which, although a natural faculty, needs to be cultivated by reading and instruction. Addison's position is recognizably a classical one, yet his use of the appetite analogy, which is increasingly employed during the subsequent decades, is fraught with danger, raising as it does the possibility of the principle of *de gustibus non est disputandum* being applied to aesthetics.

One of the problems which the neo-classicists had to face in settling upon an acceptable standard for taste was that they could no longer simply appeal to the authority of tradition, for the Enlightenment had made all sources of authority subject to the scrutiny of reason. Thus, whilst asserting that the rules enunciated by the ancients were indeed correct, they sought to find a new foundation for them on rational principles; these, of course, could only be ascertained through thoughtful introspection or by observation of that common denominator in aesthetic judgement present in all people. The abbé Dubos in his *Reflexions Critiques sur la Poesie et sur la Peinture* (translated into English in 1748) had argued that 'All that the dogmatic critics had laid down ought to be reconsidered and verified by the laws of experience',[88] and although his opinions were often the same as these 'dogmatic critics', he did open the door to a line of thinkers who (acting on his suggestion) reached rather different conclusions. These, the aesthetic empiricists, included Hutcheson, Hume, Gerard, Burke, Kames, Blair, Reynolds and Alison, all of whom, in different ways, sought through psychological investigation to discover what objects and qualities are universally pleasing to men.

These writers believed that there was an ideal and universal standard of taste, and were motivated by a desire to offset the growing feeling that this discerning faculty, based upon individual sensibility, expressed itself in such a complex and manifold way that no such measure could exist. They were not to succeed, however, and Hooker concludes from his analysis of their writings, that in the period 1750–70

there was no agreement as to the nature of beauty or as to a standard of taste; critics could agree upon no single principle as essential to beauty; and those principles which were offered, were either ambiguous and thus useless in the formation of rules, or were insusceptible of any objective test.[89]

Far from reaching a consensus these writers tended to undermine each other's arguments, thereby actually adding to the general doubt and confusion.[90]

Hooker notes that throughout the intellectual debate over taste there existed a strong current of popular opinion, which, dissatisfied with the confused and conflicting opinions manifest by the intellectuals and aestheticians, was in favour of a simple solution to the problem. As he comments,

There existed a strong conviction among the public that taste should be free from critics' laws, that beauty cannot be analysed, and that every man is competent to decide for himself, by virtue of his sensibility, on works of art.[91]

This populist current clearly reflected a growing individualism as well as the greater influence of the middle classes, who were increasingly inclined to be irritated by the aesthetic paternalism of neo-classical writers. It is therefore understandable that a new emphasis should be placed upon self-determin~tion in matters of taste.

What is more, such a position now seemed increasingly intellectually justifiable through a coming together of the doctrines of sensibility with the findings of the associational psychologists. The idea that each person had an innate and intuitive aesthetic sense which could, without the aid of judgement, unerringly 'know' what was beautiful, had not, in the thought of Shaftesbury and Hutcheson, been divorced from the belief that there was, none the less, a universal and uniform standard of beauty. But the Humean insistence that beauty was not an attribute of nature but merely a name for our reaction to it, meant that sensibility could be seen as totally subjectivist: an individual's intuitive sense was unique to him. In this way, it appeared that intellectual thought severed all connection between 'taste' and judgement, thereby legitimizing aesthetic relativism.

Now, at first sight, such a doctrine might seem highly congenial to modern consumerism with its strong emphasis upon the right of the individual to purchase whatever products satisfy his tastes without interference. It is, after all, a corollary of the doctrine of *laissez-faire*, and Hooker provides quotes to show how it was coming to be advocated in the mid-eighteenth century in place of the more traditional classical-based didacticism. He cites Dr Armstrong's poem on 'Taste' (1753), with the couplet:

> Judge for yourself; and as you find, report
> Of wit, as freely as of beef or port;[92]

together with an anonymous reviewer in the *Gentleman's Magazine* in 1767, commenting on *Tristram Shandy* to the effect that: 'In questions of taste, however, every one must determine for himself; and what is humour is as much a question of taste, as what is beauty.'[93] Certainly it was the case that popular taste was increasingly being catered for, whilst attempts to educate and improve the people in matters of aesthetic judgement, although not abandoned, were embarked upon with less and less hope of success as the century progressed.[94] Such a trend might suggest that ideas about aesthetics would become irrelevant to public taste as individuals came to act more and more upon their personal pattern of preferences.

This was, indeed, one important strand in the cultural traditions which emerged at this time. Basically, this position treated Addison's analogy linking aesthetic and gustatory taste as an identity, such that all taste was considered a purely individual and subjective matter not open to general dispute. An individual's likes and dislikes, in art as much as food and drink, were thus personal and unchallengeable. Such a view was sometimes advocated out of a spirit of liberality and freedom; an assertion of consumer (and artistic) freedom in response to those who sought to dictate what good taste should be.[95] As it was usually associated with the doctrine of innate and intuitive taste, however, it also tended to become, in effect, no more than simple philistinism. For, by excluding knowledge or judgement from any significant role in the formation of individuated taste, this position amounted to the familiar cry of, 'I may not know much about art, but I know what I like.' This exclusion of judgement from any part in the formation of taste was a widespread element in both middle- and working-class cultures in the late eighteenth and early nineteenth centuries, finding its intellectual expression in utilitarianism. Bentham, in his famous passage about push-pin and poetry, dismisses the distinction between 'good' and 'bad' taste as no more than a matter of custom and prejudice, and although he subsequently reintroduces it, it is only in relation to purely instrumental values. Thus, in effect, he completely de-aestheticizes the concept of taste.[96]

Contrary to first impressions, however, such a perspective is not especially favourable to modern consumerism, for, whilst it upholds the principle of consumer sovereignty in an extreme form, it does so at the expense of the system's essential dynamic. Taste as an ethical and aesthetic concept is indispensible to consumer behaviour, both to facilitate choice and to ensure the generation of new wants, and hence attempts to reduce it to some other dimension of experience merely promotes traditionalism. The utilitarians tried to make consumption entirely an issue of rational choice in the matter of satisfying needs, thereby seeking to eliminate the ingredient of desire entirely. Since this is an impossibility all that is actually achieved is the endorsement of whatever aesthetic values individuals acquired in their formative years, which is why those who pride themselves on their philistinism never have modern tastes.

The same result is achieved by those who endorse populism, scorning the 'authority' of connoisseurs and critics, whether they embrace utilitarianism or not, as the claim that personal taste is a purely subjective and intuitive matter is empirically false. It is, in fact, the product of ethical and aesthetic ideas, in addition to the undoubted contribution of inherited and biographical factors, and hence necessarily reflects wider intellectual and cultural changes. Whilst modern consumerism does require individuals to accept some responsibility for their tastes, this tends to carry with it the need to form aesthetic judgements, not the opportunity to avoid them. Attempts to de-aestheticize taste are likely to fail in any case because of the ineradical ethical component. Since this refers to generally desired personal qualities, it will only be those few eccentrics who do not care whether they are considered to 'lack taste' who will, in practice, be prepared to follow such a path.

In fact, in the eighteenth century at least, the idea that taste was merely a matter of direct and uninformed intuition involving little judgement, knowledge or evaluation, was rarely advanced and not, it would appear, widely held. It was common, for example, to argue that differences in taste were due to defective knowledge or judgement, and that even 'natural' good taste required training. Sometimes it was claimed that 'true taste' could only be possessed by the elite few. In any case, it seems to have become common, by the turn of the century, to distinguish between a 'natural' and a 'refined' taste, suggesting that whilst this quality may have become regarded as a more individual matter, judgement was still considered a necessary ingredient.

If the populist, subjectivist response to the problem of an agreed aesthetic standard was rejected as unworkable, then some other solution had to be found, for taste formed an indissoluble part of the prevailing ideal of character. As Hooker quotes a reviewer of Gerard's *Essays on Taste* as remarking in 1759, 'all men sought to be thought men of taste',[97] and yet as the contents of those and many others essays of the period revealed, no fixed standard could be agreed on; with the consequence that the word, 'though in almost every-body's mouth, is used in a very loose and indeterminate sense'.[98] This combination of circumstances, where a strong desire to manifest a highly valued personal quality existed, and yet no commonly agreed aesthetic standard could be found to replace the classical ideal, led to the development of modern fashion, the other crucial factor being the very real demand for novelty which the search for emotional pleasure naturally stimulated. Fashion became the *de facto* answer to the problem which none of the eighteenth-century writers on taste could solve; that is, how to find a commonly agreed, aesthetic standard, which, whilst actually catering for people's real preferences, could also continue to serve as the basis for an ideal of character. These writers, whilst perceiving the need for such a standard, had understandably assumed that it would be based upon universal and unchanging rules; the sociological necessity, however, was merely that there should be a given standard in operation at any one time (so that ordered and meaningful expressive interaction could occur) whilst the psychological necessity, arising out of the form of modern hedonism, demanded change. The consequence was the development of that institution for the continuous but orderly change in aesthetic standards which is known as the Western European fashion pattern.[99]

In fact, this pattern does embody a fixed and agreed aesthetic standard by which beauty is determined: it is the criterion of stimulative pleasure as achieved through novelty.[100] This is the basic taste which the institution reflects, and without which fashion in modern societies would be as static as it is in traditional ones. The origin and form of individual fashions, and the part played in developing and promoting them by manufacturers and designers, is really a matter of little consequence compared with the origin of this underlying predisposition, for if there was no popular demand for novelty, no new style, no matter what form it took would meet with much enthusiasm. Contrary to the view of many observers, the underlying impetus for changes in style thus comes from the consumers and not the producers,[101] taste, in this general sense, being the phenomenon upon which modern fashion is ultimately dependent.[102] But the debate over taste, precipitated by the collapse of classicism, did not lead immediately to the widespread and universal adoption of a basic attitude of this kind, as a crucial difference still existed between the middle-class and aristocratic outlooks on aesthetics; a difference which meant that, for several decades at least, two rival conceptions of taste were to be advocated.

As we have seen, the middle classes embarked upon a strenuous campaign to promote an aesthetic which served both to endorse their real preferences and to advance a character ideal which made appreciation of beauty a matter of genuine emotional sensitivity and responsiveness. Correspondingly, they advocated an interpretation of taste which presented it as a quasi-charismatic quality of near-spiritual dimensions. This was naturally not particularly to the liking of the aristocracy, who could detect the vulgar tone of 'enthusiasm' which inspired this formulation. They were still drawn to the classical ideal in which the intimate association with noble birth inevitably leads to the exclusion of all inferior classes from the possibility of aesthetic privilege. Hence they favoured restraint and refinement, even if the possibility of associating these values with a universal and unchanging standard of beauty no longer existed. Since reason had let them down, they now fell back upon social acceptability, employing the norms and conventions which prevailed within 'Society' as the basis for a workable aesthetic; good taste thus meant that form of conduct which, in an elegantly refined style, gave most pleasure to one's peers.[103]

To achieve this required the development of an exclusive, close-knit group, within which clearly agreed standards could emerge and operate, something which was easily accomplished in aristocratic circles. Such a test could only really be applied to conduct for judgement ultimately rested upon the degree of conformity to a social code and standards of decorum, good form and etiquette. Consequently, this aesthetic had very limited application; it could hardly be used, for example, in relation to nature or works of art. In fact, even dress itself was not assessed as 'art', but as an aspect of conduct.[104] Critically, however, dress and general appearance was taken as a major indication of the degree of one's mastery of good form as a whole and hence as a prime index of character. Here too, then, there is the same fundamental equation between 'taste' and goodness that existed in the middle-class cult of sensibility.

It is interesting to note that Marianne had a low opinion of anyone who did not possess 'a strong sensibility and the graces of a polished manner'.[105] The mention of sensibility is unsurprising, but its association with the graces of a polished manner is intriguing for these are essentially aristocratic virtues, and it would not have occurred to a true romantic of the later period to link them in such an unproblematic fashion. Clearly, at the time when the cult of sensibility was at its height, tension between the two contrasting formulations of the concept of taste was still largely implicit, there being little recognition of the ambiguity contained in the term. As the eighteenth century gave way to the nineteenth, however, this contradiction became more apparent until middle-class individualistic sensibility finally evolved into a Bohemian romanticism, whilst the socially oriented, exclusivist ethic of the elite developed into the stoic mannerism of the dandies.

8

The Aristocratic Ethic

For the dandy self-control and self-pride were all.

Baudelaire

We have already had occasion to note how, in the standard account of the consumer revolution in eighteenth-century England, a crucial role is attributed to the strengthening of the emulative desires of the middle classes. These are portrayed as eager to adopt the manners, customs and luxurious style of life exemplified by the aristocracy, whilst an ambition to enhance status is identified as the dynamic mechanism lying at the heart of their new propensity to consume. At the same time, we have also observed how a fresh enthusiasm for luxury goods had to be accounted for in the context of the Puritanically inspired asceticism which was such a prominent feature of the cultural inheritance of these social groups. The widely adopted approach to this problem has been to suggest that imitation of the aristocratic way of life was both cause and consequence of the decay of asceticism, a 'solution' which begs as many questions as it answers. This conclusion led to the development of an alternative view, one which concentrates upon demonstrating how Protestantism itself evolved in such a manner as to unintentionally endorse a hedonistically inclined emotionalist ethic, especially when certain neo-classicist aesthetic ideas were added to this strong moral tradition. At no point, however, has the nature of the ethic which informed the aristocratic way of life itself been the subject of consideration, and hence the basic pre-mise underlying the standard view – which is the assumption that an elite ethic is more conducive to modern consumerism than a 'bourgeois' one – has not been examined. It is now time to see if that claim can be supported.

The cavalier ethic

Once again, the Civil War and the ensuing Restoration period will be

taken as a convenient point of departure, and a start made by briefly
examining the 'cavalier ethic'. The supporters of Charles I earned this
epithet not simply through loyalty to their king but because of their
characteristic attitude to life; that is, they tended to distrust the intense
and over-earnest, favouring the casual and offhand. In this they were
influenced by the ideal of the Renaissance gentleman and courtier which
specified that a man should be accomplished as a lover, soldier, wit, man
of affairs, musician and poet; noble birth was assumed whilst the only
honourable profession was to bear arms, and although required to be
accomplished in many fields, it was important for a gentleman to do them
all with nonchalence.[1] As a courtier there was an overriding obligation to
please, and to ensure that public occasions were free of all embarrassment. Apart from this, the central feature of the cavalier ethic was the
concept of honour, to which value, nothing, except perhaps duty to the
sovereign was superior. As Richard Lovelace, one of the better known of
the Cavalier poets, expressed it:

> I could not love thee, dear, so much
> Loved I not honour more.[2]

At the same time, this ideal of a proud, independent and accomplished
man, jealous of his honour, was almost entirely secular; religion was not a
matter of great concern and there was little attempt to plumb the depths
of the soul.[3] Such an ethic certainly appears to be more favourable to
pleasure-seeking than its antithesis, and the Puritans themselves
undoubtedly regarded the Cavaliers as licentious wantons. Obviously, it
was not an ascetic outlook, the sensual pleasures that were freely indulged
being symbolized by the expensive and flamboyant clothes which are still
today associated with the Cavalier image. Yet despite this, it was not an
ethic which could have provided the basis for modern hedonism.

The primary reason for this is that no premium was placed on passion;
it was an ethic of restraint, of casual yet limited displays of sentiment. Any
excess of emotion, whether of anguish or ecstasy, would be unseemly and
ungentlemanly, representing bad manners in a courtier. It is significant
that Skelton, in his assessment of the Cavalier Poets, identifies their one
great contribution to the English lyrical tradition as the celebration of 'the
minor pleasures and sadnesses of life' (italics added).[4] This absence of
passion meant that little interest in the enjoyment of powerful emotional
stimulation was likely to emerge from this particular cluster of values. In
addition, such an ethic was necessarily other-regarding in orientation.
The courtier was required, as we have noted, to ensure that his
behaviour was pleasing to others rather than to himself, and this concern
with the effects of action naturally inhibited the degree of interest in

self-gratification. But, above all, it was the supreme importance of the concept of honour, and hence the cavalier's reputation in the eyes of others, which constrained egoistic hedonism. As Lovelace's lines imply, pride took precedence over pleasure.

These two features, the avoidance of all emotional excess in the interest of restrained, 'civilized' behaviour, and the competition for honour within a small social elite, comprise the distinctive features of the aristocratic ethic both in the seventeenth and the eighteenth centuries. It was, in effect, a 'mannered' ethic, both in the sense that stress was placed upon the way things were done, and because behaviour was itself stylized, self-conscious, and closely governed by convention. Hence even though this ethic is capable of being adapted to suit a modern consumer-oriented culture, in itself it can hardly have brought this about. The negative attitude toward strong emotion carried with it a comparative lack of interest in the 'thrill' of feeling, and although the concern with reputation can be adjusted to aesthetic spheres, there is a lack of that intense introspective imagining which facilitates longing.

One obvious reason for the absence of these features from the aristocratic ethic is the influence of a classical aesthetic, the primary characteristics of which – restraint, order and harmony, in the context of respect for Graeco-Roman authorities – have already been noted.[5] As Schucking describes it, the aristocratic impulse in the arts 'strives after difficult and artificial forms, is esoteric, abominates realism ... despises simplicity, and goes in search of humanism and culture';[6] a search which found literal expression in eighteenth-century England in the practice of the Grand Tour. Yet the nobleman of the period found more than aesthetic inspiration in the cultural artifacts of classical civilization, for he was also likely to derive his ethical inspiration from their literary monuments, and, most especially, from the writings of the Stoics.[7]

Neo-Stoicism

Mark Roberts has argued that Stoicism was 'an active and effective' moral orthodoxy in the eighteenth century, and he uses the writings of that arch-Tory, Dr Johnson, to support his claim.[8] In particular, he discusses *The Vanity of Human Wishes*, which was written in deliberate imitation of Juvenal's tenth satire, arguing that despite the addition of some Christian views, the poem represents a basically Stoical position. This is one in which the trials and tribulations of life are regarded as unavoidable, and hence the wise man merely strives to obtain the strength to bear them; to hope for happiness is folly: a life of peace is all that can reasonably be desired. The real struggle is to prevent oneself being dominated by one's passions, and in order to achieve this it is necessary to strive for a state of 'apatheia'. This meant a state of being without feeling, a detachment, especially 'that deep, emotional detachment from the concerns of this world which allows one to will that things should be as they in fact are'.[9] The modern word apathy is derived from this term although the meaning is significantly different. Apatheia does not mean a lack of interest in earthly affairs so much as that contentment which derives from a severance of all emotional connections with the environment, leading in turn to an invulnerability to distress. In effect, one determines to accept that which exists, and in consequence finds peace.[10] An obvious problem, however, is how to attain such a state, and, more particularly, which feelings and desires, if any, it is legitimate to express.

It is here that the dominant characteristics of Enlightenment thought once again become apparent, because it is nature and reason which, in tandem, are used to resolve this dilemma. Every being in the Great Chain has its own 'nature' which it is required to obey; it is, for example, in the 'nature' of fish to swim, and in the 'nature' of cats to catch mice. Similarly, Dr Johnson argues, it is in the 'nature' of man to eat and to procreate children, whilst gluttony and lust are both 'unnatural'. It is, of course, reason which is employed to determine what is or is not in the 'nature' of man, because reason is man's most distinctive and special characteristic, that which distinguishes him from animals. Hence, in neo-Stoic philosophy, a man should live in accord with the dictates of his nature, and by the light of his reason, as both will point in the same direction. Evil as such does not exist, whilst wrongdoing arises out of cognitive error; that is, from a failure to see things as they really are and to will whatever is appropriate. 'Why', asks Dr Johnson, 'do men consistently fail to do the good thing? Because Reason is continually overborne by the passions, and it is these which create misunderstandings.'[11] Emotions must therefore be placed firmly under the control of reason, otherwise not only will men not be able to perceive wisely but they will be impelled to foolish actions. Thus it is that Stoicism leads to a deep suspicion of all emotion, and consequently to efforts to minimize its role in life. As Roberts observes, 'in practice Stoicism leaves little room for emotion of any kind. The only emotion which can safely be allowed to motivate action is the wish to have a will in conformity with nature.'[12]

Pleasure is understandably also under suspicion for it accompanies the gratification of desire. Here Dr Johnson's attitude is particularly forceful. Only rationally justifiable desires are to be indulged, and even then, great care must be taken to keep these in check, for the gratification of legitimate desires, if carried out too easily or too frequently, can lead to a taste for voluptuousness. Hence his advice:

To deny early and inflexibly is the only art of checking the importunity of desire, and of preserving quiet and innocence. Innocent gratifications must be sometimes withheld; he that complies with all lawful desires will certainly lose his empire over himself, and think all his desires lawful, or dismiss his reason as troublesome and intrusive, and resolve to snatch what he may happen to wish, without enquiry about right and wrong.[13]

The reference to 'innocent gratifications' shows how similar the Stoic position on pleasure was to that of the Puritans, for here too the crucial distinction is that between those pleasures which accompany the gratification of need, and pleasure conceived of as an end in itself. Dr Johnson's view was that held by Seneca, namely that

nature has intermingled pleasure with necessary things – not in order that we should seek pleasure, but in order that the addition of pleasure may make the indispensable means of existence attractive to our eyes. Should it claim rights of its own, it is luxury[14]

This is the clearest possible prohibition upon pleasure-seeking, which, when coupled with the suppression of emotion, makes it obvious that neo-Stoicism could hardly have served to sanction modern hedonism. Rather, it must have acted as a powerful constraint upon the emergence of any such ethic, and should therefore be regarded as a current of thought which served to oppose this development. As Roberts makes clear, Dr Johnson's commitment to Stoicism was by no means exceptional; on the contrary, he can be seen as the eloquent and forceful spokesman for what was an influential current of thought throughout the eighteenth century. Periodicals such as the *Tatler*, the *Spectator* and the *Guardian* frequently manifested Stoic sentiments, or expressed judgements based upon the values of Stoicism, whilst the fact that this constituted a prevalent moral orthodoxy is attested to by the time and effort expended by the Anglican divines in attacking it in the course of their advocacy of the cult of benevolence.

They, it will be remembered, objected strongly to the Stoics' elevation of reason above emotion, as well as to the separation of the kindly act from the sympathetic identification and feeling which underlies it. This dispute goes back into the seventeenth century when the ideas of Seneca were first becoming well known, partly as a result of the translation into English of Antoine Le Grand's compendium of Stoic teaching entitled, *Man without Passion: or, The Wise Stoick, According to the Sentiments of Seneca* (1675). The religious thinkers of the Latitudiniarian School considered these views to exaggerate greatly man's rationality, failing to accord an importance to the emotions which they deserved. 'The *Stoicks*', wrote

James Lowde in 1694, 'would make Man so wholly rational, that they will scarce allow him to be sensible, and would wholly exclude all natural affections and bodily passions out of human Nature (italics in original).'[15] Against this creed of 'stoical insensibility' was asserted the Christian idea of a charity which does permit the individual to be 'inwardly disturbed', with the claim that there cannot be effective benevolence that does not spring from the tender emotions of pity and compassion.[16]

It might be claimed, as a result of examining the behaviour of English aristocrats in the eighteenth century, that they were little influenced by the kind of neo-Stoicism advocated by Dr Johnson, or, that if they were, they hypocritically combined the expression of Stoic sentiments with considerable licentiousness. After all, the popular image of the nobleman of the period is hardly that of an individual who maintained the ascetic self-control of a Seneca. Thus Habakkuk appears justified in asserting, that unless restrained by religious feeling or strong moral conventions, the 'lowest common denominator' of the English aristocracy was a certain 'dissoluteness of manners', with gout an 'occupational disease', and the mistress virtually an institution.[17] This point is an important one, but not necessarily a powerful objection.

In the first place, it is necessary to remember that the issue under debate is the nature of the aristocratic ethic, that is, those ideas which prescribed the most highly approved forms of conduct, not the actual patterns of behaviour which prevailed. In this connection, it would be more pertinent to inquire whether there were other, powerful, non-Stoic currents of thought at work,[18] than to observe that there was a gap between the ideal and reality. It would be wrong, in the second place, to assume, in an unthinkingly prudish manner, that such behaviour as that referred to by Habakkuk necessarily contravened the aristocracy's own moral code, and was hence seen by them as unethical. Raymond Williams has observed, in connection with a slightly later period, that 'in aristocratic circles, sobriety and chastity, at least in young men, were not cardinal virtues, but might even be a sign of meanness and dullness',[19] whilst it has already been noted how the pursuit of this-worldly pleasures formed a part of the cavalier ethic. This leads on to the third and last observation, which is that excessive indulgence of the appetites does not necessarily indicate the presence of hedonistic motives, and hence is not actually incompatible with a generalized stoicism; a negative attitude toward emotion, in particularly, being easily assimilated into such flamboyant 'dissoluteness'.[20] This is because such activities as heavy drinking, gambling, womanizing and engaging in energetic and dangerous sports, often represent attempts to demonstrate heroic or manly qualities; consequently they are typically communal, taking the form of character contests in which there is a predominant concern to demonstrate strength, stamina, will-power and self-control. Thus, an activity which appears to be motivated by sensory hedonism, like drinking, may well be pursued past the point at which pleasure is obtained, the object being to maintain the front of sobriety for as long as possible. Pleasure in this example has the same status as pain, both constituting forms of stimulation which have to be overcome if the individual is to ensure or enhance his reputation. Thus, whilst some interest in sensory hedonism may help to influence the choice of activities selected for such contests, it can be seen that a stoical ethic still underlies conduct;[21] a fact which is reinforced by the accompanying tendency to reject sensuousness (mainly because of its 'feminine' associations) together with any suggestions of an alliance between pleasure and spirituality. Most of these features of the aristocratic ethic of heroic stoicism can be illustrated by considering that fascinating socio-cultural phenomenon which is dandyism.

The dandy ethic

The term 'dandy' dates from the late eighteenth and early nineteenth centuries, and appears to have been English in origin, although the phenomenon itself was soon exported to France.[22] Today the word is commonly taken to refer to a man who shows a special concern for the smartness of his dress, and although the original dandies were indeed 'well-dressed men-about-town', there was more to dandyism than a concern with fashion.

The dandies constituted a small, exclusive, social group, mainly, it would appear, of men who had little real claim to aristocratic lineage and yet who had experienced a privileged education.[23] They led the leisured life of gentlemen, often on borrowed money, and typically spent their time gambling, drinking, going to the theatre, doing 'the social round', womanizing, or engaging in gentlemanly sports like boxing and tennis.[24] In addition, of course, they devoted a great deal of time and money to their clothes and general appearance.

Brummell is the one man who is taken as epitomizing the dandy, if not actually creating him in his own person. Named by Byron as one of the three greatest men of the nineteenth century (along, that is, with Napoleon and Byron himself) Brummel, the son of a civil servant, went to Eton and Oxford before joining the Tenth Hussars. Contrary to popular impression, Brummell's contribution to male fashion was not flamboyancy but quality, refinement and attention to detail. He made a few innovations in style, but he was most renowned for his obsessive concern with excellence in both the material and the fit of his clothes. He was equally fastidious about his person, and devoted an inordinate amount of time to his toilet, shaving meticulously and scrubbing himself till his skin was pink, for he took considerable pride in the fact that although he did not use perfume neither did he smell. His major concern seems to have been the extent to which he exemplified a kind of neo-classical perfection of form in appearance and deportment. He was, as Moers implies, an 'artist' in the rigid perfection of his linen and the carefully arranged symmetry of glove with hand,[25] revealing that it was not so much the fashionable style of his dress which was the secret of his success as his ability to create and maintain an overall image of refinement.

Refinement, and its expression in elegance, constituted the core of the dandy ideal, whether in dress or deportment. Dress was to be perfect, but understated, as were all gestures and expressions of feeling,[26] whilst refinement in conversation led to a premium being placed upon wit. To attain this ideal of refined behaviour was to successfully display a superiority of self, and hence arrogance was also a defining characteristic of the dandy. Naturally competition between them was intense, as each strove by means of dress, gesture, tone of voice, glance and overall manner, coupled of course, with wit, to triumph not only over all situational risks to their poise but over each other. It was the measure of Brummell's skill in this respect that he was universally acknowledged, for many years, as being the leading dandy, or in the language of his day, 'top of the male ton'.[27]

To be successful within the terms set by such an artificial and elaborately mannered ethic requires the individual to exercise continuous control over all impulses and emotions. It is not surprising, therefore, to discover that a stoic impassivity and imperturbability were major dandy characteristics, especially in circumstances of great stress. Moers refers to the dandy's need 'to tighten, to control', in order to attain his ideal,[28] whilst Baudelaire (who was actually a later romantic–dandy hybrid) said that 'the dandy' doctrine of elegance and originality is as demanding as the most rigorous monastic rule',[29] and that consequently extreme self-control was unavoidable.[30] Burnett observes that 'coolness was all' as far as conduct was concerned, 'coolness in the sense of effrontery, but also in the sense of imperturbability and reserve'.[31] This coolness was frequently required in order to triumph over the risk inherent in those social events which functioned as trials of character, even if the risk was itself self-induced, as on the famous occasion when Brummell publicly ridiculed the Prince Regent's new coat. But it was also manifest in situations of real danger; in the renowned nonchalance of the Duke of Wellington's officers, for example, many of whom were dandies. This stoical self-control was not, however, as it was with Dr Johnson, dictated by a philosophy which stated that the passions must be subjected to the sovereignty of the reason; in fact, the original dandies had no philosophy.

Rather, it was a psychological necessity in a character ideal which emphasized the achievement of restrained and self-conscious, 'mannered' conduct.[32] What is more, it was a stoicism which did not preclude indulgence of the appetites. Although Brummell never married, nor, it would appear, had any kind of love-life, this does not seem to have been normal among the dandies,[33] the majority of whom seem to have enjoyed to the full the pleasures afforded by good food, good wine and bad women, in addition to the excitement offered by sport and war. This apparent hedonism was, nevertheless, largely devoid of any emotionality. Byron, who was the only romantic acceptable in dandy circles, seems to have engaged in love affairs, whilst his more dandified friends, such as Scrope Davies, appear to have had purely physical relationships with women.[34] Moers suggests that the reason for this may lie in the dandy's self-worship and narcissism,[35] but it would probably be more pertinent to stress how a continual struggle to ensure one's reputation meant that restraint and emotional control had to be maintained at all times.[36]

The corollary of the dandy's imperturbability when faced with danger or disaster was the treatment of what might normally be regarded as trivial issues as matters of great moment. Thus, the Duke of Wellington's officers, whilst maintaining a commendable sang-froid in the face of danger, even to the extent of being able to react to the loss of a leg as if it were hardly worth mentioning, were so concerned about maintaining their uniforms in immaculate condition as to want to meet the enemy carrying umbrellas.[37] One might be tempted to say that normal emotional concern was displaced, but the truth is that the apparently minor issues of dress and deportment were of crucial importance in the dandy ethic for the same reason that more obviously aesthetic judgements were important in the cult of sensibility: they revealed one's sense of taste, and hence one's essential quality of self. Here too the ever-present danger was the loss of reputation which can follow from any manifestation of 'bad taste', except that the link is less with virtue than honour, whilst there was little room for an inner-directed judgement which was independent of the attitudes of one's peers.[38] At the same time, aesthetic judgements as such hardly mattered, for it was through conduct that taste was principally assessed. The concept of sensibility still played a part in this ethic, for a premium was placed on possession of that faculty which leads to the discernment of good taste. As far as susceptibility to stimuli was concerned, however, this was conceived of in distinctly physiological terms, to produce the strange combination of emotional impassivity with an extraordinary physical sensitivity. As Moers describes the dandy: 'His nerves are set jangling more easily than those of ordinary men, his teeth are more commonly on edge, his skin prickles and his eyes widen upon less provocation – and he boasts of his delicacy.'[39] Thus Brummell claimed to have acquired a cold through being in the same room as a damp man, and to have been prevented from eating vegetables because of his extraordinary 'sensibility'. Whilst, in part, this can be seen as a continuation of the folk myth concerning the superhuman sensitivity of those of royal or noble blood (as in the fairy-story of the princess and the pea), it is also clearly the only way in which the doctrine of a non-rational, innate, aesthetic sense can be adapted for use in an aristocratic context, the claim to special powers being loosely linked both to neo-classicism and an heroic stoicism.

Dandyism can thus be seen as a reworking of traditional aristocratic values and ideas to meet the challenge of changing circumstances. It was, at one level, quite revolutionary in its abandonment of the central principle of noble birth and its replacement with the concept of the gentleman as the possessor of an inherently noble 'self'. As Moers describes him 'the dandy . . . stands on an isolated pedestal of self. He has no coat of arms on his carriage . . . no ancestral portraits on his walls . . . no decorations on his uniform'; also typically, he had no obligations or attachments, no wife, children or relatives.[40] Yet at the same time, much of the traditional aristocratic way of life was carried forward. It was, for example, a life of leisure, with the pursuit of honour and the enjoyment of 'pleasures' the dominant activities; work and the problem of how to obtain sufficient wealth to maintain such an existence were vulgar, and hence taboo, subjects. It was exclusive and snobbish, despising all those outside its own circle; whilst what was valued was an artificial, irresponsible ethic of mannered and refined conduct. Intellectual and aesthetic interests were present, typically classical in nature, but little importance was attached to them, whilst religion was disregarded entirely.[41]

It can be seen from this brief summary of the aristocratic ethic that, neither in its cavalier nor in its dandy form, did it provide a suitable basis for the development of autonomous, self-illusory hedonism, and hence for the spirit of modern consumerism. This is not to say that the aristocracy did not engage in luxury consumption, their preoccupation with pride ensured that this would indeed be the case, and is reflected to this day in the many magnificent country houses which remain as monuments to their self-glorification. The same motive ensured that they spent lavishly on more perishable products during their lifetimes, whilst like most elites, some of this expenditure was incurred seeking pleasure with which to offset the boredom created by comfort. In this sense, Sombart was correct to stress the part played by the desire for sensory pleasure in promoting the demand for luxury goods.[42] Critically, however, the dandies did not evaluate pleasure above comfort, nor perceive that it might be necessary to sacrifice some of the latter for gains in the former, nor indeed did the nature of their ethic really allow for the development of a truly rationalized hedonism.

This development was checked in the first place by the overriding importance attached to pride, and the associated necessity to identify with a neo-classicist tradition in ethics and aesthetics. This placed the emphasis upon form, together with harmony and proportion, condemning all passion and excess. This tendency was further reinforced by the necessity to maintain social distance from the *nouveaux riches* – with their characteristic preoccupations with money and sentiment – and which served to push the aristocratic impulse yet further toward an elaborated, impassive, mannerist ethic, something which gained intellectual legitimation by appealing to Stoic philosophy. At the same time, the heroic tradition made pride, in the sense of honour, a matter of crucial importance, and this had to be built up and defended through continuous character contests with one's peers. Originally largely a matter of demonstrating valour in battle and generous hospitality in peace, an increasingly civilized society displaced chivalrous values with courtly ones, and eventually with those suited to 'Society'. Here grace and wit were prized, with the dandy every bit as concerned to defend his honour as any seventeenth-century cavalier, the difference being that reputation, instead of resting upon heroism and loyalty to the king, depended upon dedication to the sovereign power of good taste, together with success in the tourneys of wit.

Such an ethic does appear suited to the promotion of the modern fashion pattern, despite the indifference to aesthetics and, of course, fashions did change in dandy circles; with interpersonal competition providing an incentive for innovation. There is, however, no real interest in novelty to compare with that displayed by the middle classes, and, to this day, aristocratic interest in dress tends to centre upon refinement. This, in turn, stems from the comparative lack of any emphasis upon the introspective inner-directedness characteristic of the Puritan tradition. The dandy's striving did not derive from an imaginative dwelling upon ideal models, with as a consequence a guilt-driven dynamic, but from the shame-driven one which stems from other directedness. Such an ethic, with its Veblenesque overtones, facilitated the spread of fashion, but cannot be regarded as providing the intellectual origins of the modern fashion pattern as a whole.

There is an important qualification to be made, nevertheless, to this conclusion, and it stems from the exclusively masculine character of both the cavalier and dandy ethics. Both these words specifically refer to men (unlike 'Puritan' and 'Romantic', for example), and in neither case does it seem to have been possible for a woman to have exemplified fully the character ideal in question. Indeed, both ethics feature defined, 'masculine' qualities as central, thus continuing the heroic strain of traditional aristocratic thought. This obviously raises the question of the nature of the ethic which was prescribed for ladies of noble birth, and how exactly it might relate to the masculine one. Clearly, neither the heroic nor the stoic ingredients of the latter were meant to apply to 'the gentle sex' in quite the same way, although the emphasis upon refinement and the graces was, if anything, even stronger. This suggests that a greater affinity might have existed between the female aristocratic ethic and the middle-class cult of sensibility than was true for its male counterpart, and hence that conceptions of taste and attitudes toward fashion might not have been quite so dissimilar. If this was indeed the case, then it might go some way toward explaining how it was that 'sensibility and the graces of a polished manner' came to be closely associated, as well as the apparent ease with which the upper- and middle-class markets for fashionable products became integrated into one system.

9

The Romantic Ethic

The land of chimeras is alone worthy of habitation.

Rousseau

The grand elementary principle of pleasure, by which [man] knows, and feels, and lives, and moves.

Wordsworth

The decline of sensibility

The cult of sensibility reached its peak in England somewhere between 1750 and 1770, and by the early decades of the nineteenth century readers no longer found such books as Mackenzie's *The Man of Feeling* as profoundly affecting as they once had,[1] nor did they regard it as *de rigueur* to accompany the expression of their feelings with floods of tears. In retrospect, it seems inevitable that an ethic which placed such emphasis upon emotional display would be bound in time to degenerate into histrionics, and thus call forth ridicule and satire. And so it proved; with a marked reaction to melodramatic sentimentality occurring in both life and art before the end of the eighteenth century, and then continuing on into the early decades of the nineteenth.[2]

Such a reaction was not simply based on the view that frequent and uncontrolled weeping, swooning or self-prostration were unduly extravagant ways of revealing the presence of admirable emotions, but was also generated by an increasing realization that the expression of feeling had become so much the focus of attention that individuals had lost sight of the necessity for any commensurate action. Boswell mentions a certain Mr Gilbert Cooper, whom he describes as 'the last of the *benevolists*, or sentimentalists, who were much in vogue between 1750 and 1760, and dealt in *general* admiration of virtue', and, who, 'were all tenderness in *words;* [whilst] their finer feelings evaporated in the moment of expression, for they had no connection with their practice' (italics in original).[3] These remarks were prompted by the story of Mr Cooper's intense agitation upon hearing that his son was ill, agitation which made him declare that he would write an elegy (to serve as proof of the depth of his emotion) whilst it was left to a companion to suggest that a visit to his son might be a more appropriate response.[4] Clearly such behaviour was guaranteed to bring Sentimentalism into disrepute, increasingly causing people to query the sincerity of the emotions which were so conspicuously displayed. Insincerity and dissembling were, one could say, bound to become widespread in a climate in which so much importance was attached to the ability to prove oneself a person of sensibility. As a consequence of this, the cult became attacked for its tendency to generate exactly that indifference to the plight of others which it was supposed to overcome, as individuals either counterfeited their feelings, or concentrated upon the pleasures of emotional indulgence to the exclusion of any real concern for the objects of their pity. In this way, Sentimentalism became regarded as a suspect philosophy, capable as it was of serving as a pretext for essentially selfish and cruel behaviour, whilst the faith in feeling itself was also called into doubt.[5] This was the import of a cartoon on the subject of the French Revolution which appeared in the *Anti-Jacobin Review* in 1789. As described by Tompkins it included

the figure of Sensibility in a cap of liberty, weeping over a dead robin and trampling on a crowned and severed head. Feelings, runs the implicit argument, are a treacherous standard of behaviour; over-indulged, they loosen the ties of moral responsibility, destroy the sense of proportion, and, by fostering egoism, induce a fundamental callosity of heart.[6]

The nature of the attack on sensibility differed, however, depending upon whether it was undertaken in the name of common sense (as Jane Austen's title implies) or in that of true sensibility. The former tended to be part of a wide-ranging assault on emotionality and emotional indulgence of all kinds, pointing to its many and varied undesirable consequences for individuals and society at large, while extolling the superior virtues of rationality and self-control. The latter, on the other hand, whilst upholding the central tenet of a link between a person's goodness and their emotional susceptibility, concentrated upon exposing what were seen as the forces responsible for the spread of a bogus sensibility. Despite these differences, both critiques overlapped in condemning not just insincerity and dissembling but some of the grosser manifestations of a rampant Sentimentalism. Prominent among these was the sentimental romance, together with its close relative, the Gothic novel, both of which formed part of a larger industry in popular cultural products that had come into being 'on the back', as it were, of the cult of sensibility; effectively catering for that craving for the pleasures of emotional stimulation which had been unintentionally engendered in its adherents.[7]

The Gothic novel was 'the most widely read and enjoyed form of popular literature' in Britain and much of Europe between 1765 and 1840, according to Haining,[8] whilst Summers puts its heyday in the 1790s.[9] Horace Walpole is popularly credited with laying the foundations of the genre with his medieval thriller *The Castle of Otranto* (1764), although it is Ann Radcliffe who is usually recognized as having come closest to realizing the full possibilities of the form, especially in *The Mysteries of Udolpho* (1794). The novels were labelled Gothic because of the frequent choice of a medieval setting, but they were not very different in structure from the popular domestic novels which had preceded them,[10] the crucial addition being a powerful, emotionally charged atmosphere; something which was typically generated by the use of eerie locations and hints of supernatural intervention. Clearly what the genre offered the reader was the dimension of pleasurable fear,[11] as Haining frankly and eloquently confesses:

> For me, the gothic story is what it has always been, a marvelous [sic] escape from reality, an exciting journey through distant lands and strange experiences, a brush with the unknown, a footstep in the dark, a fluttering pulse and an evening's sheer entertainment.[12]

These novels were enormously popular, and led to a publishing boom in which plots were stolen, authors plagiarized and cheap, poorly written stories concerning knights, heroines and ghostly apparitions flooded the market; with, as Haining expresses it, 'all personal emotions from the cradle to the grave' worked up into the literary form of the novel of romance.

The genre, although popular, did not have public approval, and authors commonly apologized for writing these novels, whilst readers often had to stoop to subterfuge to be able to read them; sometimes publicly affecting a disdain for the very books which they had gone to great lengths to acquire.[13] All of which suggests that whilst sensibility had indeed served to create a demand for imaginatively mediated emotional pleasure, it had not given a proper legitimacy to the addiction.

For an addiction is exactly how it was portrayed in the numerous and vehement attacks made at the time, both on the Gothic novel itself, fiction in general, the reading public, and the underlying sensibility which connected them. Rogers reports how it was claimed that romances, if consumed 'in extreme', acted on the mind 'like inebriating stimulants; [to] first elevate, and at last enervate it',[14] and quotes Thomas Love Peacock as observing that the fiction-reading public 'requires a perpetual adhibition of sauce piquante to the palate of its depraved imagination'. The analogy with a drug is, of course, quite valid, as the craving for pleasure is more often stimulated than extinguished by its gratification; but it is also pertinent to note that such an addiction requires the continual acquisition of 'new' products, for as Foster observes, 'sensibility thirsted for novelty [as well as] emotional intensity'.[15] Interestingly, therefore, we can see in the nature of the attacks made upon the vogue for Gothic and sentimental fiction just those very features – a concern with self-illusory pleasure, and a taste for novelty – which have been identified as elements of the spirit of modern consumerism. What is more, the reading of these novels was portrayed as not merely addictive, and hence likely to lead to a kind of emotional and imaginative decadence, but as also creating a generalized dissatisfaction with life, leading young ladies (it was always young ladies who were singled out for mention in this connection) to expect life to be like a sentimental novel.[16]

We can now see how consumption of these novels might have helped to bring about a critical change in attitude towards the world, one characterized by the rejection of a traditional pattern of life on the grounds that it was too dull, and a consequent search for the kind of pleasure which could be experienced in imagination. Several of the satires aimed at the practice of novel-reading concentrated upon portraying the foolishness of young girls who attempted to make their lives resemble a novel,[17] and reveal that novels were typically blamed for making young women unfit for household duties, disrespectful toward their parents and betters, discontented with their social position, and generally determined to 'become heroines'[18] by striving after the unattainable. All this in addition to the predictable accusation that novels encouraged immorality and acted as 'silent instructors in the art of intrigue'.[19] As Taylor observes:

Few women have ever been beset by such extravagant fancies as were generously ascribed to the girls who patronized the eighteenth-century circulating libraries. The printed page of fiction was credited with engendering a tantalizing, an irresistible discontent. It could so 'tickle the imagination' that it caused young women to expect the unusual and bizarre instead of the common run of events.[20]

This is clearly recognizable as a description of that process through which indulgence in self-illusory hedonism works to create both a sense of dissatisfaction with the world and a generalized longing for the fulfilment of dreams. Thus making it appear very likely that the reading of novels was a major factor in the critical break with traditionalism which occurred in the second half of the eighteenth century.

The evolution of sensibility into a full-blown romanticism can be seen as following, at least in part, from the necessity of defending a philosophy of feeling against its detractors, something which placed an excessive strain upon the attempted association of the values of sincerity and propriety. For the accusation that such an ethic encouraged dissembling, hypocrisy, indifference to suffering, and even cruelty, could only really be countered by arguing that these were not the products of 'true' sensibility, but rather the outcome of behaviour governed by conventional expectations. If, therefore, people did allow themselves to be honest, and were to let their actions flow directly from their natural feelings instead of feigning that which they did not feel, such undesirable attitudes would not be created. An argument which only retains the association between emotional susceptibility and goodness at the expense of making custom and etiquette the source of all that is undesirable; consequently leading to the contrasting of 'self' and 'society', with the person of true sensibility defined as someone who is bound to be an 'outsider'. Thus, just as the dandies represented the triumph of propriety over sincerity, so the Romantics (and, especially, the romantic Bohemians) come to represent the reverse.

This development can also be seen in the popular novels of the time, which typically portray young ladies who are forced to 'suffer' by 'society' for their spirited natures and fine sensibilities, before eventually succeeding in realizing their dreams.[21] As a theme, it appears to be a muted echo of the Puritan view of the 'saintly' individual confronting the 'sinful' society, whilst also anticipating the fully romantic notion of the *poete maudit* or one 'endowed with an ambiguous gift of sensibility which makes him at the same time more blessed and more cursed than other members of a society from which he is, by the destiny of inheritance, an outcast'.[22] At the same time, such a refusal to bow the head before the sovereign powers of tradition and convention became regarded as convincing evidence that one was a person of true sensibility, possessed of a passionate and impetuous nature which would simply not permit dissembling or hypocrisy. Once again, the novels contain many examples of youthful heroines whose integrity is established in this way, often by defying parental authority, as in the interesting example given by Rogers of the 'distressed daughter, who prefers starving in a garret on a miserable pittance which she earns painting fan-mounts, to a life of affluence with a man she doesn't love'.[23] Thus, in yet one more subtle shift in the doctrine of signs, an individual's true sensibility became validated as much by their defiance of convention as by the direct manifestation of emotional susceptibility.

Certain difficulties are created by this line of argument, however, for by placing the blame for man's inhumanity to man on the tendency to compromise real feelings in the interests of orderly social intercourse, it follows that much of the whole elaborate structure of social life, with its rituals, mores and institutions, is likely to be judged to exert an 'undesirable' influence upon individuals; hence pushing the philosophy of sensibility into an increasingly 'world-rejecting' stance. This, in turn, creates a need for a source of spiritual values which can be employed to justify such a rejection, a problem which links directly with the unresolved issue of how it is that insensibility is actually to be overcome. For to argue that people would not treat each other with indifference or cruelty were they to refrain from allowing convention to dictate their conduct, is clearly to presuppose that everyone is endowed with a natural lively sensibility. But, of course, were that actually the case, it would be hard to understand how they could have come to behave conventionally in the first instance. Thus, some other factor must be identified as directly responsible for their insensibility, with a new agency invoked as the power to overcome it, and it is to resolve this problem that the rational, utilitarian ethos comes to be seen as the inhibiting force, whilst art, and more especially the faculty of imagination, is proclaimed the liberator. It is necessary to understand something of the wider changes taking place in Western European society at the end of the eighteenth and the beginning of the nineteenth centuries, however, to appreciate exactly how this cultural shift occurred.

The two most critical events in this period were the French and Industrial Revolutions, which can, for the sake of convenience, be treated as part of that same single upheaval by which the middle classes displaced the aristocracy as the leading socio-economic grouping in modern society. Originally greeted by the first generation of romantics with enthusiasm (witness Wordsworth's 'bliss was it in that dawn to be alive'), this radical change in the nature of society was quickly recognized as posing new threats, as well as presenting new opportunities. In the climate of disillusionment which ensued, that cultural disjunction between the nobility and the bourgeoisie which had characterized the eighteenth century became less significant than the divisions within the middle class itself.

The waning of the old aristocracy, and the rise to prominence of the trading and business classes, meant that the sentimentalist critique of the nobility – indicted for their emotional stoicism, frivolous extravagance, and an arrogance that hid a lack of spiritual depth – was increasingly irrelevant, and it came to be recognized that the real enemy of sensibility lay in the cold-hearted utilitarian philistinism of the *nouveaux riches*. Thus, as the sense of cultural crisis deepened, the focus of attack was shifted to deal with the greater threat, whilst a tendency to be nostalgic about the foe of yesteryear also developed. Consequently, the sentimentalists seized this opportunity to claim the mantle of moral, intellectual and spiritual leadership for themselves, and adopting along with it the previous elite's disdain for the vulgar and the useful, asserted their right to legislate for society as a whole. Such a re-drawing of the cultural lines of battle was to have a profound long-term effect on the culture of modern industrial societies, for it now became possible to counterpose explicitly conduct arising from a true sensibility with that demanded by society, the latter being identified as the realm of cold, impersonal, economic forces. Action in defiance of convention could thus now serve at one and the same time to demonstrate one's profound sensibility and membership of the true aristocracy, as well as constituting a blow for a better world.

Romanticism

It is now widely accepted that the European Romantic Movement developed out of eighteenth-century Sentimentalism, with writers such as Sterne and Mackenzie commonly described as 'proto-romantics', and recognized romantics such as Rousseau and the young Goethe identified as significant figures in the cult of sensibility. The overlap is indeed sufficiently acknowledged to make it reasonable to claim that Romanticism incorporated most of the ideas and attitudes which characterized Sentimentalism, whilst modifying and adding to them in significant ways, and thus represents a further evolution of that essentially pietistic current of feeling which we have traced back to Puritanism. Something which becomes more apparent, perhaps, when Romanticism is recognized as embracing a popular movement focusing upon emotionality and a craving for the sensational and macabre, as well as the more widely studied intellectualism and idealism of an elite.[24] Having said this, the problem of delineating, let alone defining, Romanticism, has proved an especially thorny and intractable one for cultural historians, and it would take a brave, or a foolhardy, sociologist to assert anything definite about the nature of this important movement without first considering the difficulties.

There are three good reasons why defining Romanticism should prove particularly problematic. In the first place, the phenomenon embraces developments in nearly all branches of intellectual and cultural life, together with associated shifts in social attitudes and behaviour, which occurred throughout Europe over a period of almost a century. Secondly, as Thorslev observes,[25] Romanticism has been notoriously difficult to define because the most influential definitions offered in the first decades of this century were formulated by antagonists, most noticeably, Irving Babbitt, T. E. Hulme and T. S. Eliot, with the consequence that much subsequent debate has been as concerned with defending Romanticism as defining it. Thirdly, Romanticism can justifiably be presented as more of an impulse than a unified system of ideas, and what is more, an impulse toward chaos. Logically, therefore, not only is 'a closed definition of romanticism ... not very romantic', but, 'if one important aspect of romanticism is the spirit of rebellion, then rebelling against romanticism could also be romantic'.[26] Bearing these arguments in mind, it is hardly surprising that no less an authority than A. O.

Lovejoy should have come to the conclusion that no single unified
definition was possible, and thus have advocated that one should refer to
Romanticisms not Romanticism.[27]

Such a judgement now seems unduly pessimistic, but even at the time
there were scholars who did not accept it. Prominent among these was
René Wellek, who suggested that Romanticism was recognizable as myth
and symbolism in art, organicism in philosophy and history, and the
creative imagination in all things;[28] whilst other authorities, notably
Morse Peckham[29] and H. H. Remak, have since followed in his footsteps
by offering their own definitions of this elusive phenomenon. Part of the
original difficulty stemmed, as Furst has suggested,[30] from a failure to
distinguish clearly between the spheres of reference involved – whether,
for example, one was referring to Romanticism as an archetypal,
historical, or more narrowly aesthetic, phenomenon – for, if care is taken
to do this, then it does seem possible to accept Remak's conclusion, that
'the evidence pointing to the existence in Western Europe of a
widespread, distinct and fairly simultaneous pattern of thought, attitudes
and beliefs associated with the connotation "Romanticism" is overwhelming'.[31]

Wisely employing the kind of distinctions which Furst advocates,
Halsted identifies Romanticism in the broad sense to be 'a general world
view', or 'way of answering the main questions men face';[32] more
specifically 'a name for inter-related and similar ideas and attitudes – and
related and derivative forms of behaviour – in the whole range of
intellectual concerns, in the arts, of course, but with equal import and
novelty, I suggest, in religion, history, and politics'.[33] From this
perspective, Romanticism is a general cultural movement, on a par with
the Renaissance, or the immediately preceding Enlightenment. More
narrowly, it can be seen as the name for a type of art and taste, with an
associated aesthetic theory, one normally contrasted with classicism or
realism. Finally, one might claim, as Furst does, that there have been
some individuals in all societies who displayed a 'romantic' temperament,
but that manifestations of this trait reached 'epidemic' proportions in the
late eighteenth and early nineteenth centuries.[34]

As a historical movement, Romanticism has been identified as having
its centre of gravity between 1790 and 1830, although the precise dates
vary, depending upon whether England, Germany or France is under
consideration, and whether the focus is placed on philosophy, politics,
literature, painting or music.[35] It is also commonly regarded as being a
reaction against the Enlightenment, and it is in this context that Isaiah
Berlin described Romanticism as representing, a 'shift in consciousness'
which 'cracked the backbone of European thought';[36] a view that is not
incorrect, but needs to be complemented by a recognition that the

movement also 'grew out of' the Enlightenment.[37] The reaction was, in John Stuart Mill's words, 'against the narrowness of the eighteenth century',[38] that is to say, against the culture of rationalism and the empiricist and materialist outlook which it had generated. Newton, whose discoveries were seen as representing the triumphant exemplification of this 'narrowness', was especially abhored, for his philosophy had 'clipped an angel's wings', disenchanting the world and reducing all life to the status of a machine. Such 'dissection' of experience was judged to be equivalent to 'murder', whilst the application of this approach to social and economic life resulted in a utilitarianism regarded as responsible for promoting an inhuman and calculating egoism.

Against this world-view, indeed, as a corrective to it, the romantics asserted a philosophy of 'dynamic organicism'[39] with the metaphor of growth substituted for that of the machine, and the values of change, diversity, individuality and imagination, for those of uniformitarianism, universalism and rationalism. Yet Romanticism is not really best represented as a philosophy; it is more a mode of feeling that does not lend itself easily to systematization. Thus, although Romanticism certainly had its philosophers, notable Fichte, Schopenhauer and Schelling – and also provided the basis of such later philosophical systems as existentialism and phenomenology – it is not adequately labelled a philosophy. As Gauderfroy-Demombynes expressed it, 'romanticism is a way of feeling, a state of mind in which *sensibilité* and imagination predominates over reason; it tends towards the new, towards individualism, revolt, escape, melancholy, and fantasy'.[40] Other typical characteristics of this way of feeling would be: dissatisfaction with the contemporary world, a restless anxiety in the face of life, a preference for the strange and curious, a penchant for reverie and dreaming, a leaning to mysticism, and a celebration of the irrational.[41]

A romantic theodicy

Although it is difficult to identify a romantic philosophy, it is still possible to describe a general 'theodicy', or metaphysical paradigm, shared by most romantics. This is best seen as resulting from a sentimental Deism that has been infused with the spirit of evangelical Protestantism, with beliefs about the inspirational and redeeming power of art functioning as a catalyst to unite the two streams of thought. It is, therefore, a rather special mix of Enlightenment, and more specifically Christian, ideas. We have already seen how the prosperous sections of the English middle classes reinterpreted Deism on a sentimental, rather than a rationalistic, basis, while more conventional faiths survived among the lower-middle and working classes. The decline of Sentimentalism, and the climate of religious revival created by Methodism, subsequently provided suitable circumstances for these two streams of bourgeois culture to intermingle once again, jointly opposing an increasingly influential, sceptical, utilitarian outlook.

In comparison with earlier theodicies, what distinguished Romanticism was the fact that primary emphasis was placed upon the characteristic of creativity (although love was not neglected), whilst the divine itself was no longer represented as a named, personal God, but as a supernatural force, which, whilst present throughout the natural world, also existed within each individual in the form of a unique and personalized spirit; that of his 'genius'. This resulted in two closely connected forms of religious faith: a pan-psychic mysticism, or pantheism, with regard to nature at large, combined with a purely personal drama of salvation and redemption to be acted out within the confines of the self. Abrams refers to this latter feature of Romanticism as a 'biodicy', or 'theodicy of the individual life',[42] one which clearly owed much to the traditional Christian scheme of Eden, Fall and Redemption, although it was now merged with 'the new triad of nature, self-consciousness, imagination'.[43] In fact, the two dimensions of the theodicy tended to overlap and intermingle, giving rise to a tendency, on the one hand, for individuals to retreat into an introverted mysticism, and, on the other, for the drama of redemption to be projected onto society, if not the world at large.

Such a theodicy moves art and the artist to the centre-stage of life; indeed, as Bertrand Russell observed, by generally substituting aesthetic for utilitarian values, the romantic *Weltanschauung* can reasonably be portrayed as a theory of art extrapolated into a philosophy of life.[44] Yet the romantic view of aesthetics differed not only from orthodox neo-classicism, but also from the prevailing version of middle-classicism. That, it was noted, equated the aesthetic and the ethical, using the concept of 'taste' to unite the two. This faculty was not assumed to involve any spiritual perceptiveness, however, for it was still contained within a vaguely rationalistic theology; nor, as a consequence, was 'taste' cast in direct opposition to the faculty of reason. With the ensuing reaction against an overly narrow rationalism, however, and the incorporation of an evangelical spirit into sensibility, the key attribute of 'taste' became transformed into a capacity for seeing into the nature of sacred truth, relabelled 'imagination', and used to link the aesthetic with the spiritual rather than the ethical. In consequence, the perception of beauty became linked to the gaining of privileged insights, whilst artistic creativity was assimilated back into the prophetic tradition of supernatural inspiration from which, originally, it had sprung.[45]

The romantics were sufficiently children of the Enlightenment to have been deeply imbued with a sceptical attitude toward orthodox religion, and especially toward revelation in its conventional form; doubt was, in that sense, a fundamental datum of their experience. At the same time, they still took for granted the association between nature and religious truth which had characterized Deism. They also carried forward the tendency to assume that personal discovery of the divine could be made through direct observation of nature without, or introspective journeyings into nature within, whilst treating discrepancies in any conclusions arrived at in this way as ultimately stemming from the presence of an intruding overlay of civilization. In addition, they inherited from the Leibnizian theodicy the tendency to equate the natural with the good, thus rejecting the older Christian dualistic opposition of flesh and spirit.

In contrast to the Enlightenment conception of 'nature' as that which was universal, uniform and 'rational' in man and the world, however, the romantics interpreted this term to mean either those inborn attributes 'which are most spontaneous, unpremeditated, untouched by reflection or design, and free from the bondage of social convention, or those parts of the universe which come into being independently of human effort and contrivance'.[46] Thus, instead of 'sinking' the supernatural in the natural, they chose to 'raise' the natural to the status of the supernatural,[47] and hence, as Abrams has emphasized, their religious faith is best dubbed a 'natural supernaturalism'.[48] This, of course, was in line with the central emphasis upon the metaphor of growth and the use of organicist ideas, and necessarily cast the artificial – whether in the world or in man himself – as the evil to be overcome.

The romantics also upheld the emphasis upon individualism which characterized the Enlightenment, only here too they made something rather new out of the concept. For their's was a 'qualitative' rather than a 'quantitative' individualism; a doctrine which stressed a person's uniqueness or peculiarity, rather than the features which he shared with all mankind.[49] Thus, whilst accepting that aspect of the political philosophy of the Enlightenment which emphasized the right of each individual to self-determination, their conception of the self as an essentially divine, and unique, 'creative' genius, meant that this was largely interpreted as the right to 'self-expression', or self-discovery.

In one sense, this arose logically from the view that creativity was the power which most characterized the divine, for the 'originating' faculty is that which is responsible for the unusual as well as the freshly made. The new is hence equated with the novel, and the capacity of individuals to produce cultural products identified with their idiosyncrasies. Consequently, the romantic was as fascinated by the distinctive nature of his own self as by his powers of imagination, a preoccupation clearly manifest by Rousseau in his *Confessions*.

I desire to set before my fellows the likeness of a man in all the truth of nature, and that man myself. Myself alone! I know the feelings of my heart, and I know men. I am not made like any of those I have seen. I venture to believe that I am not like any of those who are in existence. If I am not better, at least I am different.[50]

It is hardly surprising to learn that such attitudes led to a concern with individuality that bordered on egotism, or that pride in oneself and one's genius could develop into narcissism, for as Poulet observes, 'the Romantic is one who discovers himself as centre'.[51] What they tended to discover, however, lying at the centre of this centre, was the unconscious mind.[52] This was where the search for the origins of creativity was apt to lead, and this was what they were most inclined to believe – in accordance with their philosophy – was unique to them, the very heart of the private universe of self. Thus it was the forces of nature within man, the passions and promptings of the id, which came to be regarded as the ultimate source of all thought, feeling and action, the very seat of the imagination. Clearly, if this could be given full freedom of expression, then each man could become like a god.[53]

The contribution which a more distinctly Protestant tradition of thought and feeling made to Romanticism has been discussed by Gill, who has argued that Wesleyan Methodism provided a 'hidden source of strength' for the English Romantic Movement.[54] Observing that Romanticism was no mere literary phenomenon, but a general cultural renaissance, he points to the apparent coincidence that it should overlap with that other great spiritual awakening in both time and place. More specifically, he draws attention to the fact that Methodist hymns were characterized by 'lyrical passion, sincerity and spontaneity',[55] and that Wesley, like Wordsworth and Coleridge after him, advocated the use of simple and direct language similar to that employed by ordinary men and women.[56] In addition, he stresses Wesley's emphasis upon individualism, and the centrality of the view that each soul was unique in the eyes of God, together with the impetus to philanthropy which the preaching of mercy and kindness engendered. Finally, he identifies the stimulus which Methodism gave to a 'new class of devotional poetry', as revealed in the work of Cowper and Blake, and how the great romantic theme of life made perfectable through love can be seen as merely a secular version of that religion of passion, hope and conversion which was itself Methodism.[57] From all this he concludes that

The case for Methodism . . . in its relation to the English Romantic movement, appears particularly strong. No just estimate of the Romantic awakening can afford to ignore it. Whether direct or oblique, its influence was profound. Not only did it provide moral earnestness and ethical sincerity, which were soon reflected in the new forms of literature, but, what was even more important, new imaginative passion and liberated emotion. Methodism gave rise to new forms of self-expression. It contributed also its quota to the new forms of speech, the new images of Nature, and the new conceptions of personality.[58]

Such a thesis clearly deserves serious consideration, and the fact that there are connections between Wesleyanism and Romanticism, if only those evident in someone like Cowper, cannot be denied. On the other hand, Wesley had himself read Rousseau, and it is possible that some of the parallelisms noted by Gill stem from the fact that both movements were subject to similar influences rather than that the one contributed directly to the other. We have already seen how the cult of sensibility emphasized benevolence and sentiment, whilst Lecky has commented on the fact that a tradition of eighteenth-century, emotional poetry existed alongside Methodism.[59] Finally, it is important to recognize that Wesleyanism's primary appeal was to the labouring classes, and some of the *petit bourgeoisie*, rather than to the middle and *haute bourgeoisie* who seem to have responded most enthusiastically to Romanticism. Having noted these grounds for caution, however, certain crucial components of the Romantic outlook could not really have come from anywhere but the evangelical Protestant tradition, whether as represented by Wesleyan Methodism or not. These can be specified as the emphasis upon passion rather than mere sentiment, the centrality of the personal drama of conversion and salvation (in which each soul has a unique destiny) and the stress upon a prophetic stance *vis-à-vis* a 'sinful' world.

This last feature could hardly have stemmed from the world-view associated with the Enlightenment; nor indeed was the cult of sensibility a likely source. That assumed individuals had the ability to 'feel' what was right, but not to 'see' what was true, and yet it was precisely this visionary power which the Romantic prophets claimed for themselves; for the vivid scenes which their imaginations revealed were taken to be both things of exquisite beauty in themselves and glimpses of an ideal reality. As a consequence, Romanticism possessed a dynamic and radical character, quite different from the more complacent and world-accepting outlook that characterized sensibility, a dynamism which stemmed from its idealistic ontology. As Bernbaum observes:

The Romantics were keenly conscious of the difference between two worlds. One was the world of ideal truth, goodness and beauty: this was eternal, infinite, and absolutely real. The other was the world of actual appearances, which to common sense was the only world, and which to the idealist was so obviously full of untruth, ignorance, evil, ugliness, and wretchedness, as to compel him to dejection or indignation.[60]

Or, to use Abercrombie's words, 'the appearance of things is contrasted with the reality which imagination perceives, a reality which, being what is desired, is perfection'.[61] A comparison that has the consequence of making it impossible for the Romantic to accept the world as it is, compelling him to strive to transform it into the perfect reality which it should be; a response which Abercrombie distinguishes from a more purely mystical indifference toward its imperfections.[62] Thus perfectionism becomes a defining characteristic of Romanticism. Since, however, 'what the imagination seizes as Beauty must be truth',[63] insight into the real nature of the world can only be gained through powerful emotional and imaginative experience of an essentially aesthetic character. It was not just that 'feeling was a way of knowing' for the Romantics,[64] or that, as Pascal expressed it, 'the heart has reasons that reason knows not of':[65] but that myth and symbol contained more truth than any careful, 'true-to-life' observation of actuality. It was for this reason that the Romantics placed such importance on dreams – whether of the day or night variety – seeing them as essentially revelatory experiences;[66] whilst arguing that poetic truth was a matter of what was subjectively apprehended, not what was objectively described.[67]

The urge to perfect the world, which dreaming of better things gave rise to, was partially expressed in demands for the destruction of those institutions which warped the natural good nature of human beings. T. E. Hulme blames Rousseau for the emergence of this anarchistic faith:

Romantics had been taught by Rousseau that man was basically good, that it was only bad laws and customs that had suppressed him. Remove all these and the infinite possibilities of man would have a chance. This is what made them think that something positive would come out of disorder, this is what created the religious enthusiasm. Here is the root of all romanticism: that man, the individual, is an infinite reservoir of possibilities; and if you can so rearrange society by the destruction of oppressive order then these possibilities will get a chance and you will get Progress.[68]

As noted earlier, however, to regard 'bad laws and customs' as responsible for man's insensibility is to assume that ideal qualities lie dormant in everyone; in which case, why not pursue a policy of attempting to rouse these directly, rather than struggle to dismantle or reform the institutions of an unfeeling society?

In fact, the Romantics did not neglect the overtly political option, and many were active supporters of reform and revolution; whilst they were certainly not 'indifferent to the crude worldliness and materialism of politics and social affairs'.[69] But their sense of outrage at an ugly and unjust society largely caused them to redouble their efforts as artists, for they believed that the perfection they sought could only be attained through art itself; nothing else had the power to awaken the imagination in those whose feelings had become dulled by their experience of modern living. Hence, just as the Cambridge Platonists before them had argued that genuine acts of charity would not occur unless prompted by real feelings of love and compassion, so the Romantics argued that true benevolence and sympathy would only arise out of imaginative identification or empathy. As a result, imagination became invoked as the critical force which could overcome insensibility, with the failure of individuals to experience spontaneous altruistic emotions literally explicable in terms of 'a lack of imagination'.

The Romantic doctrine of moral renewal through art

The Romantics' visionary faith inspired them with the fervour to set about 'gaining converts' and 'curing souls',[70] and whilst the method they adopted owed much to the Protestant tradition of passionate preaching, it eschewed direct exhortation. For their theory of art, and, more particularly, of poetry, involved abandoning the idea that people could gain in goodness or understanding as a consequence of direct instruction. In this respect, they rejected entirely the neo-classical style of moralizing which had been exemplified by Dr Johnson. Nor did they really believe that people could be improved by having models of righteousness held up for them to imitate. What they emphasized in place of these methods was a variant of the Protestant faith in the power of 'the word', claiming that poetry could in itself work to create virtue.[71] As Abrams explains, 'in contrast to Johnson, Wordsworth maintains that, instead of telling and demonstrating what to do to become better, poetry, by sensitizing, purifying, and strengthening the feelings, directly *makes* us better' (italics in original).[72] Poetry is able to do this because it was created in the first place out of the poet's own visionary experience, and some of that 'saving grace' has been embodied in the poem, hence becoming available to be re-experienced by the reader. In this way, poetry achieves its educative and improving functions by evoking those states of feeling and imagination which are necessary for right conduct and human happiness, something the poet achieves 'by placing the reader in his own affective state of mind . . . [and] without inculcating doctrines, directly forms character';[73] the overall function of the poem being 'to foster and subtilize the sensibility, the emotions and sympathies of the reader', or generally to 'rectify men's feelings'.[74]

This same theory of personal renewal through the power of poetry is taken up even more enthusiastically by Shelley. He, however, is rather more concerned to rebut the utilitarians' condemnation of the art form,[75] than to advance a detailed account of its role as the instrument of morality. As a consequence, he not only matches the Benthamites in rhetoric, but is

anxious to place all the blame for society's ills at their door. Shelley scorns
these 'promoters of utility', or 'mere reasoners', claiming that they are to
blame for the widespread poverty and increasing inequalities which have
bred social unrest; something they have created through their advocacy
of the 'unmitigated exercise of the calculating faculty'.[76] Casting poetry
and the principle of self in the roles of God and Mammon respectively,
he argues that all problems stem from a failure to develop the creative
faculty in proportion to 'the cultivation of the mechanical arts', and that
consequently, although enough wisdom exists to build a better society,
this has not happened because of an insufficiency of imagination:

There is no want of knowledge respecting what is wisest and best in morals,
government and political economy. . . . We want the creative faculty to imagine
that which we know; we want the generous impulse to act that which we imagine;
we want the poetry of life.[77]

Then, after claiming that poetry is 'something divine', embracing as it
does all inferior forms of knowledge, and thus that poets are the 'true,
unacknowledged legislators of the world', he restates Wordsworth's
thesis by arguing that

A man, to be greatly good, must imagine intensely and comprehensively; the
pains and pleasures of his species must become his own. The great instrument of
the moral good is the imagination; and poetry administers to the effect by acting
upon the cause.[78]

A position which again takes the inherent goodness of human beings for
granted, attributing their failings to a mere lack of empathy. As Ruskin
later pithily expressed this creed, 'people would instantly care for others
as well as for themselves if only they could *imagine* others as well as
themselves' (italics in original).[79] An argument which raises imagination
to the status of a crucial 'divine', or 'magical', faculty through which all
people are to be converted into saints: for, in the words of a Victorian
defender of fiction, it can serve to 'awaken the sympathies, soften the
heart [and] excite veneration for the great, disgust for meanness'.[80]
Poems can achieve these beneficial results in individuals because 'Poetry
strengthens that faculty which is the organ of the moral nature of man, in
the same manner that exercise strengthens a limb'.[81]

   In one sense, this theory is merely a modification of the assumptions
that characterized sensibility, the addition being the introduction of the
poet as middleman. Thus, instead of individuals responding directly to
such pitiable sights as an idiot boy or a forsaken Indian woman by
bursting into tears and prostrating themselves, Wordsworth reacts on
their behalf, composing poems which artistically encapsulate such
feelings.[82] Then, when others read these works, the experience is

re-created with sufficient vividness for them to share his emotions. In this way, their capacity to both imagine and empathize is generally cultivated, with beneficial effects for them as well as for all those with whom they have dealings. At the same time, this doctrine can also be seen as a form of indirect, refined revivalism, in which the prophetic message of the spiritual virtuoso is embodied in a literary form, only to spring to life inside the head of the reader, converting him to a belief in the truth of the imaginative vision, and causing him to conduct his life differently in future.

It is noticeable how such a theory places almost as much emphasis upon the 're-creative' abilities of the reader as upon the original creative faculties of the poet, for whilst the latter must be moved by what he sees, and also capable of translating this experience into an affective, and hence effective, work of art, the former must possess sufficient imaginative skill to be able to use the words on the page to produce a convincing illusion. The reader is also, in that sense, assumed to be a creative artist, capable of conjuring up images which have the power to 'move' him.[83] There is, however, one feature of the poem which is of critical importance in facilitating this process, thereby making the reader's task simpler than the poet's was initially, and differentiating the re-created imaginary experience from any real event upon which it may have been based.

We may profitably follow Wordsworth's discussion of the processes involved in poetic creation for an identification of this ingredient, and an account of its part in the overall mechanism of character building. In the preface to the second edition of *Lyrical Ballads* (1802), he outlines the qualities which one would expect to find in a poet, who unsurprisingly, is described as 'endued with more lively sensibility, more enthusiasm and tenderness ... than the ordinary person'.[84] He is also identified as someone who

has a disposition to be affected more than other men by absent things as if they were present; an ability of conjuring up in himself passions, which are indeed far from being the same as those produced by real events, yet ... do more nearly resemble the passions produced by real events.[85]

This too is as we would expect, given the centrality, not just of imagination in the narrow sense, but of that autonomous, self-illusory faculty which can generate 'as-if' emotions. He continues by suggesting that the poet 'in bringing his feelings near to those of the persons whose feelings he describes', may actually come close to 'deluding' himself, confusing his own emotions with theirs.[86] Again, we can appreciate this emphasis on empathetic identification, as we can also that placed on creativity, with the poet 'chiefly distinguished from other men by a greater promptness to think and feel without immediate external excitement, and a greater power in expressing such thoughts and feelings as are produced in him in that manner'.[87] But there is something else that Wordsworth stresses, in addition to imagination, empathy, creativity and a generalized sensibility, something which characterizes not only the poet, the poem, and the readers' experience of it, but life itself; and that is pleasure.

A philosophy of pleasure

Having observed that 'all good poetry is the spontaneous overflow of powerful feelings', and that the composition of a poem has its origin in 'emotion recollected in tranquillity',[88] Wordsworth describes how the poet 'contemplates' that emotion until, the tranquillity disappearing, he actually experiences it. It is in this mood that composition begins. Wordsworth continues:

but the emotion, of whatever kind and in whatever degree, from various causes is qualified by various pleasures, so that in describing any passions whatever, which are voluntarily described, the mind will upon the whole be in a state of enjoyment.[89]

Hence the poet does not simply 'adopt' feelings, but 'qualifies' them so as to create enjoyment for himself, and indeed in the lines given above about the poet 'deluding' himself into confounding his feelings with those of others, there appears the clause, 'only modifying them in order to convey pleasure'.[90] It is clear from this that the poet is by no means merely a vehicle for transmitting experiences, but is crucially involved in transforming them, and the principle which governs this latter process is the production of pleasure.

Wordsworth is unambiguous on this point, stating clearly that 'the end of poetry is to produce excitement in coexistence with an overbalance of pleasure', and that the 'poet writes under one restriction only, namely, that of the necessity of giving immediate pleasure to a human being possessed of that information which may be expected from him . . . as a man'.[91] Although he does denounce those who consider poetry to be a 'matter of amusement and idle pleasure', this is because such a view does not recognize the high moral purpose which pleasure serves. Indeed, far from the need to supply it being a consideration which might 'degrade' the poet's art, pleasure reveals its essentially noble function. Pleasure is no less than the poet's medium of truth, his means of acknowledging the beauty of the universe, and his manner of giving expression to the essential dignity of man; pleasure is, in effect, 'the grand elementary principle' through which man 'knows, and feels, and lives, and moves'.[92]

Having already noted how, in the classical aesthetic tradition, the purpose of art was assumed to be the provision of pleasure in conjunction with the statement of moral truth, we can now see that the critical change proposed by Wordsworth is the claim that moral insight and improvement is achieved *through* the medium of pleasure itself, such that this becomes the moral agent; as he expresses it, 'we have no sympathy but what is propagated by pleasure'.[93] A change which implies that the poet is not simply a man of intense sensibility and imagination, but also necessarily one who is 'pleased with his own passions and volitions . . . someone who rejoices more than other men in the spirit of life that is in him'; in other words, someone who excels in his capacity to seek out and enjoy 'the pleasure which there is in life itself'.[94]

Just in case one might be tempted to feel that Wordsworth could not possibly have meant to imply that pleasure, in the full sense of the word, was the 'grand elementary principle' of life, or that the poet was, by definition, a hedonist, Lionel Trilling has forcefully supported this interpretation.[95] Noting that there were two separate 'moral ambiances' given to the word in the eighteenth century, the first standing for 'unexceptional', 'innocent', or 'domestic' pleasures, and the second, a 'very unfavourable one', to refer to where 'sensuous enjoyment becomes the chief end or object in life', he continues:

It is obvious that any badness or unfavourableness of meaning that the word *pleasure* may have relates to the primitiveness of the enjoyment that is being referred to. Scarcely any moralist will object to pleasure as what we will call a secondary state of feeling, as a charm or grace added to the solid business of life. What does arouse strong adverse judgement is pleasure in its radical aspect, as it is the object of an essential and definitive energy of man's nature. . . . Yet this is just how Wordsworth asks us to conceive of man's nature in the sentence I have spoken of – it is precisely pleasure in its primitive or radical aspect that he has in mind.[96] (Italics in original.)

This, of course, is the same distinction which we encountered in Puritanism and neo-Stoicism, and in both cases it was pleasure in this 'primitive' aspect which was so fiercely condemned. Now, for the first time, we find it directly associated with virtue, and asserted as an essential ingredient in human conduct. Indeed, individuals have the right to experience pleasure in this form, it is the essence of their 'dignity';[97] this is because it is the defining attribute of all life, and of nature, pleasure being the 'impulse from a vernal wood' which teaches us more of man and his moral being than 'all the sages can'. That most men do not experience such pleasure is an indication of their alienation from nature, and arises from the fact that 'the world' is too much with them. Only poetry, by virtue of its 'pleasurable resources', can overcome this estrangement, and thus restore them to their rightful state.

Wordsworth, as Trilling observes, hardly fits the popular image of a hedonist, largely restricting himself to such satisfactions as are offered by 'joy'.[98] He does, none the less, articulate the essential features of a philosophy of modern, rationalized hedonism, with its emphasis upon the key role played by the imagination in the creation of enjoyable emotions. The fact that he tended to limit these to the 'virtuous' feelings of pity, sorrow, sympathy, benevolence and joy, whilst largely excluding sensual gratification, demonstrates his kinship with the sentimentalists of the eighteenth century. Such restrictions do not seem consistent with his arguments, however, and it was left to the later Romantics, most especially Keats, to explore the larger implications of the claim that pleasure was the defining attribute of life.[99] This they did by widening the range of emotions from which pleasure could be obtained to include those of more dubious moral standing, such as pride, fear, horror, jealousy and hatred. In this respect, the Romantics came to emphasize that algolagnic sensibility, or 'agony', which Praz considered unique to them;[100] a delight in 'Medusean' beauty, or the pleasure that comes with pain, which he regarded as so indicative of the pathology of Romanticism. Ignoring the moral judgement which this view contains, it is clear that a man who 'rejoices in the spirit of life that is in him', whilst energetically pursuing the pleasure that there is in life itself, could indeed come to savour 'abnormal' delights, with the consequence that the qualities required of the poet may well 'not [be] incompatible with vice'.[101] The other, and closely related, discovery which the later Romantics made about the nature of pleasure, concerned its essentially elusive and self-extinguishing character; the fact that, as Trilling expresses it, 'the desire for pleasure denies itself',[102] or in Keats's words, that 'Joy . . . is ever . . . Bidding adieu'. With this understanding came the realization that whilst pleasure may be the defining attribute of life, an aching sense of pleasure lost was likely to be the defining experience of the hedonist. Disillusionment, melancholy, and an intense longing for the perfect pleasure that will not die, thus become characteristic attitudes of the dedicated romantic pleasure-seeker.

Neither of these subsequent qualifications to Wordsworth's understanding of the nature of pleasure led to any radical change in the philosophy he outlined. The tendency for the Romantic to dabble in 'vice', for example, worked to stimulate society's condemnation, thereby helping to confirm the poet's conviction of his genius; whilst recognition that pleasure was essentially fleeting acted to increase his sense of frustration with a boring, ugly and fundamentally 'unpleasant' world. Both developments thus accentuated the sense of a fundamental discrepancy between the satisfactions which life offered and those pleasures which could be enjoyed in imagination. Even the tendency to explore the more directly sensual delights which poetry can offer – so obvious when Keats is compared to Wordsworth – only served to heighten awareness of this contrast, and the realization that, whilst 'heard melodies are sweet, . . . those unheard / Are sweeter'.

It is now possible to perceive how the Romantic theodicy, as it became translated into a theory of art and the artist, led to the creation of a distinctive ideal of character, one which, although most obviously applied to the artist, was also meant to serve for the consumer or 're-creator' of his products. Since the key characteristic of the divine was taken to be creativity, both in the sense of productivity and of originality, imagination became the most significant and prized of personal qualities, with the capacity to manifest this in works of art and through an ability to enter fully into those created by others, both acting as unambiguous signs of its presence. Since, in addition, the true and perfect world which imagination revealed was necessarily the realm of beauty, any exercise of this faculty was accompanied by pleasure, such that use of the imagination and the experiencing of pleasure became largely commensurate. Thus the Romantic was someone who had an ideal sensitivity to pleasure, and indicated this fact by the spontaneity and intensity of his emotions.[103] By the same token, he was an individual who could give pleasure to others, not so much directly through his person or his actions, but indirectly, through his embodied imaginings, a pleasure which served to spiritually renew and enlighten them, as it had him. In addition, his idealistic determination and sense of obligation toward his personal 'genius', combined to make him feel estranged from an artificial, materialistic, and utilitarian society. Consequently feeling dissatisfied with a routine existence, and drawn to find consolation in 'nature', he attempts to give expression to his 'real' self whilst seeking to convert others to his vision of a more perfect world.

This ideal of character is the only one of those examined that places a high moral value directly upon the experience of pleasure, whilst actually devaluing a utilitarian preoccupation with comfort. At the same time, it is imaginatively mediated pleasure which is given a privileged position *vis-à-vis* direct sensation, with sound ethical reasons advanced to support the individual's seeking out and displaying enjoyment. Indeed, those individuals needing reassurance that they live up to this ideal will seek to transform their lives into one continuous sequence of pleasing experiences, taking delight in their own ability to enjoy the novel and the strange, as well as their general capacity for day-dreaming. They will also endeavour to manifest their hedonistic capacity in apparently uncontrolled outbursts of powerful emotion, together with a more diffuse and melancholic longing for more perfect experiences. Finally, they will attempt to reveal the unique nature of their selves through an egotistical introspection and determined eccentricity, intent on provoking a disapproving reaction from the upholders of a more conventional and 'common-sensical' morality.

It is hardly surprising that the development of this ideal of character caused the conflict between the ethics of sincerity and propriety, which had simmered throughout the late eighteenth century, to finally boil over in the first half of the nineteenth; and, transformed by the triumph of the bourgeoisie and the consequent despair of artists into a clash between genius and utilitarianism, finally solidify into the form of a clear-cut opposition between 'self' and 'society'. The range of stark alternatives presented to a person of sensibility and imagination now became those of success *or* integrity, utility *or* play, work *or* leisure, comfort *or* pleasure, 'the world' *or* 'the spirit', as estrangement became the natural state for artists and romantically inclined intellectuals. Howard E. Hugo observes that 'the real Rousseau, the fictional Werther and Harley' [the epithetical *Man of Feeling*] all shared at least two traits, 'acute emotional sensitivity, and an awareness of not belonging to the existing social order',[104] whilst he identifies Goethe's play, *Torquato Tasso* (1789), as containing one of the earliest representations in literature of the creative genius as someone who feels himself to be set apart from his fellows.[105] By the early nineteenth century such alienation had reached epidemic proportions, even displacing sensibility as the predominant trait of a truly artistic person, thus marking the widespread appearance of that type of character which Trilling dubs 'the opposing self'.[106]

There have always been selves. . . . Yet the self that makes itself manifest at the end of the eighteenth century is different in kind, and in effect, from any self that had ever before emerged. It is difficult in several notable respects, but there is one distinguishing characteristic which seems to me pre-eminently important: its intense and adverse imagination of the culture in which it has its being.[107]

This 'adverse imagination' of the culture could drive the Romantic into that form of inner exile from society which day-dreaming and fantasizing represented, finding in his 'inner eye' both the bliss which soothed despair and the inspiration necessary for renewed attempts to convert others. But disgust with a world in which people 'lay waste [their] powers' by 'Getting and spending', also caused the Romantic to distance himself physically from society, finding comfort and consolation in the natural landscape of remote places. Yet there was another form of retreat from an uncongenial world practiced by the Romantics, one in which they sought that mutual reassurance and support which cannot be found in isolation. This collective, 'other-worldly' response was that of Bohemianism, and it offered an environment in which coteries of spiritual virtuosi could develop their artistic gifts apart from the corrupting influences of the larger society, whilst also gaining reassurance of their status as members of an 'elect'.

Bohemianism

Bohemia is the social embodiment of Romanticism, with Bohemianism the attempt to make life conform to Romantic principles; therefore it is here that the most obvious and clear-cut illustrations of the Romantic ideal of character are to be found in modern society. It also serves as the best example of that fundamental and essentially modern tendency to evaluate pleasure above utility, and hence voluptuousness above opulence. The popular stereotype of a starving artist living in a bare garret, intermittently working at his art and engaging in bouts of irresponsible high-spiritedness and dissipation, reveals this basic preference very clearly. It is an inverse ranking of asceticism and indulgence to that which characterizes the commercially minded bourgeoisie, for, while the latter are apt to restrict their pleasures whilst forever adding to their comfort, the Bohemian readily embraces deprivation in the pursuit of his pleasures.

We may tentatively define Bohemianism as an unconventional and irregular way of life, voluntarily chosen, and frequently involving artistic pursuits, of those Romantics who are self-consciously in revolt against what they see as a utilitarian and philistine society, and who find mutual support against its 'corrupting' influence in coterie behaviour. It is a modern phenomenon, making its first appearance in Paris in the 1840's, and thereafter spreading to all the major cities of Europe and North America, where it has remained a permanent feature of cosmopolitan life, periodically flourishing and dying back, but never dying out.[108] It was the romantic myth of the unhappy and neglected genius, the impoverished artist whose talent goes unrecognized by society and who consequently dies in squalor, which helped to bring Bohemia into being; for its currency and appeal led many young artists to embrace suffering, and even 'martyrdom', in order that it might serve as proof of their greatness. That this should have happened first in Paris in the 1840s was probably because it was in France, in the aftermath of the Revolution, that the triumph of the bourgeoisie seemed so complete; whilst the city itself dominated the cultural life of the country to such a degree that it acted as a magnet for anyone with artistic pretensions. In addition, it was the main centre for professional training and as such attracted all those middle-class young men who, whilst marked out by their parents for the law, teaching or medicine, had hearts full of poetry and heads filled with dreams of fame.[109]

Clustering together in whichever quarter of a large city offers the lowest rents, Bohemians typically create their own social world.[110] They tend to form intellectual circles, often around a café or restaurant (such as Pfaff's in New York for the Bohemians of the 1850s and 1860s), where they meet to talk, gossip, recite, or hold verse competitions, get drunk, practise their wit, flirt, argue, or even brawl.[111] Sometimes special tables are set aside for them, or even rooms, whilst flexible opening hours are introduced to accommodate their extended arguments and parties. Often the café is home for those who cannot afford even the lowest rents, or perhaps the office from which little literary magazines and journals are produced and published on a shoe-string budget, only to appear, disappear and be replaced with lightning rapidity. Some Bohemians would be on the fringes of the commercial art world, or would actually receive an income from writing or the stage, but many, if not most, would receive little or no reward for their artistic endeavours and be forced to survive by borrowing, taking menial jobs, or by the use of their wits.[112]

Bohemians, as Parry notes, are made and not born, there being 'less of a hereditary character in their group than in any other group in society'.[113] They are nearly always the sons (and nowadays also the daughters) of fairly affluent, middle-class parents, who have eschewed a more conventional career – in preparation for which their parents would have supported them – for the more disreputable 'dabbling' in art. A choice which cuts them off from comfort, and presents them with a precarious existence on the edge of deprivation and poverty. As Murger observed, Bohemia is that stage in an artist's career which is 'the preface to the Academy, the hospital or the Morgue';[114] yet it is not a way of life which any are compelled to follow:

Many of them, if they chose, might escape the catastrophe that suddenly cuts them off at an age when life as a rule is only beginning. They need only make one or two concessions to the hard laws of necessity, which means they should learn to live in duplicate, to keep one life for the poetry in them . . . and another for the labourer that contrives to provide daily bread. But this double life . . . is not often to be met with in young men of this stamp: while pride, a bastard sort of pride, makes them proof against all counsels of common sense. And so they die young, now and again one of them leaving some piece of work behind him for the world to admire at a later day.[115]

Hence the periods of near starvation, the nights spent sleeping in the open or in unheated rooms, and the overall lack of what most civilized people would consider the ordinary decencies of life; all the results of a fierce pride which brooks no compromise.

In this respect the Bohemian resembles the monk, his poverty and comfort-asceticism stemming from a similar vow to renounce the temptations of the world.[116] Not that the Bohemian does not value the good things of life, and especially those which bring pleasure; on the contrary, these are prized most highly. Lawrence Lipton confessed that when a Bohemian in New York in the 1920s, he still had expensive tastes and coveted trips to the opera;[117] and it certainly seems to be characteristic of Bohemians, when in possession of money, to spend it lavishly on expensive forms of enjoyment, Murger referring to their tendency to drink 'the oldest and the best' wines when good fortune comes their way.[118] But it is comfort which Bohemians have renounced and especially all conduct aimed at ensuring it, to the extent that they 'will not work to the degree that threatens their way of life as artists',[119] nor will they compromise in any other way with the overriding obligation to serve the high god of Art. Thus, if their endeavours are poorly renumerated, they will not modify them in order to meet the demands of popular taste, preferring to suffer the discomfort of neglect. It is not that they have taken a vow of poverty, for a lack of wealth has little intrinsic merit, and they will happily accept money, whether as a gift or in exchange for their art.[120] It is rather that their fundamental dissatisfaction with the spiritual and aesthetic poverty of 'bourgeois' society comes to be focused upon those durable consumer goods which symbolize the life of the 'comfortably well-off', upon houses, furniture, furnishings, cars and expensive clothes. To repudiate these is to assert a commitment to pleasure as the primary means of self-expression.

The Bohemian critique of modern society emphasizes the ugliness, spiritual emptiness and general absence of heroism. The 'great flaw of the bourgeoisie' they see as being 'creative poverty', and a 'cowardice of imagination natural in men who [are] slaves to pragmatic design'.[121] Indeed, it was just those qualities which had brought the middle classes material success – their prudence, practicality and disciplined industry – which the first Bohemians took as evidence of the barrenness of their souls. For them the bougeoisie represented

ambition without passion, possessiveness without depth of desire, power without grandeur, everything that was spiritually paltry and anti-vital, everything that was inadequate and pettily self-protective, in a psychological and even a biological way. Greed was bourgeois, but so were carpet slippers and head colds.[122]

The creed which the Bohemians upheld in the face of such prosaic unimaginativeness was the very essence of Romanticism. The ideal of self-expression, for example, with the aim of realizing individuality through creativity, plus the abolition of all those laws, conventions and rules which prevented this from occurring; the pursuit of pleasure and the importance of developing to the full one's capacity for enjoyment, especially through that 'shrine . . . for the ritual of love' which is the body;[123] the idea of genius; the rejection of rational causality; world-weariness and the natural alienation of the truly talented.[124] Also, as one moves into the twentieth century, the doctrine of the equality of the sexes becomes important, together with concepts like psychological adjustment and libidinal expression, which owed their currency to the popularity of Freudianism.[125]

A comparison of the Bohemians with the dandies is helpful in revealing some of the essential features of this ethic. Like their predecessors these 'aristocrats of pleasure' adopted some upper-class values.[126] They sought, for example, to lead a leisured life, having a 'special aversion to work'.[127] Only infrequently, however, did they have sufficient money to be able to maintain an even moderately extravagent existence, though like the dandies they borrowed extensively and rarely payed their debts; consequently, at best, they resembled distressed aristocrats with little to their name but pride. But then for the Bohemians there was no shame in being poor. They also resembled the dandies in their tendency to congregate in cliques and social circles, competing with each other in word-play and delighting in provoking the bourgeoisie with their conspicuous dissipations. Unlike them, however, honour and reputation did not depend upon impeccable social conduct in the sense of mastery of good form, but on the display of commitment to romantic ideals. This could be confirmed in the company of one's peers through some evidence of a capacity to indulge in pleasure, an indifference to comfort, or simply a readiness to taunt the bourgeoisie. But the romantic Bohemian's duty to his personal genius meant that a spiritual dimension existed which transcended any mere concern with social image; hence while the dandy only really existed in the eyes of others, the Bohemian must answer to a spirit within himself, and to whose 'realization' he is obliged to devote his life. The critical importance of this feature of the romantic ethic is also highlighted by comparing Bohemianism with that later hybrid of dandyism and Romanticism which was aestheticism.

Identifiable largely by the slogan 'art for art's sake', aestheticism was a phenomenon of the late nineteenth century and is generally associated with such artists and writers as Pater, Whistler and Wilde.[128] Although the image of the aesthete brings to mind the dandy, aestheticism was a development out of Romanticism in which the logical incompatibility of art and utilitarianism was taken to the point of stripping the former of even its moral and spiritual functions. As Schucking explains,

It divorced art from all influence over life except the purely aesthetic, and so confined it within a sacred grove whose priests were the artists. Artist-priests performed their offices, often, like Gautier and later his emulator Oscar Wilde, entirely removed from the common herd by the extravagances in which they indulged at times. The ordinary man could not follow them, could not conceive why any sensible man should spend a whole day in the pursuit of the only right adjective or in the attuning of a couple of vowels.[129]

This separation of the artist from the public can be seen as a logical extension of the romantic's claim to belong to a special race of men. The aesthete, however, has no evangelical fervour, no message of salvation to bring to the people, and cannot contemplate art being 'reduced' to a means of moral renewal. In this sense, the original classical conception of art as that which should please and instruct, and which has been changed by the romantics to the theme of instruction through pleasure, was now changed once again into the doctrine that art should merely please. As Johnson observes, aestheticism causes art to be valued 'solely for the immediate aesthetic pleasure it affords'.[130] On the other hand, the artist, in his capacity as aesthetic virtuoso and critic, is the only one properly qualified to judge what is 'true pleasure', or 'correct taste'.[131]

Ironically, such a development gives less impetus to modern hedonism than did the Romantic Movement. For although aestheticism specifies that the giving of pleasure is the sole purpose of art, and then goes on to suggest that life itself should be approached, 'in the spirit of art',[132] these teachings do not cause the artist to plunge into an orgy of hedonistic activity. This is because the treatment of life as art leads to an attitude of detachment, one in which events are appraised as 'spectacle', something to be judged with the eye of a critic and connoisseur; at the same time, the gap between art and life is recognized as irreducible, with the result that there is a tendency to withdraw into a contemplative mode. Unlike the romantic, however, this is largely to escape from the ugliness of the real world and not to find the inspiration with which to change it. Most crucial of all, the aesthete's ultimate responsibility to art means that he has a duty to make an art object of himself, something that would bring him pleasure as well as others. Hence the popular image of the aesthete as narcissistic and effeminate, with Wilde's comment, 'we watch ourselves, and the mere wonder of the spectacle enthralls us', epitomizing the consequent egotism.[133]

It is in this respect that aestheticism comes closest to the dandy ethic, with its overwhelming stress on self-image. Here, though, the concern is predominantly aesthetic and there is little emphasis upon etiquette, although a preoccupation with the one kind of 'good form', can, in practice, merge into the other. What they do have in common is reliance upon a close-knit social group for the necessary reassurance that one has attained the ideal, as well as the same personal catastrophe consequent on exclusion.[134] Of greater significance is the similar need to exercise self-control and discipline, for art is taken to be a matter of skill, not feeling. There is thus a form of emotional stoicism in aestheticism resembling that which characterized dandyism, although without the 'heroic' element. Baudelaire illustrates this ingredient with his expressed dislike of the romantics for their storminess, high-flung spontaneity and desire to let every emotion take its course.[135] Wilde also rejected the romantic identification of the natural with the aesthetic, reversing Wordsworth's observation by claiming that 'all bad poetry springs from genuine feeling', and describing a sunset as a very second-rate Turner.[136] Hence aestheticism becomes the cult of the artificial as the aesthete struggles to turn himself into an object of beauty. Thus the irony that, if art is to please, then the aesthete must subdue his passions at all times, arranging his behaviour with great deliberateness so that it will bring pleasure to all; his own satisfaction deriving both from his 'reflection', and the knowledge that he does delight others. It is consequently a largely contemplative and appreciative stance, with little impetus to action or expression.[137]

It follows from this that aestheticism does not represent a powerful impulse to reject 'the world'. There is a repudiation of utilitarianism, but not materialism, for luxury, in the form of exquisite, rare and beautiful objects of little use, actually symbolizes the aesthetic attitude. Consequently, although aestheticism helps to promote the phenomenon of fashion by making individuals aware of themselves as objects of beauty, and did have an impact upon taste and patterns of consumption at the turn of the century, it does not create the restless longing, that dissatisfaction with experience and yearning for the dream, which underpins the spirit of consumerism.[138]

Indeed, by attempting to make art a 'morality-free zone', independent of society's larger taboos and restrictions, the aesthetes lost that power to defy convention which the Bohemians possessed.[139] The claim that art imposed a 'higher' morality on those few souls who could appreciate it merely led to such 'precious' individuals withdrawing from involvement with the larger society in order to cultivate their special talent. There was, therefore, no basis for asserting the supremacy of art over other areas of life, as like the dandies, the aesthetes just assumed their own superiority; and although they could condemn society for being ugly, they could not condemn it as 'evil'.[140] Thus whilst the aesthete was likely to be indifferent to society's conventions, he lacked good reasons for flouting them. Indeed, since he was probably dependent upon 'Society' in the narrow sense for his reputation and livelihood, he would be disinclined to defy it too openly. The Bohemian, by contrast, as we have seen, needed to flout convention, and it is precisely this difference which indicates that only Romanticism could have supplied that dynamic so necessary to modern consumerism.

The romantic ideal of character, together with its associated theory of moral renewal through art, functioned to stimulate and legitimate that form of autonomous, self-illusory hedonism which underlies modern consumer behaviour. At the same time, romantic ideas concerning the role and function of the artist served to ensure that a continuous supply of novel and stimulating cultural products would be forthcoming, and that via Bohemia, the limits to prevailing taste would repeatedly be tested and overthrown. The romantic world-view provided the highest possible motives with which to justify day-dreaming, longing and the rejection of reality, together with the pursuit of originality in life and art; and by so doing, enabled pleasure to be ranked above comfort, counteracting both traditionalistic and utilitarian restraints on desire.

More specifically, Romanticism provided that philosophy of 'recreation' necessary for a dynamic consumerism: a philosophy which legitimates the search for pleasure as good in itself and not merely of value because it restores the individual to an optimum efficiency. In this respect, the philosophy of self-expression and self-realization most commonly attributed to the influence of Freud and which has served to introduce intrinsic hedonism into areas such as education and therapy, can be seen to be fundamentally romantic in inspiration. At the same time, Romanticism has ensured the widespread basic taste for novelty, together with the supply of 'original' products, necessary for the modern fashion pattern to operate; something best illustrated by a recognition of the central function which Bohemia fulfils as the social and cultural laboratory for modern society, as crucial in connection with consumption as science and technology is for production. In all these ways, Romanticism has served to provide ethical support for that restless and continuous pattern of consumption which so distinguishes the behaviour of modern man.

10

Conclusion

The bourgeois were once the deadly enemies of the Romantics. Or rather, they only seemed to be. Now we know that the Romantics were bourgeois, and that the bourgeois were Romantics, to a considerable extent, far more than we (and of course, than they themselves) were accustomed to think.

John Lukács

The problem posed at the beginning of this book was that of accounting for the consumer revolution which accompanied the onset of industrialization in eighteenth-century England. Noting that economic historians had identified the importance of rising demand as a crucial factor initiating that revolution, and located its principal cause in a 'new propensity to consume', the origins of this propensity were then taken as the focus of discussion. Whilst the evidence showed that this stemmed from changes in values and attitudes, being in some way related to such innovations as the rise of modern fashion, romantic love and the novel, it soon became clear that existing accounts of these changes were either reductionist or circular. This problem was then shown to be a general feature of those theories of consumer behaviour current within the social sciences, with neither the instinctivist, manipulationist nor Veblenesque perspectives supplying satisfactory explanations of that dynamic generation of new wants which is so characteristic of modern consumerism. Indeed, these perspectives were seen to be seriously deficient in their ahistorical treatment of the subject, as well as in their common tendency to regard wanting as an irrational, involuntary and 'unworthy' form of behaviour.

It therefore proved necessary, in order to resolve this historical problem, not only to provide a more adequate conceptualization of the nature of modern consumerism, but to develop a theory which, while not reducing this aspect of human conduct to a matter of instinctive impulsiveness or environmental manipulation, nevertheless compensated for the inability of utilitarianism to consider the question of the origin of wants. The solution adopted was to turn to a hedonistic model of human action, and eschewing the misleading habit of treating this term as a synonym for utility, focus upon that feature of human conduct in which pleasure and not satisfaction is the goal. Recognition of the fundamental and extensive differences between behaviour directed toward these two ends, and hence the fact that individuals living above the level of subsistence are likely to be faced with a choice between them, made it possible to distinguish traditional from modern hedonism. The former was identified as a preoccupation with sensory experience, with 'pleasures' regarded as discrete and standardized events, and in the pursuit of which there is a natural tendency for the hedonist to seek despotic powers. Modern hedonism is marked, in contrast, by a preoccupation with 'pleasure', envisaged as a potential quality of all experience. In order to extract this from life, however, the individual has to substitute illusory for real stimuli, and by creating and manipulating illusions and hence the emotive dimension of consciousness, construct his own pleasurable environment. This modern, autonomous, and illusory form of hedonism commonly manifests itself as day-dreaming and fantasizing.

Hedonism of this kind is seen as providing the answer to the problem of the distinctive features of modern consumerism, for it explains how the individual's interest is primarily focused on the meanings and images which can be imputed to a product, something which requires novelty to be present. At the same time, the joys of longing rival those of actual gratification, with disillusionment the necessary concomitant of the purchase and use of goods; characteristics which also help to explain the dynamic and disacquiring nature of modern consumer behaviour. Such a model not only makes it possible to understand precisely how a consumer creates (and abandons) 'wants', and why it is that this has become a never-ending process, but also directs attention to the character of consumption as a voluntaristic, self-directed and creative process in which cultural ideals are necessarily implicated. It is then argued that not only is modern consumerism to be understood in these terms, but that romantic love and the crucial modern phenomenon of dynamic fashion should also be viewed as dependent upon autonomous, self-illusory hedonism.

Attention was turned in Part Two to the cultural, historical and sociological (rather than the economic and psychological) dimensions of the original problem. These, it will be remembered, concerned the fate of the Protestant ethic and the enigma set by the discovery that the new propensity to consume took the form of a demand for luxury goods by the middle sections of society. How, if these classes were indeed the carriers of an ascetic and puritanical 'Protestant ethic', itself essential to that ordered, regular pattern of productive work constitutive of capitalism, could they also be responsible for a form of consumerism based on hedonism? It was a sociological puzzle previously resolved through separating the production and consumption revolutions by more than a century, and hence attributing the ascetic and hedonistic roles to very different generations. This solution – always logically suspect – was now shown to be empirically doubtful; and as a consequence, Protestantism and its connection with pleasure became the object of investigation.

Whilst Weber's original analysis of Protestantism was not directly challenged, it was noted how it effectively ceased at the end of the seventeenth century, with little attention given to the revolution in Christianity after the great dogmatic synthesis achieved by Calvin. By examining the Arminian reaction, however, together with the arguments of the Cambridge Platonists and Leibniz's alternative theodicy, it proved possible to trace the emergence of a new religious ethic of benevolence; one in which virtue was associated with the charitable feelings of pity and sympathy and linked the manifestation of these with the Calvinist teaching that a melancholy sensibility constituted a sign of God's grace. This was the basis of an emotionalist deistic ethic in which the good man or woman revealed their virtue – in the form of a profound sensibility to the plight of others – through a display of frequent and profound emotions, especially those of pity and melancholy. With the ensuing shift from the spiritual significance of emotions to their intrinsic pleasures (itself a product of decaying eschatological beliefs) sentimentalism proper was born.

It was at this point that some attention was given to the popular claim that the hedonistic ingredient in modern society stemmed from the emphasis which the aristocracy had always placed upon the pleasures of life, and that any new enthusiasm for luxury which the middle classes displayed in the second half of the eighteenth century should be seen as deriving from an emulation of their more 'liberated' social superiors. This argument was shown to be unconvincing in light of the fundamentally traditional nature of upper-class hedonism, centring as it did (at least for men) upon a stoic, virility ethic which denied emotionality; something which was shown to be true of both the earlier 'cavalier', and the later 'dandy' versions, each being social, 'mannered' ethics lacking the moral inner-directedness so characteristic of the middle classes.

Consideration of the aristocratic ethic did, however, serve to draw attention to a crucial new ingredient present in the cult of sensibility but largely alien to the Protestant tradition, which was 'imported' from the nobility. This was a concern with aesthetics, which, long central to classical thought and hence to the aristocratic outlook, now brought radical changes to the previously exclusively moral and spiritual middle-class ethic, causing the aspiring bourgeoisie to develop their own 'middle-classicist' aesthetic, and, drawing upon the ideas of Lord Shaftesbury, substitute intuition and feeling for traditional authority and reason. By doing this, however, they came close to equating goodness and beauty; with pleasure, as manifested in emotion, serving as an index of both.

In part, this was a response to the problem of finding an agreed and fixed aesthetic standard which had been posed by the decline of classicism; a problem which the aristocracy solved by equating 'taste' with conformity to carefully defined standards of propriety. The middle classes, by contrast, true to their religious heritage, regarded 'taste' as a sign of moral and spiritual worth, with an ability to take pleasure in the beautiful and to respond with tears to the pitiable equally indicative of a man (or woman) of virtue. It was an ethic which inevitably provided powerful legitimation for the pursuit of emotional pleasure. Although there was, for a time at least, an attempt to hold both the aristocratic and bourgeois conceptions of taste in balance, the tensions between propriety and sincerity soon forced them apart, with artistic 'genius' coming to displace the former emphasis on the more passive concept of 'taste'.

This shift marked the move into Romanticism, and with the cult of sensibility under attack for the manifest hypocrisies and dissembling which it encouraged, a theodicy of creativity finally displaced the existing theodicy of benevolence. This had the effect of casting the individual of true virtue in the role of an opponent to 'society', whose conventions he must deny if only to secure proof of his genius and passion. At the same time, he becomes not merely a virtuoso in feeling but also in pleasure, something he must prove by creating cultural products which yield pleasure to others. Pleasure indeed becomes the crucial means of recognizing that ideal truth and beauty which imagination reveals – it is the 'grand elementary principle' of life – and thus becomes the means by which enlightenment and moral renewal can be achieved through art. These are urgently needed in a society now thoroughly imbued with the life-denying philosophy and institutions of a materialistic utilitarianism. Not only, therefore, must the romantic be an outsider in order to manifest his genius, but any consistent attempt to live in accord with his ideals necessarily forces him into the inner exile of Bohemia.

It is now possible to state the general nature of the conclusion reached concerning the relationship between the romantic ethic and the spirit of modern consumerism. The latter, labelled self-illusory hedonism, is characterized by a longing to experience in reality those pleasures created and enjoyed in imagination, a longing which results in the ceaseless consumption of novelty. Such an outlook, with its characteristic dissatisfaction with real life and an eagerness for new experiences, lies at the heart of much conduct that is most typical of modern life, and underpins such central institutions as fashion and romantic love. The romantic ethic can be seen to possess a basic congruence, or 'elective affinity', with this spirit, and to have given rise to a character type and ethical conduct highly conducive to the adoption of such attitudes. In particular, romantic teachings concerning the good, the true and the beautiful, provide both the legitimation and the motivation necessary for modern consumer behaviour to become prevalent throughout the contemporary industrial world.

The thesis advanced in this book is not merely that the Romantic Movement assisted crucially at the birth of modern consumerism; it is also maintained that romanticism has continued in the two centuries or so since that time to work in such a way as to overcome the forces of traditionalism and provide a renewed impetus to the dynamic of consumerism. This general fact can be observed in the close association, both in time and place, between romanticism, especially in its social form of Bohemianism, and a dynamic upsurge in cultural consumerism. Paris, for example, is both the spiritual home of Bohemianism and the historic fashion capital of the world, whilst California, long-regarded as the site of the most advanced experiments in consumerism, has been the centre of both the beat and the hippie Bohemian movements of the 1950s and 1960s. In fact, taking a longer time-span into account, it is possible to discern a close correspondence between outbursts of Bohemianism and periods of creative consumer boom. Apart from their initial association in the early nineteenth century, one can observe such connections in the 1890s, the 1920s and the 1960s; the 'naughty nineties', the 'jazz age' and the 'swinging sixties' all revealing essentially the same characteristic features. Each period witnessed a 'moral revolution', in which a 'new spirit of pleasure' emerged to challenge what was identified as a restrictive 'puritanism'; a spirit most evident among the educated young, who sought pleasure and self-expression through alcohol, drugs, sex and art, whilst an intense moral idealism went hand-in-hand with an unrestrained commercialism.[1]

Such a thesis raises several problems in its wake, the most central of which are naturally similar to those identified as arising from Weber's original argument linking Protestantism with capitalism. What, for example, is the precise nature of the claimed connection, and how, in particular, are ethical attitudes and patterns of economic conduct understood to be linked? Perhaps the direction of implied causality should be reversed, with the hedonistic impulses of consumers regarded as more instrumental in effecting the growth of romanticism than vice versa?[2] Such queries quickly lead into fundamental issues in sociological theory, issues concerning the nature of action and cultural change which can hardly be fully explored in this context; on the other hand, it would be foolish to pretend they are not present. In order to consider them, therefore, if only briefly, it will be helpful to start by stressing, as did Weber, the essentially ironic nature of the relationship between the advocacy of ethical ideals and the forms of conduct which they serve to promote.

The irony of social action

Neither the first Romantics, nor their successors in subsequent decades, ever intended to grant legitimacy to modern consumerism or to that spirit of self-interested hedonism upon which it is based. Nor, indeed, did they seek to act in such a way as to overcome traditional objections to pleasure-seeking merely in order to allow the commercial exploitation of new areas of hedonistic interest. Pleasure-seeking, whether engaged in by the original creator or the subsequent re-creator of cultural products, was not, as we have seen, regarded as an end in itself, but as a means to moral and spiritual renewal. Consequently, the Romantics were scathing in their attacks upon those who engaged in the search for mere stimulation and excitement, being just as quick to condemn those trashy, Gothic novels 'full of sensational action and tawdry sentiment' which flooded the market in the late eighteenth and early nineteenth centuries as any neo-classical critic. Wordsworth himself inveighed against those 'frantic novels, sickly and stupid German tragedies, and deluges of idle and extravagant stories in verse'[3] which he considered to have caused the neglect of all literature of quality. His objection against these works was not that they provided pleasure – for, as we have seen, this was also his intention – but that 'excitement is carried beyond its proper bounds';[4] with emotional stimulation engaged in for 'idle' reasons, and not for the sole and noble purpose of conveying truth or creating a moral sensibility.

That pleasure should be put to work corruptly in the service of self-seeking ends in this fashion was in turn blamed upon the widespread acceptance of a utilitarian, *laissez-faire* philosophy, and the consequent unchecked operation of commercial forces. Hence, far from endorsing consumerism, the first Romantics initiated that form of mass culture critique so characteristic of modern intellectuals, in which the unrestrained pursuit of profit and personal gain is seen as the primary factor which acts to prevent people from experiencing that spiritual enlightenment which is their birthright.[5] In this respect, one can say that Wordsworth and Shelley no more approved of the modern consumer's endless striving to satisfy new wants than Luther and Calvin applauded the entrepreneur's efforts to amass profits; indeed, on the contrary, all four had the true moralist's horror of any society organized around such blatantly selfish principles.

This is not to say that the Romantics failed to recognize how their own works might be consumed in a manner other than they intended, or that their advocacy of a moral philosophy of pleasure might serve the interests of groups whom they opposed. After all, in comparison with neo-classicism, Romanticism represented a major concession to what effectively constituted popular taste, and thus could easily be employed as an element in a populist critique of traditional values. Wordsworth had himself rejected difficult forms and abstruse subject-matter in poetry, advocating the language 'really used by men',[6] whilst Coleridge pioneered the treatment of exotic topics. Authors like Scott and Poe followed in their footsteps, finding an eager market for their simply told stories of mystery, horror and romance. It was hardly surprising, therefore, that Stendhal should observe (somewhat tongue-in-cheek, no doubt) that Romanticism 'is the art which gives the public those literary works, which, with its present outlook on life, afford it the greatest possible pleasure'.[7]

Whilst the recognition that the Romantics could be said to have brought about a state of affairs generally conducive to modern consumerism is certainly not tantamount to suggesting that this was ever their intention, it does direct attention to the fact that there is a sense in which one can see Romanticism as the 'ideology' of a new artist class. For, just as Romanticism as a general world-view can reasonably be seen as both a rejection of the traditional, aristocratic ethic and a reaction against an emerging, bourgeois utilitarianism, so the Romantic theory of art can be regarded as an attempt to find a middle path between the restrictiveness of neo-classicism and the philistine tyranny of a populist commercialism. The fine artist, whilst identifying with the classical tradition in European art, was able to turn to popular, vernacular cultures, especially those identified with the 'folk', both in order to obtain fresh material with which to please his new middle-class audiences, and to gain some degree of artistic freedom to experiment outside the constraints imposed by a classical aesthetic. At the same time, the commercial artist, forced to adapt to both the lowest common denominator and the fickle character of public taste, could invoke more elite, classical conceptions of the role and function of the artist in order to salvage some integrity and independence of action. By thus playing off these two traditions against one another, the artist with fundamentally romantic inclinations might succeed in negotiating a position which offered some possibility of integrity and success.

This possibility existed because of the emphasis placed upon the theory of moral renewal through art, which, whilst enabling the artist to cater for the public's demand for pleasure, also permitted him to claim a holy purpose for his art and a 'spiritual' role for himself. Compared with neo-classicism, however, Romanticism involved concessions to popular taste, concessions which served to ensure the continued economic survival of the artist under the new 'free market' conditions. This is not, however, to claim that Romanticism was little more than the ideological representation of the interests of a bourgeois artist class, nor that their professional idealism was merely a cover for self-interest; for a degree of correspondence can be taken for granted between the 'interests' of a group and the ideals it espouses without there being any necessity to assume that the one is explicable in terms of the other.[8] In any case, as we have already seen in the discussion of Bohemianism, Romanticism could also create a very real tension between the 'ideal' and 'material' interests of the artist.

Having made these qualifications concerning a degree of *post hoc* recognition of functions and the presence of an 'ideological' interest, it still remains the case that Romanticism's connection with modern consumerism must be viewed as ironic, for although the Romantics certainly did intend both to provide pleasure and to promote day-dreaming, they cannot be regarded as having sought an outcome in which these combined to facilitate the restless pursuit of goods and services. Hence it is possible to observe that precisely the same irony of history was associated with the emergence of modern rationalized consumption as accompanied modern production. It is the same 'cunning of reason', as Mitzman calls it, by which people may intend one thing but actually attain something entirely different,[9] even indeed, results diametrically opposed to their initial intentions.

This ironic feature of human action was one Weber emphasized in his work, with the consequence that his analyses frequently demonstrated how 'the idea works against its original meaning . . . and thus destroys itself'.[10] He did incline however, toward a cultural pessimism, and hence had a tendency to give an especially negative interpretation to this notion, emphasizing the manner in which high-minded and idealistic conduct functioned to undermine itself, both in the sense that supremely meaningful action becomes in time meaningless, and in the sense that conduct which was morally impeccable changes into that which is morally low and mean;[11] good intentions constantly leading to evil consequences. There would seem to be no good reason, however, for accepting this gloomy and restricted notion of irony, and a proper understanding of social action requires a study of all unintended consequences and unrealized intentions no matter what their moral significance.[12] In fact, we have already had cause to note Bernard de Mandeville's 'optimistic' version of irony, in which social benefits flow directly from the practice of vice, a tradition of largely satirical analysis in which one can also place

Veblen. Hence, whilst accepting the reality of a 'demoralizing' irony in the sense identified by Weber, it is also important to recognize that it can be found in more 'constructive' forms.[13]

To imply that the irony of history might operate in the reverse direction to that traced by Weber, however, is to suggest both that 'meaningless' action might regain its ideal and transcendent significance, and that conduct undertaken for petty or self-seeking ends could develop into idealistic or altruistic action; specifically, in the case in question, that self-illusory hedonism might develop into a genuine romantic idealism. This, indeed, is precisely what it could be argued has happened periodically in the years since the first Age of Romanticism; most recently, during the late 1960s and early 1970s. To claim this is not to deny Weber's observation concerning the 'degeneration' of idealism, for that too has necessarily been the fate of these self-same movements: it is merely to point to the essentially two-way nature of this ironic interchange, and that whilst romantic idealists may act in such a way as to unintentionally promote a self-seeking hedonism, the self-illusory pleasure-seeker may also find that his pattern of behaviour leads unwittingly in the direction of an idealistic commitment.[14]

Now the thrust of the discussion throughout this work has been to indicate precisely how changing conceptions of the good, the true and the beautiful have, through the medium of ideals of character, worked to modify the typical patterns of conduct manifested by 'the good man', or 'the good woman', in the middle and upper classes of society at different periods in English history. To suggest, therefore, that action prompted mainly by hedonistic self-interest could, in turn, result in idealistic conduct, might appear to constitute something of a volte-face, indicative perhaps of a general sympathy with more materialistic or even deterministic traditions in the study of culture and cultural change. Nothing could actually be further from the truth, for the reason that stress is placed on the fundamentally two-way nature of social irony is precisely because it is considered more valuable and pertinent to shed light on the actual dynamic mechanisms of socio-cultural change than it is to engage in the largely sterile debate over the comparative influence of 'material' or 'ideational' factors. In order to do this, however, it is necessary to consider the difficult twin concepts of 'motivation' and 'legitimation', for these are the terms which are typically called upon to do the heavy work of linking the realm of beliefs and values with that of purposive social action.

Motivation and legitimation

In the discussion of theories of consumption we had occasion to be critical of those assumptions concerning motivation to be found not merely in classical economics, but also in the writings of Sombart and Veblen. Basically, the objection was that in all cases 'motive' is interpreted psychologically to refer either to an emotion – such as pride, greed, ambition or lust – or to a tendency to maximize satisfaction. At the same time, such a 'springs of action' view of 'motives' leads to them being ascribed universally to all human beings, rather than located in specific historical and socio-cultural sites. It is clearly necessary to reject this conception of the nature of motivation and to recognize its essentially created character as a product of human self-conscious intention, with ethical ideas central to those processes through which motivated conduct is constructed.

Weber himself was among the first to emphasize the fact that individuals needed to have 'good reasons' for their conduct and seek to satisfy themselves as well as others concerning this 'goodness'.[15] A fact which, as Quentin Skinner notes, means that an actor has to 'tailor his projects in order to fit the normative language available', as well as his language to fit his projects.[16] This recognition of the importance played by a 'vocabulary of motives' in enabling social action to occur was subsequently taken up by Gerth and Mills, and has led to a general recognition that the availability of suitable normative language is as much a constraint upon an individual's freedom of action as more 'concrete' biological or economic forces.[17] What is more, it has also led to a growing awareness that the very distinction between 'motivation' and 'legitimation' cannot, in practice, be sustained; since, as Marshall observes, 'legitimations may simply be the actor's articulation of his or her motives'.[18]

This perception has led to a tendency to discard the concepts of 'motive' and 'legitimation' (or 'justification') in favour of the more neutral 'account', and the substitution of the study of these for consideration of motivated action itself.[19] It is a development which has the advantage of stressing the fact that motive is an achieved concept, but the prevalence of methodological interactionism and the associated preoccupation with talk means that little light has been shed on how it is that individuals come to construct their own motives. It is, also, however, a perspective which recognizes the fundamentally rhetorical nature of motive talk,[20] and if this insight is extended to that form of private language which we call thinking, then it is possible to see how individuals might come to construct motives through basically self-rhetorical processes.[21] This, of course, links with common-sense notions of how people decide upon courses of action, as well as with the assumption contained in classical economics about the manner in which individuals calculate their own interests. But if this insight is linked to Marshall's observation concerning the identity of motivation and legitimation, it becomes possible to see that much of this self-rhetorical talk must concern, not the identification of self-interest, but the recognition of moral obligation. Being rhetorical in character, the purpose of these silent conversations can be taken to be the achievement of an effect, to exert influence in such a way as to generate movement and action, whilst a central feature of these exercises in persuasion must be the generation of a desire to do that which is right and good, to come to 'want', in effect, to do good for goodness' sake.

Looked at in this light, it is possible to see how ethical ideas and values might enter directly into those processes through which social conduct is itself constructed, much as it has always been assumed was the case with interest, whilst the widespread tendency to accord some form of ontological priority to the latter is avoided. Expressed crudely, it means that a generalized desire to 'do good', or to 'do the right thing', can be assumed to be just as much an intrinsic feature of human conduct as any tendency to self-seeking. If, however, this is the case, how are these two aspects of behaviour related?

In this work it has proved convenient to employ the distinction between self-seeking and idealistic conduct in order to discuss the nature of consumer behaviour and the development of cultural systems. Consumer behaviour itself has, following convention, been treated as stemming from a self-seeking disposition (albeit heuonistic rather than utilitarian), whilst discussion of such movements as Puritanism, Sentimentalism and Romanticism have taken the reality of both moral and idealistic conduct for granted. It is now necessary, however, in order to examine their relationship, to abandon this stark antithesis, and by recognizing their intimate interdependence in real action, to trace some of the – fundamentally ironic – interconnections between them.

Hedonistic self-interest and romantic idealism

The manner through which genuinely idealistic or moral action might decay over time into a mere hedonistic self-concern is readily appreciated, and has already been referred to in discussing the decline of the cult of sensibility. There it was suggested that an exaggerated display of sentimentality might not indicate either genuine feelings of pity or concern, nor lead to appropriate benevolent or sympathetic action, being mainly a symptom of self-love. Joyce Tompkins provides a good description of this phenomenon:

again and again we find that enormity of self-congratulation with which the weeper at once luxuriates in the beguiling softness of tears and compliments himself on his capacity for shedding them, seeing in his mind's eye not only the object of his attention [that is whatever prompted the display of emotion] but himself in a suitable attitude in front of it.[22]

Even earlier, we had occasion to note what David Fordyce called that 'self-approving joy' which is open to the benevolent man, and which Isaac Barrow dubbed 'virtuous voluptuousness'. Crane labelled it 'egoistic hedonism' of the kind that leads individuals to 'entertain themselves with pleasant Reflections upon their own Worth'.[23] It is especially easy to see how Puritanism might lead to this kind of hypocrisy and self-love, given the repeated injunctions to examine one's spiritual condition, coupled with the urgent need to have confirmation of one's status as a member of the elect. Such continual reflection on oneself and one's conduct was bound to provide ample opportunities for self-admiration.[24]

It generally requires a greater effort, on the other hand, to recognize how it is that action of an essentially hedonistic kind may also develop into ethical and idealistic forms. Here it is critically important to recognize that ideals are necessarily implicated in that variety of imaginatively mediated hedonism which has been taken to constitute the spirit of consumerism, and this for the simple reason that perfected or 'idealized' images naturally offer the greatest pleasure. This is clearly revealed in both Walter Mitty's and Billy Liar's fantasies for in each case idealized self-images are the central means through which pleasure is attained. Obviously, if it is pleasant to contemplate perfect images, then it is especially pleasant to contemplate ourselves as embodying that perfection. Walter Mitty obtains pleasure from his fantasies because he envisages himself as a dare-devil flying ace or world-famous surgeon, whilst the heroine of Virginia Woolf's story 'sees' herself as the epitome of beauty. We may choose to regard such day-dreams as evidence of self-love, or even childishness, but one cannot escape the fact that they do involve the imaginative realization of ideals, and, as such, can, under appropriate circumstances, become the basis for self-idealistic activity in reality. Conduct directed at realizing perfection in oneself arising out of imaginative exercises of this kind thus manifests a mixture of hedonistic and idealistic features. Striving to make oneself beautiful is perhaps the most obvious and common example of such behaviour, and although it can justifiably be labelled 'self-interested', it also constitutes 'idealism' in the sense of being activity aimed at fulfilling an ideal.[25] Such self-directed idealism becomes especially important, however, when the moral rather than the aesthetic dimension is the focus of attention.

Morally idealized self-images can be just as much sources of pleasure as aesthetic ones, as Simone de Beauvoir revealed in her autobiography. There she disclosed how, as a child, she played fantasy games with her sister, using exemplary figures as the basic props for their hedonism. She describes how, in the course of playing these character games, she often imagined herself to be Mary Magdalene, 'drying Christ's feet with her long hair', or alternatively, a heroine such as Joan of Arc, or Geneviève de Brabant, women who 'only attained to bliss and glory in this world or in the next after sufferings inflicted on them by males'.[26] These roles enabled her to enjoy all manner of imaginary sufferings, and 'revel in the delights of misfortune and humiliation', her 'piety' disposing her 'towards masochism'.[27] Here we can see how encouraging children to emulate 'saintly' figures provides ample opportunity for self-illusory hedonism. Although Simone de Beauvoir shared these games with her sister it is also clear that she could easily have acted them out in isolation, or even covertly; the pleasure itself deriving from the 'fatefulness' of the situations accompanying the achievement of saintliness, as well as the simple contemplation of oneself in an idealized persona.

However, whilst the habit of identifying with ideal images may be embarked on in the first instance largely because of the opportunities which this provides for imaginative pleasure-seeking, the hedonist's sense of identity can easily become so moulded by this process as to come to depend upon a belief in a real similarity. Although the element of pretence remains – there is usually no desire to *be* the person imagined, and certainly not to actually experience their fate – the pleasure gained from contemplation of the idealized self-image encourages the belief that one possesses similar qualities. This can only be regarded as true, however, if the individual obtains some external proof, and this must necessarily take the form of conduct in the world. In order to bolster and protect the idealized self-image the individual must now engage in some character-confirming conduct; it becomes necessary to 'do good' in order to retain the conviction that one is good. Hence the irony by which 'disinterested', idealistic action eventually becomes required in order to protect the ideal self-image which the pursuit of pleasure has been instrumental in constructing.[28]

A similar result can occur if imagination is put to work realizing the ideal in all those with whom one comes into contact, thereby casting oneself in the role of a pathetic and worthless person. The emotional satisfactions provided by such self-denigration and debasement are similar to those which were noted earlier to derive from Calvinism. Goethe makes the melancholic young Werther declare that 'Our imagination, impelled by nature to assert itself, nourished by the fantastic images of the poet's art, invents a hierarchy of being of which we are the lowest, while everyone else appears more splendid, more perfect.'[29] Although there may be a perverse tendency in some people for conduct to be directed to the 'realization' of such 'masochistic' anti-ideals, the use of imagination in this way typically works to assist the development of idealism for it is the real self which is judged unfavourably as a consequence of these comparisons. The dreamer realizes only too well how he is failing to live up to his own ideal image, whilst on the other hand, 'everyone else appears more splendid, more perfect'. In either case, however, whether the ideal is projected onto the self or onto others, awareness of the ever-widening gap between that ideal and the nature of the real self becomes a critical feature of life.

A central problem for the imaginative hedonist, therefore, is his awareness of this widening disjunction between the constructed ideal and the experienced reality; the more the hedonistic impulse causes images to be idealized, the greater the discrepancy becomes between these and the real-self. It is as if the pleasures gained by dreaming on the ideal are 'taken out' of those experienced in reality, which is judged to be more and more unsatisfactory in consequence. In this case, however, the reality which is thus 'degraded' is the individual's perception of himself as a virtuous person, leading to a deepening sense of worthlessness and demoralization. Indeed, for the morally sensitive, inner-directed person the powerful feelings of guilt which are generated may spark off intense self-condemnation. This, then, in turn, adds an extra intensity to the need for reassurance that one is indeed good.

It can be seen from this analysis how forms of self-illusory hedonism can link up with a self-centred, moral idealism; while the search for pleasure may itself lead to the generation of guilt and a consequent need for signs of one's goodness. It merely remains to observe that since virtue is usually defined in terms of conduct which does transcend concern with the self, or at least involves some subordination of self to a higher goal, it is nearly always necessary actually to perform some genuinely disinterested act in order to obtain such reassurance. Self-interested hedonism and altruistic idealism are thus connected via images of the self as 'virtuous', with, in both cases, character-confirming conduct acting as the critical fulcrum around which behaviour turns.

The concept of character forms a common thread running through the multitude of modern vocabularies which are applicable to human actions. Used to refer to that aspect of behaviour for which individuals accept responsibility, it enables all action to be viewed as moral, with judgements made about the 'goodness' of each individual actor in the light of prevailing ideals. It is not suggested here, however, that it is people's direct desire to 'do the good thing' which is most affected by changes in conceptions of the good, the true and the beautiful, so much as the indirect effect exerted via the need for character confirmation. It is the need people have to be convinced that they are good which is crucial, something which is especially relevant in the case of those social groups which have inherited a tradition of moral inner-direction, and hence are attuned to the importance of membership of a moral elite or 'elect'.

By recognizing that social conduct is typically a composite product of hedonistic self-interest and altruistically inclined idealism, with an overriding concern with self-image serving to articulate the two, it becomes possible to see how the spirit of modern consumerism and the romantic ethic might be connected; hedonistic concerns leading into self-idealism and ethical preoccupations creating opportunities for hedonism. Indeed, the two forms are not merely connected but must be seen as inextricably interlocked, bound together by processes through which a desire for pleasure develops into a genuine concern for ideals, and ethical impulses 'degenerate' into mere narcissism. If, then, such individual processes are aggregated and viewed in macro-social terms as socio-cultural movements, it becomes possible to perceive how a modern consumerist outlook and a romantic ethic may be linked in both generative and degenerative directions; that is to say, by tendencies for periods of commercial dynamism to develop into idealistic 'reformations', and idealistic upheavals to degenerate into sentimentalistic self-seeking. As there is no good reason for assuming that a one-way trend governs such changes, it would seem reasonable to postulate a *recurso* pattern of generation–degeneration–regeneration to have typified the past two hundred years. Thus, if Romanticism did originally make modern hedonism possible, then the spirit of hedonism has subsequently also functioned to give rise to further outbursts of romantic fervour.

This is a conclusion which allows us to observe that the Romantics were not necessarily wrong in assuming that people could be morally improved through the provision of cultural products that yielded pleasure. Nor indeed were they wrong in seeing this process as one which relied upon individuals dreaming about a more perfect world. Such activity can reasonable be viewed as creating opportunities for the generation of idealism. This is only one possible outcome, however, of encouraging people to pursue imaginative pleasure, and would seem to depend for its success upon the prior acceptance of a more general romantic outlook. For it is also clear that where this is absent, and largely materialistic and utilitarian beliefs prevail, then it seems only too likely that romantic poems, novels and music, will be employed as little more than the raw material for a leisure and recreation industry; with dreams used less to raise the vision of an imaginatively apprehended ideal world with which to counter this one, than to overcome boredom and alienation. As we have had occasion to note, however, irony pervades the human condition, connecting intention and consequence in strange and unanticipated ways, hence while romantics may sometimes have assisted commercialism, commercial interests may also have unwittingly acted so as to promote romanticism.[30]

Puritan and romantic: conflict or symbiosis?

If this overall analysis is correct, then 'romantic' and 'puritan' cannot represent the cultural polar types which many sociologists and psychologists seem to regard them as being. Certainly, Romanticism and Puritanism have traditionally embodied contrasting beliefs, especially those relating to the divine, human nature and man's destiny; beliefs which, in turn, frequently lead into a direct conflict of attitude. At the same time, many values central to the one perspective are clearly denigrated in the other, thus lending support to the view that they should be regarded as, in effect, contradictory. This is certainly how Taylor perceives the romantic and puritan personality types, defining them oppositionally through such contrasts as 'inhibited–uninhibited, authoritarian–democratic, and pessimistic–optimistic'.[31] Although it is easy to see why he, among others, is tempted to conceptualize the two types in purely contrasting terms, our historical and sociological understanding of their relationship should make us wary of following suit. Or, at least, it should cause us to recognize that such differences do not signify the absence of similarities. Indeed, our analysis has suggested that much of the Puritan tradition was carried forward into Romanticism, and whilst beliefs were transmuted and alien ingredients introduced, a historical kinship is still discernible. Even Taylor is forced to recognize this when noting a common tendency toward morbidity and melancholia, although he then treats the fact of this similarity as a reason for rejecting this characteristic as relevant to the formulation of either of the two personality types.[32] Yet to dismiss such similarities in this fashion is unjustifiable, and creates an unnecessary risk of misunderstanding the place of these influential traditions within the culture of modern societies.

The prevailing belief that 'romantic' and 'puritan' (or 'Protestant') cultural ethics and personality types are inversions of each other, which can be seen in such analyses of contemporary culture as those advanced by Bell and Martin, for example,[33] generally gains its credence from a combination of Weber's influence and the success of recent generations of romantics in persuading social scientists to adopt their mythic world-view. Two misconceptions, in particular, stem more or less directly from the acceptance of Weber's thesis. The first is the common treatment of the words 'Puritan' and 'Puritanism', and even, most unforgivably, 'Protestant', as if they referred merely to that highly rationalistic and ascetic strand of Christian thought which Weber considered attained its apotheosis in Calvinism. Such a view necessarily distorts the real historical character of both Protestant and Puritan religious thought, causing the equally prominent (and, as argued here, influential) Pietistic Puritan tradition to be overlooked. It is as a consequence of this distortion that 'Puritan' is commonly taken to imply someone who is emotionally impoverished, when it could just as reasonably mean someone of the most intense but controlled passion. Such an interpretation cannot be judged entirely wrong, reflecting as it does, existing usage; but if, as appears to be the case, this meaning is not only projected backwards in time, but also used as a guide to existing trends, then it leads to a gross distortion of the true nature of this religiously inspired movement, and thus to the obscuring of its close connections with Romanticism.

Secondly, Weber's brief treatment of the spirit of capitalism and his rather unfortunate tendency to appear to define this and the Protestant ethic in terms of each other, has given rise to a cavalier indifference to the distinction between them on the part of the majority of social scientists. All too often, the term 'Protestant ethic' is used to refer to what Weber identified as the 'Spirit of Capitalism', with the natural consequence that the Romantics are presented as primarily opposed to that ethic, when their real hostility was toward the spirit which Weber considered it to have ironically generated.[34]

This can be best appreciated by recognizing that it was Franklin, not Calvin, who was seen as epitomizing all that the Romantics hated most. In North America, where the Romantic Movement took the form of Transcendentalism, it was such inheritors of the pietistic and intensely moral Puritan tradition as Emerson, Thoreau, Melville and Poe, who repeatedly criticized what they saw as the shallow and immoral nature of Franklin's utilitarianism. Emerson, in particular, repeatedly attacked the selfish doctrine of the market-place, advocating in its place an ideal of the self as being and becoming;[35] whilst Thoreau, an especially bitter critic of the capitalist spirit, declared that 'nothing, not even crime, is more opposed to poetry, to philosophy, ay to life itself, than this incessant business'.[36] In England, Shelley's attack on utilitarianism and the self-centred commercial spirit which it engendered, was continued by subsequent generations of romantics, D. H. Lawrence, for example, being prominent among those who chose to pour scorn on Franklin's creed.[37] This is not, of course, to imply that the Romantics actually approved of Calvinism, or of that ascetic religious ethic which Weber associated with its teachings, but at least it had the merit in their eyes of being a religious system, and hence could be credited with directing men's gaze toward eternity.[38]

While the words 'Puritan' and 'Protestant' have become increasingly restricted to refer merely to the ascetic, rationalist element in that broad religious movement, and more and more closely identified with a materialistic and self-seeking outlook in business, so the terms 'Romantic' and 'Romanticism' have also proved unreliable tools for cultural analysis. It was noted earlier that 'rebelling against romanticism could also be romantic', and that as a result romanticism could be specified as a 'tradition against tradition';[39] whilst the romantic himself, with his penchant for legend and myth, is inevitably a poor authority on the nature of such an elusive movement. Both of these tendencies have acted as obstacles to clear-sightedness in the social sciences, especially given the modern tendency to prefer the subjective categories of meaning employed by 'the folk' to those which sociologists have good reason to devise. Thus, whilst each new generation of romantics establish their credentials by denying that they are indeed romantics – that is to say, by asserting their uniqueness as a generation – the analyst has had to accept the emotional truth of such claims whilst repudiating their literal meaning, thus recognizing that continuity in rebellion which is the romantic tradition. This is an understandably difficult position to attain, with the consequence that sociologists have not only fallen out among themselves over the issue of whether the latest romantic renaissance is 'unique', but have also been tempted to ignore the evidence for historical precedents and hence endorse the myth.[40]

What needs to be asserted most forcibly is that there existed within Protestantism, and even within that especially harsh and vigorous branch of it known as Puritanism, two major strands of thought, ones which correspond generally to Weber's distinction between Calvinism and Pietism, and that whilst the former subsequently evolved into rationalism and utilitarianism, the latter developed into Sentimentalism and Romanticism;[41] a division which may indeed be regarded as having been precipitated by the emergence out of the former of the 'spirit of capitalism' itself. As John William Ward observes,

In Puritan religious thought there was originally a dynamic equipoise between two opposite thrusts, and tension between an inward, mystical, personal experience of God's grace and the demands for an outward, sober, socially responsible ethic, the tension between faith and works, between the essence of religion and its outward show. Tremendous energy went into sustaining these polarities in the early years, but as the original piety wained, itself undermined by the worldly success that benefitted from the doctrine of the calling, the synthesis split in two and resulted in the eighteenth century in Jonathan Edwards and Benjamin Franklin, similar in so many ways, yet so radically unalike.[42]

Although Jonathan Edwards was no 'romantic', and even defended Calvinism against its Arminian critics, his brand of cosmic optimism, influenced as it was by the thought of the Cambridge Platonists, laid the basis for the later Transcendentalist movement in New England. It was therefore via such advocacy as his that Puritanism made the transition to 'romantic religion', this being as much a logical development out of the Reformation – as much a descendant of Protestant ethics – as Franklin's 'spirit'.[43] A proper appreciation of this cultural lineage allows one to see that, whilst the rationalistic puritan and romantic traditions differ, and in some respects are even opposed, it is really a form of sibling rivalry which divides them, joined as they are through a kinship which can be discerned psychologically and sociologically as well as historically.

This can be seen most clearly in their shared nature as deeply idealistic, ethical systems which impose a 'calling' upon the individual. In this respect both are 'ascetic' movements in Weber's terminology, that is, they demand that the individual engage in action in the world, rather than retreat into mysticism. There is a mystical strand in Romanticism, of course, but the more typical 'world-rejecting' stance, as exemplified by Wordsworth's 'The world is too much with us', is a rejection of the artificial, social world of 'getting and spending', and bears a close affinity to the orthodox Puritan's suspicion of that imperfect reality which is the product of man's sinfulness. In addition, both are individualistic, inner-directed ethics, requiring intense introspection and soul-searching, and whilst what is located in each case as 'the real self' is different, it is this inner reality which is appealed to as the ultimate authority for resisting what are seen as unwarrantable demands from without. Roszak, for example, refers to that characteristic 'quality of sober introspection' displayed by the young hippies of the 1960s, and how they engaged in 'lint-picking analyses of motivation' during sessions of 'soul-searching';[44] whilst Oden sees exactly the same zealous pursuit of honesty through self-examination as characteristic of the modern encounter movement as typified traditional Puritan pietism.[45]

It remains true that considered as social ethics or ideals of character, the rationalistic Protestant and Romantic versions do stand opposed to each other in the central values which they assert. This is bound to be the case with ideals, for they constitute uniquely systematized patterns of conduct in which all actions are envisaged as undertaken in accord with one given, coherent set of values. It is a fundamental mistake, however, to confuse such a cultural ideal type with that total pattern of behaviour which might be identified as characterizing the conduct of individuals or social groups, and hence to confuse an ethic with a type of personality or the behaviour typical of a given social position. In theory, individuals cannot conform to two ethics; in practice, it may not be so difficult. This is because conduct is patterned as much by psychological and sociological considerations as logical ones. There is thus no good reason for assuming any one-to-one relationship between character ideals and personality types, or between social ethics and ways of life. There will be a strain toward consistency in the light of whatever ideals operate, but one personality type may well be 'consistent' with more than one ideal of character. At the same time the culture of a class grouping may successfully incorporate and transmit more than one social ethic, the complex and differentiated patterns of social action permitting behaviour governed by contrasting values to be incorporated into one overall style of living. Something of the manner in which this is accomplished for the modern middle classes with respect to 'puritan' and 'romantic' values can be illustrated by briefly considering the sphere of child-rearing.

There is a widespread tendency to assume that an ideal of character derived from a secularized version of the Protestant ethic has long prevailed among the middle classes, determining both the nature of their child-rearing practices and being itself perpetuated as a consequence of them. It is an ideal which, while now largely lacking the original supernatural sanctions, still emphasizes such values as thrift, industry, independence and internalized self-discipline, whilst presenting success in a vocation as evidence of an individual's moral worth. Increasingly, however, this ideal is reported as being under attack, either directly, by an alternative 'hedonistic', 'expressive', 'remissive', or 'fun' ethic, or indirectly, as a result of changing fashions in child-rearing and education.[46] Such an attack is generally seen to have begun some time after the First World War, becoming largely successful after 1945. It is an argument which all too easily equates a conflict of ethics with contradictory patterns of conduct, and, by failing to specify carefully precisely what forms of behaviour might follow from acceptance of the alternative, 'non-puritan' ethic, fails to recognize how ethically contrasted but psychologically symbiotic traits may be generated from one overall pattern of child-rearing. This conflict is commonly presented as centring around the twin polarities of deferred versus instant gratification and the inhibited as opposed to the uninhibited expression of emotion; these being the two dimensions of personality along which the ethics are seen as primarily distinguishable. It is not at all clear, however, that, in practice, such forms of behaviour should be presented as being 'at odds' with each other.

These terms are, in the first place, definitionally interdependent and could have little meaning without their 'partners'; something which would also seem to be true behaviourally, as acquaintance with both forms is a fundamental prerequisite for either action, and most certainly before one can adopt a conscious preference for one as opposed to the other.[47] It follows from this that the very practice of the one kind of conduct creates the circumstances necessary for the performance, as well as the positive valuation of, the other. We have already seen how the practice of 'real' deferred gratification is not necessarily anti-hedonistic in either intention or effect. This is because the tendency to gratify desires as and when they arise reveals little commitment to hedonism so long as the occurrence of desire is itself beyond the individual's control; what is distinctive of modern rational hedonism and of the behaviour of the real romantic is the tendency to seize opportunities to create desire, not merely to satisfy it; and it is here that the postponement of real gratification becomes essential. It follows from this that a pattern of child-rearing practice which stresses deferred gratification serves to stimulate day-dreaming and fantasizing, hence developing within the individual exactly those skills necessary to become an expert in manipulating desire. It also creates the circumstances under which the individual is most likely to come to place a value upon 'instantaneous' gratification.

A similar relationship can be said to exist between the practice of inhibiting the expression of emotion and the valuation of deep passion. Here too the price paid for restraining behavioural impulses is their deflection into other channels, ones largely imaginative and covert, with the consequence that the possibility of a different kind of conduct is created. In fact, both the delaying of gratification and the suppression of emotion work together to create a rich and powerful, imaginative inner life within the individual, the necessary prerequisite for a 'romantic' personality.

It seems clear that the overall pattern of child-rearing which has been considered characteristic of the middle classes, with its emphasis upon literacy, privacy, individual responsibility, self-denial, emotional inhibition and intellectual accomplishment, is conducive to the development of romantic personality traits. The common mistake has been to confuse the values which parents might wish to instil in their children with the personality traits which result from their child-rearing practices. Hence the failure to recognize that attempts to raise children as 'puritans', by encouraging deferred gratification and emotional restraint, may actually give rise to both day-dreaming and suppressed passion, thereby providing the conditions necessary for the development of a romantic personality. To this extent, the psychological links between Puritanism and Romanticism can be said to reflect the historical ones.

This is not to suggest that Protestant ethic values are not transmitted from one generation to the next, merely that the ironic consequence of striving to ensure this can be to help create individuals with 'romantic' tendencies. These may, of course, be negatively valued and thus held in check, such that a 'puritan' character is constructed; alternatively, romantic beliefs may be adopted, justifying the explicit creation of a 'romantic' one. The evidence suggests, however, that no matter which character type is chosen the necessary personality traits are interdependent. Introversion, for example, facilitates day-dreaming, as does privacy and a stress upon silent reading,[48] whilst the inhibition of emotion appears to be a precondition for artistic or 'creative' expression. 'Puritans' and 'romantics' can be said to have the same personality traits;

they merely value them differently. Thus to the 'puritan', introverted day-dreaming and fantasizing is an example of exactly that kind of temptation to idleness and indulgence which must be resisted, whilst to the 'romantic' it is the most valued aspect of experience. For the 'puritan' control over desire has to be secured so that it too can be resisted; for the 'romantic' control is needed so that desire can be created and accentuated at will. Thus, whilst a 'puritan' will regard his tendency to day-dream as bad, because, although enjoyable, it is time-wasting and interferes with work and the acceptance of reality (or even, if the theological version survives, is evidence of sinfulness) the 'romantic' will regard this activity as the most central and significant aspect of his life.[49]

This strongly suggests that the middle-class individual is 'double'; that there are two beings inside him. An observation which brings to mind Murger's comment on the necessity of living in duplicate if one is to avoid a Bohemian life of poverty and deprivation, as well as an earlier remark of Barfield's on the 'imaginative double life' of the typical eighteenth-century gentleman. That age was noted for both reason and sentiment, and Fairchild has suggested that these two principles might have met in the self-same individuals. He writes,

The eighteenth-century bourgeois is not merely utilitarian; he is also sentimental. He preserves clear traces of those deeply emotional hopes and fears which moved his Puritan forebears. He, in turn, of course, is the ancestor of the modern business man, who exhibits similar streaks of hardness and softness.[50]

This last suggestion is endorsed by Houghton, who observes how in Victorian society 'sensibility could complement utilitarianism'.[51] In the light of these remarks, it would seem appropriate to view these two sets of traits as complementary rather than contradictory, jointly comprising one overall 'purito-romantic' personality system.

This conclusion also naturally leads to the suggestion that those puritan and romantic values institutionalized in the social roles and statuses of modern society should not be regarded as constituting a 'contradiction' of any sort, but be seen, on the contrary, as serving to integrate discrete patterns of behaviour into a larger, and fundamentally balanced, system. It is certainly necessary to recognize that a cultural contradiction can easily be a sociological compatibility. That is to say, attitudes and beliefs which directly contrast, will, nevertheless, not lead people to experience tension or conflict if their expression is successfully separated in time and place; something which is generally true of the way puritan–utilitarian and romantic–sentimental values are institutionalized in contemporary middle-class society. Perhaps the most pertinent illustration of this is the way in which the middle-class life cycle is divided into a Bohemian youth followed by a bourgeois middle-age, thus leading to a serial form of integration.

At the very end of Murger's *Scenes from Bohemian Life,* Marcel confesses to Rudolph that he has become corrupted by living with his relatives and that he now 'no longer cares for anything but what is good and comfortable'.[52] This, it would seem, is the destiny of most of those Bohemians who do not die young, Bohemianism itself being not merely a 'stage of the artist's career' but a phase in the bourgeois life cycle, similar in many ways to that which Keniston defines as 'youth'.[53] Of course, this stage of life is also, for many of the middle class, largely coincidental with the status of student, which is also clearly an institutionalized site of romantic values in modern society; several studies of student protest in the 1960s highlighting the essentially 'romantic' nature of these movements.[54] The crucial point, in either case, is that the Bohemianism of youth in no way conflicts with the 'bourgeois' nature of later life.

There is a more far-reaching version of the claim that romantic and rational-utilitarian values are serially institutionalized in the life-cycle of bourgeois man, one which asserts that the romanticism of youth is but the culmination of an entire childhood of exposure to such values. It is the complete 'ethos of childhood' which embodies romanticism, and hence stands opposed to that 'ethos of bureaucracy' which represents adulthood.[55] It is for this reason that 'youth', poised as it is between the two, is so prone to be a time of rebellion and protest.[56]

Such a view has some truth, for there is indeed a direct link between romantic teachings and liberal or progressive thinking about the needs of children, and hence ideas about the correct way in which they should be reared and educated.[57] In the twentieth century especially, this body of thought has been so influential that even parents committed to a strictly 'puritan' ethos are likely to modify the obligations which they impose upon the child, with the result that it is one of the two crucial ascribed statuses in modern society in which 'romantic' attitudes are prescribed as well as permitted. This does not necessarily mean that they predominate to the exclusion of 'puritan' values, however, as some observers seem to assume. The other crucial status, vital to the transmission of quasi-romantic, expressive values from one generation to another over the past 200 years, has, of course, been that of female.

We have already had cause to note the prominence of women among the readers of romantic and sentimental fiction in the eighteenth century, something which has remained true for that genre down to the present day; whilst many of the activities identified as most compatible with romantic values – notably education, child-care, welfare work and, to a degree, the fine arts – have all traditionally been regarded as 'women's work'. Obviously, if one sex is viewed as the principal carrier of 'puritan' values, and the other the carrier of 'romantic' ones, then it becomes a little easier to understand how these two apparently incompatible cultures have come to be incorporated into the experience of a single class grouping. To a considerable extent this identification appears to be supportable; after all, the middle-class woman's role has long been defined in terms of emotional sensitivity or 'sensibility', especially with regard to such emotions as pity, gentleness and kindness, most particularly towards children and animals, whilst traditionally she is also credited with an intuitive sense and a responsiveness to 'atmosphere'. At the same time, there is a tendency for her to be portrayed as idealistic rather than realistic, as well as romantic in the narrow sense. Finally, this role is credited with a primary aesthetic responsibility, especially with regard to furnishings and dress. The wife and mother is thus often considered the specialist in 'taste', the connoisseur in non-appetite pleasure.[58] Since women and children have had comparatively little power in comparison with adult males, theirs has been a minority ethic, regarded as fundamentally subservient to the 'puritanical', utilitarian one endorsed by the patriarchy. But its presence has, nevertheless, been significant, becoming more so in recent times as the power differential between these status groups has decreased. All too often, the close association between 'the Protestant ethic' and masculinity has been forgotten in sociological discussions of cultural change, with a consequent tendency to overlook how inappropriate this ethic is as a description of the character ideal advocated for half the middle class. Of critical importance is the fact that its presence has meant that males, alienated in adolescence from the unemotional ethic embodied in their fathers, have, through strong nurturent identification with their mothers, been able to find some legitimation for the adoption of a romantic idealism; a 'romantic' being a male who, almost by definition, has refused to 'grow up' by the yardstick of normal 'bourgeois' standards. What strongly supports this inter-pretation is Keniston's evidence that those middle-class male youths who are most drawn to espouse romantic Bohemian values and attitudes are precisely the ones who regard their mothers sympathetically, but consider their fathers to be cold, withdrawn, 'success men' who have 'sold out' on idealism.[59] This differential pattern of parent identification is specifically made the basis of the contrast between 'puritan' and 'romantic' personality types drawn up by Taylor,[60] whilst Hudson's work also shows how differences in attitudes towards parents is associated with the choice of the arts or sciences as spheres of specialization.[61]

All of which suggests that the presence of the romantic ethic is of greater significance for adolescents and 'youthful' males than for the women and children for whom it is meant to apply. This is because, as implied, the attempt to develop a 'puritan' character actually creates 'romantic' personality traits whilst denying their legitimation. By identify-ing with his mother rather than his father, however, an adolescent boy can gain some legitimation for his latent romanticism. Since the rearing of girls as 'sentimentalists' probably does not produce latent 'puritan' traits to the same extent, the reverse process is perhaps less likely to be as culturally significant.

The conclusion to be drawn from this is that middle-class families successfully transmit both rational utilitarian and romantic values to their offspring, the father and the mother having a different responsibility in this respect. The 'romantic' values are likely to be given expression first, probably under the mother's overall guidance, and the more 'puritanical' ones imposed later (when the father becomes more important). If for various reasons, however, the romantic values remain dominant into adulthood, then the individual will probably enter a career in the arts, education, or the caring professions, even, in extreme cases, spending a period in Bohemia; whilst in the majority of instances, the predominance of a 'capitalist spirit' will cause 'romantic' values to be consigned to the recreational side of life, with the individual devoting his energies to the pursuit of a career in commerce, business or administration.

Of course, the characterization of the adult male world as one in which there is no room for romantic beliefs and values is itself inaccurate. Not all occupational roles give expression to the 'ethos of bureaucracy' or to the rational, utilitarian spirit of capitalism. It follows, for example, from what has already been said, that opportunities exist in the fields of education, therapy and child-care to pursue a career in which self-development and self-expression is approved. The same can be said of the caring professions, and, up to a point, for the churches, where that sentimentalist tradition of charitable concern and philanthropy which we saw connected Puritanism with Romanticism has continued down to the present day.[62]

But the most important cluster of occupations within modern society in which romantic values are institutionalized is naturally enough that which relates to the arts, something which is still true even when one has set aside the largely unpaid artistic vocation of the 'Bohemian'. In fact, elements of the Bohemian image are attached to successful artists, as well as to those who teach the arts in schools, colleges and universities, because the very image of the arts is an essentially romantic one, with art itself, although valued, being rarely rewarded. Hudson's work on stereotyped images of the artist and the scientist shows quite clearly how young schoolboys see the typical arts graduate as 'pleasure-seeking and irresponsible', whilst the science graduate is 'the more puritanical', the application of semantic differentials revealing that while the artist is 'warm, exciting, imaginative, feminine, smooth and soft', the scientist is 'valuable, dependable, intelligent, manly, hard and rough'.[63] Clearly a career in the arts would seem to allow the middle-class 'Bohemian' child to pass through youth into adulthood without there being much necessity to adopt the commercial, utilitarian attitudes of a 'bourgeois'.[64]

Just as 'puritan' and 'romantic' stand for contrasting character ideals which can, none the less, be successfully incorporated into one personality system, so too do they stand for apparently opposed cultural traditions which comprise the single cultural system of modernity; a system of which their symbiotic relationship is the central feature. For even though they generate ideals which individuals may occasionally feel the need to choose between,[65] and which intellectuals continually seek to champion against each other,[66] these outlooks are differentially institutionalized along the lines of age, gender, occupation and social roles; as well as differentially internalized in such a way as to eliminate any acute experiences of conflict from all but the most ethically reflective of individuals.[67] As a result, these twin cultures ensure the continued performance of those contrasted but interdependent forms of behaviour essential to the perpetuation of industrial societies, matching consumption with production, play with work. Hence, while the contrast may indeed represent a 'contradiction' within the culture, it is not a contradiction within capitalism itself;[68] on the contrary, this form of cultural differentiation has characterized such societies from their birth, and appears essential to their continued existence.

The cultural logic of modernity is not merely that of rationality as expressed in the activities of calculation and experiment; it is also that of passion, and the creative dreaming born of longing.[69] Yet, more crucial than either is the tension generated between them, for it is upon this that the dynamism of the West ultimately depends. The main source of its restless energy does not derive from science and technology alone, nor yet from fashion, the avant-garde and Bohemia, but from the strain between dream and reality, pleasure and utility. This is the source of the tune to which these twin cultural traditions dance their cultural tango in time, as it is of the conflicting tensions which many individuals experience in their daily lives. In struggling to cope with the necessity of making trade-offs between need and pleasure, whilst seeking to reconcile their Bohemian and bourgeois selves, modern individuals inhabit not just an 'iron cage' of economic necessity, but a castle of romantic dreams, striving through their conduct to turn the one into the other.

Notes

Chapter 1   Introduction

1   *Oxford English Dictionary*, 1969 ed, *s.v.* 'romantic'.
2   Not all advertising makes use of 'romantic' copy, of course, but then not all consumption is 'modern' in character.
3   One can find this view expressed, for example, in Pease's discussion of the growth of modern advertising. See Otis Pease, *The Responsibilities of American Advertising: Private Control and Public Influence, 1920–1940* (New York: Arno Press, 1976), pp. 40–1.
4   Examples of some of these responses can be found in *Anarchy and Culture: The Problem of the Contemporary University*, ed. David Martin (London: Routledge and Kegan Paul, 1969).
5   Compilations I found especially useful were *Counter Culture*, ed. Joseph Berke (London: Peter Owen, 1969); *The Hippy Papers: Notes from the Underground Press*, ed. Jerry Hopkins (New York: Signet Books, 1968); and *BAMN: Outlaw Manifestos and Ephemera 1965–70*, ed. Peter Stansill and David Zane Mairowitz (Harmondsworth, Middx.: Penguin Books, 1971).
6   The main texts here were Kenneth Westhues (ed.), *Society's Shadow: Studies in the Sociology of Countercultures* (Toronto: McGraw-Hill Ryerson, 1971), and Frank Musgrove, *Ecstasy and Holiness: Counter Culture and the Open Society* (London: Methuen, 1974).
7   This comparison can be found in Booker, who comments on the 'close parallel' between the atmosphere of the 1960s and that of the first age of Romanticism (Christopher Booker, *The Neophiliacs* (London: Fontana, 1970), p. 52), declaring indeed that 'there is nothing in which we see the fever of our times so clearly fore-shadowed as in the dreams, delusions and the excesses of the late eighteenth and nineteenth century phenomenon known as Romanticism' (ibid., p. 54). Martin is another commentator who regards the counter culture of the sixties as 'a continuing working out of the principles of Romanticism which had rooted themselves in North American and Western European culture at the outset of the modern age', the counter culture itself embodying 'certain crucial Romantic values' in an especially

dramatic fashion (Bernice Martin, *A Sociology of Contemporary Cultural Change* (Oxford: Blackwell, 1981), pp. 1–2. Then again, Musgrove comments on the fact that 'Nineteenth-century Romanticism was strikingly like the contemporary counter culture' and employs what he sees as an important division within Romanticism as the basis for two separate sub-scales for the measurement of counter cultural commitment (Musgrove, *Ecstasy and Holiness*, p. 65).

8 A general discussion of the part played by Romanticism in the development of modern thought can be found in H. Stuart Hughes, *Consciousness and Society* (Brighton: Harvester Press, 1979).

9 As Hughes observes, both Freud and Weber 'sought to curb the romanticism they found within themselves' (ibid., p. 35).

10 Karl Mannheim, *Essays on the Sociology of Culture* (London: Routledge and Kegan Paul, 1956), pp. 87–90.

11 See David Riesman, Nathan Glazer and Reuel Denny, *The Lonely Crowd: A Study in the Changing American Character* (New York: Anchor Books, 1966), and William H. Whyte, *The Organization Man* (New York: Doubleday Anchor Books, 1957).

12 Winston White, *Beyond Conformity* (Glencoe, Ill.: Free Press, 1961).

13 See the critique of such studies by Elizabeth Long, 'Affluence and After: Themes of Success in American Best-Selling Novels, 1945–1975', in Robert Alun Jones and Henrika Kuklick (eds), *Knowledge and Society: Studies in the Sociology of Culture Past and Present*, vol. 3 (Greenwich, Conn.: Aljai Press, 1981), pp. 257–301, see esp. pp. 258–9.

14 Bell asserts that 'The major intellectual attack on Puritanism came in the first decade of the twentieth century' and associates it with the 'Young Intellectuals' such as Walter Lippmann, Van Wyck Brooks, John Reed and Harold Stearns (Daniel Bell, *The Cultural Contradictions of Capitalism* (London: Heinemann, 1976, p. 61). Whyte also sees an intellectual assault on the Protestant ethic occurring around the turn of the century, but for him the relevant names are William James, John Dewey, Charles Beard and Thorstein Veblen, whilst he considers that the Protestant ethic had 'taken a shellacking from which it would not recover', 'By the time of the First World War' (*The Organization Man*, pp. 22–4). Carroll sees what he calls the Puritan character type as attaining 'maturity' historically 'before the First World War' (John Carroll, *Puritan, Paranoid, Remissive: A Sociology of Modern Culture* (London: Routledge and Kegan Paul, 1977), p. 10). For Cowley, however, the real assault on Puritanism occurred *after* the First World War, and was conducted in the name of Freud (Malcolm Cowley, *Exile's Return: A Literary Odyssey of the 1920s* (New York: Viking Press, 1956), p. 66). Lavers also places the revolt against Puritanism in the 1920s and credits Freud as the major influence (James Lavers, *Between the Wars* (Boston, Mass.: Houghton Mifflin, 1961), p. 113). Richard le Gallienne, however, places the intellectual revolt against Puritanism and conventionally as occurring in the 1890s, led by such artists as Aubrey Beardsley and Oscar Wilde (Richard Le Gallienne, *The Romantic Nineties* (London: G. P. Putnam, 1926), p. 167). We can see from this that whilst some observers place the reaction against the Protestant ethic at the end of the nineteenth

century or at the beginning of the twentieth, some place it in the 1920s, and others after the Second World War.

15   Neil McKendrick, John Brewer and J. H. Plumb, *The Birth of a Consumer Society: The Commercialization of Eighteenth-Century England* (London: Europa Publications, 1982), p. 13.

16   The key works here are Thorstein Veblen, *The Theory of the Leisure Class: An Economic Study of Institutions* (London: George Allen and Unwin, 1925), and Werner Sombart, *Luxury and Capitalism*, introduction by Phil Siegelman (Ann Arbor, Mich.: University of Michigan Press). Both are discussed in chapters 3 and 4.

17   Veblen, *The Theory of the Leisure Class;* Riesman et al., *The Lonely Crowd;* Kenneth Galbraith, *The Affluent Society* (Harmondsworth, Middx: Penguin Books, 1958); Herbert Marcuse, *One Dimensional Man* (London: Routledge and Kegan Paul, 1964); Daniel Bell, *The Cultural Contradictions of Capitalism.*

18   For evidence that sociologists typically employ Weberian theory in a peripheral fashion, or even restrict themselves to ceremonial citations, see Kiku Adatto and Stephen Cole, 'Classical Theory in Contemporary Sociological Research: The Case of Max Weber', *Knowledge and Society: Studies in the Sociology of Culture Past and Present,* 3 (1981), 137–62.

19   As John Rex has observed, Weber possessed 'a range of comparative and historical knowledge which has probably had no equal in modern time' *Makers of Modern Culture: A Biographical Dictionary,* ed. Justin Wintle (London: Routledge and Kegan Paul, 1981), *s.v.* 'Weber, Max'.

20   This is clearly revealed by Steve Baron's assertion, at the end of his survey of the study of culture in British sociology, that 'Cultural Studies relies on the concept of ideology as a central part of its problematic' 'The Study of Culture: Cultural Studies and British Sociology Compared', *Acta Sociologica,* 28, 2 (1985), 71–85, see esp. p. 84).

21   It might prove equally valuable to apply the broader Durkheimian perspective to nominally 'non-religious' movements of the pre-modern period.

22   The phrase is from Ortega y Gasset. Cited by Franklin Baumer, *Modern European Thought: Continuity and Change in Ideas, 1600–1950* (New York: Macmillan, 1977), p. 9.

23   Arthur O. Lovejoy, *The Great Chain of Being: A Study of the History of an Idea* (Cambridge, Mass.: Harvard University Press, 1961), chap. 1.

24   Ibid., p. 7.

25   This becomes a less justifiable exclusion as one moves into the twentieth century, but a largely acceptable restriction as far as the eighteenth and nineteenth centuries are concerned.

26   Ibid., p. 16.

27   Some scholars may indeed feel that there has been an overly cavalier disregard for the disciplinary proprieties in this respect, with consequent widespread distortion and error. This is an obvious risk, but worth running, if, in the process, it is possible to gain some insights into the workings of the cultural systems of modern societies.

28 In many respects, this work could rightly be considered as little more than a footnote (if an over-extended one) to Weber's original essay.
29 It should perhaps be noted that, following Weber, this work espouses a general methodological individualism (as opposed to the methodological interactionism currently much favoured by sociologists), and also focuses more upon the cultural production of social action than upon the social construction of knowledge.

Chapter 2   Accounting for the consumer revolution in eighteenth-century England

1 Elizabeth Waterman Gilboy, 'Demand as a Factor in the Industrial Revolution', in R. M. Hartwell (ed.), *The Causes of the Industrial Revolution in England* (London: Methuen, 1967), pp. 121–38; Eric L. Jones, 'The Fashion Manipulators: Consumer Tastes and British Industries, 1660–1800', in Louis P. Cain and Paul J. Uselding (eds), *Business Enterprise and Economic Change* (Kent State, Ohio: Kent State University Press, 1973), pp 198–226.
2 Jones, 'The Fashion Manipulators', p. 199.
3 Gilboy, 'Demand as a Factor', p. 122.
4 Neil McKendrick, John Brewer and J. H. Plumb, *The Birth of a Consumer Society: The Commercialization of Eighteenth-Century England* (London: Europa Publications, 1982), p. 9.
5 Gilboy, 'Demand as a Factor', pp. 122–3.
6 There was a related controversy over whether the home or the overseas market played the more significant role in contributing to the increased demand for goods. This appears to have been settled in favour of the home market, with, as McKendrick observes, the export thesis no longer commanding general support (see McKendrick, Brewer and Plumb, *The Birth of a Consumer Society*, p. 180). For further discussion and confirmation of this opinion, see A. H. John, 'Aspects of English Economic Growth in the First Half of the Eighteenth Century', *Economica*, 28 (May 1961), 176–90; D. E. C. Eversley, 'The Home Market and Economic Growth in England, 1750–1780', in E. L. Jones and Edmund Mingay Gordon (eds), *Land, Labour and Population in the Industrial Revolution* (London: Edward Arnold, 1967), pp. 206–59; and W. A. Cole, 'Factors in Demand, 1700–1780', in Roderick Floud and Donald McCloskey (eds), *The Economic History of Britain since 1700* (Cambridge: Cambridge University Press, 1981), pp. 36–65.
7 Harold Perkin, *The Origins of Modern English Society* (London: Routledge and Kegan Paul, 1969), p. 91.
8 Elizabeth E. Hoyt, 'The Impact of a Money Economy upon Consumption Patterns', *Annals of the American Academy of Political and Social Science*, 305 (May 1956), pp. 12–22; Kusum Nair, *Blossoms in the Dust: The Human Factor in Indian Development* (New York: Frederick A. Praeger, 1962), p. 56.
9 This has long been recognized as the problem of economic traditionalism as manifested in the backward-sloping supply curve of labour. What has not

been given equal emphasis, however, is the fact that such traditionalism is an equally effective obstacle to modern consumer behaviour.

10 Jones, 'The Fashion Manipulators', p. 200 (italics as in original).
11 William Cobbett, *Rural Rides . . . with Economical and Political Observations,* ed. E. W. Martin (London: Macdonald, 1958), p. 222.
12 Joan Thirsk, *Economic Policy and Projects: The Development of a Consumer Society in Early Modern England* (Oxford: Clarendon Press, 1978), p. 23; Walter Minchinton, 'Convention, Fashion and Consumption: Aspects of British Experience since 1750', in Henri Baudet and Henk van der Meulen (eds), *Consumer Behaviour and Economic Growth in the Modern Economy* (London: Croom Helm, 1982), p. 22; Jones, 'The Fashion Manipulators', p. 216.
13 For further discussion of this important dimension of the problem see pp. 38–57 below.
14 McKendrick, Brewer and Plumb, *The Birth of a Consumer Society,* p. 11.
15 Perkin, *Origins of English Society,* pp. 96–7.
16 See, in addition, Eric Pawson, *The Early Industrial Revolution: Britain in the Eighteenth Century* (London: Batsford Academic, 1978), pp. 77–8.
17 McKendrick, Brewer and Plumb, *The Birth of a Consumer Society,* p. 10.
18 Ibid., p. 56.
19 Ibid., p. 38.
20 Ibid., pp. 14–16.
21 Ibid., pp. 20–1.
22 Ibid., p. 22.
23 Ibid., pp. 22–3.
24 Ibid., p. 98.
25 Ibid., p. 41.
26 Ibid., p. 54.
27 Ibid., p. 56.
28 Ibid., p. 60.
29 Ibid., p. 74.
30 Ibid., p. 92.
31 Ibid., p. 36.
32 The repeal of sumptuary legislation cannot be held to be a significant factor facilitating this new propensity to consume luxury goods for this had occurred a good deal earlier. As Baldwin observes, 'the reign of Elizabeth marked the zenith of sumptuary legislation in England'; whilst James I's accession to the throne heralded the abolition of the majority of the penal laws relating to dress (see Frances Elizabeth Baldwin, *Sumptuary Legislation and Personal Regulation in England* (Baltimore: John Hopkins Press, 1926), p. 249). Although isolated attempts were made during the first half of the seventeenth century to impose restrictions on what were regarded as excesses in apparel, these received little support and appear in any case to have been largely ignored.
33 McKendrick, Brewer and Plumb, *The Birth of a Consumer Society,* p. 63.
34 Ibid., p. 69.
35 Georg Simmel, 'Fashion', *American Journal of Sociology,* 62 (May 1957), 541–58, reprinted from *International Quarterly* 10 (1904). See also

International Encyclopedia of the Social Sciences, David L. Sills (ed.), 1968, *s.v.* 'Fashion', by Herbert G. Blumer.

36 McKendrick, Brewer and Plumb, *The Birth of a Consumer Society*, p. 171.
37 Ibid., p. 172.
38 Ibid.
39 Pawson, *The Early Industrial Revolution*, p. 77.
40 Thirsk, *Economic Policy and Projects*, pp. 7–8.
41 Ibid., p. 14.
42 See, for example, J. H. Plumb, 'Commercialization and Society', in McKendrick, Brewer and Plumb, *The Birth of a Consumer Society*, pp. 265–335.
43 Ibid., pp. 265–85.
44 Ibid., pp. 282, 284.
45 Ian Watt, *The Rise of the Novel: Studies in Defoe, Richardson and Fielding* (Berkeley: University of California Press, 1957); Leo Lowenthal and Marjorie Fiske, 'The Debate over Art and Popular Culture in Eighteenth-Century England', in Mirra Komarovsky (ed.), *Common Frontiers of the Social Sciences* (Glencoe, Ill.: Free Press, 1957), pp. 33–96; J. M. S. Tompkins, *The Popular Novel in England 1770–1800* (Lincoln, Nebr.: University of Nebraska Press, 1961).
46 John Tinnon Taylor, *Early Opposition to the English Novel: The Popular Reaction from 1760–1830* (New York: King's Crown, 1943), p. 40.
47 Ibid., p. 54.
48 Ibid., p. 65.
49 Lawrence Stone, *The Family, Sex and Marriage in England 1500–1800* (London: Weidenfeld and Nicolson, 1977), p. 284.
50 Ibid., p. 282.
51 Ibid.
52 See, in this respect, Denis de Rougemont, *Passion and Society*, trans. (Montgomery Belgion, rev. edn (London: Faber and Faber, 1956), and, for a slightly different view, John Alan Lee, 'The Romantic Heresy', *Canadian Review of Sociology and Anthropology*, 12 (1975), 514–28.
53 That these various phenomena are closely interrelated would seem to be fairly obvious. Not only did romantic love form the main subject-matter of novels, it was also a principal leisure-time activity. At the same time, the rapid turnover in the popularity of novels matched that of fashions in dress, which, in their turn, played an important part in attracting potential lovers. Dances, concerts and race-meetings were, of course, important occasions for establishing such liaisons. A final common factor is the prominent part played by women in all these spheres, something which was also true of the consumer revolution itself. See Neil McKendrick, 'Home Demand and Economic Growth: A New View of the Role of Women and Children in the Industrial Revolution', in Neil McKendrick (ed.), *Historical Perspectives: Studies in English Thought and Society in Honour of J. H. Plumb* (London: Europa Publications, 1974), pp. 152–210.
54 Thirsk, *Economic Policy and Projects*, p. 23.
55 Minchinton, 'Convention, Fashion and Consumption', p. 22.
56 McKendrick, Brewer and Plumb, *The Birth of a Consumer Society*, pp. 14–16.

57   Ibid.
58   Ibid., p. 13.
59   To 'justify' consumption in terms of its contribution to production is not
     really to 'justify' consumption at all for the moral superiority of work values
     remains intact. It is rather to point to the inescapable conclusion that some
     level of luxury consumption has to be tolerated. Unless one is going to
     claim, however, that individual consumers were successfully able to use this
     argument to counter their own ascetic tendencies, it is necessary to look
     elsewhere for the beliefs and values which justified the new propensity to
     consume luxury goods.
60   For evidence of the strength of opposition to luxury consumption on moral
     and ascetic grounds see Gordon Vichert, 'The Theory of Conspicuous
     Consumption in the Eighteenth Century', in Peter Hughes and David
     Williams (eds), *The Varied Pattern: Studies in the Eighteenth Century*
     (Toronto: A. M. Hakkert, 1971), pp. 253–67.
61   Ibid., p. 256.
62   *Boswell's Life of Johnson*, ed. George Birkbeck Hill, rev. and enlarged edn by
     L. F. Powell, 6 vols (Oxford: Clarendon Press, 1934), vol. 2, pp. 291–2.
63   Quoted in Vichert, 'The Theory of Conspicuous Consumption', p. 260.
64   There is also something rather strange about this concentration upon the
     justification of luxury consumption *per se* given the emphasis in the standard
     account upon the role of emulative motives. One would have imagined that
     the focus would have been on those writers who justified emulation.
65   Stone, *The Family, Sex and Marriage*, pp. 224–5.
66   Haller has identified 'spiritual equalitarianism' as the 'central force of
     revolutionary Puritanism' in England. See William Haller, *The Rise of
     Puritanism, or the Way to the New Jerusalem as set forth in Pulpit and Press from
     Thomas Cartwright to John Lilburne and John Milton, 1570–1643* (New York:
     Harper, 1957), p. 86.
67   Even if one accepts that the Restoration signalled the defeat of the harsher
     forms of Protestantism, and Calvinism in particular, it still seems improbable
     that deeply ingrained moral attitudes would be swept away quite so quickly.
68   This view does present the bourgeoisie as inheriting the power and wealth
     of the aristocracy, and thus, to some extent, those objects which are their
     symbols. But to concentrate on seeing the process in these terms is, in
     effect, to 'de-ethicize' consumption and fail to regard it as a form of
     conduct which is expressive of basic values.

Chapter 3   The puzzle of modern consumerism

1   There has been a tendency to leave the subject of consumption to the
     discipline of economics, which, in turn, is largely a product of that tradition
     of utilitarian thought that began to take shape in the eighteenth century.
     Since economics is a notoriously ahistorical discipline it has been able to
     avoid confronting the issue of explaining the consumer revolution which
     coincided with its birth.
2   It goes without saying that modern consumerism has only been made possible

through the introduction of a variety of economic, social and technological innovations. Mass production itself is one of these, as too is advertising and credit selling. None the less, even when all these contributory factors have been identified, it still appears that modern consumerism remains unexplained; unexplained that is as a pattern of meaningful conduct.

3   Erich Fromm, 'The Psychological Aspects of the Guaranteed Income', in Robert Theobald (ed.), *The Guaranteed Income: Next Step in Economic Evolution?* (New York: Doubleday, 1964), pp. 175–84, see esp. 179.

4   John O'Neill, 'The Productive Body: An Essay on the Work of Consumption', *Queen's Quarterly*, 85 (Summer 1978), 221–30, see esp. 225.

5   Rom J. Markin Jr, *Consumer Behaviour: A Cognitive Orientation* (New York: Macmillan, 1974), p. 195.

6   Interestingly, if, at times like Christmas or prior to a birthday, an individual responds to a query concerning what he would like for a present by intimating that there is nothing that he wants, this is treated not only as an infraction of the norm of reciprocity but also as a false report of psychological reality.

7   Obviously some wants relate to products which service recurrent needs like those for food and clothing and hence their cyclical reappearance is understandable. The form taken by a want is, however, independent of the need which gives rise to it. Thus, whilst the need for food will be experienced at regular intervals, this may lead, at different times, to a want for a hamburger, a Chinese meal or merely a bar of chocolate. A specific want thus reflects the expression of a preference within the context of a need and the recurrent nature of needs does not explain the ever-changing nature of wants.

8   Daniel Lerner, *The Passing of Traditional Society: Modernizing the Middle East* (Glencoe, Ill.: Free Press, 1958).

9   See comments in Richard Martin, Steven Chaffee and Fausto Izcaray, 'Media and Consumerism in Venezuela', *Journalism Quarterly*, 56 (1979), 296–304.

10 Hazel Kyrk, *A Theory of Consumption* (London: Isaac Pitman, 1923), p. 4.

11 The fact that modern consumers rarely seem to find their own behaviour bewildering is testimony to the powerful taken-for-granted nature of the values and attitudes upon which it rests. It is just these unquestioned assumptions which should have been the main focus of attention for social scientists. Unfortunately, despite a vast amount of investigation into the socio-demographic preferences of consumers, together with extensive, commercially supported, psychological and psycho-analytic inquiry into buying habits, few comparative and historical studies have been undertaken which could have shed light upon the spirit of modern consumerism. Only in social anthropology does one sometimes encounter an awareness of the extent to which modern consumer behaviour remains a mystery. See, in this connection, Mary Douglas and Baron Isherwood, *The World of Goods: Towards an Anthropology of Consumption* (Harmondsworth, Middx.: Penguin Books, 1978).

12 David Riesman and Daniel Lerner, 'Self and Society: Reflections on some

Turks in Transition', in David Riesman, *Abundance for What? And Other Essays* (New York: Anchor Books, 1965), pp. 382–96, see esp. p. 391.

13 George M. Foster, 'Peasant Society and the Image of Limited Good', *American Anthropologist*, 67 (1965), 293–315, see esp. p. 297.

14 Lerner, *Passing of Traditional Society*, p. 400.

15 Georg Simmel, 'Fashion', *American Journal of Sociology*, 62 (May 1957), p. 546.

16 A fundamental reason why the insatiable nature of modern consumerism has tended to be ignored by social scientists is because classical economics deemed the origin of consumer wants and tastes to be beyond its sphere of inquiry. This has not only had the unfortunate consequence of diverting attention from this crucial question, but, in presenting the rationality of instrumental action as the typical characteristic of modern consumerism, economics has succeeded in making the endless pursuit of wants appear to be both 'natural' and 'irrational'. As far as understanding the nature of modern consumerism is concerned it would have been better for social science if more attention had been paid to the apparent irrationality of ends and less to the postulated rationality of means. This treatment of the ends of action as effectively random, is, as Parsons observed, both a major characteristic of utilitarian social thought and a principal weakness. See Talcott Parsons, *The Structure of Social Action: A Study in Social Theory with Special Reference to a Group of Recent European Writers* 2nd edn (Glencoe, Ill.: Free Press, 1949), pp. 59–60.

17 For early critiques see Henry Waldgrave Stuart, 'The Phases of the Economic Interest', in John Dewey (ed.), *Creative Intelligence: Essays in the Pragmatic Attitude* (New York: Henry Holt, 1917), pp. 282–353 and Kyrk, *A Theory of Consumption*. A contemporary critique can be found in Douglas and Isherwood, *The World of Goods*. A noteworthy exception to the economists' general neglect of these problems and a promising attempt to construct a theory of consumption on more realistic assumptions is to be found in Tibor Scitovsky, *The Joyless Economy: An Inquiry into Human Satisfaction and Consumer Dissatisfaction* (New York: Oxford University Press, 1976).

18 Stuart, 'Phases of Economic Interest', p. 347.

19 Ibid., p. 309. Whilst it could be argued that it is not irrational to believe others when they inform us that a new product will provide greater satisfaction than one currently consumed, this is to assume some standard for comparing satisfactions provided by different products as well as the idea that the tastes of individuals are equatable. Both of these assumptions are rejected by marginal utility theory. Equally, it could be suggested that it is not irrational for a consumer whose disposable income has grown to employ his surplus in trying a new product since he is not in this way losing any existing gratification. It is still the case, even here however, that a more rational strategy would be to use the new wealth to consume more of what is already known to be satisfying. This is indeed what traditional consumers typically do, as has already been noted. See pp. 18–19 above.

20 Kenneth Galbraith, *The Affluent Society*, 3rd edn rev. (Harmondsworth, Middx.: Penguin Books, 1979).

21 Ibid., p. 136.
22 Ibid., p. 143.
23 Ibid., pp. 137–45 *passim.*
24 Ibid., pp. 147–8.
25 Ibid., p. 147. Galbraith seems to overlook the fact that much of this expenditure is incurred in attempts to persuade consumers to want one brand of cereal or detergent rather than another.
26 Ibid., p. 144.
27 McKendrick, Brewer and Plumb, *Birth of a Consumer Society*, p. 14.
28 Ibid., pp. 35, 63, 28.
29 Ibid., p. 16.
30 Although the idea that human beings possess some pre-formed or innate disposition to acquire products, as, for example, jackdaws would seem to be endowed with where shiny objects are concerned, is a popular view, it is clearly untenable. Apart from the fact that what is characteristic of human behaviour is its extreme plasticity, and hence the great variety of goods for which there has been some demand at one time or another, this argument overlooks the equally marked tendency of modern consumers to 'disac-quire' or dispose of goods.
31 The idea that human motivation can be understood in terms of needs at all is now considered by some psychologists to be highly doubtful. See, for an instance of this scepticism, Michael A. Wallach and Lise Wallach, *Psychology's Sanction for Selfishness: The Error of Egoism in Theory and Therapy* (San Francisco: W. H. Freeman, 1983), pp. 217–25.
32 Markin, *Consumer Behaviour*, p. 195.
33 Galbraith, *Affluent Society*, p. 136.
34 For evidence that 'higher' needs such as social status and prestige may displace 'lower' biological ones, see Herskovits's reference to competitive yam growing among the Ponapean in Micronsia and the observation that 'families of a man aspiring to great prestige may go hungry' (Melville J. Herskovits, *Economic Anthropology: A Study in Comparative Economics* (New York: Alfred A. Knopf, 1960), p. 462).
35 This hierarchy of needs perspective also has strong overtones of an evolutionary ethnocentricism, suggesting, as it appears to, that only in modern society do the 'highest' needs find proper expression.
36 Stuart, 'Phases of Economic Interest', p. 347.
37 Vance Packard, *The Hidden Persuaders* (London: Longmans, 1957).
38 This is merely a restatement of the view encountered earlier which presents demand as a reflex phenomenon with an awareness of increased supply automatically triggering a consumer response. It is a view which bypasses the critical issue of the origin of wants.
39 The adoption of this position is usually clearly signalled by the designation of consumers' wants as 'false'; see, for one of many examples of this usage, Mike Featherstone, 'The Body in Consumer Culture', *Theory, Culture and Society*, 1 (1982), 18–33.
40 Even here it is important to note that promoters of rival products commonly seek to undermine each other's influence.

41 To claim, as some writers do, that all groups in modern society represent the interests of the producers of goods either directly or indirectly is to confuse the aims of individual manufacturers with the continued existence of a particular form of society, whilst to observe that individual consumers only have the wants they do because of the socialization they have experienced is a self-evident and unhelpful truth which applies in all cultures.

42 For a useful summary discussion of the effects of advertising see Gillian Dyer, *Advertising as Communication* (London, Methuen, 1982), pp. 72–86 *passim*.

43 The manipulationist position thus gains its strength by ignoring the interest which the consumer has in the symbolic meanings of the product and contrasting an assumed utilitarian outlook with the advertisers' symbolic manipulation.

44 Just as price is no more than a symbolic meaning attached to a product the manipulation of which affects the consumer's willingness to buy, so too is desirability a symbolic meaning attached to a product, the manipulation of which affects a consumer's willingness to buy. To assume that individuals are deceived if they buy a product out of a liking for its image, but not if they buy it out of a liking for its price, is strangely contradictory.

45 John P. Diggins, *The Bard of Savagery: Thorstein Veblen and Modern Social Theory* (Brighton: Harvester Press, 1978), p. 100.

46 Thorstein Veblen, *The Theory of the Leisure Class: An Economic Study of Institutions* (London: George Allen and Unwin, 1957).

47 Ibid., p. 85.

48 Ibid., p. 25.

49 Ibid., p. 31.

50 See David Seckler, *Thorstein Veblen and the Institutionalists: A Study in the Social Philosophy of Economics* (London: Macmillan, 1975).

51 Harvey Leibenstein, 'Bandwagon, Snob, and Veblen Effects in the Theory of Consumers' Demand', in Edwin Mansfield (ed.), *Microeconomics: Selected Readings*, 4th edn (New York: Norton, 1982), pp. 12–30.

52 For material on reference group theory see Robert K. Merton, *Social Theory and Social Structure*, rev. and enlarged edn (Glencoe, Ill: Free Press, 1968), pp. 225–386, and for its use in the examination of consumer behaviour see A. Benston Cocanougher and Grady D. Bruce, 'Socially Distant Reference Groups and Consumer Aspirations', in Harold H. Kassarjian and Thomas S. Robertson, *Perspectives in Consumer Behaviour* (Glenview, Ill.: Scott, Foresman, 1973), pp. 309–14.

53 The fundamental inadequacy of these explanations is clearly revealed when Leibenstein refers to what he calls 'irrational demand', that is, 'purchases that are neither planned nor calculated but are due to sudden urges, whims, etc., and that serve no rational purpose but that of satisfying sudden whims and desires' ('Bandwagon, Snob, and Veblen Effects', p. 14); the explanation of consumer behaviour presented in the Veblen effects hypotheses is only marginally less vacuous than this.

54 It is interesting to speculate upon why, although economists generally look with approval upon the individual who acts rationally in pursuit of his own

satisfaction and material self-interest, they tend to look with some disapproval upon the individual who acts rationally in pursuit of prestige or social status.

55 Veblen, *Theory of the Leisure Class*, p. 103.
56 Merton, *Social Theory and Social Structure*, pp. 225–386 *passim*.
57 For the use of these terms see Roger S. Manson, *Conspicuous Consumption: A Study of Exceptional Consumer Behaviour* (Farnborough, Hants.: Gower, 1981) p. 11.
58 It can be noted at this point that the widespread tendency to use the phrase 'keeping up with the Joneses' to refer to a competitive striving for higher status is misguided. If the efforts of consumers were limited to maintaining their social position in this way there would be little change in consumption patterns; 'getting ahead of the Joneses' is clearly what Veblen had in mind.
59 Veblen, *Theory of the Leisure Class*, p. 70.
60 It is pertinent in this respect to observe that envy often includes hostility or dislike, and hence that it is not uncommon for an individual to contest another's claim to superior status by denying its legitimacy.
61 That the failure to perceive the extent to which consumption is expressive in this sense is a main shortcoming of Veblen's work is a point made by Arthur K. Davis. See 'Veblen on the Decline of the Protestant Ethic', *Social Forces*, 22 (1944), 282–6, and esp. p. 282.
62 David Riesman and Howard Roseborough, 'Careers and Consumer Behaviour', in David Riesman, *Abundance for What? And Other Essays* (New York: Doubleday Anchor Books, 1965), pp. 107–130, see esp. p. 120.
63 Edward O. Laumann and James S. House, 'Living-Room Styles and Social Attributes: The Patterning of Material Artifacts in a Modern Urban Community', in Kassarjian and Robertson, *Perspectives in Consumer Behaviour*, pp. 430–40.
64 For further evidence that the arbiters of taste belong to the upper middle or lower upper classes and are not members of the societal elite, see Russell Lynes, *The Tastemakers* (New York: Grosset and Dunlop, 1959).
65 It is interesting to speculate on what the motive for inconspicuous consumption might be in Veblen's theory. Although the obvious answer is that it is guided merely by the desire for utility this would be to deny the validity of his insight into the cultural significance of the act of consumption. If, however, it is recognized as having symbolic meaning for the consumer then this opens up the possibility that conspicuous consumption may also manifest these 'inner-directed' concerns.
66 Diggins suggests that it was Boas's account of the potlatch which provided Veblen with his inspiration for the theory of conspicuous consumption (Diggins, *The Bard of Savagery*, p. 98).
67 Veblen assumes that changes in patterns of visible consumption derive from an attempt to aspire to higher social status simply on the grounds that consumption is a form of behaviour which has significance as an indicator of status, but those who use his theory often write as if he had proved that modern consumers act out of emulative motives. Veblen did not, in fact, provide much evidence of people's motives.

68 As we have already seen the evidence does not support this model as fashionable innovations are not necessarily introduced by the social elite.

69 *International Encyclopaedia of the Social Sciences*, David L. Sills (ed.), 1968, *s.v.* 'Fashion', by Herbert G. Blumer, p. 342.

Chapter 4   Traditional and modern hedonism

1 Werner Sombart, *Luxury and Capitalism* (Ann Arbor: University of Michigan Press, 1967), p. 59.

2 Neil McKendrick, John Brewer, and J. H. Plumb, *The Birth of a Consumer Society: The Commercialization of Eighteenth-Century England* (London: Europa Publications), p. 98.

3 See Otis Pease, *The Responsibilities of American Advertising : Private Control and Public Influence, 1920–1940* New York: Arno Press), p. 22.

4 Lionel Trilling, 'The Fate of Pleasure: Wordsworth to Dostoevsky', *Partisan Review*, 30 (Summer 1963) 73–106, reproduced in Lionel Trilling, *Beyond Culture: Essays on Literature and Learning* (Oxford: Oxford University Press, 1980) p. 56.

5 Sombart, *Luxury and Capitalism*, p. 61.

6 Tibor Scitovsky, *The Joyless Economy: An Enquiry into Human Satisfaction and Consumer Dissatisfaction* (New York: Oxford University Press, 1976).

7 If only because of the logical difficulty of equating an aspect of experience with a class of objects.

8 The outstanding exception, of course, is that tradition of thought which derives from the work of Freud. It should be obvious, however, that the hedonistic theory of action proposed here has little in common with those theories which have been labelled 'hedonistic' but which are instinctivist or behaviourist in character. The view that pleasure is some kind of dominant universal motivating force underlying human conduct is specifically rejected. One may assume that human beings often prefer pleasure to boredom without being committed to the assumption that all behaviour is hedonistic. Motives are social constructs, not psychological or physiological predispositions, and hence the crucial questions concern the circumstances under which 'pleasure' becomes the self-conscious and deliberate goal of human action. The position adopted here is that there are no 'instrinsically' unpleasant activities (although there may well be acts which humans commonly experience as pleasant), and hence that hedonistic action refers to conduct in which pleasure is pursued as a deliberate and self-conscious goal, the form which this takes being determined by the critical cultural concept of 'taste'.

9 Jeremy Bentham, 'An Introduction to the Principles of Morals and Legislation', in Jeremy Bentham and John Stuart Mill, *The Utilitarians*, 1823 edn (New York: Doubleday, Dolphin Books, 1961), p. 15.

10 There would seem to be something of a central ambiguity within utilitarian thought concerning the concept of pleasure, as this discussion suggests. Whilst, on the one hand, there is the tendency to incorporate the concept of

pleasure into that of utility, there also exists the tendency to see pleasure as a 'luxury' and hence as something which is 'unnecessary'. Whether human beings can be said to have a 'need' for pleasure is hard to determine. Sensory deprivation experiments suggest the presence of a need for stimulation, but it would appear to be difficult to demonstrate a need for pleasure as such.

11 See, for support for this view, Gilbert Ryle, *Dilemmas* (Cambridge: Cambridge University Press, 1954), pp. 54–67.

12 Of course, sexual activity can also be described as being 'pushed' by need, whilst hunger may be aroused by contact with food. These examples are chosen merely to illustrate the different ideal-type models of motivated behaviour involved.

13 Ryle, *Dilemmas*, pp. 58–9.

14 Ibid. For further discussion of some of the issues raised here see David L. Perry, *The Concept of Pleasure* (The Hague: Mouton, 1967).

15 Joy or ecstasy can perhaps be best viewed as a whole-body experiental condition built-up through prolonged exposure to a pleasing pattern of stimulation.

16 If it is indeed the patterned nature of stimuli which makes us aware of pleasure, whilst it is their intensity which brings pain, then this could be a reason why awareness appears to play a more critical role in relation to the former than the latter; that is, painful stimuli are likely to demand our attention in a way which is simply not true of pleasurable ones, where a more active process of discernment is involved.

17 See Scitovsky, *The Joyless Economy*, pp. 63–4.

18 It might be thought that the 'hierarchy of needs' perspective which was rejected earlier (see pp. 44–5), is here being resurrected in a modified form through the claim that the pursuit of pleasure arises as an explicit end in itself in human affairs once basic needs have been satisfied. Apart, however, from the fact that no biological or psychological 'need' for pleasure is postulated, the process outlined here is one in which a loss of pleasure is experienced as a consequence of activity undertaken to satisfy basic needs. The emergence of systematic pleasure-seeking can thus be seen as a compensatory innovation, and implies nothing about a supposed 'hierarchy' of inherent needs.

19 Incidentally experienced pleasure can be labelled 'secondary'; where this is the primary purpose of conduct, behaviour can be said to be directed towards 'primary' pleasure.

20 Such 'action hedonism' is a feature of most delinquent sub-cultures found in modern industrial societies, where the 'search for kicks' or 'thrills' is a manifest concern. See David Matza, 'Subterranean Traditions of Youth', *Annals of the American Academy of Political and Social Science*, 338 (November 1961), 102–18. Here, too, fighting is a central activity, as are various legal and illegal, dangerous acts. It is important to note, however, that a concern with the hedonistic ingredient in these activities is severely curtailed by their status-signifying functions. Hence the pleasurable quality of the experience may be extensively compromised in the interests of manifesting strength, bravery, virility, loyalty or daring. Thus, although such activities may well be

prompted by boredom, and there is some concern with the enjoyment gained, the rationalization of pleasure-seeking is greatly curtailed by the primacy of these other values.

Drama is, at one level, an attempt to experience some of the pleasurable qualities associated with real-life 'action' experiences without the 'fatefulness' which usually accompanies them. The technique for doing this is via the artistic reproduction of the experience together with audience–actor identification. A similar 'reproduction' and 'identification' technique for extracting pleasure from the material of real life occurs with simple story-telling, and may also be a significant ingredient in the visual arts. This is the most promising future path for the development of hedonism.

21 Whilst it is true that some emotions may be more commonly accompanied by feelings of pleasantness than others, this does not mean that such emotions as anger, fear or sorrow cannot become sources of pleasure under the right conditions.

22 It is pertinent in this context to note the common stem to the words 'emotion' and 'motion'.

23 Strictly speaking, all aspects of emotional arousal could be considered to constitute 'behaviour', even that which is subcutaneous. In the context of social interaction, however, overt manifestations of arousal clearly have a far greater significance than any covert indications.

24 Where the suppression of emotion extends beyond the control of overt actions to embrace all subjective dimensions of the experience, as it does in the stoical ideal of *apathea* or emotionlessness, it would be more correct to speak of emotional extinction than control. This path clearly leads directly away from modern hedonism.

25 In one sense, the power to inhibit the expression of emotion logically implies an ability to express it when desired. All that would seem to be required is the cessation of the effort of suppression. Individuals do not normally live, however, in a state of permanent suppressed emotional excitement, and hence there will be occasions when something more than the abandonment of inhibition will be necessary. In addition, full emotional control implies the ability to chose the emotion desired.

26 As long as emotion remains locked in to a behavioural complex which includes motor activity of an extravagant and dramatic kind, there can be little hope of gaining control of the subjective dimension of that experience. All that one can do is to try and adjust one's real experiences, or alternatively try to shut out information about the world, as children often do by hiding their eyes (or covering their ears) when frightened.

27 Owen Barfield, *History in English Words*, new edn (London: Faber and Faber, 1954;, pp. 169–70.

28 Contemporary linguistic usage suggests the continuing influence of the idea that emotion is an attribute of situations rather than of persons as references to 'sad' or 'happy' occasions imply. Usually, however, this is interpreted to mean that individuals feel themselves under an obligation to experience the required emotion, and hence is not really comparable with situations in which there is no voluntaristic ingredient present.

29 Max Weber, *The Sociology of Religion*, trans. Ephraim Fischoff (London: Methuen, 1965), chapters 2, 3, *passim*.
30 Those thinkers and artists who were part of the Romantic Movement in Europe in the eighteenth and nineteenth centuries can be said to have been well to the fore in accomplishing this process (see pp. 179–87 below), with the 'self' and 'genius' twin focii of their 'spiritualizing' endeavours.
31 Barfield, *History in English Words*, pp. 165–9.
32 Ibid., p. 165.
33 See pp. 123–31 below.
34 The phrase is, of course, Coleridge's. The full quote is 'That willing suspension of disbelief for the moment, / which constitutes poetic faith' (see Coleridge, *Biographia Literia, or Biographical Sketches of my Literary Life*, 2 vols, first edn repr. (London: Rest Fenner, 1817), vol. 2, p. 6).
35 It might be objected that the ancient profession of acting had always presupposed possession of the ability to employ imagination to successfully manifest a chosen emotion at will. Whilst this seems a plausible claim, it would be anachronistic to assume that acting, either in Graeco-Roman, Renaissance or Elizabethan times, necessarily involved the ability to actually experience chosen emotions at will. For the fact that a character was undergoing a given emotion was typically conveyed by stylized gestures and expressions (in addition to utterances), and it was not necessary to the performance for either the actor to actually experience, or for the audience to believe that he really was experiencing, that emotion for the portrayal to be accepted. Thus, although acting has always encompassed imitation and mimickry, it is only in modern times that it has also typically embraced the ability to voluntarily 'become' another person in the sense of taking over their experience of reality; something which is perhaps most associated with the ideas of Konstantin Stanislavski.

Chapter 5   Modern autonomous imaginative hedonism

1 James Thurber, *The Thurber Carnival* (London: Hamish Hamilton, 1945), pp. 47–51.
2 Ibid., p. 49.
3 Willis Hall and Keith Waterhouse, *Billy Liar (The Play)* (Glasgow: Blackie, 1966), p. 8.
4 Ibid., p. 48.
5 Ibid., p. 21.
6 Although the fact that fantasizing possesses continuity and often builds cumulatively is not apparent in the case of Walter Mitty, it is commonly reported by imaginative fantasizers. See W. H. Auden, 'Freedom and Necessity in Poetry: My Lead Mine', in Jerome S. Bruner, Allison Jolly and Kathy Sylva (eds), *Play – Its Role in Development and Evolution* (Harmondsworth, Middx.: Penguin Books, 1976), pp. 584–5.
7 Thurber, *The Thurber Carnival*, p. 47.
8 Hall and Waterhouse, *Billy Liar*, pp. 16–17.

9   Ibid., p. 102.
10 It is important to note in this respect that there is no suggestion that either Walter Mitty or Billy Liar commonly lapse into delusion, for although addicted to fantasizing, both still possess the ability to distinguish between dream and actuality.
11 Thurber, *The Thurber Carnival*, p. 47.
12 See, for example, the discussion of Bohemianism on pages 195–8 below.
13 Hall and Waterhouse, *Billy Liar*, p. 75.
14 Sigmund Freud, *The Future of an Illusion*, trans. by W. D. Robson-Scott, revised and newly edited by James Strachey (New York: Doubleday, Anchor Books, 1964), p. 49. Freud cites Columbus's belief that he had found a new sea-route to India as a case of 'illusion' because wish-fulfilment played such a prominent part in its formation, whereas Aristotle's belief that vermin developed out of dung he describes as an 'error' because wish-fulfilment played no part in its development. It would seem preferable to call the first example a 'delusion', and retain the term 'illusion' for those instances where individuals are aware of the contrast between what they perceive and what they know.
15 Indeed they can be said to be in a better position to know that these images are false than in the case of such 'objective' illusions as mirror-depth or perspective for they have consciously created them. However, this observation plunges us into the murky waters of the debate over the ontological status of different categories of sense data, and hence is an issue which is perhaps best not pursued here. Suffice to say that there is no intention of implying that mental phenomena are 'unreal' in a philosophical sense, merely that actors typically operate with a clear distinction between their existing situation and those imaginary ones which they can call into being.
16 The assumption underlying this discussion is that much private, covert day-dreaming is a pleasurable experience deliberately engaged in for its own sake. This is not to claim that all fantasizing or image-making is pleasant, nor that it occurs merely in response to a desire for pleasure. The recall of memories, and the imaginative anticipation of events, constitutes a large part of the continuing stream of consciousness which characterizes the mental life of human beings, and these activities necessarily merge into and blend with enjoyable fantasies. Some of this activity will be distressful, as when we suddenly have vivid recall of a painful event, and much of it may focus upon matters which cause anxiety or guilt. Even when contemplating disastrous and morbid images, however, there is a distinct possibility that we might dwell upon them because of the frisson of horror which they can provide. It does seem reasonable to suggest, therefore, that, in so far as our daily routines permit us to develop mental images without being subject to external demands, there will be a tendency for these to develop in ways which provide pleasure, and it is in this respect that Freud's observations on the motivational significance of wishes seems most pertinent.

It should be clear, however, that what is not accepted is the traditional psycho-analytic view that day-dreaming is necessarily a regressive and cathartic phenomenon arising out of suppressed desires. Although some fantasies may indeed be a way of giving expression to wishes which are denied gratification by social taboos and have their origin in childhood experiences, it cannot be assumed that these constitute the bulk of a normal individual's imaginative inner-life. Day-dreaming should be regarded as an integral part of the mental experience of normal healthy individuals. There is little evidence, for example, to support the common assumption that fantasizing performs a cathartic function in the reduction of arousal, and is hence best viewed simply as a skill or faculty of human beings which is 'just there'. See Jerome L. Singer, *The Child's World of Make-Believe: Experimental Studies in Imaginative Play* (New York: Academic Press, 1973), p. 119.

17 There is no particular reason why one should not 'day-dream' about the past. Such exercises in imaginative reconstruction typically involve modifying what actually happened to make it more acceptable and pleasing, along a 'what might have happened if' line of thought. This still approximates to a day-dream rather than a fantasy in so far as it stays within the bounds of the possible, whilst such retrospective exercises are very likely to merge into anticipatory ones on the basis of 'next time' scenarios.

18 One of the key features of day-dreaming is the fact that the scene which is viewed in the mind's eye is taken as being a possible, real, future event to such an extent that the act has some of the qualities of second sight. This sense of looking into the future helps to give the images a greater flavour of actuality, whilst also increasing the desire for the envisaged events to occur. In this latter connection, day-dreaming must be considered a highly significant force helping to motivate social conduct.

19 The pleasures of day-dreaming can also be regarded as double in another respect for there is an aesthetic pleasure to be gained from viewing the imagined scenario 'from the outside' as if it were a work of art, as well as that gained from being a participant acting 'on the inside'.

20 Obviously longing cannot be an integral feature of fantasizing without the individual running the risk of being considered (or indeed, becoming) mentally ill; someone who longs to be invisible or to 'become' Winston Churchill is not likely to be regarded as normal.

21 An epicurean appreciation of the fact that delaying satisfaction heightens the pleasure accompanying eventual gratification has always been a feature of hedonistic conduct. What is novel is the readiness to accept a postponement of gratification in order that the intervening period might be devoted to the joys of imaginative, anticipatory dreaming.

22 'Ode on a Grecian Urn', in *The Poetical Works of John Keats*, ed. H. W. Garrod, 2nd. edn (Oxford: Clarendon Press, 1958), pp. 260–2.

23 This, of course, is precisely what happens when individuals 'fall in love at first sight', a process which involves associating the realization of one's most cherished dreams with the 'possession' of one particular, real person.

24 To this extent Veblen was essentially correct in emphasizing the cultural meaning of products rather than their utility. Unfortunately, he chose to emphasize merely one, highly specific, form of meaning, relating it to a very dubious theory of human nature.

25 In practice, individual dream experiences probably do not vary greatly, but

tend to be minor variants of a standard theme, as is the case, for example, with the stories in popular romantic novels or westerns. In a similar fashion, new products do not have to be very different from the old in order to serve as the focus for fresh desire.

26	The idea that acquisition of a long-desired product has actually fulfilled a dream may, of course, persist for a while after purchase, most especially in that interval between purchase and use, whilst the desire to believe that this is the case may cause disillusionment to be slow in dawning. Indeed, through the process of the displacement of goals, acquisition itself might have become the focus of the dream. None of this alters the fact that reality-pleasure will not live up to expectations which the experience of dream-pleasure has created.

27	Virginia Woolf, *A Haunted House and Other Stories*, 1962 edn (London: The Hogarth Press, 1944), pp. 49–58.

28	Ibid., pp. 51–2.

29	Ibid.

30	Although it has long been recognized that people gain 'psychic gratification' from advertisements, the tendency among social scientists has been to treat this as a comparatively trivial fact, of no great consequence in the understanding of socio-economic conduct.

31	It is, of course, true that one must be able to 'use' any new product imaginatively before being convinced that it is worth buying. One must 'imagine' the desk in the study in order to appreciate that it is too big, and one must 'imagine' the red shoes together with the burgundy dress in order to realize that the colours might clash. In this respect the possession of an imaginative faculty is an obvious necessity for any modern consumer, although it is not something which a traditional consumer would necessarily require. But this is a different – fundamentally impersonal – use of imagination from that egocentric form which is essential to the generation of desire. These imaginative exercises are relevant only to the more precise specification of the parameters of need; thus it is obvious that one 'needs' a desk which will fit in the study and one's need is for shoes which will not clash with the dress one has already bought. In order, however, to feel desire for the desk or the shoes they must be related, however vaguely, to a dream-vision of self. One must be able to gain pleasure from the picture of oneself working at the desk or wearing the shoes.

32	To stress that desire is dependent upon egocentric dreams is not to imply that all consumption is motivated by purely selfish concerns, only that desire for a product is related to the consumers' ability to create a pleasant, imaginative scene in which it features. Many of those objects, such as flowers, chocolates or jewellery, which are commonly bought in order to be presented to others as gifts are still capable of being cast in this light.

33	See Auden, 'Freedom and Necessity', in Bruner, Jolly and Sylva, *Play*, pp. 584–5.

34	The pleasures which self-illusory hedonism supplies are largely aesthetic and emotional, the scenes created in imagination having the characteristics of both works of art and drama. It follows, therefore, that it is those products which present the greatest possibilities for aesthetic and emotional dream projection which are central to the phenomenon of fashion.

35 Obviously, young people can only attach their day-dreams to products which are differentiated, in terms of strangeness, from those which predominate in the parental home, as the very familiarity of the latter excludes them from being objects of dream-induced desire. This is why major changes in fashion are so intimately associated with generations.

36 Daniel Bell, *The Cultural Contraditions of Capitalism* (London: Heinemann, 1976), pp. 55–7.

37 It would be a mistake to imagine that modern consumerism depends upon consumers adopting a specific dream – that is, one which outlines a given style of life for all to aspire to. Whilst particular dreams may prevail among some sections of the population, it is really only the general practice of individualistic, covert day-dreaming which is crucial to the system as a whole.

Chapter 6   The other Protestant ethic

1 See the discussion on pp. 28–35.
2 Max Weber, *The Protestant Ethic and the Spirit of Capitalism*, trans. Talcott Parsons (London: Unwin University Books, 1930), p. 74.
3 To which one can add the even more intriguing question of how it was possible for these two processes to be occurring at approximately the same time, and in connection with the same critical class of culture carriers.
4 Weber, *The Protestant Ethic*, p. 53.
5 Ibid., p. 119.
6 Ibid., p. 166.
7 Ibid., p. 167.
8 Ibid.
9 Ibid., p. 263.
10 Ibid., p. 168.
11 Ibid., p. 275.
12 Samuel Eliot Morison, *The Intellectual Life of Colonial New England* (Ithaca, NY: Great Seal Books, 1960) p. 10.
13 John Carroll, *Puritan, Paranoid, Remissive: A Sociology of Modern Culture* (London: Routledge and Kegan Paul, 1977), p. 6.
14 Weber, *The Protestant Ethic*, p. 169.
15 Ibid., p. 274. This marked hostility to all decorative intent in clothing makes it especially difficult to understand the enthusiasm for fashion which gripped the middle classes in the eighteenth century.
16 Ibid., p. 171.
17 Ibid.
18 *Encyclopedia of Religion and Ethics*, ed. James Hastings (1908), *s.v.* 'Puritanism', by H. G. Wood (Edinburgh: T. and T. Clark, 1908).
19 Weber, *The Protestant Ethic*, p. 171–2.
   It becomes important, as we shall see, to be able to assess the relative

extent to which Puritanism condemned opulence as opposed to voluptuousness, that is to say, comfort-luxury as contrasted with pleasure-luxury;
for although, in its initial stages as a reforming movement these were not
only both condemned but also closely associated, as Calvinist teachings lost
their grip on the population, currents of thought emerge which differentially evaluate these 'evils'. Many writers have taken it for granted that
Puritan thought led to a tendency for pleasure to be regarded as a greater
evil than excessive comfort (see Tibor Scitovsky, *The Joyless Economy : An
Inquiry into Human Satisfaction and Consumer Dissatisfaction* (New York:
Oxford University Press, 1976), pp. 205–6) but contrary currents of thought
existed, outlasting the religious framework of ideas which gave rise to them.

20 For a summary discussion of this controversy, see Gordon Marshall, *In
Search of the Spirit of Capitalism: An Essay on Max Weber's Protestant Ethic
Thesis* (London: Hutchinson University Library, 1982), pp. 82–96.

21 Weber, *The Protestant Ethic*, p. 259.

22 Ibid., p. 252.

23 Even, in places, references to teachings such as predestination which
persisted. See the mention of A. Kohler's study on p. 226.

24 The primary source for this argument is Elie Halevy, *The Growth of
Philosophical Radicalism*, new edn (Boston, Mass.: Beacon Press, 1955); but
see also Basil Willey, *The Eighteenth Century Background: Studies on the Idea of
Nature in the Thought of the Period* (London: Chatto and Windus, 1961), pp.
10–11.

25 The term 'theodicy' appears to have been coined by Leibniz in the 1690s to
refer to the defence of God against charges brought about by a
consideration of both moral and natural evil (see *Dictionary of the History of
Ideas: Studies of Selected Pivotal ideas*, ed. Philip P. Wiener, *s.v.* 'Theodicy',
by Leroy E. Leomker, New York: Charles Scribner's Sons, 1968). It rapidly
came to be used in a somewhat broader sense to mean the study of the
compatability of the idea of God with the existence of evil, and, more
generally still, as a synonym for philosophical theology. Weber keeps fairly
close to the original meaning, and it is especially puzzling, therefore, that
there is no reference to Leibniz in *The Protestant Ethic and the Spirit of
Capitalism*, or in any of his monographs on the world religions.

26 There are several dimensions to this problem of theodicy. There is, first of
all, the general issue of natural evil and the difficulty of reconciling this with
the idea of an omnipotent benevolent god. Secondly, there is the problem of
explaining the individual distribution of this evil between persons; why
should it be, for example, that some suffer more than others. Thirdly, and
lastly, there is the associated question of socially structured inequalities and
injustices and what kind of supernatural justification can be assumed to
legitimate them. These three dimensions may, for convenience, be dubbed
the philosophical, moral and ideological aspects of the single problem of
theodicy. The focus of this discussion is on the first two of these, as it tends
to be in Weber's writings. For a consideration of the third dimension, see
Bryan Turner, *For Weber* (London: Routledge and Kegan Paul, 1981), pp.
142–76.

27 Max Weber, *The Sociology of Religion*, trans. Ephriam Fischoff, introduction by Talcott Parsons (London: Methuen, 1965), p. 139.
28 Ibid.
29 Ibid., p. 143.
30 Ibid., p. 144.
31 Ibid., p. 147.
32 John Hick, *Evil and the Love of God* (London: Macmillan, 1966).
33 Weber, *Sociology of Religion*, p. 144.
34 It might be argued that Weber did not discuss the later, more deistical, versions of Protestantism because they did not conform to his conception of a 'salvation religion', but, on the contrary, tended to eliminate the need for salvation through their acceptance of this world as 'good'. Even if this argument were to be accepted, however (and, in fact, the concept of salvation was retranslated rather than eliminated), the problem of theodicy remains.
35 The only one of these writers to be cited more than once by Weber in *The Protestant Ethic and the Spirit of Capitalism* is Pascal. Neither Spinoza nor Leibniz are mentioned, whilst there is one intriguing reference to Kant, where it is suggested that 'many of his formulations concerning ethics are closely related to ideas of ascetic Protestantism' (p. 270).
36 Gerald R. Cragg, *From Puritanism to the Age of Reason: A Study of Changes in Religious Thought within the Church of England 1660–1700* (Cambridge: Cambridge University Press, 1950), p. 13.
37 As Cragg observes, Calvinism failed to 'win the hearts and minds' of the English people, alienating them with 'its reckless lack of moderation and undisciplined exuberance' (ibid., p. 31).
38 John Tulloch, *Rational Theology and Christian Philosophy in England in the Seventeenth Century*, 2 vols (Edinburgh: William Blackwood, 1874), vol. 1, pp. 8–9.
39 For a discussion of these issues see D. P. Walker, *The Decline of Hell: Seventeenth-Century Discussions of Eternal Torment* (London: Routledge and Kegan Paul, 1964).
40 Gerald R. Cragg, *The Church and the Age of Reason 1648–1789* (London: Hodder and Stoughton, 1962), p. 144.
41 Tulloch, *Rational Theology and Christian Philosophy*, p. 25.
42 Ibid., p. 31.
43 There has naturally been some difference of opinion over who should rightly be deemed members of this group but Benjamin Whichcote, John Smith, Ralph Cudworth and Henry More appear in nearly everyone's list.
44 Gerald R. Cragg, *The Cambridge Platonists* (New York: Oxford University Press, 1968), p. vii.
45 Tulloch, *Rational Theology and Christian Philosophy*, p. 31.
46 Cragg, *The Cambridge Platonists*, p. 8.
47 Bredvold rather charmingly describes the Cambridge Platonists as 'those gentle and modest divines whose gracious charitableness and humanity are a refreshment to the weary scholar who comes upon them' (see Louis I. Bredvold, *The Natural History of Sensibility* (Detroit, Mich.: Wayne State University Press, 1962), p. 8).

48   Cragg, *The Cambridge Platonists*, p. 10.
49   Ernst Cassirer, *The Platonic Renaissance in England*, trans. James P. Pettegrove (New York: Gordian Press, 1970), p. 81.
50   Tillotson, quoted by Cragg, *From Puritanism to the Age of Reason*, p. 34.
51   Cassirer, *The Platonic Renaissance*, p. 82.
52   R. S. Crane, 'Suggestions toward a Genealogy of the "Man of Feeling"', *A Journal of English Literary History*, 1 (1934), republished in R. S. Crane, *The Idea of the Humanities and other Essays Critical and Historical* (Chicago: University of Chicago Press, 1967), vol. 1, pp. 188–213, see esp. p. 189.
53   From Ward's *Life of More*, quoted in Cassirer, *The Platonic Renaissance*, p. 81.
54   See Cragg, *The Cambridge Platonists*, p. 10.
55   The popular image of the Puritans as individuals who were hostile to the arts and classical learning is a distortion. As Dowden observes, the Puritan gentleman could well be 'a scholar, a lover of music, a lover of letters', and he points out that Cromwell's chaplain, Peter Sterry, was a lover of the works of Titian and Van Dyke, whilst Milton's father composed madrigals and encouraged his son to read the poets of Greece and Rome (see Edward Dowden, *Puritan and Anglican: Studies in Literature* (London: Kegan Paul, Trench, Trubner, 1910), p. 21). Morison also notes, of the Puritans in New England, that although they proscribed the theatre, they actually stimulated an interest in 'the classics, belles-lettres, poetry and scientific research' (Morison, *The Intellectual Life of New England*, p. 4). This is not to say, however, that they were prepared to accept classical writers as authoritative sources in theological matters. As Weber notes, Calvin was deeply distrustful of Aristotle and classical philosophy in general, as too was Luther in his early years, whilst the Westminster Confession incorporated the doctrine that everything necessary for salvation was contained in the Scriptures (Weber, *The Protestant Ethic*, p. 244).
56   Cragg, *The Cambridge Platonists*, p. 15.
57   Basil Willey, *The English Moralists* (London: Chatto and Windus, 1964), p. 172.
58   Cassirer, *The Platonic Renaissance*, p. 38.
59   Ibid., p. 83.
60   Willey, *The English Moralists*, p. 183.
61   G. Macdonald Ross, *Leibniz* (Oxford: Oxford University Press, 1984), p. 103.
62   It is of interest that, in the course of this discussion, Leibniz attacks Calvinist predestination and enters into the Supralapsarian versus Infralapsarian debate on the Arminian side.
63   Gottfried Wilhelm Leibniz, *Theodicy*, trans. E. M. Hughes from C. J. Gerhardt's edition 1875–90, edited, abridged and with an introduction by Diogenes Allen (Don Mills, Ontario: J. M. Dent, 1966), p. 35.
64   Referred to by Diogenes Allen, ibid., p. 16.
65   Arthur O. Lovejoy, *The Great Chain of Being: A Study of the History of an Idea* (Cambridge, Mass.: Harvard University Press, 1961), pp. 52–64. Diogenes Allen feels that there is little support for Lovejoy's claim, arguing that Leibniz, 'does not need and does not use the idea of a great chain of being' (*Theodicy*, p. xix).

66 This possibility only exists if one accepts Lovejoy's claim concerning the centrality of the idea of the Great Chain of Being, which could, at a pinch, be regarded as a 'frozen' version of the doctrine of *karma.*

67 Weber did note that 'a religion of predestination obliterates the goodness of god', but he did not explore the consequences of this fact for the development of Protestantism (Weber, *Sociology of Religion*, p. 202).

68 Cassirer, *The Platonic Renaissance*, p. 50. See also the references cited on p. 249 above.

69 Willey, *The English Moralists*, pp. 174–82.

70 Ibid., p. 179.

71 *Leviathan*, cited by Crane, 'Suggestions toward a Genealogy', p. 205.

72 Ibid., p. 206.

73 Ibid., p. 207.

74 Weber, *The Protestant Ethic*, p. 232.

75 See Crane, 'Suggestions toward a Genealogy', p. 200.

76 See, for a discussion of the role of Enlightenment ideas upon the rise of irreligion and unbelief, Franklin L. Baumer, *Religion and the Rise of Scepticism* (New York: Harcourt Brace, 1960). For the nineteenth and twentieth centuries see Colin Campbell, *Toward a Sociology of Irreligion* (London: Macmillan, 1971), chapter 3.

77 Arthur O. Lovejoy, *Essays in the History of Ideas* (New York: George Braziller, 1955), pp. 82–6.

78 The change in religious thought brought about by the Enlightenment went much deeper than this, constituting a virtual paradigmatic revolution in Thomas Kuhn's terms – see Thomas S. Kuhn, *The Structure of Scientific Revolutions* (Chicago: University of Chicago Press, 1962). Lovejoy has outlined how the general world-view which we associate with the Enlightenment can be understood as derived from one of the two fundamental strains in Platonic thought. These he dubs 'otherworldliness' and 'thisworldliness', meaning by the former an assumption that the world of sense is in some way unreal, and that true reality and goodness exist only in another, 'ideal', realm; whilst by the latter he means the acceptance of the world of sense as truly real in its own right (Lovejoy, *The Great Chain of Being*, pp. 26–8). It was the former, 'otherworldly' strand, which, he claims, dominated Christian and Western thought up to the eighteenth century, but that at this point, the rejection of Christian theology based on revelation coincided with a switch of emphasis to the other, 'thisworldly', one. This contrast of Lovejoy's, and indeed the very terminology he employs, suggests some comparison with Weber's analysis of the world's religions (even though there is an obvious contrast in usage). Central to this latter discussion is the fundamentally contrasting conception of the relationship between the world of empirical reality and the divine which mark occidental and oriental religions. Predominant in the West is the concept of a transcendental omnipotent god, implying, 'the utterly subordinate and creaturely character of the world created by him out of nothing' (Weber, *Sociology of Religion*, p. 178). Such a view tends, as Weber emphasizes, to rule out any real possibility of religion taking the path of self-deification or

any 'genuinely mystical subjective possession of god ... because this appeared to be a blasphemous deification of a mere created thing' (ibid.). In the East, however, the world of sense was not regarded as a special creation, but merely as 'something presented to man', something which has been in the nature of things from all eternity, and this concept of a real empirical world was not abandoned as in the West but taken as the starting point for 'insight into the ultimate consequences of the *karma* chain of causality, to illumination, and hence to a unity of knowledge and action' (ibid., p. 179). As Weber comments, 'this way remained forever closed to every religion that faced the absolute paradox of a perfect god's creation of a permanently imperfect world' (ibid.). Now this would appear to be the very distinction which the Enlightenment revolution in thought reversed, as Lovejoy suggests, with Leibniz's theodicy having the unintended effect of making the world seem 'near-perfect' and thus making self-deification, pantheism and forms of mysticism, real possibilities in Western culture.

79　The thinkers of the Enlightenment were greatly influenced in this respect by the views of such classical writers as Plato and Aristotle, whom they considered to be less prejudiced than modern men because their judgements were less overlaid by history and custom.

80　Crane, 'Suggestions toward a Genealogy', p. 193.

81　Willey, *The English Moralists*, p. 217.

82　Crane, 'Suggestions toward a Genealogy', p. 194.

83　It was also argued that the mere contemplation of God's goodness would move a man to charitable feelings, and that if it did not, then there was little hope of such a person experiencing any benevolent feelings. As Barrow expressed it, 'what can we esteem, what can we love, if so admirable goodness does not affect us? how prodigiously cold and hard is that heart, which cannot be warmed and softened into affection by so melting a consideration?' (see Isaac Barrow, *The Works of the Learned Isaac Barrow ... being all his English Works; published by his Grace Dr. John Tillotson, late Archbishop of Canterbury*, 5th edn, 3 vols (in 2) (London: A. Miller, 1741), vol. 3, pp. 299–300).

84　Ibid., p. 195.

85　Ibid., pp. 206–7.

86　Ibid.

87　Ibid., p. 211.

88　Quoted by Crane, 'Suggestions toward a Genealogy', p. 211.

89　Ibid., p. 212.

90　Although this discussion is focused upon currents of thought which were essentially English in character, it is important to recognize the important contribution made to the developments under consideration by thinkers of the Scottish Enlightenment. Apart from the very obvious influence of Hume and Adam Smith, men such as Francis Hutcheson, Dugald Steward, Adam Ferguson, Lord Kames and Lord Monboddo all contributed significantly to the intellectual debates of the period. See Louis Schneider, *The Scottish Moralists: On Human Nature and Society* (Chicago: University of Chicago Press, 1967), and Gladys Bryson, *The Scottish Inquiry of the Eighteenth Century* (New York: Augustus M. Kelly, 1968).

91 Quoted by Crane, 'Suggestions toward a Genealogy', p. 188.

92 Weber, *The Protestant Ethic*, p.119.

93 Ibid., p. 104.

94 As Weber notes, 'Calvin viewed all pure feelings and emotions, no matter how exalted they might seem to be, with suspicion.'

95 William Haller, *The Rise of Puritanism, or the Way to the New Jerusalem as set forth in Pulpit and Press from Thomas Cartwright to John Lilburne and John Milton, 1570–1643* (New York: Harper Bros., 1957), pp. 84–5.

96 Ibid., p. 27.

97 Ibid.

98 One only needs to read *Pilgrim's Progress*, or, perhaps better still, John Bunyan's largely autobiographical *Grace Abounding to the Chief of Sinners* to realize something of the frequent and violent passions which could beset the Puritan.

99 Weber, *The Protestant Ethic*, p. 261.

100 Quoted by Amy Louise Reed, *The Background of Gray's Elegy: A Study in the Taste for Melancholy Poetry 1700–1751* (New York: Russell and Russell, 1962), p. 12.

101 Gordon Rattray Taylor, *The Angel-Makers: A Study in the Psychological Origins of Historical Change 1750–1850* (London: Heinemann, 1958), p. 117.

102 Charles Wesley illustrates these attitudes in the lines: 'Ah, lovely Appearance of Death / No Sight upon Earth is so fair', and 'Pain, my old companion, Pain / Seldom parted from my Side / Welcome to thy Seat again / Here, if GOD permits, abide' (quoted by Rattray Taylor, ibid., p. 119).

103 Weber, *The Protestant Ethic*, p. 110.

104 Ibid., p. 111.

105 Ibid., p. 112.

106 Ibid., pp. 113–14.

107 Ibid., pp. 115.

108 Weber links the idea of the religious believer as a 'vessel of the Holy Spirit' with a preoccupation with the inward mystical and personal experience of God's grace, whilst the idea of the religious believer as a tool of the divine will is associated with concentration upon an outward, sober, responsible ethic of works. Lutheranism is then seen as embodying the former model and Calvinism the latter. Even within Calvinism, however, certainty that one possessed saving grace was never, in practice, assessed by the individual on the basis of external criteria alone, but was recognized as involving a distinctive subjective state.

109 John Bunyan, *The Pilgrims [sic] Progress, From this World to that which is to come* (London: George Virtue, 1848), p. 35.

110 It is important to recognize the different role which emotional sensibility had within Calvinism compared with the more pietistic and mystical forms of Protestantism. Whereas in the latter, intense emotional states were primarily the means of attaining experience of, or union with, God, in the former emotionality is critically merely a sign of one's elect status.

111   Edmund S. Morgan, *Visible Saints: The History of a Puritan Idea* (New York: New York University Press, 1963), p. 34.

112   Herbert Wallace Schneider, *The Puritan Mind* (Ann Arbor, Mich.: University of Michigan Press, 1958), p. 20.

113   Weber does refer, in his discussion of Pietism, to the practice of attempting to assess the subjective state of grace of a believer, but he does not seem to consider this to be an important ingredient in any developing doctrine of signs (Weber, *The Protestant Ethic*, p. 244).

114   Morgan, *Visible Saints*, p. 67.

115   Ibid., p. 72.

116   Ibid., p. 89.

117   Ibid., p. 91.

118   Ibid., p. 70.

119   Haller, *The Rise of Puritanism*, p. 88.

120   Ibid., p. 92.

121   Ibid., pp. 95–6.

122   Ibid., p. 115.
       Interestingly, in view of Weber's remarks on the consequences of the abolition of the confessional for the development of a Protestant ethic (see *The Protestant Ethic*, pp. 106 and 124), Haller suggests that the Puritan habit of committing the details of all sins to paper served the same psychological function 'as that of auricular confession'; that is to say, having balanced his spiritual books, the Puritan could go to bed with a good conscience (see Haller, *The Rise of Puritanism*, p. 100).

123   Haller, *The Rise of Puritanism*, pp. 90–1.

124   There was a natural tendency for signs of the experience of saving grace to be associated in the popular mind with extraordinary and intense emotional experiences, especially of an hysterical nature, with the consequence that screaming, fainting and manifesting convulsions were commonly considered proof of the gift of grace. The Puritan divines had to issue repeated warnings against these erroneous beliefs (see Schneider, *The Puritan Mind*, pp. 124–5). The prevalence of these unorthodox ideas indicates something of the widespread need for a clear doctrine of signs, and of the difficulty in distinguishing 'true' from 'false' symptoms of saving grace. In fact, the former were meant to be 'gracious affections' rather than intense forms of emotional expression, something which was important for the development of a sentimental theology.

125   John W. Draper, *The Funeral Elegy and the Rise of English Romanticism* (London: Frank Cass, 1929, repr. 1967), p. 319.

126   Ibid., p. 67. Draper, in fact, describes the psychological ideal of the Puritans as 'a tumultuous and exalted depression' (ibid., p. 320).

127   Ibid., pp. 236 and 238.

128   Quoted by Hoxie Neale Fairchild, *Religious Trends in English Poetry*, 3 vols (New York: Columbia University Press, 1939–49), vol. 1, p. 41.

129   Cragg, *From Puritanism to the Age of Reason*, p. 36.

130   Peter Burke, *Popular Culture in Early Modern Europe* (London: Temple Smith, 1978), p. 257.

131 Quoted by Weber, *The Protestant Ethic*, p. 175.
132 Ibid., p. 174.
133 Draper, *The Funeral Elegy*, p. 237.
134 Ibid., p. 239.
135 Quoted by Eleanor M. Sickels, *The Gloomy Egoist: Moods and Themes of Melancholy from Gray to Keats* (New York: Octagon Books, 1969), p. 150.
136 Draper, *The Funeral Elegy*, p. 246.
137 Ibid., p. 309.
138 Ibid., p. 93.
139 Ibid., p. 236.
140 Sickels, *The Gloomy Egoist*, p. 157.
141 Draper, *The Funeral Elegy*, p. 241.
142 Sickels, *The Gloomy Egoist*, p. 157.
143 Insufficient attention has been paid to this critical psychological consequence of the loss of religious conviction as far as what might be called the 'negative' Christian beliefs are concerned – that is, belief in the devil, sin, hell and eternal damnation. For, whilst individuals may experience great relief in being freed from the tremendous burden of fear and anxiety which such beliefs typically create, they may also experience a psychic sense of loss. This is because fear and its associated emotions of dismay, awe and terror, constitute powerful states which are experienced as intensely stimulating; consequently there is a kind of 'pleasure' which attends them even if the individual concerned is not fully able to appreciate this at the time. Life without such emotions can therefore come to be regarded as unexciting. The parallel here is with soldiers who have been exposed to fire in battle. Although they may sensibly prefer to remain out of the firing line, it is not uncommon for them to feel a considerable sense of loss when returned to a peacetime existence, and that loss is connected, in part, with the pleasurable intensity of living which even powerful, negative emotions can bring.
144 Sickels, *The Gloomy Egoist*, p. 345.
145 Bredvold, *The Natural History of Sensibility*, p. 85.
146 Draper, *The Funeral Elegy*, p. 22.
147 See p. 122 above.
148 Fairchild, *Religious Trends in English Poetry*, vol. 1, p. 545.
149 Haller, *The Rise of Puritanism*, pp. 89–90.
150 Fairchild, *Religious Trends in English Poetry*, vol. 1, p. 546.
151 Draper, *The Funeral Elegy*, p. 18.
152 Fairchild, *Religious Trends in English Poetry*, vol. 1, p. 545. P. M. Masson has indeed claimed that Rousseau's sentimental belief in his own innate goodness was derived from the Calvinist doctrine of election (see P. M. Masson, *La Religion de J. J. Rousseau*, 3 vols (Paris: Hachette, 1916), vol. 1, p. 37).

Chapter 7   The ethic of feeling

1 Louis I. Bredvold, *The Natural History of Sensibility* (Detroit, Mich.: Wayne

State University Press), p. 5.

2 Owen Barfield, *History in English Words*, new edn (London: Faber and Faber, 1954), p. 177.

3 It is important to recognize that the ethic of feeling identified here as sensibility constituted an entirely novel cultural phenomenon. As Crane comments, 'it was not a philosophy which the eighteenth century could have derived full fledged from ancient or Renaissance tradition. It was something new in the world – a doctrine, or rather a complex of doctrines – which a hundred years before 1750 would have been frowned upon, had it ever been presented to them, by representatives of every school of ethical or religious thought. Neither in antiquity, nor in the Middle Ages, nor in the sixteenth century, nor in the England of the Puritans and Cavaliers had the "man of feeling" ever been a "popular type"' (see R. S. Crane, 'Suggestions toward a Genealogy of the "Man of Feeling"', *A Journal of English Literary History*, 1 (1934), pp. 189–90.

4 Raymond Williams, *Keywords: A Vocabulary of Culture and Society* (Glasgow: Fontana/Croom Helm) 1976), p. 237.

5 *Collins Dictionary of the English Language* (1979), *s.v.* 'sentimental'.

6 Alex Preminger (ed.) *Princeton Encyclopedia of Poetry and Poetics*, enlarged edn (Princeton, NJ: Princeton University Press, 1974).

7 Eleanor M. Sickels, *The Gloomy Egoist: Moods and Themes of Melancholy from Gray to Keats* (New York: Octagon Books, 1969), p. 195.

8 Both references are to be found in Lodwick Hartley, *Laurence Sterne in the Twentieth Century: An Essay and a Bibliography of Sternean Studies 1900–1965* (Chapel Hill, NC: University of North Carolina Press, 1966), p. 38.

9 Erik Erämetsä, *A Study of the Word "Sentimental" and of Other Linguistic Characteristics of Eighteenth-Century Sentimentalism in England* (Helsinki: Annals Academiae Scientiarum Fennicae Ser. B, 74 (1951), no. 1).

10 Ibid., p. 39.

11 Ibid., p. 59.

12 J. M. S. Tompkins, *The Popular Novel in England 1770–1800* (Lincoln: University of Nebraska Press, 1961), p. 92.

13 Whilst some individuals were considered to possess 'natural' sensibility it was also considered possible to develop or cultivate such tendencies. This generally involved exposing oneself to those stimuli considered likely to produce an emotional reaction in a person of true sensibility, and then striving to bring forth such a response in oneself. Such a regime could obviously provide its own opportunities for emotional indulgence. The distinction naturally brings Weber's discussion of charisma to mind (see Max Weber, *The Sociology of Religion*, trans. Ephraim Fischoff (London, Methuen, 1965), pp. 2–3).

14 The phrase is the title of a book by Henry Mackenzie, first published in 1771.

15 Bredvold, *The Natural History of Sensibility*, p. 32.

16 Sickels, *The Gloomy Egoist*, p. 195.

17 Ibid.

18 Brian Vickers, Introduction to Henry Mackenzie, *The Man of Feeling* (London: Oxford University Press, 1967), p. ix.

9 René Wellek, *A History of Modern Criticism: 1750–1950*, vol. 1, *The Later Eighteenth Century* (London: Jonathan Cape, 1955), p. 73.
20 Maximillian E. Novak, *Eighteenth-Century English Literature* (London: Macmillan, 1983), p. 157.
21 Joseph Texte, *Jean-Jacques Rousseau and the Cosmopolitan Spirit in Literature: A Study of the Literary Relations between France and England during the Eighteenth Century* (New York: Burt Franklin, 1899), p. 289.
    This shows clearly how the Calvinist doctrine of signs has become carried forward into the secular ethic of sensibility. In fact, Sterne, who probably did more than any other writer to popularize the ideal of sensibility, was a clergyman, and thereby forms an obvious link between the two.
22 There are grounds for believing that this ideal was more enthusiastically adopted by women than men.
23 Vickers, Introduction to *The Man of Feeling*, p. viii.
24 For further evidence and a discussion of contemporary attempts to explain why emotions should be the source of pleasure, see A. O. Aldridge, 'The Pleasures of Pity', *A Journal of English Literary History*, 16, 1 (March 1949), 76–87, and Earl R. Wasserman, 'The Pleasures of Tragedy', *A Journal of English Literary History*, 14, 4 (December 1947), 283–307.
25 Tompkins, *The Popular Novel in England*, p. 103.
26 Ibid.
27 Darrel Mansell, *The Novels of Jane Austen: An Interpretation* (London: Macmillan, 1973), pp. 46–7.
28 Jane Austen, *Sense and Sensibility* (London: Avalon Press, 1949), p. 31.
29 Ibid., p. 80.
30 Interestingly, this self-referential form of emotional triggering is still identified by the use of the adjective 'sentimental'; objects which have special resonance for given individuals being said to possess 'sentimental value'.
31 Austen, *Sense and Sensibility*, p. 52.
32 Ibid., p. 71.
33 Ibid., p. 76. The satiric tone does not negate the truth of this observation.
34 Ibid., p. 92.
35 Ibid., p. 48.
36 Ibid., p. 49.
37 Ibid., p. 44.
38 Ibid., p. 78.
39 Ibid., p. 173.
40 Ibid., p. 179.
41 Ibid., p. 75.
42 Ibid., p. 76.
43 Ibid., p. 209. It follows from this analysis that Marianne's behaviour is not at all impetuous in the sense of being action undertaken without consideration; she knows what she is doing and she considers it right to behave in that way. To that extent, her behaviour could justly be said to be premeditated (although pre-imagined or pre-rehearsed would probably be better terms). It is only from a utilitarian and consequentialist ethical perspective that Marianne's conduct is unproblematically dubbed 'impetuous'.

44   Ibid., pp. 211–12.
45   Ibid., p. 250.
46   Ibid., p. 54.
47   Ibid., p. 241.
48   Ibid., p. 191.
49   Lawrence Stone, *The Family, Sex and Marriage in England 1500–1800* (London: Weidenfeld and Nicolson, 1977), p. 282.
50   *First Impressions* appears to have been Jane Austen's original title for *Pride and Prejudice,* and is referred to by Mansell as 'a conventional phrase for love at first sight' (Mansell, *The Novels of Jane Austen,* p. 78). He also cites a contemporary work on landscape gardening to show both the currency and importance of this idea: 'There is no principle of the art [of landscape gardening] so necessary to be studied as the effects produced . . . by . . . that general disposition of the human mind, by which it it capable of receiving *first impressions*' (ibid., p. 48; italics in original).
51   Stone, *The Family, Sex and Marriage,* p. 282.
52   Austen, *Sense and Sensibility,* p. 81.
53   Mansell, *The Novels of Jane Austen,* p. 14.
54   Ibid.
55   Ibid.
56   Ibid., p. 16. As Mansell notes, a similar sudden friendship is intimated in *Sense and Sensibility* when Elinor first meets Lucy Steele. True to her commitment to 'sense' Elinor does not respond (*Sense and Sensibility,* p. 113).
57   Austen, *Sense and Sensibility,* p. 301.
58   Ibid., p. 23.
59   Ibid., p. 56.
60   Ibid., p. 54. Marianne is, however, decidedly unlike most heroines portrayed in the novels of the period, for she neither elopes nor actually expresses herself in favour of doing so. Colonel Brandon does confess to Elinor that in his youth he loved a girl very much like Marianne in temperament, and that they planned to elope (ibid., p. 168).
61   Ibid., p. 41.
62   Religion does play a part in justifying the cult of sensibility – natural religion, as opposed to Christianity, serving to legitimate the cult of sentiment in the same general fashion that it served to legitimate the cult of reason. This connection became more indirect, however, as systems of ethics and aesthetics developed independently of the world-view which generated them.
63   Ibid., p. 64.
64   Arthur O. Lovejoy, 'The Parallel of Deism and Classicism', in *Essays in the History of Ideas* (New York: George Braziller, 1955), p. 92.
65   Ibid.
66   This term comes to be the very focus of the dispute, with the aristocracy and the middle classes attributing a different meaning; see pp. 154–60 below.
67   Hoxie Neale Fairchild, *Religious Trends in English Poetry,* 3 vols (New York: Columbia University Press, 1939–49), vol. 1, p. 202. As Fairchild notes,

Pietistic Christianity is essentially an anti-neo-classical force (ibid., p. 218). Given a weakening of religious convictions, however, combined with the middle-class determination to be considered as good as the aristocracy, elements of this movement became mixed with neo-classicism. The ensuing aesthetic revolution constituted the second major development in the evolution of modern hedonistic culture accomplished through the introduction of classical ideas into the Protestant tradition (the first, as we have seen, involved the development of natural religion).

68   This is less ironic than it might seem as middle-class culture was itself made up of rationalistic utilitarianism and sentimental Pietism, with the consequence that aristocratic attacks on the former often tended to assist the latter, and vice versa. Shaftesbury was, in fact, opposing the Hobbesian tradition in ethics and did not intend to lend support to a bourgeois, anti-aristocratic aesthetic.

69   Quoted by Bredvold, *The Natural History of Sensibility*, p. 13.

70   Ibid., p. 14.

71   Shaftesbury's philosophy of ethics was a good deal more complicated than is implied here. There was, for example, a considerable stoic ingredient (see Esther A. Tiffany, 'Shaftesbury as Stoic', *PMLA*, 38 (March 1923), no. 1, 642–84), whilst he never endorsed the excessive displays of emotion that became the hallmark of sentimentalism. Nevertheless, his arguments in favour of an intuitive moral sense, which was 'felt' rather than rationally apprehended, clearly did a great deal to supply that movement with its necessary intellectual support. For details of Shaftesbury's philosophy see Stanley Grean, *Shaftesbury's Philosophy of Religion and Ethics: A Study in Enthusiasm* (Athens: Ohio University Press, 1967); Basil Willey, *The English Moralists* (London: Chatto and Windus), pp. 216–32; as well as Bredvold, *The Natural History of Sensibility*.

72   Bredvold, *The Natural History of Sensibility*, p. 15. A more elegant restatement of this same position is, of course, subsequently encountered in Keats, but then the idea of an innate moral sense and its intimate association with the apprehension of beauty and truth is taken up by Rousseau in France, from whom it enters directly into the mainstream of romantic thought, and also by Francis Hutcheson, who transmitted it to Hume, Adam Smith and other members of the Scottish group of moral philosophers.

73   Another critical consequence of Shaftesbury's teachings and the development of a philosophy of sensibility was that pleasant emotions could themselves now be cited as acceptable reasons for conduct. The fact that one gained pleasure from a given emotion indicated that the action which it prompted was right and good, and thus that experience of the emotion could itself be cited as sufficient grounds for the action; indeed the more powerful the emotion or the more intense the pleasure, the greater the claim for virtuousness which could be made. This was, of course, exactly what happened in the emergent cult of romantic love, where 'passion' became the only acceptable justification for conduct, but it also had significant repercussions for consumerism, as it meant that a rhetoric of liking could now suffice to legitimate purchases.

74   That virtue and beauty were closely associated, if not identified, in eighteenth-century thought, is revealed by some of the phrases in common use at the time, such as 'virtue's sweet charms', 'moral grace' and 'moral beauty' (see Bredvold, *The Natural History of Sensibility*, p. 19).

75   The middle-class tradition of philanthropic concern, with its distinctive sentimental concern for children and dumb animals, can be seen to have its origins in this dimension of eighteenth-century sensibility (see Tompkins, *The Popular Novel in England*, pp. 105–6 and Appendix II).

76   The list of authors is interesting for the indication it gives about the literary tastes of the person of sensibility. It is not surprising that Cowper and Scott should figure prominently, whilst Pope is admired 'no more than is proper' (Austen, *Sense and Sensibility*, p. 48).

77   Ibid., p. 23.

78   Mario Praz, *The Romantic Agony*, 2nd edn, trans. Angus Davidson (Oxford: Oxford University Press, 1970) p. 21; B. Sprague Allen, *Tides in English Taste (1619–1800): A Background for the Study of Literature*, 2 vols (New York: Rowman and Littlefield, 1969), vol. 2, pp. 228–9; Tompkins, *The Popular Novel in England*, Appendix IV.

79   Austen, *Sense and Sensibility*, p. 82.

80   Ibid., p. 86.

81   Neil McKendrick, John Brewer and J. H. Plumb, *The Birth of a Consumer Society: The Commercialization of Eighteenth-Century England* (London: Europa Publications, 1982), p. 28.

82   Ibid., p. 40.

83   It is a matter of regret that social scientists have neglected to consider this important phenomenon in any detail. Apart from such occasional descriptive studies as Russell Lynes, *The Tastemakers* (New York: Grosset and Dunlop, 1959), the topic has been left to aestheticians and cultural historians.

84   *Princeton Encyclopedia of Poetry and Poetics*, *s.v.* 'Taste'.

85   Wellek, *A History of Modern Criticism*, p. 24.

86   *Princeton Encyclopedia of Poetry and Poetics*, *s.v.* 'Taste'.

87   Ibid.

88   E. N. Hooker, 'The Discussion of Taste, from 1750–1770, and the New Trends in Literary Criticism', *PMLA*, 49 (June 1934), no. 2, 577–92, see esp. p. 579.

89   Ibid., p. 585.

90   Various lines of thought contributed to this generally confused state of affairs. The problem posed by the concept of the sublime, for example, as that which, whilst pleasing, was outside the rules of traditional aesthetics, was one. Another was that school of thought which, emphasizing the *je ne sais quoi* quality in works of art, treated beauty and hence taste as fundamentally indefinable. Of growing significance, however, was the influence exerted by associational psychology, which emphasized the relationship between ideas of beauty and the distinctive experience of the individual mind. As each man's education and experience was peculiar to him, he would respond in an essentially individual manner when brought face to face with beauty. Hume was the major figure in this tradition, and in

his essay 'On the Standard of Taste' he argued that beauty does not belong to things in themselves but merely reflects the mind's reaction to them. This aesthetic subjectivism was to become an important influence upon the thinking of the Romantics.

91 Hooker, 'The Discussion of Taste', p. 591.

92 Ibid., p. 589.

93 Ibid.

94 See Leo Lowenthal and Marjorie Fiske, 'The Debate Over Art and Popular Culture in Eighteenth Century England', in Mirra Komarovsky (ed.), *Common Frontiers of the Social Sciences* (Glencoe, Ill.: Free Press, 1957), pp. 66–9.

95 See the argument in Francis Gallaway, *Reason, Rule and Revolt in English Classicism* (New York, Octagon Books, 1974), p. 286.

96 *Princeton Encyclopedia of Poetry and Poetics*, p. 845. Bentham actually tries to make satisfaction the basis of taste, which is the mistake, as noted earlier, of confusing comfort with pleasure.

97 Hooker, 'The Discussion of Taste', p. 588.

98 Ibid.

99 Terminology can be a problem here. A fashion usually means the prevailing style, whilst the fashion typically means that one which is the latest or most approved. In contrast to these, the term 'fashion pattern' is used to imply the overall system of rapidly changing aesthetic standards which serves, in modern societies, to generate an endless sequence of individual fashions.

100 Changes in aesthetic standards succeed in opening up new areas of hedonistic experience because of pleasure's intimate association with a change in stimulus.

101 The idea that designers and manufacturers 'make' fashion in the sense of foisting unwanted products on consumers is to confuse the appearance of a new fashion with the mechanisms which allow the pattern as a whole to operate. Mandel, for example, observes that 'fashion is a typically social phenomenon, with the impetus coming from the side of the producers (the designers), not from that of the consumers. It is the few important *couturiers* in Paris who "make" fashion, not the "public"' (see Ernest Mandel, *Marxist Economic Theory*, trans. Brian Pearce, 2 vols (London: Merlin Press, 1970), p. 66). Obviously the *couturiers* are critical in effecting the introduction of a given style, but in doing so they are responding to the popular demand for novelty.

102 Taste refers both to an actual and to an ideal pattern of preferences. As an actual pattern it points to the consistency of liking and disliking which characterizes our choice of stimuli: it thus represents the nature of our pleasures, or more accurately our judgement of the comparative intensity of pleasure to be obtained from different sources of stimulation. This actual pattern will, of course, he significantly influenced by past experience, as most 'tastes' are 'acquired'. On the other hand, taste also refers to an ideal pattern of preferences, those which reveal the individual's ability to discern and appreciate aspects of the environment which aesthetic theory has indicated are beautiful. Thus whilst individuals simply 'have' taste in the

first sense (and nobody can be without it unless their sense organs are impaired) in this second sense an individual may or may not have 'good taste'. We may assume that individuals will try and bring these two senses of taste together, either trying to change their real preferences in order to bring them in accord with the ideal, or arguing that their real choices should be made the standard for assessing aesthetic value.

103   This division arises out of a contradiction which lies at the very heart of the concept of sensibility: the tension which is bound to arise between being sensitive to the actual plight and real feelings of others, and being oneself susceptible to displays of intense emotion. The assumption made by the original advocates of sensibility appears to have been that these would be congruent with one another; that is, through empathetic identification with the 'sufferings' of others one would be bound to feel that pity and sympathy which prompts benevolent conduct. It is clear, however, that a self-interested concern to display the correct emotions can easily come to interfere with a person's ability to successfully empathize with another's plight, just as an overriding concern to identify another's feelings correctly may inhibit one's own exhibition of emotion. These self-regarding and other-regarding tendencies are hard to keep in balance, and it is therefore unsurprising that the key concept of 'taste' became subject to contrasting interpretations, the tension ultimately manifesting itself as a conflict between sincerity and propriety.

104   This is, in its effect, a process of de-aestheticization similar to that advocated by the utilitarians.

105   Austen, *Sense and Sensibility*, p. 164

Chapter 8   The aristocratic ethic

1   Maria Ossowska, *The Social Determinants of Moral Ideas* (London: Routledge and Kegan Paul, 1971), p. 141.

2   R. Skelton, *Cavalier Poets: Writers and their Work, no. 117* (published for the British Council and the National Book League by Longmans, Green, London, 1960), p. 656.

3   Ibid., p. 10.

4   Ibid., p. 656.

5   It is not intended to give the impression that the constraints imposed by classicism were such as to remove all possibility of individuals expressing themselves in intense or passionate ways. As Barzun observes, there were some 'energetic manifestations of feeling tolerated under classicism' (Jacques Barzun, *Classic, Romantic and Modern*, 2nd edn rev. (Chicago: University of Chicago Press, 1961), p. 47, and he cites king-worship, love-making, intrigue, etiquette, duelling, as well as the playhouse, watching public executions, sport, gaming, hunting and the playing of murderous practical jokes (ibid., p. 46). He also points to the very real and powerful feelings experienced by such exemplars of Stoicism as Pope and Dr Johnson (ibid., p. 47). The key word in the above quote, however, is 'tolerated', for what is at issue here is the degree to which the expression

of strong emotion was given ethical approval. Individuals are likely to experience strong emotions, and find ways of expressing them, in all cultures; but this does not mean that such conduct finds equal approbation. It is also notable how many of the above activities are public and communal in character, lacking the isolated and introspective dimension of, say, novel-reading.

6 Levin L. Schucking, *The Sociology of Literary Taste* (London: Kegan Paul, Trench, Trubner, 1944), p. 12.

7 Although Greek authorities were commonly cited in aesthetic matters, Roman writers were preferred when moral issues were under debate, and the anthropology and ethics of the Roman Stoics were, in particular, employed by Enlightenment thinkers as the basis for a critique of existing society. See *The Dictionary of the History of Ideas: Studies of Selected Pivotal Ideas*, ed. Philip P. Wiener, *s.v.* 'Enlightenment', by Helmut O. Pappe, and 'Neo-Classicism', by David Irwin.

8 Mark Roberts, *The Tradition of Romantic Morality* (London: Macmillan, 1973), p. 81.

9 Ibid., p. 38.

10 There are obvious similarities with Buddhism, and one feels that neo-Stoicism offers another suitable opportunity for extending Weber's discussion of theodicy.

11 Quoted by Roberts, *The Tradition of Romantic Morality*, p. 47.

12 Ibid., p. 48. As has been argued, this is a more rigidly anti-emotionalist ethic than Calvinism for the thrust is toward extinction rather than control.

13 Ibid., pp. 56–7.

14 Ibid., p. 48.

15 Quoted by Crane, 'Suggestions toward a Genealogy of the "Man of Feeling"', *A Journal of English Literary History*, 1 (1934), p. 198.

16 Ibid., p. 200.

17 H. J. Habakkuk, 'England's Nobility', in Daniel A. Baugh (ed.), *Aristocratic Government and Society in Eighteenth-Century England: The Foundations of Stability* (New York: Franklin Watts, 1975), pp. 97–115, see esp. p. 114.

18 The assumption made here is that there were none of any significance which stemmed from religious thought, and although there were strands in the pagan classical tradition which could have had such an effect, they were largely overlooked in favour of a neo-Stoic philosophy.

19 Raymond Williams, *The Long Revolution* (London: Chatto and Windus, 1961), p. 38.

20 In this respect Dr Johnson's version of Stoicism does seem to have been influenced by Christianity, and cannot be taken as accurately reflecting that 'heroic' form which was more congenial to the aristocracy.

21 In fact, there is a logic which links the two, for activities must be 'fateful' in some way if they are to serve to reveal character, and this in turn means that there has to be an element of risk; see, Erving Goffman, 'Where the Action is', in *Interaction Ritual: Essays on Face-to-Face Behaviour* (Harmondsworth, Midd.: Penguin Books, 1967), pp. 149–270. Consequently, activity will also be arousing and serve to combat boredom, although the need for

concentration and the fear of failure act as strong inhibitors upon pleasure-seeking.

22   Lavers suggests that a change in men's fashions occurred first in England because the aristocracy were not required, as they were in France, to be courtiers, and hence could wear more casual clothes. It was this 'English' style which the young *Incroyables* of the *Directoire* period were subsequently to adopt (see James Lavers, *Dandies* (London: Weidenfeld and Nicolson, 1968), pp. 12–13).

23   The fact that the dandies were not, in this sense, true aristocrats, does not diminish their importance for this discussion, as their intense aspiration to be considered members of society's elite made them 'more royal than the king' in their adherence to what they saw as elitist principles.

24   T. A. J. Burnett, *The Rise and Fall of a Regency Dandy: The Life and Times of Scrope Berdmore Davies* (London: John Murray, 1981), pp. 52–60 *passim.*

25   Ellen Moers, *The Dandy: Brummell to Beerbohm* (London: Secker and Warburg, 1960), p. 35.

26   The dandies were not fops and scorned extravagance in dress if not in expenditure; as Lavers notes, dandyism is 'the *repudiation* of fine feathers' (*Dandies*, p. 10; italics in original).

27   Moers, *The Dandy*, p. 18.

28   Ibid.

29   Ibid., p. 282.

30   Cesar Grana, *Bohemian versus Bourgeois: French Society and the Man of Letters in the Nineteenth Century* (New York: Basic Books, 1964), p. 151. Grana's suggestion that the dandy is a descendant of the Bohemian must be judged rather bizarre given that the first type antedates the second by half a century. This strange idea seems to derive from his exclusive concern with French society and such literary figures as Stendhal, Flaubert and Baudelaire. Even in France, however, dandyism emerged in the *Directoire* period and thus predated Bohemianism. In fact, it is a third category, the aesthete, who provides the sociological link between the dandy and the Bohemian.

31   Burnett, *The Rise and Fall of a Regency Dandy*, p. 51.

32   Interestingly, Taylor identifies the essential feature of dandyism as a refusal to betray suffering, quoting Baudelaire as saying, 'a dandy may be bored, he may even be ill and in pain. But he will keep smiling all the time with Spartan serenity'. He comments: 'it will be seen that in some respects dandyism resembles both religious faith and stoicism. . . . This is the attitude, not quite identical with stoicism, of one who has been made to suffer sadistically: he refuses to give his tormentor the satisfaction of betraying his suffering. It seems the logical product of a certain type of parental treatment' (Gordon Rattray Taylor, *The Angel Makers: A Study in the Psychological Origins of Historical Change 1750–1850* (London: Heinemann, 1958, p. 250). The evidence would suggest, however, that a childhood spent at a public school may have had more to do with exposure to sadism than treatment received at the hands of parents (see, Burnett, *The Rise and Fall of a Regency Dandy*, pp. 20–1).

33   Burnett, *The Rise and Fall of a Regency Dandy*, pp. 42–53 *passim.*

34 Ibid.
35 Moers, *The Dandy*, p. 17.
36 It seems clear, for example, that Scrope Davies was more concerned with cultivating his reputation as a womanizer than with the actual pleasures of seduction. See Burnett, *The Rise and Fall of a Regency Dandy*, p. 37.
37 Moers, *The Dandy*, p. 116.
38 The dandy is utterly dependent upon the exclusive social group to which he belongs; once expelled or forced to flee by his creditors, he effectively ceases to exist. This was the sad fate or both Brummell and Scrope Davies.
39 Ibid., pp. 20–1.
40 Ibid., p. 17.
41 The essence of Carlyle's condemnation of the dandy was that as a mere 'Clothes-wearing Man' he lacked any spiritual awareness (see Thomas Carlyle, *Sartor Resartus: Hero-worship and the Heroic in History*, Everyman Library edn (London: J. M. Dent, 1921), pp. 204–10).
42 Werner Sombart, *Luxury and Capitalism* (Ann Arbor, Mich.: University of Michigan Press, 1967).

Chapter 9   The romantic ethic

1 Vickers, Introduction to Henry Mackenzie, *The Man of Feeling* (London: Oxford University Press, 1967), p. viii.
2 Winfield H. Rogers, 'The Reaction against Melodramatic Sentimentality in the English Novel 1796–1830', *PLMA*, 49 (March 1934), 98–122.
3 James Boswell, *Boswell's Life of Johnson*, ed. Birkbeck Hill, revised by L. F. Powell, 2nd edn (Oxford: Oxford University Press, 1934), vol. 3, p. 149.
4 Ibid.
5 Lecky comments on the growing realization that 'The exaggerated sentimentality which sheds passionate tears over the fictitious sorrows of a novel or a play is no certain sign of a benevolent and unselfish nature, and is quite compatible with much indifference to real sorrows and much indisposition to make efforts for their alleviation' (quoted by Walter E. Houghton, *The Victorian Frame of Mind 1830–1870* (New Haven, Conn.: Yale University Press, 1957), p. 278). In fact, Mackenzie, the author of *The Man of Feeling*, warned against this very danger, saying, 'In morals as in religion, there are not wanting instances of refined sentimentalists, who are content with talking of virtues which they never practice, who pay in words what they owe in actions; or perhaps what is as fully dangerous, who open their minds to *impressions* which never have any effect upon their *conduct*, but are considered as something foreign and distinct from it' (Louis I. Bredvold, *The Natural History of Sensibility* (Detroit, Mich.: Wayne State University Press, 1962), p. 85, italics in original).
6 J. M. S. Tompkins, *The Popular Novel in England 1770–1800* (Lincoln, Nebr.: University of Nebraska Press, 1961), p. 111.
7 Ian Watt's carefully expressed judgement that, whilst 'people have always . . . read for pleasure and relaxation . . . there seems to have arisen in the

eighteenth century a tendency to pursue these ends more exclusively than before', must be judged over cautious in face of the evidence. But then he is not clear about what reading for pleasure might involve (Ian Watt, *The Rise of the Novel: Studies in Defoe, Richardson and Fielding* (Berkeley: University of California Press), p. 48).

8   Peter Haining, *Gothic Tales of Terror: Classic Horror Stories from Great Britain, Europe and the United States* (Harmondsworth, Middx.: Penguin Books, 1973), p. 10.

9   Montague Summers, *The Gothic Quest: A History of the Gothic Novel* (New York: Russell and Russell, 1964), p. 12. See also Devendra P. Varma, *The Gothic Flame* (New York: Russell and Russell, 1957).

10 Summers cites a contemporary satirist on how one could turn a domestic novel into a Gothic one. Essentially it amounts to no more than a process of substituting ingredients, a castle for a house, for example, and a giant for a father (Summers, *The Gothic Quest*, p. 35).

11 Foster notes that the main object of the Gothic novel or 'sentimental tale of adventure' was to create an emotional effect in the reader, especially tears and shudderings, whilst there was a 'pathological craving for fearful experiences' on the part of the readers (see James R. Foster, 'The Abbé Prevost and the English Novel' *PMLA*, 42 (June 1927), 443–64, see esp. p. 443 and p. 461).

12 Haining, *Gothic Tales of Terror*, p. 124.

13 John Tinnon Taylor, *Early Opposition to the English Novel: The Popular Reaction from 1760–1830* (New York: King's Crown Press, 1943), pp. 8–10.

14 Rogers, 'The Reaction against Melodramatic Sentimentality', p. 110.

15 Foster, 'The Abbé Prevost and the English Novel', p. 453.

16 See Taylor, *Early Opposition to the English Novel*, pp. 62–75 *passim*, and Rogers, 'The Reaction against Melodramatic Sentimentality', pp. 110–11.

17 For a good example see 'Polly Honeycombe' in Richard W. Bevis (ed.), *Eighteenth Century Drama: Afterpieces* (London: Oxford University Press, 1970), pp. 137–61.

18 Taylor, *Early Opposition to the English Novel*, p. 62; Rogers, 'The Reaction against Melodramatic Sentimentality', p. 106.

19 Taylor, *Early Opposition to the English Novel*, p. 65.

20 Ibid., p. 69.

21 Rogers, 'The Reaction against Melodramatic Sentimentality', pp. 101–2.

22 M. H. Abrams, *The Mirror and the Lamp: Romantic Theory and the Critical Tradition* (New York: Oxford University Press, 1953), p. 103.

23 Rogers, 'The Reaction against Melodramatic Sentimentality', p. 101.

24 G. S. R. Kitson Clark, 'The Romantic Element 1830–1850', in J. H. Plumb (ed.), *Studies in Social History: A Tribute to G. M. Trevelyan* (London: Longmans, Green, 1955), p. 90.

25 Peter L. Thorslev Jr, 'Romanticism and the Literary Consciousness', *Journal of the History of Ideas*, 36 (July–September 1975), no. 3, pp. 563–72, see esp. p. 563.

26 Kenneth B. Klaus, *The Romantic Period in Music* (Boston, Mass.: Allyn and Bacon, 1970), pp. 13–14. One can also note, as Baumer does, that since the

romantics loved the mysterious and celebrated paradoxes, it is not always easy to know what they are talking about (see Franklin L. Baumer, *Modern European Thought: Continuity and Change in Ideas 1600–1950* (New York: Macmillan, 1977), p. 269.

27   Arthur O. Lovejoy, 'On the Discrimination of Romanticisms', *PMLA*, 39 (June 1924), 229–53, reprinted in *Essays in the History of Ideas* (New York: George Braziller, 1955). He does appear to modify this position in the later book *The Great Chain of Being: A Study of the History of an Idea* (Boston, Mass.: Harvard University Press, 1936), as Baumer observes (*Modern European Thought*, p. 269).

28   Wellek's position, outlined in various publications, is summarized in this form by Thorslev, 'Romanticism and the Literary Consciousness', p. 563.

29   Morse Peckham, 'Toward a Theory of Romanticism', *PMLA*, 66 (March 1951), 5–23, and *Beyond the Tragic Vision: The Quest for Identity in the Nineteenth Century* (New York: Braziller, 1962).

30   Lilian R. Furst, *The Contours of European Romanticism* (London: Macmillan, 1979), p. 2.

31   H. H. Remak, 'West-European Romanticism: Definition and Scope', Newton P. Stallnecht and Horst Frenz (eds), *Comparative Literature: Method and Perspective* (Carbondale, Ill.: Southern Union University Press, 1961), pp. 223–59, see esp. p. 226.

32   John B. Halsted (ed.), *Romanticism* (New York: Walker, 1969), p. 2.

33   Ibid.

34   Furst, *The Contours of European Romanticism*, p. 5.

35   Lovejoy, for example, dates Romanticism in England from the 1740s ('On the Discrimination of Romanticisms', p. 241), whilst Klaus (*The Romantic Period in Music*) sees the terminal dates as 1820 and 1920. Shenck gives details for most of the other countries of Europe – see H. G. Shenck, *The Mind of the European Romantics: An Essay in Cultural History* (London: Constable, 1966).

36   Quoted in Lilian R. Furst, *Romanticism* (London: Methuen, 1969), p. 27.

37   Baumer, *Modern European Thought*, p. 268.

38   Ibid., p. 270.

39   The phrase is Morse Peckham's (see 'Toward a Theory of Romanticism', p. 11–12).

40   J. Gaudefroy-Demombynes, 'The Inner Movement of Romanticism', in Anthony Thorlby (ed.), *The Romantic Movement*, (London: Longmans, 1966), pp. 188–142, see esp. p. 138.

41   See Anthony Thorlby (ed.), *The Romantic Movement* (London: Longmans, 1966), Part Two, pp. 145–61, for documents illustrating these attitudes.

42   Cited in Thorslev, 'Romanticism and the Literary Consciousness', p. 566.

43   The phrase is Geoffrey Hartman's, quoted by Thorslev (ibid.).

44   Bertrand Russell, *A History of Western Philosophy: And its Connections with Political and Social Circumstances from the Earliest Times to the Present Day* (London: Allen and Unwin, 1946), p. 707.

45   The traditional association between poetic inspiration and supernatural possession is discussed by Abrams, *The Mirror and the Lamp*, p. 189; Weber

also mentions it but rather tends to assume that prophetic religion and art are necessarily opposed and irreconcilable (see Max Weber, *The Sociology of Religion*, trans. Ephriam Fischoff (London: Methuen, 1965), pp. 244–5).

46   The words are Arthur Lovejoy's, quoted by Abrams, *The Mirror and the Lamp*, p. 198.

47   The expression is Carlyle's (see Baumer, *Modern European Thought*, pp. 275–6).

48   M. H. Abrams, *Natural Supernaturalism: Tradition and Revolution in Romantic Literature* (New York: W. W. Norton, 1971).

49   The qualitative versus quantitative notion of individualism derives from Simmel (see Georg Simmel, *The Sociology of Georg Simmel*, ed. Kurt H. Wolff (New York: Free Press, 1964), p. 81), whilst it is Shenck who refers to singularity or peculiarity (*The Mind of the European Romantics*, p. 21).

50   Cited by Howard Mumford Jones, *Revolution and Romanticism* (Cambridge, Mass.: Harvard University Press, 1974), p. 233. Jones also goes on to observe that, 'The great, the unique contribution of romanticism to modernity is the insistence that every human being is a distinct and autonomous entity' (p. 463).

51   G. Poulet, 'Romanticism', pp. 40–2 in Thorlby (ed.), *The Romantic Movement*, p. 40.

52   For evidence that the Freudian concept of the unconscious has its origins in romantic thought see W. Riese, 'The Pre-Freudian Origins of Psychoanalysis', *Science and Psychoanalysis*, 1 (1958), 24–32, and Lancelot Law Whyte, *The Unconscious before Freud* (London: Tavistock, 1959), esp. chapter 4.

53   The fact that under Romanticism the divine commonly takes the form of a unique personal genius means that self-deification can occur in a form not regarded by Weber as possible within the Western religious tradition. For this is different from both 'possession' and spiritual suffusion, as it is also from the mere manifestation of divine characteristics. It is, in fact, a process of emanation, or genius-realization, in which the individual actualizes that particular divine being which he has it in himself to become (cf. Weber's discussion in *The Sociology of Religion*, pp. 158–9).

54   Frederick C. Gill, *The Romantic Movement and Methodism: A Study of English Romanticism and the Evangelical Revival* (London: The Epworth Press, 1937), p. 17.

55   Ibid., p. 29.

56   Ibid., pp. 37–8.

57   Ibid., p. 147.

58   Ibid., p. 17.

59   Lecky actually refers to the emotional poetry of the eighteenth century as 'the poetic counterpart of Methodism'. The reference is from John Draper, *The Funeral Elegy and the Rise of English Romanticism* (London: Frank Cass, 1967).

60   Ernest Bernbaum, 'The Romantic Movement', in Robert F. Gleckner and Gerald E. Enscoe (eds), *Romanticism: Points of View* (Englewood Cliffs, NJ: Prentice-Hall, 1962), pp. 88–96, see esp. p. 91.

61   Lascelles Abercrombie, *Romanticism* (London: Martin Secker, 1963) p. 89.

62   Ibid. The distinction brings Weber's ascetic–mystic contrast to mind, and it is the case that Romanticism has much in common with that form of religious response which Weber dubbed, 'inner-worldly asceticism'. This is because the individual is under an obligation to his 'god', to do his bidding; that is to 'realize' his 'true self', a process similar to the 'perpetual externalization of the divine' which Weber associates with asceticism (see Weber, *The Sociology of Religion*, p. 171).

63   The quotation is, of course, from Keats. See Abrams, *The Mirror and the Lamp*, p. 315.

64   Halsted (ed.), *Romanticism*, p. 21.

65   Ibid., p. 13.

66   As Hayter observes, 'All the Romantic writers thought that there was a strong link between dreams and the processes of literary creation. Dream theory, dreams as sources, dreams as techniques, were important to them, and they valued and used their own dreams' (see Althea Hayter, *Opium and the Romantic Imagination* (London: Faber and Faber, 1968), p. 67).

67   Such epistemological subjectivism did not mean that truth was considered to be relativistic in character, for the world of ideal truth, beauty and goodness which imagination revealed was assumed to be essentially one and the same.

68   T. E. Hulme, 'Romanticism and Classicism', in Gleckner and Enscoe (eds), *Romanticism*, pp. 34–44, see esp. pp. 35–6.

69   The phrase is Raymond Williams's and he continues by observing that apart from 'the poets from Blake and Wordsworth to Shelley and Keats there have been few generations of creative writers more deeply interested and more involved in study and criticism of the society of their day.' He then lists the various political activities engaged in by the Romantic poets (see Raymond Williams *Culture and Society 1780–1950* (Harmondsworth, Middx.: Penguin Books, 1962), p. 48).

70   It was Fairchild who suggested that the English romanticist was 'a parish priest with a cure for souls' (quoted by Abrams, *The Mirror and the Lamp*, p. 328), but, for reasons given above (see p. 185), a comparison with the prophets would have been more appropriate.

71   It seems to have been the influence of this faith in 'the word' which caused them to emphasize the power of poetry rather than that of art in general. This latter claim emerged somewhat later.

72   Abrams, *The Mirror and the Lamp*, p. 330.

73   Ibid., p. 329. Just in case there might be those who doubt the efficacy of this mechanism, Wordsworth refers them to the 'true tale' of *Goody Blake and Harry Gill*. This recounts how a man, hard-hearted enough to try and prevent a poor woman from using his hedge for firewood, and experiencing her 'curse', is, in consequence, thereafter never able to feel warm (see *Preface to Lyrical Ballads* (1802), in Harold Bloom and Lionel Trilling (eds), *Romantic Poetry and Prose* (New York: Oxford University Press, 1973), p. 609).

74   Abrams, *The Mirror and the Lamp*, p. 103.

75   The utilitarians had attacked poetry for being 'misrepresentation', and dangerous misrepresentation at that, their single-minded obsession with

utility even leading them to such observations as, 'ledgers do not keep well in rhyme' (see Abrams, *The Mirror and the Lamp*, p. 302).

76 Percy Bysshe Shelley, 'A Defence of Poetry', in Bloom and Trilling (eds), *Romantic Poetry and Prose*, pp. 746–62, see esp. p. 756.

77 Ibid., p. 757.

78 Ibid., p. 750.

79 *Selections from the Writings of John Ruskin, Second Series 1860–1888* (Orpington: George Allen, 1899), p. 231.

80 Quoted in Richard D. Altick, *The English Common Reader: A Social History of the Mass Reading Public 1800–1900* (Chicago: University of Chicago Press, 1957), p. 115.

81 Shelley, 'In Defence of Poetry', p. 750.

82 It is noticeable that whilst the typical man or woman of feeling was simply 'acted on' by external forces, the Romantic is expected to respond creatively to events in the world.

83 Very little seems to be known about the precise mechanisms involved in the reading of fiction. For a brief discussion of some of the issues, see D. W. Harding, 'Psychological Processes in the Reading of Fiction', *The British Journal of Aesthetics*, 2 (1962), 133–47.

84 Bloom and Trilling (eds), *Romantic Poetry and Prose*, p. 601.

85 Ibid., p. 602.

86 Ibid.

87 Ibid., p. 607.

88 Ibid., p. 608.

89 Ibid.

90 Ibid., p. 602.

91 Ibid., pp. 607, 603.

92 Ibid., p. 603.

93 Ibid.

94 Ibid., *Michael*, line 77.

95 Lionel Trilling, 'The Fate of Pleasure: Wordsworth to Dostoevsky', *Partisan Review*, 30 (Summer 1963), 73–106, and reprinted in *Beyond Culture: Essays on Literature and Learning* (Oxford: Oxford University Press, 1980), pp. 50–76 (page references are to the latter).

96 Trilling, *Beyond Culture*, p. 52.

97 It is interesting to note that Trilling continues by commenting on the connection between pleasure and luxury, defining the latter as 'the means of pleasure made overt and conspicuous' (ibid., p. 55). Wordsworth's emphasis on pleasure as constituting the 'dignity' of man he thus sees as a version of the growing belief that all men were entitled to a life which transcended subsistence and embraced some degree of 'affluence'.

98 Ibid., p. 53.

99 Wordsworth's views on the role of pleasure and of the psychology of moral behaviour owed a good deal to Hartleyan associationism, a current of thought derived from Locke which was both materialistic and deterministic (see Baumer, *Modern European Thought*, pp. 175–6). It was also highly optimistic, and tended to assume that ideas imprinted on the mind through

pleasurable association would inevitably lead from the 'lower' to the 'higher'. Perhaps this goes some way toward explaining Wordsworth's failure to perceive that pleasure might also be an agent of moral degradation.

100 Mario Praz, *The Romantic Agony*, trans. Angus Davidson, 2nd edn (Oxford: Oxford University Press, 1979).

101 Abrams, *The Mirror and the Lamp*, p. 103. This has naturally been a principal focus for the many critics of Romanticism, who have regarded such 'unhealthy' tendencies as eventually leading to 'sensationalism, satanism [and] sadism' (see F. R. Lucas, 'Faeries and Fungi; Or the Future of Romanticism', in Thorlby (ed.), *The Romantic Movement*, pp. 62–4, see esp. p. 61). The intriguing question raised here is how far the desire to enjoy such 'abnormal' pleasures in life is dependent upon their prior enjoyment in imagination; if this is the case, then the essence of this critique must be accepted as valid. On the other hand, it seems wrong to associate de Sade's name with this tendency as he was not really a romantic but a follower of the Enlightenment faith in rational self-determination. He despised sensibility and set no value on emotional or imaginatively mediated pleasure; in this respect he epitomizes traditional rather than modern hedonism. See *The Marquis de Sade: The Complete Justine, Philosophy in the Bedroom and other Writings*, compiled and trans. by Richard Seaves and Austryn Wainhouse (New York: Grove Press, 1966;, esp. pp. 177–367.

102 Trilling *Beyond Culture*, p. 53.

103 Considerable ethical significance is still attached to the display of emotions, as it was in the cult of sensibility, but now they are less significant in themselves than as an index of hedonistic capacity.

104 Howard E. Hugo, 'Components of Romanticism', in John B. Halsted (ed.), *Romanticism: Problems of Definition, Explanation and Evaluation* (Boston, Mass.: D. C. Heath, 1965), pp. 30–6, see esp. p. 31.

105 Ibid., p. 36.

106 Lionel Trilling, *Sincerity and Authenticity* (Cambridge, Mass.: Harvard University Press, 1971), p. ix.

107 Ibid.

108 Grana suggests that the origin of Bohemianism represents something of 'a sociological riddle' because it coincides with the rise to power and influence of the bourgeoisie. 'How did it happen', he asks, 'that while one section of the bourgeoisie was efficiently gathering profits with unbending matter-of-factness, another was giving itself over to philosophical despair, the cult of sensitivity, and the enthronement of the nonutilitarian virtues?' (see Cesar Grana, *Bohemian versus Bourgeois: French Society and the French Man of Letters in the Nineteenth Century* (New York: Basic Books, 1964), p. 17). As we have seen, this is not really a 'riddle' because the culture of the middle classes had long been divided into Pietistic sentimentalist and rationalistic utilitarian strands, and hence the perceived triumph of the latter sparked a reaction from the former. At the same time, the middle classes had to attain economic dominance before they were in a position to 'afford' the 'luxury' of Bohemia.

109 This point is made by Grana, ibid., pp. 26–7.

110 This summary discussion of Bohemianism draws on material from France,

the United States and Britain, from the 1840s up to the early 1960s. The principal sources are: Henry Murger, *The Latin Quarter (Scènes de la Vie Bohème)*, trans. Ellen Marriage and John Selwyn, introduction by Arthur Symons (London: Greening, 1908); Arthur Ransome, *Bohemia in London* (Oxford: Oxford University Press, 1984; first published by Chapman and Hall, 1907); Albert Parry, *Garrets and Pretenders: A History of Bohemianism in America* (New York: Dover Publications, 1960; first published 1933); Francis J. Rigney and L. Douglas Smith, *The Real Bohemia: A Social and Psychological Study of the 'Beats'* (New York: Basic Books, 1961); R. Mills, *Young Outsiders* (London: Routledge and Kegan Paul, 1973).

111   See Parry, *Garrets and Pretenders*, pp. 14–61.

112   Murger asserts that 'genuine Bohemians live on their wits' (*The Latin Quarter*, p. xxx).

113   Parry, *Garrets and Pretenders*, p. xxiii.

114   Murger, *The Latin Quarter*, p. xxi.

115   Ibid., pp. xxiii–xxiv.

116   It is interesting to compare the economic basis of Bohemianism with that of monasticism. Like the monk the Bohemian tends to either rely on charity or establish semi-self-sufficient communities, whilst also attempting to sell his 'spiritual insights'. The charity, however, comes from relatives and friends rather than strangers, whilst communities are rarely sufficiently well organized to guarantee a permanent income; casual employment being a frequent resort when these means fail.

117   Lawrence Lipton, *The Holy Barbarians* (New York: Julian Messner, 1959), p. 286.

118   Murger, *The Latin Quarter*, p. xxx.

119   Rigney and Smith, *The Real Bohemia*, p. 23.

120   Lipton has claimed that the American beat-Bohemians of the 1950s attributed special spiritual significance to the state of poverty, and although it is possible that this might have been a consequence of their interest in Buddhist thought, Rigney and Smith's evidence does not support him (see Lipton, *The Holy Barbarians* p. 264, and Rigney and Smith, *The Real Bohemia*, p. 23).

121   Grana, *Bohemian versus Bourgeois*, p. 65.

122   Ibid., p. 69.

123   Malcolm Cowley, *Exile's Return: A Literary Odyssey of the 1920's* (New York: Viking Press, 1956), p. 60.

124   Grana, *Bohemian versus Bourgeois*, pp. 67–8.

125   In fact, the first Romantics were pioneers in the movement for sexual equality, whilst Freud's debt to Romanticism has already been noted. It might appear from the statement of this creed as if Bohemianism represented a clear rejection of the spirit of deferred gratification, and Cowley does mention 'The idea of living for the moment' as an item (*Exile's Return*, p. 60). Although this is true up to a point, and a real pressure to engage in sensory enjoyments exists, both to manifest freedom from convention and to demonstrate hedonistic potential, postponement of consummation is still necessarily built in to the Bohemian way of life and

hence provides limitless opportunities for day-dreaming. The manner of existence itself guarantees frequent deprivation, whilst the repudiation of conventional routes to 'success' ensures the continuous dreaming of fame.

126   The phrase is Murger's, *The Latin Quarter*, p. 42.

127   Parry, *Garrets and Pretenders*, p. 26.

128   This discussion of aestheticism draws heavily on R. V. Johnson, *Aestheticism* (London: Methuen, 1969), together with William Gaunt, *The Aesthetic Adventure* (London: Jonathan Cape, 1945) and Graham Hough, *The Last Romantics* (London: Gerald Duckworth, 1949).

129   Levin L. Schucking, *The Sociology of Literary Taste* (London: Kegan, Paul, Trench, Trubner, 1944), p. 24.

130   Johnson, *Aestheticism*, p. 14.

131   Thus although the aesthete has no prophetic message to impart, he does act as an instructor in the fine art of self-cultivation.

132   Johnson, *Aestheticism*, p. 19.

133   Ibid., p. 42.

134   The fate of Brummell and Wilde is similar in this respect.

135   Grana, *Bohemian versus Bourgeois*, p. 153.

136   Johnson, *Aestheticism*, p. 80.

137   As Houghton notes, 'being as distinct from doing is the pure aesthetic attitude' (*The Last Romantics*, p. 281).

138   For details of aestheticism's impact upon fashion, especially in association with the Pre-Raphaelites, see Johnson, *Aestheticism*, and Hough, *The Last Romantics*, as well as Alison Adburgham, *Shops and Shopping 1800–1914: Where, and in what Manner the Well-dressed Englishwoman bought her Clothes* (London: George Allen and Unwin, 1964), chapter 16.

139   Indeed, their tendency to ignore morality made them especially vulnerable to charges of corruption.

140   In fact, aestheticism tended to espouse an amorality which led into decadence. For a discussion of the relationship of decadence to aestheticism see the essays in Ian Fletcher (ed.), *Decadence and the 1890's* (London: Edward Arnold, 1979).

Chapter 10   Conclusion

1   See, for example, Richard le Gallienne, *The Romantic Nineties* (London: G. P. Putnam, 1926); Douglas Goldring, *The Nineteenth Twenties: A General Survey and some Personal Memories* (London: Nicholson and Watson, 1945), and James Lavers, *Between the Wars* (Boston, Mass.: Houghton Mifflin, 1961). Material for comparison with the 1960s can be found in Christopher Booker, *The Neophiliacs* (London: Fontana, 1970), Frank Musgrove, *Ecstasy and Holiness: Counter Culture and the Open Society* (London: Methuen, 1974), and Bernice Martin, *A Sociology of Contemporary Cultural Change* (Oxford: Basil Blackwell, 1981).

2   For a discussion of the problems presented by Weber's thesis and the criticisms commonly made of it, see Gordon Marshall, *In Search of the*

Spirit of Capitalism: An Essay on Max Weber's Protestant Ethic Thesis (London: Hutchinson University Library, 1982), chapters 5 and 6.

3   Harold Bloom and Lionel Trilling (eds), *Romantic Poetry and Prose* (New York: Oxford University Press, 1973).

4   Ibid., p. 607.

5   The elitist romantic form of this critique has been best expressed in modern times by F. R. Leavis – see *Nor shall my Sword: Discourses on Pluralism, Passion and Hope* (London: Chatto and Windus, 1977) – and, in a more populist form, by Richard Hoggart, *The Uses of Literacy* (Harmondsworth, Middx.: Penguin Books, 1958). More explicitly socialist and neo-Marxist versions of this critique, which nevertheless still draw their inspiration from the Romantic tradition, have been developed by members of the Frankfurt School (see essays in B. Rosenberg and D. M. White (eds), *Mass Culture: The Popular Arts in America* (Glencoe, Ill.: Free Press, 1957), and A. Arato and E. Gebhardt (eds), *The Essential Frankfurt School Reader* (Oxford: Blackwell, 1978), Part 2).

6   Bloom and Trilling (eds), *Romantic Poetry*, p. 595.

7   John B. Halsted (ed.), *Romanticism* (New York: Walker, 1969), p. 92.

8   There is also no particular reason for assuming that such reduction will necessarily be from ideals to interests; the 'interests' which individuals and groups come to have can equally be considered a product of their 'ideals'. The relationship between these two concepts is taken up below (see pp. 212–16).

9   Arthur Mitzman, *The Iron Cage: An Historical Interpretation of Max Weber* (New York: Alfred A. Knopf, 1970), p. 183.

10 Louis Schneider, 'Ironic Perspective and Sociological Thought', in Lewis A. Coser (ed.), *The Idea of Social Structure: Papers in Honour of Robert K. Merton* (New York: Harcourt Brace Jovanovich, 1975), pp. 323–37, see esp. p. 336.

11 See Werner Stark, 'Max Weber and the Heterogony of Purposes', *Social Research*, 34 (Summer 1967), 249–64, see esp. pp. 253–8 *passim*.

12 For a general discussion of these issues in sociology see: R. K. Merton, 'The Unanticipated Consequences of Purposive Social Action', *American Sociological Review*, 1 (1936), 894–904; R. K. Merton, *Social Theory and Social Structure* (New York: Free Press, 1949), Part 1; Colin Campbell, 'A Dubious Distinction: An Inquiry into the Value and Use of Merton's Concepts of Manifest and Latent Function', *American Sociological Review*, 47 (February 1982), no. 1, 29–43; and Albert O. Hirschman, *The Passions and the Interests: Political Arguments for Capitalism before its Triumph* (Princeton, NJ: Princeton University Press, 1977), pp. 130–6.

13 In fact, Werner Stark claims that it was Weber's tendency to espouse a general cultural pessimism which caused him to invert that more 'progressive' notion of the heterogony of purpose associated with such writers as Adam Smith and Bernard de Mandeville (Stark, 'Max Weber and the Heterogeny of Purposes', p. 253).
   There are clear differences between consequential and transformational irony; that is, between observing that actions have unintentional and opposed consequences, and noting that conduct itself may change its character over

time. Weber refers to both types in his work. The fact that an anti-materialistic Protestantism helped to bring modern capitalism into being is an example of consequentialist irony. On the other hand, the fact that the actual behaviour of Puritan entrepreneurs also becomes transformed from meaningful moral action into 'meaningless' moral profit-seeking with the loss of a genuine Calvinist faith can be seen as an example of transformational irony.

14 The process through which idealistic commitments are created is clearly related to Weber' discussion of charisma.

15 Max Weber, *The Theory of Social and Economic Organization,* trans. A. M. Henderson and Talcott Parsons, edited and with an introduction by Talcott Parsons (New York: Free Press, 1964), pp. 98–9.

16 Quentin Skinner, *The Foundations of Modern Political Thought,* vol. 1: *The Renaissance* (Cambridge: Cambridge University Press, 1978), pp. xii–xiii.

17 Hans Gerth and C. Wright Mills, *Character and Social Structure: The Psychology of Social Institutions* (London: Routledge and Kegan Paul, 1954), pp. 112–30.

18 Marshall, *In Search of the Spirit of Capitalism,* p. 258.

19 See C. Wright Mills, 'Situated Action and the Vocabulary of Motives', *American Sociological Review,* 6 (December 1940), 904–13; M. Scott and S. Lyman, 'Accounts', *American Sociological Review,* 33 (February 1968), no. 1. 46–62; Alan F. Blum and Peter McHugh, 'The Social Ascription of Motives', *American Sociological Review,* 36 (February 1971), 98–109; and Anthony Wootton, *Dilemmas of Discourse: Controversies about the Sociological Significance of Language* (London: Allen and Unwin, 1975), pp. 86–92.

20 The principal influence here has been the work of Kenneth Burke; see his *A Grammar of Motives and A Rhetoric of Motives* (Cleveland, Ohio: World Publishing, 1962).

21 Interestingly, Scott and Lyman state that their concept of an account includes 'those non-vocalized but lingual explanations that arise in an actor's "mind" when he questions his own behaviour', but they go on to restrict their concern to vocalized accounts, and especially those given in face-to-face relations (see Scott and Lyman, 'Accounts', p. 47).

22 Joyce Tompkins, *The Popular Novel in England 1770–1800* (Lincoln: University of Nebraska Press, 1961), p. 101.

23 See pp. 121f.

24 It is not being argued that idealistic conduct is, at root, self-interested, merely that it can decay into such a form. This fact should not be taken as indicative that all moral action is basically little more than selfishness. This is no more reasonable than the assumption that selfish behaviour is merely a disguise, adopted for reasons of modesty, for conduct which is truly altruistic.

25 Idealistic is not, of course, the opposite of self-interested conduct; 'other-interested' or 'altruistic' conduct is the opposite of self-interested, whilst 'realistic' is the opposite of idealistic. Ideals are, however, generally presented as transcending self by their very nature as 'non-actual' entities and although it is possible to concentrate upon realizing the ideal in oneself

whilst making no effort to realize it in any other form, systems of ideals are interlinked and it may prove more difficult than imagined to limit one's efforts to realize them in oneself without being forced to pay attention to their more generalized forms. It is in this way that idealistic concerns can function to exert a 'pull' away from pure self-interest.

26 Simone de Beauvoir, *Memoirs of a Dutiful Daughter*, quoted by Jerome Bruner, Alison Joly and Kathy Sylva (eds), *Play – Its Role in Development and Evolution* (Harmondsworth, Middx.: Penguin Books, 1976), p. 587.

27 Ibid.

28 Such behaviour must be 'genuine' if it is to fulfil the function of providing the individual with reassurance concerning his goodness; that is, it must be an intrinsically self-justifying act in which the desire to do good predominates over the desire for confirmation of one's goodness.

29 Johann Wolfgang von Goethe, *The Sufferings of Young Werther*, trans. Bayard Quincy Morgan (London: John Calder, 1976), pp. 80–1.

30 For an example of how commercial institutions can provide the necessary framework for the generation of a romantic idealism, see the authors' introductory essay, 'From Romance to Romanticism', in Colin Campbell and Allan Murphy, *Things We Said Today: The Complete Lyrics and a Concordance to The Beatles' Songs 1962–1970* (Ann Arbor, Mich.: Pierian Press, 1980), pp. xxi–xxxi.

31 Gordon Rattray Taylor, *The Angel-Makers: A Study in the Psychological Origins of Historical Change 1750–1850* (London: Heinemann, 1958).

32 Ibid.

33 See Daniel Bell, *The Cultural Contradictions of Capitalism* (London: Heinemann, 1976) and Martin, *A Sociology of Contemporary Cultural Change.*

34 There has been much debate in sociology over the exact nature of this distinction and how far it is reasonable to accuse Weber of defining the one in terms of the other (see Marshall, *In Search of the Spirit of Capitalism*, pp. 119–22). The validity of these criticisms is not at issue here, given that, however the two are defined, the 'spirit' which animates economic productive activity cannot encompass all a religious ethic is intended to cover.

35 Brian M. Barbour, 'Franklin and Emerson', in Brian M. Barbour (ed.), *Benjamin Franklin: A Collection of Critical Essays* (Englewood Cliffs, NJ: Prentice-Hall, 1979), pp. 25–9, see esp. p. 28.

36 Irvin G. Wyllie, *The Self-Made Man in America: The Myth of Rags to Riches* (New York: Free Press, 1954), p. 140, and Barbour, 'Benjamin Franklin', in Barbour (ed.), *Benjamin Franklin*, pp. 63–74.

37 Unfortunately, Freud's ideas, as they became modified in the course of their assimilation into popular thought during the 1920s, further worked to reinforce the tendency to blur the Protestant ethic with the spirit of capitalism. As a consequence, the Bohemians of Greenwich Village regarded themselves as deliberately opposing what they defined as 'a business-Christian ethic' (see Malcolm Cowley, *Exile's Return: A Literary Odyssey of the 1920's* (London: Hodder and Stoughton, 1962), p. 62).

38 It is important to remember that Romanticism, like Puritanism, was also a movement of deep moral concern.

39 The phrase is Oden's (see Thomas C. Oden, 'The New Pietism', in Eileen
Barker (ed.), *New Religious Movements: A Perspective for Understanding Society*
(New York: Edwin Mellen Press, 1982), pp. 86–106, see esp. p. 86. In fact,
Oden shows rather well how that aspect of the 1960s cultural revolution
which went under the label 'encounter movement', whilst ostensibly
rebelling against Calvinistic Puritanism, was actually 'reappropriating' the
pietistic wing of the puritan Protestant tradition (ibid., pp. 93–4).

40 For examples of the dispute over the uniqueness of the counterculture see
Kenneth Westhues, *Society's Shadow: Studies in the Sociology of Countercultures* (Toronto: McGraw-Hill Ryerson, 1972), and Kenneth Keniston,
Youth and Dissent: The Rise of a New Opposition (New York: Harcourt Brace
Jovanovich, 1971), whilst for an overview see Colin Campbell, 'Accounting
for the Counter Culture', *The Scottish Journal of Sociology*, 4 (January 1980),
no. 1, 37–51. A plea to accept the 'romantics'' own definition of reality and
not resort to sociological 'imputation' is to be found in Brian Salter,
'Explanations of Student Unrest: An Exercise in Devaluation', *British
Journal of Sociology*, 24 (September 1973), no. 3, 329–40. Roszak's apologia
for the counter-culture also reveals the extent to which history has become
distorted by the prevalence of romantic myth. He indicts Christianity, for
example, in the form of a 'Protestant ethic' for bringing about a
materialistic, ratiocinative culture in which feeling and sensibility are
suppressed and nature disparaged (see Theodore Roszak, *The Making of a
Counter-Culture* (Garden City: Doubleday Anchor Books, 1969), pp.
250–1). He appears to see no contradiction, however, between this view and
his approval of writers like Blake who drew their inspiration from the
self-same Protestantism (ibid., pp. 127–201).

41 The tendency to view seventeenth-century Puritanism through the
distorting screen of Victorian evangelicalism may be partly to blame for the
failure to recognize its profoundly pietistic character, although the very
emotionalism and sentimental humanitarianism characteristic of this later
movement ultimately derives from the former.

42 John William Ward, 'Benjamin Franklin: The Making of an American
Character', in Barbour (ed.), *Benjamin Franklin*, pp. 50–62, see esp. p. 61.

43 This observation was made by Hoxie Neale Fairchild, *Religious Trends in
English Poetry* (New York: Columbia University Press, 1939–49), vol. 3, p.
12.

44 Roszak, *The Making of a Counter-Culture*, p. 62.

45 Oden, 'The New Pietism', pp. 95–7.

The general failure to perceive that the 'opposite' of the Protestant ethic
is every bit as inner-directed as that which it rejects, stems, at least in part,
from the mistake of regarding individualism as the key feature of that ethic.
This is an error contained in the arguments of both William H. Whyte (*The
Organisation Man*, New York: Doubleday Anchor Books, 1957) and
Riesman (David Riesman, Nathan Glazer and Reuel Denny, *The Lonely
Crowd*, New York: Doubleday Anchor Books, 1966) and naturally leads to
the assumption that whatever ethos has replaced it must be 'social', or
'other-directed' in form.

46 The terms are from Bell, *The Cultural Contradictions of Capitalism;* Martin, *A Sociology of Contemporary Cultural Change;* John Carroll, *Puritan, Paranoid, Remissive: A Sociology of Modern Culture* (London: Routledge and Kegan Paul); and Martha Wolfenstein, 'The Emergence of Fun Morality', in Eric Larrabee and Rolf Meyersohn, (eds), *Mass Leisure* (Glencoe, Ill.: Free Press, 1958), pp. 86–95.

47 Thus although one can impute a 'natural uninhibitedness' to a person's conduct (as, for example, the Romantics did with the 'noble savage'), no one can choose to behave in that fashion. To be 'uninhibited' is to reject an inhibited pattern of behaviour; it is therefore deliberate and not 'unthinking' conduct.

48 Jerome L. Singer, *The Child's World of Make-Believe: Experimental Studies of Imaginative Play* (New York: Academic Press, 1973), pp. 73 and 198.

49 Part of the failure to perceive how fundamentally interdependent are the nature of the personality traits necessary for the construction of 'puritan' and 'romantic' character types stems from the persuasive force of the romantic myth. This specifies that a romantic is someone who is 'naturally' impulsive, uninhibited, passionate and creative, when, in reality romantics are merely those people who deliberately choose to behave in this way.

50 Fairchild, *Religious Trends in English Poetry*, vol. 2, p. 9.

51 Walter E. Houghton, *The Victorian Frame of Mind 1830–1870* (New Haven, Conn.: Yale University Press, 1957), p. 277.

52 Henry Murger, *The Latin Quarter (Scènes de la Vie Bohème)*, trans. Ellen Marriage and John Selwyn (London: Greening, 1908), p. 329.

53 Kenneth Keniston, *Youth and Dissent: The Rise of a New Opposition* (New York: Harcourt Brace Jovanovich, 1971), p. 160; Jeanne H. Block, Norma Haan and M. Brewster Smith, 'Activism and Apathy in Contemporary Adolescents', in James F. Adams (ed.), *Understanding Adolescence: Current Developments in Adolescent Psychology* (Boston, Mass.: Allyn and Bacon, 1968), pp. 198–231, see esp. p. 215. Interestingly, Keniston's evidence, as well as that of Block, Haan and Smith, suggests that Bohemian youths are the offspring of parents who were themselves 'Bohemian' in their youth, thus somewhat qualifying Parry's remark about there being 'less of an hereditary character' in this group than any other in society.

54 See, in addition to Booker, Musgrove, and Westhues, Nathan Adler, *The Antinomian Stream: New Life Styles and the Antinomian Personality* (New York: Harper and Row, 1972).

55 Peter L. Berger and Richard J. Neuhaus, *Movement and Revolution* (New York: Doubleday Anchor Books, 1970), p. 35.

56 It is important to recognize that not all students, let alone all youths, accept 'romantic' values. On the contrary, there is evidence that the majority espouse conventional 'bourgeois' success values. See, for example, the evidence provided by R. Mills, *Young Outsiders: A Study of Alternative Communities* (London: Routledge and Kegan Paul, 1973), p. 22.

   This is a perspective which stresses the 'strange unevenness between developmental and humanist themes in American educational and child-rearing philosophies' on the one hand, and 'the weakness of these same themes in commerce and politics' on the other (see Charles Hampden-Turner, *Radical Man* (London: Duckworth, 1971), p. 419). For an argument which has clear links with the popular idea that permissive child-rearing was the cause of the student rebelliousness which occurred in the 1960s, see Richard Flacks, 'The Liberated Generation: An Exploration of the Roots of Student Protest', *Journal of Social Issues*, 23 (July 1967), no. 3, 52–75; reprinted in Kenneth Westhues, *Society's Shadow: Studies in the Sociology of Countercultures* (Toronto: McGraw-Hill Ryerson, 1972).

57   Rousseau is the great seminal influence here (although again Freud is the one who is most commonly cited), his ideas having been taken up and incorporated into educational practice by Pestalozzi and Froebel. The Freudian revolution imparted a new impetus to the introduction of progressive (or largely 'romantic-inspired') ideas and practices into child-rearing, and especially infant care, something which Wolfenstein has documented for the period 1914–45 in the United States (see Wolfenstein, 'The Emergence of Fun Morality', 1958). To suggest that the widespread adoption of 'permissive' child-rearing practices has been a major factor in the creation of a new generation of 'romantics' is to overlook the obvious fact that only romantically inclined parents would be likely to adopt such practices in the first place. It is therefore simpler to regard the child's values as directly inherited from the parents.

58   This is most clearly revealed in those 'refined' activities long considered most suitable for upper-middle class woman to pursue; activities such as playing the piano, singing, drawing, arranging flowers and, of course, engaging in philanthropic work.

59   Kenneth Keniston, *The Uncommitted: Alienated Youth in American Society* (New York: Dell Publishing, 1960), pp. 116–17.

60   See, Taylor, *The Angel-Makers*, Part Five.

61   Liam Hudson, *Frames of Mind: Ability, Perception and Self-Perception in the Arts and Sciences* (London: Methuen, 1968).

62   The prevalence among the middle classes of moral crusades and movements of reform, such as anti-slavery, pacifism and, more recently, nuclear disarmament, testify to the strength of this tradition. See Parkin on the middle-class preference for 'expressive politics' – Frank Parkin, *Middle Class Radicalism: The Social Basis of the British Campaign for Nuclear Disarmament*, (Manchester: Manchester University Press, 1968).

63   Hudson, *Frames of Mind*, pp. 36 and 45.

64   It would be wrong to give the impression, however, that all artists have espoused a 'romantic' aesthetic in the narrow sense. Some have asserted a classical or neo-classical aesthetic against what they regarded as the excessive emotionalist or expressive tendencies of Romanticism. Their perception of the role of the artist in society, however, did not necessarily depart very much from a romantic position.

65   Students in art colleges would seem to be among those most aware of this choice. Tom Nairn and Jim Singh-Sandhu comment, for example, on how they see themselves as confronted with the choice between 'being a Great Artist' or a 'Success', and that 'while some students dream of being

Rembrandts, more assume they are going to be Mary Quants, David Baileys, or David Hockneys' ('Chaos in the Art Colleges', in Alexander Cockburn and Robin Blackburn (eds), *Student Power: Problems, Diagnosis, Action* (Harmondsworth, Middx.: Penguin Books, 1969), pp. 103–185, see esp. p. 107).

66 Evidence of the conflict between these two ethics can be found in the intellectual history of modern societies. In Britain conflict between the 'romantic' and 'rational-utilitarian' perspectives has largely taken the form of what Raymond Williams has called 'the culture and society debate'. He traces this from its origins in the dispute between Romantics and Benthamites down to the twentieth century, placing on the one side such writers as Blake, Coleridge, Arnold, Carlyle, Ruskin, Henry James, D. H. Lawrence and F. R. Leavis, whilst on the other he identifies Bentham, J. S. Mill, T. H. Huxley, H. G. Wells, Bertrand Russell and C. P. Snow (Raymond Williams, *Culture and Society 1780–1950*, Harmondsworth, Middx.: Penguin Books, 1961). Indeed, the so-called 'Two Cultures Debate', initiated by Snow in the early 1960s, and in which Leavis took such strong exception to Snow's account of the cultural topography of the modern world, starkly revealed the extent to which this intellectual conflict still characterizes modern society. The most significant feature of that debate was not the pronouncement that the intellectual life of the West was increasingly split into the two groups of scientists and literary intellectuals, but the way in which the ensuing controversy revealed that the mutual hostility stemmed from a fundamental contrast in ethical outlooks – for details see David K. Connelius and Edwin St Vincent (eds), *Cultures in Conflict: Perspectives on the Snow-Leavis Controversy* (Chicago, Ill.: Scott, Foresman, 1964). It was not merely a question of mutual antipathy and misunderstanding born of intellectual specialization, rather it was a moral conflict, born of contrasting (indeed inverted) definitions of the good, the true and the beautiful; definitions which, at base, involved the differential ranking of 'utility' and 'pleasure'. Life is not an intellectual system, however, and this intellectual conflict should not be mistaken for a cultural 'contradiction'. On the contrary, intellectuals help to ensure the dynamic evolution of the cultural system of modernity by advancing these rival claims.

67 As Weber emphasized, the source of rationalization within an individual's status-set is the consistent application of one set of values derived from a single ideal of character. It is this ethically prompted source of 'integration' which can come to challenge the situationally differentiated application of values to conduct.

68 This latter claim concerns a disjunction of norms, that is behaviour required 'in the economic realm' and that 'central in the culture' (see Bell, *The Cultural Contradictions of Capitalism*, p. 15). It is hard to make sense of such claims, but it would seem that 'economic realm' excludes the activity of consumption and that 'culture' excludes the area of science and technology, as it is only by interpreting Bell's terms in this way that it is possible to arrive at the strange conclusion that the 'two realms which had historically been

joined to produce a single character structure – that of the Puritan and his calling – have now become unjoined' (ibid.). Clearly the economy and the culture of modern society can only be considered 'unjoined' if one assumes the complete victory of romanticism and the complete absence of any consumption activity; if, on the other hand, one recognizes that the economic realm necessarily comprises consumption and production, whilst the culture contains both puritan-utilitarian and romantic traditions, then 'contradiction' is no more a fair description than compatability.

69 As Denis de Rougemont has pointed out, passion is *the* distinctive feature of the European psyche, and a prime source of that restlessness and strenuousness so characteristic of the West (*Passion and Society*, trans. Montgomery Belgion, rev. edn (London: Faber and Faber, 1956), p. 316).

References

Abercrombie, Lascelles, *Romanticism* (London: Martin Seeker, 1963).

Abrams, M. H., *The Mirror and the Lamp: Romantic Theory and the Critical Tradition* (New York: Oxford University Press, 1953).

———, *Natural Supernaturalism: Tradition and Revolution in Romantic Literature* (New York: W. W. Norton, 1971).

Adatto, Kiku and Cole, Stephen, 'Classical Theory in Contemporary Sociological Research: The Case of Max Weber', *Knowledge and Society: Studies in the Sociology of Culture Past and Present*, (1981), 137–62.

Adburgham, Alison, *Shops and Shopping 1800–1914: Where, and in what Manner the Well-dressed Englishwoman bought her Clothes* (London: George Allen and Unwin, 1964).

Adler, Nathan, *The Antinomian Stream: New Life Styles and the Antinomian Personality* (New York: Harper and Row, 1972).

Aldridge, A. O., 'The Pleasures of Pity', *A Journal of English Literary History*, 16 (March 1949), no. 1, 76–87.

Allen, B. Sprague, *Tides in English Taste (1619–1800): A Background for the Study of Literature*, 2 vols (New York: Rowman and Littlefield, 1969).

Altick, Richard D., *The English Common Reader: A Social History of the Mass Reading Public 1800–1900* (Chicago, Ill.: University of Chicago Press, 1957).

Arato, A. and Gebhardt, E. (eds), *The Essential Frankfurt School Reader* (Oxford: Blackwell, 1979).

Auden, W. H. 'Freedom and Necessity in Poetry: My Lead Mine', in Jerome S. Bruner, Allison Jolly and Kathy Sylva (eds), *Play – Its Role in Development and Evolution* (Harmondsworth, Middx.: Penguin, 1976), pp. 584–5.

Austen, Jane, *Sense and Sensibility* (London: Avalon Press, 1949).

Baldwin, Frances Elizabeth, *Sumptuary Legislation and Personal Regulation in England* (Baltimore, Md.: Johns Hopkins Press, 1926).

Barbour, Brian M., 'Franklin and Emerson', in Brian M. Barbour (ed.), *Benjamin Franklin: A Collection of Critical Essays* (Englewood Cliffs, NJ: Prentice-Hall, 1979), pp. 25–9.

Barfield, Owen, *History in English Words*, new edn (London: Faber and Faber, 1954).

References 283

Baron, Steve, 'The Study of Culture: Cultural Studies and British Sociology Compared', *Acta Sociologica*, (1985), no. 2, 71–85.

Barrow, Isaac, *The Works of the Learned Isaac Barrow . . . being all his English Works; published by his Grace Dr. John Tillotson, late Archbishop of Canterbury*, 5th edn, 3 vols (in 2) (London: A. Miller, 1741).

Barzun, Jacques, *Classic, Romantic and Modern*, 2nd edn rev. (Chicago, Ill.: University of Chicago Press, 1961).

Baumer, Franklin, L., *Religion and the Rise of Scepticism* (New York: Harcourt Brace, 1960).

——, *Modern European Thought: Continuity and Change of Ideas 1600–1950* (New York: Macmillan, 1977).

Beauvoir, Simone de, *Memoirs of a Dutiful Daughter*, trans. by James Kirkup (Harmondsworth, Middx.: Penguin Books, 1963).

Bell, Daniel, *The Cultural Contradictions of Capitalism* (London: Heinemann, 1976).

Bentham, Jeremy, 'An Introduction to the Principles of Morals and Legislation', in Jeremy Bentham and John Stuart Mill, *The Utilitarians*, 1823 edn (New York: Doubleday Dolphin Books, 1961).

Berger, L. Peter and Neuhaus, Richard J., *Movement and Revolution* (New York: Doubleday Anchor Books, 1970).

Berke, Joseph, *Counter Culture* (London: Peter Owen, 1969).

Bernbaum, Ernest, 'The Romantic Movement', in Robert F. Gleckner and Gerald E. Enscoe (eds), *Romanticism: Points of View* (Englewood Cliffs, NJ: Prentice-Hall, 1962), pp. 88–96.

Bevis, Richard W. (ed.), *Eighteenth Century Drama: Afterpieces* (London: Oxford University Press, 1970).

Block, Jeanne H., Haan, Norma and Smith M. Brewster, 'Activism and Apathy in Contemporary Adolescents', in James F. Adams (ed.), *Understanding Adolescence: Current Developments in Adolescent Psychology* (Boston, Mass.: Allyn and Bacon, 1968), pp. 198–231.

Bloom, Harold and Trilling, Lionel (eds), *Romantic Poetry and Prose* (New York: Oxford University Press, 1973).

Blum, Alan F. and McHugh, Peter, 'The Social Ascription of Motives', *American Sociological Review*, 36 (February 1971), 98–109.

Booker, Christopher, *The Neophiliacs* (London: Fontana, 1970).

Boswell, James, *Boswell's Life of Johnson*, 6 vols, ed. by Birkbeck Hill, revised by L. F. Powell, 2nd edn (Oxford: Oxford University Press, 1934).

Bredvold, Louis I., *The Natural History of Sensibility* (Detroit, Mich.: Wayne State University Press, 1962).

Bruner, Jerome, Jolly, Alison and Sylva, Kathy (eds), *Play – Its Role in Development and Evolution* (Harmondsworth, Middx.: Penguin Books, 1976).

Bryson, Gladys, *The Scottish Inquiry of the Eighteenth Century* (New York: Augustus M. Kelly, 1968).

Bunyan, John, *The Pilgrims [sic] Progress, From this World to that which is to come* (London: George Virtue, 1848).

Burke, Kenneth, *A Grammar of Motives and a Rhetoric of Motives* (Cleveland, Ohio: World Publishing, 1962).

Burke, Peter, *Popular Culture in Early Modern Europe* (London: Temple Smith, 1978).

Burnett, T. A. J., *The Rise and Fall of a Regency Dandy: The Life and Times of Scrope Berdmore Davies* (London: John Murray, 1981).

Campbell, Colin, *Toward a Sociology of Irreligion* (London: Macmillan, 1971).

——, 'Accounting for the Counter Culture', *The Scottish Journal of Sociology*, 4 (January 1980), no. 1, 37–51.

——, 'A Dubious Distinction: An Inquiry into the Value and Use of Merton's Concepts of Manifest and Latent Function', *American Sociological Review*, 47 (February 1982), no. 1, 29–43.

—— and Murphy, Allan, *Things We Said Today: The Complete Lyrics and a Concordance to The Beatles' Songs 1961–1970* (Ann Arbor, Mich.: Pierian Press, 1980).

Carlyle, Thomas, *Sartor Resartus: Hero-worship and the Heroic in History*, Everyman Library edn (London: J. M. Dent, 1908).

Carroll, John, *Puritan, Paranoid, Remissive: A Sociology of Modern Culture* (London: Routledge and Kegan Paul, 1977).

Cassirer, Ernest, *The Platonic Renaissance in England*, trans. James P. Pettegrove (New York: Gordian Press, 1970).

Clark, G. S. R. Kitson, 'The Romantic Element 1830–1850', in J. H. Plumb (ed.), *Studies in Social History: A Tribute to G. M. Trevelyan* (London: Longmans, Green, 1955).

Cobbett, William, *Rural Rides . . . with Economical and Political Observations*, ed. E. W. Martin (London: Macdonald, 1958).

Cocanougher, A. Benston and Bruce, Grady D., 'Socially Distant Reference Groups and Consumer Aspirations', in Harold H. Kassarjian and Thomas S. Robertson (eds), *Perspectives in Consumer Behaviour* (Glenview, Ill.: Scott, Foresman, 1973), pp. 309–14.

Cockburn, Alexander and Blackburn, Robin (eds), *Student Power: Problems, Diagnosis, Action* (Harmondsworth, Middx.: Penguin Books, 1969).

Cole, W. A., 'Factors in Demand, 1700–1780', in Roderick Floud and Donald McCloskey (eds), *The Economic History of Britain since 1700* (Cambridge: Cambridge University Press, 1981), pp. 36–65.

Coleridge, Samuel Taylor, *Biographia Literia, or Biographic Sketches of my Literary Life*, 2 vols, first edn repr. (London: Rest Fenner, 1817).

Connelius, David K. and Vincent, Edwin St (eds), *Cultures in Conflict: Perspectives on the Snow-Leavis Controversy* (Chicago, Ill.: Scott, Foresman, 1964).

Cowley, Malcolm, *Exile's Return: A Literary Odyssey of the 1920s* (New York: Viking Press, 1956).

Cragg, Gerald R., *The Church and the Age of Reason 1648–1789* (London: Hodder and Stoughton, 1962).

——, *From Puritanism to the Age of Reason: A Study of Changes in Religious Thought within the Church of England 1660–1700* (Cambridge: Cambridge University Press, 1950).

——, *The Cambridge Platonists* (New York: Oxford University Press, 1968).

Crane, R. S., 'Suggestions toward a Genealogy of the "Man of Feeling" ', *A Journal of English Literary History*, vol. 1 (1934), republished in R. S. Crane,

The Idea of Humanities and other Essays Critical and Historical (Chicago, Ill.: University of Chicago Press, 1967), vol. 1, pp. 188–213.

Davis, Arthur K., 'Veblen on the Decline of the Protestant Ethic', *Social Forces*, 22 (1944), 282–6.

Diggins, John P., *The Bard of Savagery: Thorstein Veblen and Modern Social Theory* (Brighton: Harvester Press, 1978).

Douglas, Mary and Isherwood, Baron, *The World of Goods: Towards an Anthropology of Consumption* (Harmondsworth, Middx.: Penguin Books, 1978).

Dowden, Edward, *Puritan and Anglican: Studies in Literature* (London: Kegan Paul, Trench, Trubner, 1910).

Draper, John W., *The Funeral Elegy and the Rise of English Romanticism* (London: Frank Cass, 1929, repr. 1967).

Dyer, Gillian, *Advertising as Communication* (London: Methuen, 1982).

Erämetsä, Erik, *A Study of the Word "Sentimental" and of Other Linguistic Characteristics of Eighteenth-Century Sentimentalism in England* (Helsinki: Annals Academiae Scientiarum Fennicae Ser. B, (1951), no. 1).

Eversley, D. E. C., 'The Home Market and Economic Growth in England, 1750–1780', in E. L. Jones and Edmund Mingay Gordon (eds), *Land, Labour and Population in the Industrial Revolution* (London: Edward Arnold, 1967), pp. 206–59.

Fairchild, Hoxie Neale, *Religious Trends in English Poetry*, 3 vols (New York: Columbia University Press, 1939–49).

Featherstone, Mike, 'The Body in Consumer Culture', *Theory, Culture and Society*, 1 (1982), 18–33.

Flacks, Richard, 'The Liberated Generation: An Exploration of the Roots of Student Protest', *Journal of Social Issues*, 23 (July 1967), no. 3, 52–75.

Fletcher, Ian (ed.), *Decadence and the 1890's* (London: Edward Arnold, 1979).

Foster, George M., 'Peasant Society and the Image of Limited Good', *American Anthropologist*, 67 (1965), 392–315.

Foster, James R., 'The Abbé Prevost and the English Novel', *PMLA*, (June 1927), 443–64.

Freud, Sigmund, *The Future of an Illusion*, trans. by W. D. Robson-Scott, revised and newly edited by James Strachey (New York: Doubleday Anchor Books, 1964).

Fromm, Erich, 'The Psychological Aspects of the Guaranteed Income', in Robert Theobald (ed.), *The Guaranteed Income: Next Step in Economic Evolution?* (New York: Doubleday, 1964).

Furst, Lilian R., *The Contours of European Romanticism* (London: Macmillan Press, 1979).

Galbraith, Kenneth, *The Affluent Society*, 3rd edn rev. (Harmondsworth, Middx.: Penguin Books, 1979).

Gallaway, Francis, *Reason, Rule and Revolt in English Classicism* (New York: Octagon Books, 1974).

Gaudefroy-Demombynes, J., 'The Inner Movement of Romanticism', in Anthony Thorlby (ed.), *The Romantic Movement* (London: Longmans, 1966), pp. 138–42.

Gaunt, William, *The Aesthetic Adventure* (London: Jonathan Cape, 1945).

Gerth, Hans and Mills, C. Wright, *Character and Social Structure: The Psychology of Social Institutions* (London: Routledge and Kegan Paul, 1954).

Gilboy, Elizabeth Waterman, 'Demand as a Factor in the Industrial Revolution', in R. M. Hartwell (ed.), *The Causes of the Industrial Revolution in England* (London: Methuen, 1967), 121–38.

Gill, Frederick C., *The Romantic Movement and Methodism: A Study of English Romanticism and the Evangelical Revival* (London: The Epworth Press, 1937).

Goethe, Johann Wolfgang von, *The Sufferings of Young Werther*, trans. Bayard Quincy Morgan (London: John Calder, 1976).

Goffman, Erving, 'Where the Action Is', in *Interaction Ritual: Essays on Face-to-Face Behaviour* (Harmondsworth, Middx.: Penguin Books, 1967), pp. 149–270.

Goldring, Douglas, *The Nineteen Twenties: A General Survey and some Personal Memories* (London: Nicholson and Watson, 1945).

Grana, Cesar, *Bohemian versus Bourgeois: French Society and the Man of Letters in the Nineteenth Century* (New York: Basic Books, 1964).

Grean, Stanley, *Shaftesbury's Philosophy of Religion and Ethics: A Study in Enthusiasm* (Athens, Ohio: Ohio University Press, 1967).

Habakkuk, H. J., 'England's Nobility', in Daniel A. Baugh (ed.), *Aristocratic Government and Society in Eighteenth-Century England: The Foundations of Stability* (New York: Franklin Watts, 1975), pp. 97–115.

Haining, Peter, *Gothic Tales of Terror: Classic Horror Stories from Great Britain, Europe and the United States* (Harmondsworth, Middx.: Penguin Books, 1973).

Halevy, Elie, *The Growth of Philosophical Radicalism*, new edn (Boston, Mass. Beacon Press, 1955).

Hall, Willis and Waterhouse, Keith, *Billy Liar (The Play)* (Glasgow: Blackie, 1966).

Haller, William, *The Rise of Puritanism, or the Way to the New Jerusalem as set forth in Pulpit and Press from Thomas Cartwright to John Lilburne and John Milton, 1570–1643* (New York: Harper, 1957).

Halsted, John B. (ed.), *Romanticism*, Documentary History of Western Civilization Series (New York: Walker, 1969).

Hampden-Turner, Charles, *Radical Man* (London: Duckworth, 1971).

Harding, D. W., 'Psychological Processes in the Reading of Fiction', *The British Journal of Aesthetics*, 2 (1962), 133–47.

Hartley, Lodwick, *Laurence Sterne in the Twentieth Century: An Essay and a Bibliography of Sternean Studies 1900–1965* (Chapel Hill, NC: University of North Carolina Press, 1966).

Hayter, Althea, *Opium and the Romantic Imagination* (London: Faber and Faber, 1968).

Herskovits, Melville, J., *Economic Anthropology: A Study in Comparative Economics* (New York: Alfred A. Knopf, 1960).

Hick, John, *Evil and the Love of God* (London: Macmillan, 1966).

Hirschman, Albert O., *The Passions and the Interests: Political Arguments for Capitalism before its Triumph* (Princeton, NJ: Princeton University Press, 1977).

Hoggart, Richard, *The Uses of Literacy* (Harmondsworth, Middx.: Penguin Books, 1958).

Hooker, E. N., 'The Discussion of Taste, from 1750–1770, and the New Trends in Literary Criticism', *PMLA*, 49 (June 1934), no. 2, 577–92.

Hopkins, Jerry (ed.), *The Hippy Papers: Notes from the Underground Press* (New York: Signet Books, 1968).

Houghton, Walter E., *The Victorian Frame of Mind 1830–1870* (New Haven, Conn.: Yale University Press, 1957).

Hoyt, Elizabeth E., 'The Impact of a Money Economy upon Consumption Patterns', *Annals of the American Academy of Political and Social Science*, 305 (May 1956), 12–22.

Hudson, Liam, *Frames of Mind: Ability, Perception and Self-Perception in the Arts and Sciences* (London: Methuen, 1968).

Hughes, H. Stuart, *Consciousness and Society* (Brighton: Harvester Press, 1979).

Hugo, Howard E., 'Components of Romanticism', in John B. Halsted (ed.), *Romanticism: Problems of Definition, Explanation and Evaluation* (Boston, Mass. D. C. Heath, 1965), pp. 30–6.

Hulme, T. E., 'Romanticism and Classicism', in Robert Francis Gleckner and Gerald E. Enscoe (eds), *Romanticism: Points of View* Englewood Cliffs, NJ: Prentice-Hall, 1962), pp. 34–44.

John, A. H., 'Aspects of English Economic Growth in the First Half of the Eighteenth Century', *Economica*, (May 1961), 176–90.

Johnson, R. V., *Aestheticism* (London: Methuen, 1969).

Jones, Eric L., 'The Fashion Manipulators: Consumer Tastes and British Industries, 1660–1800', in Louis P. Cain and Paul J. Uselding (eds), *Business Enterprise and Economic Change* (Kent State, Ohio: Kent State University Press, 1973), pp. 198–226.

Jones, Howard Mumford, *Revolution and Romanticism* (Cambridge, Mass: Harvard University Press, 1974).

Keats, John, *The Poetical Works of John Keats*, ed. H. W. Garrod, 2nd edn (Oxford: Clarendon Press, 1958).

Keniston, Kenneth, *The Uncommitted: Alienated Youth in American Society*, (New York: Dell Publishing, 1960).

——, *Youth and Dissent: The Rise of a New Opposition* (New York: Harcourt Brace Jovanovich, 1971).

Klaus, Kenneth B., *The Romantic Period in Music* (Boston: Allyn and Bacon, 1970).

Kuhn, Thomas S., *The Structure of Scientific Revolutions* (Chicago, Ill.: University of Chicago Press, 1962).

Kyrk, Hazel, *A Theory of Consumption* (London: Isaac Pitman 1923).

Laumann, Edward O. and House, James S., 'Living-Room Styles and Social Attributes: The Patterning of Material Artifacts in a Modern Urban Community', in H. H. Kassarjian and T. S. Robertson, *Perspectives in Consumer Behaviour* (Glenview, Ill.: Scott, Foresman, 1973), pp. 430–40.

Lavers, James, *Between the Wars* (Boston, Mass. Houghton Mifflin, 1961).

——, *Dandies* (London: Weidenfeld and Nicolson, 1968).

Leavis, F. R. *Nor shall my Sword: Discourses on Pluralism, Passion and Hope* (London: Chatto and Windus, 1977).

Lee, John Alan, 'The Romantic Heresy', *Canadian Review of Sociology and Anthropology*, 12 (1975), 514–28.

Le Gallienne, Richard, *The Romantic Nineties* (London: G. P. Putnam, 1926).

Leibenstein, Harvey, 'Bandwagon, Snob, and Veblen Effects in the Theory of Consumers' Demand', in Edwin Mansfield (ed.), *Microeconomics: Selected Readings* 4th edn (New York: Norton, 1982), pp. 12–30.

Leibniz, Gottfried Wilhelm, *Theodicy*, trans. by E. M. Hughes from C. J. Gerhardt's edition 1875–90, edited, abridged and with an introduction by Diogenes Allen (Don Mills, Ontario: J. M. Dent, 1966).

Lerner, Daniel, *The Passing of Traditional Society: Modernizing the Middle East* (Glencoe, Ill.: Free Press, 1958).

Lipton, Lawrence, *The Holy Barbarians* (New York: Julian Messner, 1959).

Long, Elizabeth, 'Affluence and After: Themes of Success in American Best-Selling Novels, 1945–1975', in Robert Alun Jones and Henrika Kuklick (eds), *Knowledge and Society: Studies in the Sociology of Culture Past and Present* (Greenwich), Conn.: Aljai Press, 1981), vol. 3, pp. 257–301.

Lovejoy, Arthur O., 'On the Discrimination of Romanticisms', *PMLA*, (June 1924) 229–53; reprinted in *Essays in the History of Ideas* (New York: George Braziller, 1955).

—— 'The Parallel of Deism and Classicism', in *Essays in the History of Ideas* (New York: George Braziller, 1955), pp. 78–98.

——, *Essays in the History of Ideas* (New York: George Braziller, 1955).

——, *The Great Chain of Being: A Study of the History of an Idea* (Cambridge, Mass.: Harvard University Press, 1961).

Lowenthal, Leo and Fiske, Marjorie, 'The Debate Over Art and Popular Culture in Eighteenth Century England', in Mirra Komarovsky (ed.), *Common Frontiers of the Social Sciences* (Glencoe, Ill.: Free Press, 1957), pp. 33–96.

Lucas, F. R., 'Faeries and Fungi; Or the Future of Romanticism', in A. Thorlby (ed.), *The Romantic Movement* (London: Longmans, 1966), pp. 62–4.

Lynes, Russell, *The Tastemakers* (New York: Grosset and Dunlop, 1959).

McKendrick, Neil, 'Home Demand and Economic Growth: A New View of the Role of Women and Children in the Industrial Revolution', in Neil McKendrick (ed.), *Historical Perspectives: Studies in English Thought and Society in Honour of J. H. Plumb* (London: Europa Publications, 1974), pp. 152–210.

——, Brewer, John and Plumb, J. H., *The Birth of a Consumer Society: The Commercialization of Eighteenth-Century England* (London: Europa Publications, 1982).

Mandel, Ernest, *Marxist Economic Theory*, 2 vols, trans. Brian Pearce (London: Merlin Press, 1970).

Mannheim, Karl, *Essays on the Sociology of Culture* (London: Routledge and Kegan Paul, 1956).

Mansell, Darrel, *The Novels of Jane Austen: An Interpretation* (London: Macmillan, 1973).

Manson, Roger S., *Conspicuous Consumption: A Study of Exceptional Consumer Behaviour* (Farnborough, Hants.: Gower Publishing, 1981).

Marcuse, Herbert. *One Dimensional Man* (London: Routledge and Kegan Paul, 1964).

Markin, Rom J., Jr, *Consumer Behaviour: A Cognitive Orientation* (New York: Macmillan, 1974).

Marshall, Gordon, *In Search of the Spirit of Capitalism: An Essay on Max Weber's Protestant Ethic Thesis* (London: Hutchinson University Library, 1982).

Martin, Bernice, *A Sociology of Contemporary Cultural Change* (Oxford: Basil Blackwell, 1981).

Martin, David, *Anarchy and Culture: The Problem of the Contemporary University* (London: Routledge and Kegan Paul, 1969).

Martin, Richard, Chaffee, Steven and Izcaray, Fausto, 'Media and Consumerism in Venezuela', *Journalism Quarterly*, 56 (1979), 296–304.

Masson, Pierre-Maurice, *La Religion de J. J. Rousseau*, 3 vols (Paris: Hachette, 1916).

Matza, David, 'Subterranean Traditions of Youth', *Annals of the American Academy of Political and Social Science*, 338 (November 1961), 102–18.

Merton, R. K., 'The Unanticipated Consequences of Purposive Social Action', *American Sociological Review*, (1936), 894–904.

——, *Social Theory and Social Structure*, revised and enlarged edn (Glencoe, Ill.: The Free Press, 1968).

Mills, C. Wright, 'Situated Action and the Vocabulary of Motives', *American Sociological Review*, 6 (December 1940), 904–13.

Mills, R., *Young Outsiders: A Study of Alternative Communities* (London: Routledge and Kegan Paul, 1973).

Minchinton, Walter, 'Convention, Fashion and Consumption: Aspects of British Experience since 1750', in Henri Baudet and Henk van der Meulen (eds), *Consumer Behaviour and Economic Growth in the Modern Economy* (London: Croom Helm, 1982), pp. 207–30.

Mitzman, Arthur, *The Iron Cage: An Historical Interpretation of Max Weber* (New York: Alfred A. Knopf, 1970).

Moers, Ellen, *The Dandy: Brummell to Beerbohm* (London: Secker and Warburg, 1960).

Morgan, Edmund S., *Visible Saints: The History of a Puritan Idea* (New York: New York University Press, 1963).

Morison, Samuel Eliot, *The Intellectual Life of Colonial New England* (Ithaca, NY: Great Seal Books, 1960).

Murger, Henry, *The Latin Quarter (Scènes de la Vie Bohème)*, trans. Ellen Marriage and John Selwyn, introduction by Arthur Symons (London: Greening, 1908).

Musgrove, Frank, *Ecstasy and Holiness: Counter Culture and the Open Society* (London: Methuen, 1974).

Nair, Kusum, *Blossoms in the Dust: The Human Factor in Indian Development* (New York: Frederick A. Praeger, 1962).

Novak, Maximillian E., *Eighteenth-Century English Literature* (London: Macmillan, 1983).

Oden, Thomas C., 'The New Pietism', in Eileen Barker (ed.), *New Religious Movements: A Perspective for Understanding Society* (New York: The Edwin Mellen Press, 1982), pp. 85–106.

290 *References*

O'Neill, John, 'The Productive Body: An Essay on the Work of Consumption', *Queen's Quarterly*, 85 (Summer 1978), 221–30.
Ossowska, Maria, *The Social Determinants of Moral Ideas* (London: Routledge and Kegan Paul, 1971).
Packard, Vance, *The Hidden Persuaders* (London: Longmans, 1957).
Parkin, Frank, *Middle Class Radicalism: The Social Basis of the British Campaign for Nuclear Disarmament* (Manchester: Manchester University Press, 1968).
Parry, Albert, *Garrets and Pretenders: A History of Bohemianism in America* (New York: Dover, 1960 edn, first published in 1933).
Parsons, Talcott, *The Structure of Social Action: A Study of Social Theory with Special Reference to a group of recent European Writers*, 2nd edn (Glencoe, Ill.: Free Press, 1949).
Pawson, Eric, *The Early Industrial Revolution: Britain in the Eighteenth Century* (London: Batsford Academic, 1978).
Pease, Otis, *The Responsibilities of American Advertising: Private Control and Public Influence, 1920–1940* (New York: Arno Press, 1976).
Peckham, Morse, 'Toward a Theory of Romanticism', *PMLA*, (March 1951), 5–23.
——, *Beyond the Tragic Vision: The Quest for Identity in the Nineteenth Century* (New York: George Braziller, 1962).
Perkin, Harold, *The Origins of Modern English Society* (London: Routledge and Kegan Paul, 1968).
Perry, David L., *The Concept of Pleasure* (The Hague: Mouton, 1967).
Plumb, J. H., 'Commercialization and Society', in N. McKendrick, J. Brewer and J. H. Plumb, *The Birth of a Consumer Society: The Commercialization of Eighteenth-Century England* (London: Europa Publications, 1982), pp. 265–335.
Poulet, G., 'Romanticism', in A. K. Thorlby (ed), *The Romantic Movement* (London: Longmans, 1966), pp. 40–2.
Praz, Mario, *The Romantic Agony*, trans. by Angus Davidson, 2nd edn (Oxford: Oxford University Press, 1979).
Ransome, Arthur, *Bohemia in London* (Oxford: Oxford University Press, 1984; first published by Chapman and Hall, 1907).
Reed, Amy Louise, *The Background of Gray's Elegy: A Study in the Taste for Melancholy Poetry 1700–1751* (New York: Russell and Russell, 1962).
Remak, H. H., 'West-European Romanticism: Definition and Scope', in Newton P. Stallnecht and Horst Frenz (eds), *Comparative Literature: Method and Perspective* (Carbondale, Ill.: Southern Union University Press, 1961), pp. 223–59.
Riese, W. 'The Pre-Freudian Origins of Psychoanalysis', *Science and Psychoanalysis*, 1 (1958), 24–32.
Riesman, David, and Lerner, Daniel, 'Self and Society: Reflections on some Turks in Transition', in *Abundance for What? And Other Essays* (New York: Doubleday Anchor Books, 1965), pp. 382–96.
—— and Roseborough, Howard, 'Careers and Consumer Behaviour', in *Abundance for What? And Other Essays* (New York: Doubleday Anchor Books, 1965), pp. 107–30.

——, Glazer, Nathan and Denny, Reuel, *The Lonely Crowd: A Study in the Changing American Character* (New York: Doubleday Anchor Books, 1966).

Rigney, Francis J. and Smith, L. Douglas, *The Real Bohemia: A Social and Psychological Study of the 'Beats'* (New York: Basic Books, 1961).

Roberts, Mark, *The Tradition of Romantic Morality* (London: Macmillan, 1973).

Rogers, Winfield H., 'The Reaction against Melodramatic Sentimentality in the English Novel 1796–1830', *PMLA*, 49 (March 1934), 98–122.

Rosenberg, B. and White, D. M. (eds), *Mass Culture: The Popular Arts in America* (Glencoe, Ill.: Free Press, 1957).

Ross, G. Macdonald, *Leibniz* (Oxford: Oxford University Press, 1984).

Roszak, Theodore, *The Making of a Counter-Culture* (New York: Doubleday Anchor Books, 1969).

Rougemont, Denis de, *Passion and Society*, trans. by Montgomery Belgion, rev. edn (London: Faber and Faber, 1956).

Ruskin, John, *Selections from the Writings of John Ruskin, Second Series 1860–1888*, (Orpington: George Allen, 1899).

Russell, Bertrand, *A History of Western Philosophy: And its Connections with Political and Social Circumstances from the Earliest Times to the Present Day* (London: Allen and Unwin, 1946).

Ryle, Gilbert, *Dilemmas* (Cambridge: Cambridge University Press, 1954).

Sade, Marquis de, *The Complete Justine, Philosophy in the Bedroom and other Writings*, compiled and trans. by Richard Seaves and Austryn Wainhouse (New York: Grove Press, 1966).

Salter, Brian 'Explanations of Student Unrest: An Exercise in Devaluation', *British Journal of Sociology*, 24 (September 1973), no. 3, 329–40.

Schneider, Herbert Wallace, *The Puritan Mind* (Ann Arbor, Mich.: University of Michigan Press, 1958).

Schneider, Louis, *The Scottish Moralists: On Human Nature and Society* (Chicago, Ill.: University of Chicago Press, 1967).

——, 'Ironic Perspective and Sociological Thought', in Lewis A. Coser (ed.), *The Idea of Social Structure: Papers in Honour of Robert K. Merton* (New York: Harcourt Brace Jovanovich, 1975), pp. 323–37.

Schucking, Levin L., *The Sociology of Literary Taste* (London: Kegan Paul, Trench, Trubner, 1944).

Scitovsky, Tibor, *The Joyless Economy: An Inquiry into Human Satisfaction and Consumer Dissatisfaction* (New York: Oxford University Press, 1976).

Scott, M. and Lyman, S., 'Accounts', *American Sociological Review*, 33 (February 1968), no. 1, 46–62.

Seckler, David, *Thorstein Veblen and the Institutionalists: A Study in the Social Philosophy of Economics* (London: Macmillan, 1975).

Shelley, Percy Bysshe, 'A Defence of Poetry', in H. Bloom and L. Trilling (eds), *Romantic Poetry and Prose* (New York: Oxford University Press, 1973), pp. 746–62.

Shenck, H. G., *The Mind of the European Romantics: An Essay in Cultural History* (London: Constable, 1966).

Sickels, Eleanor M., *The Gloomy Egoist: Moods and Themes of Melancholy from Gray to Keats* (New York: Octagon Books, 1969).

Simmel, Georg, 'Fashion', *American Journal of Sociology*, 62 (May 1957), 541–58; reprinted from *International Quarterly* 10 (1904).
——, *The Sociology of Georg Simmel*, ed. Kurt H. Wolff (New York: Free Press, 1964).
Singer, Jerome L., *The Child's World of Make-Believe: Experimental Studies of Imaginative Play* (New York: Academic Press, 1973).
Skelton, R., *Cavalier Poets: Writers and their Work, no. 117* (published for the British Council and the National Book League by Longmans, Green, London, 1960).
Skinner, Quentin, *The Foundations of Modern Political Thought*, vol. 1: *The Renaissance* (Cambridge: Cambridge University Press, 1978).
Sombart, Werner, *Luxury and Capitalism*, introduction by Philip Siegelman (Ann Arbor, Mich.: University of Michigan Press, 1967).
Stansill, Peter and Mairowitz, David Zane (eds), *BAMN: Outlaw Manifestos and Ephemera 1965–70* (Harmondsworth, Middx.: Penguin Books, 1971).
Stark, Werner, 'Max Weber and the Heterogony of Purposes', *Social Research*, 34 (Summer 1967), 249–64.
Stone, Lawrence, *The Family, Sex and Marriage in England 1500–1800* (London: Weidenfeld and Nicolson, 1977).
Summers, Montague, *The Gothic Quest: A History of the Gothic Novel* (New York: Russell and Russell, 1964).
Taylor, Gordon Rattray, *The Angel-Makers: A Study in the Psychological Origins of Historical Change 1750–1850* (London: Heinemann, 1958).
Taylor, John Tinnon, *Early Opposition to the English Novel: The Popular Reaction from 1760–1830* (New York: King's Crown Press, 1943).
Texte, Joseph, *Jean-Jacques Rousseau and the Cosmopolitan Spirit in Literature: A Study of the Literary Relations between France and England during the Eighteenth Century* (New York: Burt Franklin, 1899).
Thirsk, Joan, *Economic Policy and Projects: The Development of a Consumer Society in Early Modern England* (Oxford: Clarendon Press, 1978).
Thorlby, Anthony (ed.), *The Romantic Movement* (London: Longmans, 1966).
Thorslev, Peter L., Jr, 'Romanticism and the Literary Consciousness', *Journal of the History of Ideas*. 36 (July–September 1975), no. 3, 563–72.
Thurber, James, *The Thurber Carnival* (London: Hamish Hamilton, 1945).
Tiffany, Esther A., 'Shaftesbury as Stoic', *PMLA*, 38 (March 1923), no. 1, 642–84.
Tompkins, J. M. S., *The Popular Novel in England 1770–1880* (Lincoln, Nebr.: University of Nebraska Press, 1961).
Trilling, Lionel, *Sincerity and Authenticity* (Cambridge, Mass.: Harvard University Press, 1971).
——, 'The Fate of Pleasure: Wordsworth to Dostoevsky', *Partisan Review*, 30 (Summer 1963) 73–106; reproduced in Lionel Trilling, *Beyond Culture: Essays on Literature and Learning* (Oxford: Oxford University Press, 1980).
Tulloch, John, *Rational Theology and Christian Philosophy in England in the Seventeenth Century*, 2 vols (Edinburgh: William Blackwood, 1874).
Turner, Bryan, *For Weber* (London: Routledge and Kegan Paul, 1981).
Varma, Devendra P. *The Gothic Flame* (New York: Russell and Russell, 1957).

Veblen, Thorstein, *The Theory of the Leisure Class: An Economic Study of Institutions* (London: George Allen and Unwin, 1925).

Vichert, Gordon, 'The Theory of Conspicuous Consumption in the Eighteenth Century', in Peter Hughes and David Williams (eds), *The Varied Pattern: Studies in the Eighteenth Century* (Toronto: A. M. Hakkert, 1971), pp. 253–67.

Vickers, Brian, Introduction to Henry Mackenzie, *The Man of Feeling* (London: Oxford University Press, 1967).

Walker, D. P., *The Decline of Hell: Seventeenth Century Discussions of Eternal Torment* (London: Routledge and Kegan Paul, 1954).

Wallach, Michael A. and Wallach, Lise, *Psychology's Sanction for Selfishness: The Error of Egoism in Theory and Therapy* (San Fransisco, Calif.: W. H. Freeman, 1983).

Ward, John William, 'Benjamin Franklin: The Making of an American Character', in Brian M. Barbour (ed.), *Benjamin Franklin: A Collection of Critical Essays* (Englewood Cliffs, NJ: Prentice-Hall, 1979), pp. 50–62.

Wasserman, Earl R., 'The Pleasures of Tragedy', *A Journal of English Literary History*, 14 (December 1947), no. 4, 283–307.

Watt, Ian., *The Rise of the Novel: Studies in Defoe, Richardson and Fielding* (Berkeley, Calif.: University of California Press, 1957).

Weber, Max, *The Protestant Ethic and the Spirit of Capitalism*, trans. Talcott Parsons (London: Unwin University Books, 1930).

——, *The Theory of Social and Economic Organization*, trans. A. M. Henderson and Talcott Parsons, edited and with an introduction by Talcott Parsons (New York: Free Press, 1964).

——, *The Sociology of Religion*, trans. Ephriam Fischoff, introduction by Talcott Parsons (London: Methuen, 1965).

Wellek, René, *A History of Modern Criticism: 1750–1950*, vol. 1: *The Later Eighteenth Century* (London: Jonathan Cape, 1955).

Westhues, Kenneth, *Society's Shadow: Studies in the Sociology of Countercultures* (Toronto: McGraw-Hill Ryerson, 1972).

White, Winston, *Beyond Conformity* (Glencoe, Ill.: Free Press, 1961).

Whyte, Lancelot Law, *The Unconscious before Freud* (London: Tavistock, 1959).

Whyte, William H., *The Organization Man* (New York: Doubleday Anchor Books, 1957).

Willey, Basil, *The Eighteenth Century Background: Studies on the Idea of Nature in the Thought of the Period* (London: Chatto and Windus, 1961).

——, *The English Moralists* (London: Chatto and Windus, 1964).

Williams, Raymond, *The Long Revolution* (London: Chatto and Windus, 1961).

——, *Culture and Society 1780–1950* (Harmondsworth, Middx.: Penguin Books, 1962).

——, *Keywords: A Vocabulary of Culture and Society* (Glasgow: Fontana/Croom Helm, 1976).

Wolfenstein, Martha, 'The Emergence of Fun Morality', in Eric Larrabee and Rolf Meyersohn (eds), *Mass Leisure* (Glencoe, Ill.: Free Press, 1958), pp. 86–95.

Woolf, Virginia, *A Haunted House and Other Stories* (London: The Hogarth Press, 1962).

Wootton, Anthony, *Dilemmas of Discourse: Controversies about the Sociological Significance of Language* (London: Allen and Unwin, 1975).

Wyllie, Irvin G., *The Self-Made Man in America: The Myth of Rags to Riches* (New York: Free Press, 1954).

Reference works

Collins Dictionary of the English Language, s.v. 'Romantic', 'Sentimental' (London: Collins, 1979).

Dictionary of the History of Ideas: Studies of Selected Pivotal Ideas, s.v. 'Enlightenment' by Helmut O. Pappe, 'Neo-Classicism' by David Irwin, and 'Theodicy' by Leroy E. Leomker (New York: Charles Scribner's Sons, 1968).

Encyclopedia of Religion and Ethics, s.v. 'Puritanism' by H. G. Wood (Edinburgh: T. and T. Clark, 1908).

International Encyclopaedia of the Social Sciences, ed. David L. Sills, s.v. 'Fashion' by Herbert G. Blumer (New York: The Macmillan Company and The Free Press, 1968).

Makers of Modern Culture: A Biographical Dictionary, s.v. 'Weber, Max' by John Rex (London: Routledge and Kegan Paul, 1981).

Princeton Encyclopaedia of Poetry and Poetics, ed. Alex Preminger (Princeton, NJ: Princeton University Press, 1974), s.v. 'Sensibility', 'Sentimentality' and 'Taste'.

Index

Appendix A

Colin Campbell,
Selected Publications
on Consumption

'The Craft Consumer: Culture, Craft and Consumption in a Postmodern Society', *Journal of Consumer Culture* 5:1 (2005).

'I Shop Therefore I Know That I Am: The Metaphysical Foundations of Modern Consumerism', in *Elusive Consumption*, Karin Ekstrom and Helen Brembeck (eds.), Oxford: Berg, 2004.

'On Understanding Modern Consumerism and Misunderstanding the Romantic Ethic Thesis: A Reply to Boden and Williams, *Sociology* 37:4 (2003).

'Shopaholics, Spendaholics and the Question of Gender' in April Lane Benson (ed.) *I Shop Therefore I Am: Compulsive Buying and the Search for Self*, Jason Aronson Press: Northvale, N.J., 2000.

'Consumption and the Rhetorics of Need and Want' *Journal of Design History* 11:3 (1998).

'The Romantic Ethic and The Spirit of Modern Consumerism: Reflections on the Reception of a Thesis Concerning the Origin of the Desire for Goods' in Susan M Pearce (ed.) *Experiencing Material Culture*. Leicester: Leicester University Press, 1997.

'When the Meaning is not a Message: A Critique of the Consumption as Communication Thesis' in Mica Nava et al., *Buy This Book: Studies in Advertising and Consumption*. London: Routledge, 1997.

'Shopping, Pleasure and the Sex War', in *The Shopping Experience* Pasi Falk and Colin Campbell (eds.), London: Sage, 1996.

'Romanticism, Introspection and Consumption: Some Comments on Professor Holbrook's Paper', in Russell W. Belk, Nikhilesh Dholakia and Alladi Venkatesh (eds.) *Consumption and Marketing: Macro Dimensions*, Cincinnati, Ohio: South-Western College Publishing, 1996.

'The Meaning of Objects and the Meaning of Actions: A Critical Note on the Sociology of Consumption and Theories of Clothing' *Journal of Material Culture* 1:1 (1996).

'Conspicuous Confusion? A Critique of Veblen's Theory of Conspicuous Consumption' *Sociological Theory* 13:1 (1995).

'The Sociology of Consumption' in Daniel Miller (ed.) *Approaching Consumption*, London: Routledge, 1995.

'Consuming Goods and the Good of Consuming' *Critical Review* 8:4 (1994).

'Capitalism, Consumption and the Problem of Motives: Some issues in the understanding of conduct as illustrated by an examination of the treatment of motive and meaning in the works of Weber and Veblen', in Jonathan Friedman (ed.), *Consumption and Identity*, Reading: Harwood Academic Publishers, 1994.

'Understanding Traditional and Modern Patterns of Consumption in Eighteenth Century England: A Character-Action Approach' in John Brewer and Roy Porter (eds.) *Consumption and The World of Goods*, London: Routledge, 1993.

'The Desire for the New: Its Nature and Social Location as Presented in Theories of Fashion and Modern Consumerism' in *Consuming Technologies: Media and Information in Domestic Spaces*, edited by Roger Silverman and Eric Hirsch, London: Routledge, 1992.

'Consumption: The New Wave of Research in the Humanities and Social Sciences' in F.W. Rudmin (ed.) 'To Have Possessions: A Handbook on Ownership and Property' (Special Issue) *Journal of Social Behaviour and Personality* 5:5 (1991).

'Character and Consumption: An Historical Action Theory Approach to the Understanding of Consumer Behaviour' *Culture and History* 7 (1990).

'Romanticism and the Consumer Ethic: Intimations of a Weber-style thesis' *Sociological Analysis* 44:4 (1983).

Lightning Source UK Ltd.
Milton Keynes UK
03 November 2009

145760UK00001B/179/A